UNIVERSITY OF CALGARY
LCR Publishing Services

TRANSFORMING SOCIAL WORK FIELD EDUCATION

New Insights from Practice Research and Scholarship

Julie L. Drolet, Grant Charles,
Sheri M. McConnell, and Marion Bogo

EDITORS

LCR Publishing Services
An imprint of University of Calgary Press
2500 University Drive NW
Calgary, Alberta
Canada T2N 1N4
press.ucalgary.ca

LIBRARY AND ARCHIVES CANADA CATALOGUING IN PUBLICATION

Title: Transforming social work field education : new insights from practice research and
    scholarship / Julie L. Drolet, Grant Charles, Sheri M. McConnell, and Marion Bogo (editors).
Names: Drolet, Julie, 1971- editor. | Charles, Grant, 1953- editor. | McConnell, Sheri M., editor.
    | Bogo, Marion, editor.
Description: Includes bibliographical references and index.
Identifiers: Canadiana (print) 20220427569 | Canadiana (ebook) 20220427631 | ISBN 9781773854380
    (hardcover) | ISBN 9781773854397 (softcover) | ISBN 9781773854410 (PDF) | ISBN
    9781773854403 (Open Access PDF) | ISBN 9781773854427 (EPUB)
Subjects: LCSH: Social work education. | LCSH: Social service—Fieldwork. | LCSH: Fieldwork
    (Educational method) | LCSH: Social service—Research.
Classification: LCC HV11 .T73 2022 | DDC 361.3071/55—dc23

The University of Calgary Press acknowledges the support of the Government of Alberta through the Alberta Media Fund for our publications. We acknowledge the financial support of the Government of Canada. We acknowledge the financial support of the Canada Council for the Arts for our publishing program.

Alberta Government   Canada   Canada Council for the Arts   Conseil des Arts du Canada

Cover image: Colourbox 5509580
Copyediting by Francine Michaud
Cover design, page design, and typesetting by Melina Cusano

TRANSFORMING
SOCIAL WORK
FIELD EDUCATION

This book is dedicated to the memory of our respected colleague
Marion Bogo,
a trailblazer in social work field education and research,
whose passion, dedication, and generosity will
continue to inspire current and future generations of
social work educators, students, and researchers.

Contents

List of Figures

List of Tables

Acknowledgements

Many people have worked together to bring this book to publication, and we are grateful for their support and commitment throughout this project. This book is a publication of the Transforming the Field Education Landscape (TFEL) project. We would like to thank the contributors in the book for sharing their field research in TFEL's Field Research Scholar program in 2020–2021 and with a broader audience in this collection.

The development of the book was supported by members of the Transforming the Field Education Landscape (TFEL) project, which held a Summer Institute on Academic Writing in Field Education in 2021. We acknowledge the role of faculty mentors in the Institute that provided writing guidance and support to contributing authors: Jill Hanley (McGill University), David Nicholas (University of Calgary), Sally St George (University of Calgary), Tamara Sussman (McGill University), Christine Walsh (University of Calgary), and Dan Wulff (University of Calgary). We especially thank Telford-Anthony Pattinson, Paul Papin, Lee-Ann Penalua, and Lucy Amadala for facilitating writing workshops on strategies for writing literature reviews, procrastination and time management, critical thinking and scholarly writing, academic integrity, and stress management.

We also benefited greatly from the many student research assistants and postdoctoral scholars who assisted in the Field Research Scholars program and in the book at various stages: Mohammad Idris (Omid) Alemi, Wasif Ali, Evalyna Bogdan, Tara Collins, Hilary Daum, Vibha Kaushik, Godfrey Makoha, and Mohammed Nurudeen Musah. We are grateful to Emmanuel Chilanga and Olena Babenko for coordinating the project. We would especially like to thank Erin Leveque for copy editing and proofreading the manuscripts with great skill and diligence. We are thankful to Brian Scrivener at The University of Calgary Press for his support and enthusiasm.

We would like to acknowledge the contribution of our co-editor Marion Bogo who suddenly passed away in the fall of 2021. She actively participated in the development of the book process, attentively reviewed chapters, provided comments to the authors, and supported the project. We hope that she would have been pleased with the outcome of the book.

Transforming the Field Education Landscape (TFEL) project is supported in part by funding from the Social Sciences and Humanities Research Council.

Julie L. Drolet, Grant Charles, and Sheri M. McConnell

Introduction: Field Research Scholarship in Social Work Education

Julie L. Drolet, Grant Charles, and Sheri M. McConnell

This book brings together diverse perspectives on field education and practice research within academia and across the public and not-for-profit sectors to enhance knowledge and applied skills development. Social work scholars, practitioners, service users, and students offer new insights, practice experiences, case studies, and reflections which have the potential to transform social work field education. The book features contributors at various stages of their careers to foster a meaningful dialogue on the dynamic, complex, and multi-faceted nature of social work practice, research, and innovation in field education. Critical issues in social work field education are explored through field research scholarship. Current theoretical concepts and perspectives that shape social work field education are presented using practice research and case studies grounded in the experiences of diverse communities and countries.

Field education or practicum is a critical component of social work education. The Canadian Association for Social Work Education (CASWE) engages in activities to promote and support field education as a central component of social work education (CASWE, 2022). It is recognized as the signature pedagogy in social work education (Council on Social Work Education [CSWE], 2015). It is through practicum that students learn to integrate and apply the values, knowledge, complex practices, and skills of the social work profession. Field education experiences ensure that new professionals are entering the field practice in an ethical manner and with an established level of competence (Bogo, 2015). In terms of their professional training, it is critical that students enrolled in social work programs across Canada have opportunities for positive, educational, and quality field education experiences. This said, however, there is a crisis in the imagining and provisioning of field placements that needs to be addressed to ensure that quality learning experiences are provided to students at the undergraduate and graduate levels.

The collection of literature in this book focuses on the scholarly activity in field education that contributes to the resolution of this crisis by revisioning how the profession can prepare the next generation of social workers. With the recognition that the crisis is coupled with the impacts of the COVID-19 pandemic, there is a need to adopt more innovative and sustainable models in social work field education (Drolet et al., 2020). Many social work field educators report challenges with a high demand for field placements, due in part to rising student admissions, as well as increased pressures on field agencies that typically provide practicums to social work students (Ayala et al., 2019; Bogo, 2015). The onset of the COVID-19 pandemic in 2020 created additional pressures for many students, social work field education programs, and field agencies. Despite these challenges, new opportunities and innovative approaches to field education, which are potentially beneficial in the current context, are emerging. The book adopts an inquiry-based learning and transformational approach that contributes innovative understandings of field education by providing new open access resources to inform social work field education, and specifically the integration of research in practice and field education.

New understandings and approaches are urgently needed to address the crisis in social work field education. As professionals, social workers are expected to use research to inform their practice and to contribute to the production of research. Yet many social workers are reticent to integrate research into their practice and into field education. The book is a product of the Transforming the Field Education Landscape (TFEL) partnership funded by a Social Sciences and Humanities Research Council's Partnership Grant.

Transforming the Field Education Landscape Partnership

The Transforming the Field Education Landscape project brings together social work academic researchers, field educators, students, professional social work associations, and partners who share concerns about the state of field education in Canada and internationally. The project is built on an inquiry-based learning and a transformational approach to create "opportunities for students and postdoctoral fellows to explore, identify, and develop promising practices for integrating research training in social work practice" (Drolet, 2020, p. 7). The goal of the TFEL project is:

> To integrate research and practice in the preparation of the next generation of social workers by developing partnered research training initiatives, both within academia and across the public and not-for-profit sectors, that enhance student research practice knowledge and applied skill development. (Drolet, 2020, p. 3)

With the onset of the COVID-19 pandemic, the TFEL project's research and related activities shifted online in March 2020. Research and related activities, training, and mentorship were supported using Microsoft Teams and Zoom. Field placements were also disrupted and moved online due to the pandemic, and TFEL generated new practicum opportunities for students by creating sub-projects, including group projects and research on the impacts of COVID-19 on field education. TFEL supervised 29 practicum students (20 graduate practicum students and nine undergraduate practicum students) between April 2019 and May 2022. Recognizing the importance of establishing the next generation of researchers, the Field Research Scholars Program was created by the project to facilitate research, knowledge exchange, and dialogue on research in field education.

Field Research Scholars Program

The Field Research Scholars program is a unique opportunity for emerging scholars and early career social work academics to present their research and obtain feedback from their peers in virtual seminars. In the 2020–2021 academic year, the program hosted 48 participants, including graduate, PhD, postdoctoral scholars, and early career faculty members. Each participant was invited to present on their research, and the Zoom recordings and PowerPoint presentations were published on the TFEL website (see www.tfelproject.com). Bi-weekly seminars were held on Zoom during the COVID-19 pandemic, which expanded access for many participants.

This book is an outcome of the Field Research Scholars program and offers an original contribution to the literature on the integration of research into practice and field education. The book is organized in four sections and includes 16 chapters written by 30 scholars as contributing authors. Each section of the book was edited by a Canadian social work faculty member serving as a section editor: Julie Drolet, University of Calgary; Grant Charles, The University of British Columbia; Sheri M. McConnell, Memorial University; and Marion Bogo, University of Toronto.

The book aims to stimulate interest in and discussion on the critical role of research and scholarship in social work field education in Canada and internationally, by creating a space for dialogue and collaboration around the integration of research in field education. Overall, the book adopts a mixed methods research approach. Several chapters report on qualitative studies, present case study research grounded in specific communities or country contexts, and narrative reflections to inform their writing in the chapters.

The book development and writing process was supported by the TFEL partnership through the Summer Institute 2021 on Academic Writing in Field Education, which was designed to provide support and mentorship to the contributors in their writing process. Workshops were held throughout the summer. The contributions in this collection work together to create a coherent whole in discussing research and scholarship in the context of field education. In this book, authors explore how social work engages in practice, policy, and research, and the implications for field education in diverse contexts.

Outline of the Book

This book is organized in four parts: field education practice, research, and theory; anti-racist and Indigenous knowledges, methodologies, and perspectives; social justice, advocacy, and international social work; and new developments and approaches in field education. Collectively, these sections provide a picture of the challenges and possibilities around the world, as social work field education intersects with research. As a collection, the chapters demonstrate the ways in which the social work profession is navigating and challenging the status quo towards social development and social justice.

Field Education Practice, Research, and Theory

The first section of the book focuses on field education practice, research, and theory. Many longstanding practices in field education are being critically analyzed given the realities of the COVID-19 pandemic. The need for quality and accessible placements that provide learning opportunities for students in diverse sites remains an important concern for many social work education programs. The development of new practices and ways of conducting field have emerged for discussion and debate given the significant challenges of the global pandemic. This section of the book situates key concerns in addressing barriers to accessing practicums, field supervision by non-social work practitioners, enhancing equity and accessibility through the field placement process, and development social work theory in Africa.

In chapter 1, Natalie Beck Aguilera, William Lamar Medley, C. Gage, and Annelise Hutchison discuss the social and economic implications of unpaid practicums for social work students. The chapter begins by situating the current reality of the COVID-19 pandemic, which has demonstrated significant and disparate experiences for members of systematically oppressed communities and social groups. The authors argue that students also have been affected by the social and economic implications of the pandemic, including economic marginalization. The authors trace the history of the social work profession beginning with a discussion about the early perception of social workers as not "deserving" financial compensation for their care work given their gender roles as women. This early tradition influenced the tension between today's academic and direct service demands of the social work practicum, and how many field agencies continue to rely on students' unpaid labour. The authors discuss unpaid internships as a practice that perpetuates inequality among students along class divides that benefit students who can afford to independently finance their studies, or who are supported by others, while pursuing their education. Furthermore, the authors show how students who juggle competing responsibilities during their practicum face financial hardships and experience economic oppression created in part by practicum requirements and policies. The consequences and implications of unpaid practicums for students are discussed, and a case study illustrates the challenges experienced from a student perspective. Recommendations are provided by the authors, including the need for a safety net to mitigate exclusionary practices and to support paid practicums in the form of stipends or wages allocated to students. The authors demonstrate how the global pandemic has created new opportunities for rethinking previous field practices with the goal of dismantling barriers experienced by students through an equity lens. With the increasing costs of tuition and rising living expenses due to inflation, the authors suggest that universities can play a role in funding social work practicums. The practices discussed in the first chapter of the book aim to improve students' access to social work practicum, offering important implications for field education programs that can ultimately increase diversity in social work education and the profession while supporting economic justice.

In chapter 2, Karen Lok Yi Wong presents an ongoing debate in the field of social work on whether social work students should be matched with non-social work field supervisors during their placements. The author outlines the benefits for students in learning from non-social work field supervisors, such as new approaches and perspectives with diverse and multidisciplinary backgrounds in a community senior service setting. The chapter also outlines several concerns with respect to the development of one's social identity as a social worker. Drawing on personal experience as a graduate practicum student during the COVID-19 pandemic, the author presents a critical self-reflection using reflexivity on her placements in two agency settings. The first field agency was a community senior service centre in Downtown Vancouver, the second was a university research institute on ageing and technology. As the only social worker in both field agencies, the author presents the role of the field supervisors, the field education coordinator, and the faculty liaison in her placements. The chapter highlights the importance of collaboration and relationships in working with non-social work supervisors, particularly in healthcare and social services. Reciprocal learning was reported as a feature, given that field supervisors were exposed to the scope of social work practice and the benefits associated with a social work perspective within the agency context. Frequent communication and prior supervision experience were factors that contributed to the successful practicum experience at the graduate level. The chapter shares fruitful learning experiences on the benefits and challenges associated with non-social work field supervision.

In chapter 3, Alise de Bie, Janice Chaplin, and Jennie Vengris consider issues of equity and accessibility in the field placement process particularly for students from equity-deserving groups including racialized, Indigenous, 2SLGBTQ+, and disabled students. The School of Social Work at McMaster University is located in the urban centre of Hamilton which served as the site of placement learning for this chapter. The chapter discusses how members of the field education team and a field instructor created student-led caucus groups for racialized, Indigenous, queer/trans, and disabled students, which resulted in student-led research projects, reports, presentations, and events on 2SLGBTQ+ inclusiveness in field education, accessibility, and disability inclusion in the social work program. Social work students' experiences of racism also were discussed. An online survey and in-person focus groups and interviews were conducted in 2017 with 30 racialized, Indigenous, 2SLGBTQ+, and/or disabled students and recent alumni to learn about their field education experiences. The chapter focuses on how the findings from the study were used to enhance equity and accessibility in field education by preparing students for placement; recruiting and training field instructors to provide effective supervision; spending time matching students for placement leading to more positive experiences; considering identity-related student and field instructor matching processes; and creating pre-placement interview guides to facilitate student disclosures and equity/identity-related needs.

Also, an important dimension raised in this chapter is the importance of relationality in field education, which is explicitly discussed. The authors explain how new placements opportunities were explored in organizations that do racial justice work with 2SLGBTQ+ communities and Indigenous community partners; yet they noted that these opportunities still present some significant challenges owing to funding precarity in a neoliberal context. High staff turnover due to under-resourcing and unsustainable placements require ongoing connection and negotiation, and, oftentimes, additional supervision and support to non-social work field supervisors. The chapter highlights a reality whereby colleagues from equity-deserving groups are already over-subscribed to represent and provide access to their communities within the university context. Increased representation of faculty from equity-deserving groups would be conducive to an equitable labour load, while facilitating new placement-generating connections. The chapter provides many insights into the approaches adopted by the field team to engage alumni, the complexities of placing equity-deserving students in new field opportunities, and the preparation of students as future field instructors. Further, this chapter demonstrates the importance of engaging in change-oriented field research and evaluation projects to enhance equity and accessibility in field education teaching and learning.

In chapter 4, Emmanuel Chilanga considers development social work theory in Africa, and how social work theory, practice, and policy should shift from Eurocentric to Afrocentric pedagogies. Using a scoping review of the literature, the author examines developmental social work pedagogies in Africa. He then discusses the need for social work education to address quality of life factors on the continent that are influenced by poverty, unemployment, food insecurity, HIV/AIDS, malaria, and the COVID-19 pandemic. The author calls for localized and Indigenous approaches in developmental social work to facilitate human development. The results of the scoping review discuss curriculum-related activities including field education, social development, teaching methods, student projects and assignments, and extracurricular activities, such as creating Indigenous teaching materials, locally relevant research, and networking. Similar to other chapters in this book, field education is identified as a critical component of social work education. A number of universities in South Africa, Lesotho, Ghana, Zimbabwe, Nigeria, and Malawi have adopted a developmental social work perspectives in social work education, despite some common challenges including inadequate local resources, limited research, field education challenges, and lack of social work regulatory bodies. Consistent with Kelemua Zenebe Ayele and Ermias Kebede's contribution in this volume, which explores social work education in Ethiopia, Chilanga calls for locally relevant and Indigenous knowledge in development social work theory and field education in Africa. Social work is a rapidly growing profession in Africa, and social work academics and field educators are encouraged to adopt developmental social work to effectively address social problems and challenges.

Anti-racist and Indigenous Knowledges, Methodologies, and Perspectives

Section two of the book brings together chapters on anti-racist and Indigenous knowledges, methodologies, and perspectives. The section begins with Zipporah Greenslade's reflection on her search of anti-racism education as a graduate student in social work education. This discussion on anti-racism is followed by three chapters, each taking a unique approach to how social work needs to recognize culturally responsive practices, intersectionality, and critical race and social identity perspectives.

In chapter 5, Greenslade presents her anti-racism education research journey, informed by an autoethnographic research project and her location as a Black researcher and practicum student. She presents on the vital role of critical conversations in anti-racist education and how social work field education can play an integral role in connecting theory to practice. She begins her discussion by exposing the context and the need for anti-racist social work education and field education. Critical race theory is proposed as a foundation to engage in anti-racist social work education, and to address racism and examine structural inequalities. A practicum case example is presented to set the context for the author's narrative reflection: entitled "A Conversation with Myself," it explores a practicum incident in depth through questions raised about racism and the emotional burdens placed on racialized students. By giving voice to her experience, the author is contributing valuable knowledge to field research scholarship in anti-racist field education.

Alexandra K. Mack poignantly demonstrates in chapter 6 racial and ethnic disproportionality and disparity within the modern-day child welfare system. To address the overrepresentation of racial and ethnic populations in child welfare, her chapter proposes culturally responsive practices in service engagement. The author argues that building a culturally responsive workforce is a development process that includes workforce diversity, the assessment of strengths and growth, and anti-racism training. The chapter presents four pillars of the child welfare system as implemented in the United States: (1) Front Door pillar, (2) Temporary Safe Haven pillar, (3) Well-Being pillar, and (4) Exit to Permanence pillar. Drawing from a field practicum at a Child and Family Services Agency in the US, she provides insights and implications for promoting culturally responsive practices in field practicum settings.

In chapter 7, Endalkachew Taye Shiferaw, Helen Asrate, and Afework Eyasu discuss the lived gender disparities of three Ethiopian women in their pursuit of education. As social work doctoral students, themselves from Ethiopia, they collaborated in an exploratory study with three Ethiopian women in order to understand the experiences and meanings of earning a PhD. Intersectionality theory is used to consider the various multilayered identities of the participants in the study and to discuss the social identity factors, such as spirituality, family background, economic situation, culture, and personal values that influenced their educational and personal journeys. Each case in the chapter provides the context, background, and quotes in the voices of the women participants to illustrate salient and key points. It also provides a cross-case analysis that illustrates how the three women, in the pursuit of higher education, faced significant challenges, traveling away from their families, overcoming health concerns requiring special supports, and, in one case, experiencing forced migration due to political conflicts. The women academics were found to be engaged in multiple activities and responsibilities, including caregiving for children and parents, and managing domestic work. They experienced economic hardships, marital separation, and discrimination from family members, friends, and other faculty members, instructors, and classmates during their studies. Despite these challenges, the women in the study attributed their academic success to support provided by parents, family members, spouse(s), and their dedicated pursuit of their education. Spirituality, family support, and personal strengths were seen as contributing factors towards their success and education. The chapter concludes with a call to address gender-based discrimination in accessing higher education, and the need for field education programs to consider the recruitment of rural placements for practicum students to mitigate accessibility barriers to education and, at the same time, address local realities.

In the final chapter of this section, Anita R. Gooding, a licensed clinical social worker and researcher, demonstrates the importance of use of self in relation to social work identity, values, and knowledges. Chapter 8 begins with a discussion on the need for critical questioning about key assumptions and dominant identities, like Whiteness, in the social work classroom. Critical race theory and social identity theory provide the framework for exploring race as a component of use of self, and the author demonstrates its applicability in all areas of social work practice. Specifically, race and racial categories affect the ways in which social workers, particularly BIPOC (Black, Indigenous, and People of Colour) social workers, engage with use of self in their work with students and within the supervisory space. The profession of social work is called to do more to uplift the subjugated knowledges, advance marginalized voices, and create space for counter-narratives to offer a deeper understanding of social structures in the process of social change. This chapter connects with Zipporah Greenslade's in the same section in considering the supervisory relationship and how racial categorizations affect how a social worker is perceived, and when race is activated as a social identity in the context of field education. Anita R. Gooding demonstrates how both theories (critical race theory and social identity theory) contribute to explaining how race may influence use of self in the context of the student-field instructor relationship. By naming race, field instructors and students co-create an opening to engage in meaningful conversations about race and how a racialized identity informs use of self in building relationships in social work practice.

Social Justice, Advocacy, and International Social Work

The contributions in this section focus on social justice, advocacy, and international social work. The section begins with Vibha Kaushik's examination of the need for social workers to learn about immigrant and newcomers' settlement and integration experiences. Chapter 9 focuses on the development and integration of immigration content in the curriculum, and, specifically, the need for practitioners to respond to the challenges faced by immigrants and refugees in field education. A discussion of voluntary and forced international migration provides the context for this exploration. Immigration, Refugees, and Citizenship Canada (IRCC) funds the Settlement Program to offer a variety of services and supports offered by the immigrant serving sector, which are designed to benefit immigrants and help them integrate into Canadian communities. In Canada, there has been an increasing interest in building capacity in the social work profession for working with immigrants and newcomers. Despite the critical role of field education in preparing students for social work practice, there is a dearth of field placements in immigrant serving agencies and organizations. This chapter also speaks to the challenges raised in chapter 2 by Karen Lok Yi Wong on whether social work students should be matched with non-social work field supervisors during their placements. The chapter explores this practice challenge and offers some questions and options to consider in support of the development of practicum placements with immigrant serving agencies.

In this section, the authors of chapter 10, Kelemua Zenebe Ayele and Ermias Kebede, offer an overview of social work and field education in Ethiopia. In their study, they consider the opportunities and challenges in social work field education with respect to promoting social justice. Drawing on their experiences at the University of Gondar, a partner in the TFEL project, the authors discuss the historical context of social work in Ethiopia and the resurgence of social work education in recent years. As new social work education programs are launched in Ethiopian post-secondary institutions, a number of challenges have emerged for field education programs. The lack of trained social work field instructors, the lack of sufficient numbers of placements for students, and the lack of dedicated financial resources for field education programs are discussed. The chapter situates social justice as central to the social work profession and distinguishes the profession from other disciplines, as "social workers" in Ethiopia are hired despite a lack of social work credentials or training. This discussion complements Chilanga's articulation of developmental social work in the African context in chapter 4.

Chapter 11 focuses on community development field placements in Pakistan and presents a case study on community drinking water. Wasif Ali emphasizes the importance of community development to enhance human and environmental well-being in Pakistan. He demonstrates how local and international development agencies are engaged with schools of social work in research and training while contributing to the development of the social work profession. Field practicums, or internships, provide student learning opportunities in community development projects. In this chapter, a community drinking water project exemplifies the training of practicum students to engage in conducting needs assessments, community mobilization, participatory action research, building capacity, and monitoring and evaluation. The Punjab Community Water Supply Project aims to provide clean drinking water and health hygiene education during a time of severe water crisis in Pakistan. Social work practicum students are engaged in advancing the basic human right that is the provision of clean drinking water by working directly with affected communities. Ali's chapter reports on the student learning opportunities in the project, demonstrating the importance of collaboration to address social and environmental justice issues in local communities. His study also draws attention to the context of social work and the history of social welfare and community development in Pakistan, where social work and field education face similar challenges experienced in other countries featured in this book. For example, Western influence in social work education is considered suspect by local populations, and the lack of formal arrangements to facilitate field education presents a serious obstacle for field coordination.

In chapter 12, Margaret Janse van Rensburg, Courtney Weaver, Christine Jenkins, Morgan Banister, Edward King, Sheila Bell, and the Ottawa Adult Autism Initiative discuss an advocacy practicum to establish a framework for virtual community consultations. The chapter presents a doctoral level advocacy practicum of 130 hours that was created by Carleton University's School of Social Work. This chapter outlines the processes where members of the Ottawa Adult Autism Initiative were accompanied by an advocacy practicum student to create a strategy to host virtual consultations with the adult autism community in Ottawa, Canada. The chapter is informed by critical autism studies, which centres autistic persons as experts in autism, and critical pedagogy, which considers critical consciousness as a means for political participation. Together, the authors created an *Instructions and Guidance Document* and a set of recommendations to engage the adult autism community in virtual consultations. The chapter demonstrates the important contributions of a practicum student working in partnership with community members in a volunteer grassroots organization that aims to assist adults on the autism spectrum and their families in finding the support and services they need.

The chapter shares the problem-posing education model that includes a four-phase process for consultations through dialogue that ultimately informs the future virtual community consultations. The importance of facilitation strategies, fostering positive attitudes and atmospheres, and leadership is explored. The COVID-19 pandemic has demonstrated the importance for students to develop virtual social work practice skills such as the virtual consultation process described and explained in this chapter.

In chapter 13, Nicole Balbuena presents an important challenge facing social workers and social service providers when undocumented people are deemed ineligible for social services. The chapter critically examines how intimate partner violence (IPV) agencies that claim to offer services to all, regardless of race, sexuality, gender, and legal status, encounter institutional policies and practices that restrict the ability of service providers to deliver supports and services. Drawing on 12 in-depth interviews with IPV service providers, a study was conducted to examine how the legal status of the victims influenced the manner in which providers deliver their (in)formal services and resources in Orange County, California. The chapter reveals how restrictive eligibility and selection processes, fear of deportation while accessing services, and the lack of a valid social security number present structural barriers in a tense political environment that contributes, ultimately, to eliminate undesirable (prospective) clients. IPV agencies face internal and external structural and political barriers that result in the exclusion of undocumented clients. Social workers are advised to pay attention to legal and ethical challenges arising from oppressive systems and punitive immigration policies that shape the experiences of how undocumented immigrants receive and respond to services; these challenges additionally hinder social workers' ability to provide formal support to the undocumented population. Further research and continued discussion about unjust immigration policies and discriminatory ideologies from institutionalized systems are needed for social workers to advocate and assist undocumented immigrants to overcome political, social, and legal barriers when accessing IPV services. This discussion has important implications with respect to undocumented immigrants and migrants accessing other health and social services. As stated earlier in this section by Vibha Kaushik, it is important to acknowledge immigration status as a component of diversity in social work practice.

New Developments and Approaches in Field Education

In the final section of this book, authors consider new developments and approaches in field education. The section begins with a chapter that considers field education during the COVID-19 pandemic. In chapter 14, Kaltrina Kusari considers social work field education and the abrupt shift to virtual course delivery and field placements during the onset of the pandemic. As a field instructor supervising social work students in the disability sector, she reflects on critical disability theories, the importance of field education, and the use of Information and Communication Technologies to facilitate practicum placements. She observes that the disruptions created by COVID-19 to field education provided both challenges and opportunities for innovation. Within the disability field, the shift to a virtual format created new opportunities for student learning. Despite the challenges that COVID-19 presented, it also offered a space to experiment with field education opportunities which were conceptualized as unconventional. Kusari suggests that virtual program and service delivery might be helpful in the future post-pandemic.

In the next chapter, Emma De Vynck, Jill Ciesielski, and Heather M. Boynton discuss how to support the development of spiritual competencies in field education and practice.

Chapter 15 is written collaboratively from the perspective of three social workers and researchers at varying stages in their professional and academic paths, each with a passion for increasing spiritual awareness and spiritually sensitive field practice in social work. Spirituality and spiritual struggles and trauma are informed by the authors' personal practice and research endeavours, with implications for field education. The authors argue that the social work classroom rarely includes adequate exploration of spiritual and religious matters, and often students first encounter the spiritual elements of social work when they embark on their field placements. As they begin to engage with clients in the field setting, students may encounter spiritual and religious matters in clients' narratives implicitly or explicitly. Apart from religiously affiliated agencies, practicum students often lack exposure to spirituality, and students may be ill-prepared to address the spiritual struggles or distress, trauma, grief, and loss that impact well-being. The authors explore the implications for a spiritually sensitive framework for field education.

In chapter 16, the section concludes with Ricardo Diego Suárez Rojas's reflection on how to enhance brain potential in fieldwork education through the multimodal integration of imagination and trauma (MIIT) framework. Drawing on his community practice experience in Mexico and the United States, Rojas introduces nine working principles, with recommendations for field education. Field education is recognized as the signature pedagogy of the social work profession, representing the space in which students develop their professional capabilities and integrate theory and practice. The theoretical framework presented in this chapter recognizes that perception and movement rely on and depend upon multimodal integration (MI). The concluding chapter of the book provides a summary of the themes discussed in the book, in addition to an analysis of what was learned, what strengths were applied or developed, and the challenges faced by those who initiated or implemented field research activities. Implications and recommendations for social work field research scholarship are presented.

Conclusion: Transforming Field Education Research and Scholarship

The present book offers a number of unique features by focusing on research and scholarship in social work field education. This topic area has not received much attention in the field of social work. With the need for evidence-based practice, it is necessary to better understand how students and field educators can integrate research into their practice and develop new research skills and knowledge in the profession.

This collaborative work focuses on social work research in practice contexts and highlights the implications for field education. It especially brings together case studies, field research, and reflections from contributors located in diverse geographic regions such as Canada, United States, Ethiopia, Kosova, Mexico, and Pakistan. The chapters explore the social work values and ethics that guide social work practice in diverse contexts. Unique to the book is the range of international contributions and the breadth of knowledge displayed by the contributors at diverse stages of career (graduate and PhD students, postdoctoral scholars, and early career researchers). Training and mentorship too are a unique feature of the book, the process of which contributed to establish and strengthen the relationships between the contributors while making linkages between the chapters. The editors are convinced that this collection is the first scholarly work that responds to the contemporary realities and needs to showcase research and scholarship in social work field education.

REFERENCES

Ayala, J., Drolet, J., Fulton, A., Hewson, J., Letkemann, L., Baynton, M., Elliott, G., Judge-Stasiak, A., Blaug, C., Tetrault, A., & Schweizer, E. (2019). Restructuring social work field education in the 21st century in Canada: From crisis management to sustainability. *Canadian Social Work Review, 35*(2), 45–65. https://doi.org/10.7202/1058479ar

Bogo, M. (2015). Field education for clinical social work practice: Best practices and contemporary challenges. *Clinical Social Work Journal, 43*(3), 317–324. https://doi.org/10.1007/s10615-015-0526-5

Canadian Association for Social Work Education [CASWE]. (2022). *About us – Activities.* CASWE. https://caswe-acfts.ca/about-us/

Council on Social Work Education [CSWE]. (2015). *Report of the CSWE summit on field education 2014.* CSWE. https://www.cswe.org/Centers-Initiatives/Initiatives/Summit-on-Field-Education-2014

Drolet, J. (2020). A new partnership: Transforming the field education landscape – Intersections of research and practice in Canadian social work field education. *Field Educator, 10*(1). 1–18. https://www.proquest.com/openview/ef6ccf9ae80c58aa736fc0340d68bc48

Drolet, J., Alemi, M. I., Bogo, M., Chilanga, E., Clark, N., Charles, G., Hanley, J., McConnell, S., McKee, E., St. George, S., Walsh, C., & Wulff, D. (2020). Transforming field education during COVID-19. *Field Educator, 10*(2), 1–9. https://fieldeducator.simmons.edu/article/transforming-field-education-during-covid-19

PART I:
Field Education Practice, Research, and Theory

Addressing Class in Field: Economic Justice and Unpaid Social Work Practicums

Natalie Beck Aguilera, William Lamar Medley, C. Gage, and Annelise Hutchison

Social work students, while serving on the front lines addressing the fall-out of the COVID-19 pandemic throughout their practicums, have also been affected by it. The economic impact of the crisis has highlighted the disparate experiences between social groups, and students are part of these groups. As a profession, we can no longer ignore the impact that unpaid practicums have on our students, especially those from systemically oppressed communities. Moving forward from this crisis, we cannot go back to "how it used to be" in many ways, including the practice of unpaid practicums being the norm for the most vulnerable social work students. Our "new normal" should include a safety net of paid internships for low-income students, much as the pandemic has underscored the need for social safety nets in many areas of our society. This is an ethically and socially just way to proceed that would also increase the representation of marginalized groups in the professional field of social work.

The Council on Social Work Education (CSWE) declared field the signature pedagogy of social work education in 2008 (Boitel & Fromm, 2014), and field practicums undoubtedly play a critical role in allowing students the opportunity to link theory to practice and to learn by doing (Caldararu, 2019). While field is highly regarded for its educational value, what is rarely addressed is the economic context in which it takes place. However, in one study that does demonstrate this context, 80% of students reported that their practicum had a negative impact on their financial situation (Johnstone et al., 2016). Especially for students from economically oppressed communities, the resulting practice of unpaid practicums runs counter to the profession's belief in economic justice. This is the idea that inequalities in economic opportunities should be addressed by giving more to those with fewer native assets and those born into less favorable social positions (Reisch, 2002). The cost of unpaid internships should be a matter of concern for the entire social work community, not just those who are currently students (Johnstone et al., 2016). Our values and practice need to better align within the profession moving forward.

History

The profession of social work started out voluntary and unpaid, as future social workers would learn directly within the agencies, instead of within an organized learning context, such as post-secondary education programs (Lager & Hamann, 2010). As they ventured into academic settings before developing their own discipline, social science-focused faculty instructed early social work students to study rather than to intervene with the clients at their agencies. However, this was not in accord with what the agencies desired, which was direct help with the work at hand (Royse et al., 2016). The early tension between the academic and direct service demands of the social work practicum is still apparent today. Furthermore, this tension reflects the ongoing reality whereby agencies have historically capitalized on student labour. This continues to manifest today as students are required, typically, to complete unpaid field placements to meet graduation requirements.

Many early social workers (usually women) were viewed as "well-intentioned, committed volunteers who would soon get married" and therefore seen as not deserving more than a modest stipend (Austin, 1983, p. 361). This demonstrates that compensation for work has always been an issue for social workers, even those practicing professionally after completing their education. Additionally, this early social work context indicates that the professional field of social work itself has had to grapple with inequity in the past. Funding for professional social work arose through laws and government support for specific programs, causes, and settings (Lager & Hamann, 2010). However, this did not extend to internships: in 1947 the United States Supreme Court had ruled that trainees were not employees and did not have to be paid (Bacon, 2011; Waxman, 2018). This tradition carries on in social work education today. Though CSWE establishes current standards for many aspects of social work education, they may also situate themselves more on tradition than on the evidence of what is most beneficial to students (Hemy et al., 2016).

Students and professors contend with social work's professional history throughout the entirety of social work education programs. Investigating the power imbalances that are inherent to how social work was originally created, such as women's devalued labour as discussed above, is a valuable exercise in the foundation of social work education. A tenet of social work practice includes alleviating power imbalances within both the profession and those which negatively impact our client populations. Therefore, being familiar with the origins of the profession informs the path forward for current students as they prepare to enter the professional field. As stated in the *Code of Ethics of the National Association of Social Workers* preamble, it is imperative to have a "dual focus on individual well-being in a social context and the well-being of society" (National Association of Social Workers, 2017, para. 1), as work is done to create a more just and equitable world. That work should, and does, begin by looking inward at certain aspects of social work education which uphold harmful societal norms regarding unpaid internships that perpetuate inequality among students.

Currently

Higher education systems today replicate and reflect inequality and oppression, even though the social work departments within them teach students to fight against these social issues. Although the profession of social work espouses anti-oppressive practice, aspects of the implicit curriculum of social work, such as the structure of field practicums, replicate systems of dominance (Bhuyan et al., 2017). A characteristic that distinguishes social work practicums from internships in many other disciplines is that practicums are tied to specific learning outcomes and are, therefore, required components of the educational program. Mandating mostly unpaid internships as a condition for graduation reinforces preexisting class divides among students, benefitting those who can afford to independently finance their studies or who are supported by others while pursuing their education.

Students who must work to support themselves (and sometimes their families) must do so in addition to their practicum, not to mention other classes they may be taking or personal caregiving responsibilities. The need to work a paid job while in practicum not surprisingly leads to substantial levels of additional stress and fatigue for students in this situation (Hemy et al., 2016). Students may also be forced to take on extra debt to cover living expenses incurred during their practicum, in addition to the debt they are acquiring to enroll in the practicum course itself (Caldararu, 2019) and any other courses they are taking. Furthermore, when they must start repaying their loans, students are often in low-paying jobs (Smith et al., 2021). Though education is supposed to be the great equalizer, preexisting class divides are replicated within and beyond college (Bacon, 2011).

Research demonstrates that juggling these multiple competing responsibilities can severely impact not only students' finances, but also family responsibilities, employment stability, health, and attrition rates (Hodge et al., 2020). The stress associated with unpaid internships and financial hardship has even been found to compromise the learning experience (Hodge et al., 2020). This demonstrates that, at times, unpaid internships are self-defeating, as the learning which is the ultimate purpose of the practicum is negatively impacted by the financial situation created. While having academic discussions about how to serve economically oppressed people in the field, some social work students themselves are simultaneously experiencing economic oppression, which is then exacerbated by practicum requirements. This experience can be harmful in several ways beyond the obvious financial impact, such as potentially leading to feelings of isolation or alienation from classmates, decreased time to study and prepare for exams, and higher levels of physical exhaustion due to added labour as the student navigates both paid and unpaid work to complete their degree.

In working directly with oppressed populations, students gain a better understanding of discrimination and oppression. However, because they serve marginalized populations, the agencies in which social work students practice are often marginalized themselves, usually operating on shoestring budgets with poorly paid staff (Wiebe, 2010). This leaves little room in the budget to pay interns for their time and labour, which negatively impacts not only the students, but also other employees. As entry-level positions are converted to unpaid ones, employees are essentially pushed out (Bacon, 2011). Therefore, the consequences of unpaid practicums are complex, with significant outcomes affecting not only the student, but also current and prospective employees, and the agencies themselves.

The ways that social work practicums currently operate have been argued to meet the requirements of the Fair Labor Standards Act (FLSA; Council on Social Work Education, 2014; Slaymaker, 2014), but that makes the practice codified, not ethical. Also, the FLSA does not apply to non-profit and governmental organizations, where most social work practicums take place. In these settings, students are not considered employees but volunteers, and therefore, under the FLSA, they are not legally protected against harassment and discrimination in the workplace. This leads to social work interns working in the lowest-status positions at their organizations to gain educational experience, and the recommendations of their field instructors, without compensation (Bacon, 2011). This situation is rife with inequity.

Case Study

Sam is a senior BSW student entering her field internship placement. As a first-generation student from a single parent family, she has seen the amount of hard work and dedication it takes to support a family. She has been placed at a local non-profit organization supporting the needs of families like hers through case management and group work. Along with her internship, Sam is taking a full class load as well as working part-time as a server at a local restaurant.

Prior to the beginning of the semester, Sam attends a meeting where the field director explains the policies and procedures of the internship. During this meeting, the field director stresses that it is not recommended that practicum students work during their internship and that their internship should take priority. Knowing that her job has always been flexible and happy to work around her school schedule in the past, Sam does not worry too much about it.

Sam starts her internship and quickly falls in love with it. She is helping people, learning new things, and finally putting the information she has gained in her classes to use. Sam's field supervisor, Helen, notices the way that Sam has excelled at every task given to her and decides that she should take on more responsibility. Helen assigns Sam to co-facilitate a support group for newly single mothers as well as taking on more casework clients. Sam is excited to be part of the group until she realized that it is scheduled for the same time that she is normally scheduled to work at the restaurant.

Sam goes to her manager at the restaurant and tells her that she needs to change her availability due to the growing demands at her internship. Her manager tells her she has wanted to have this conversation with Sam for a while now. She has noticed Sam's performance slipping and that she seems distracted at work, making easily avoidable mistakes. She tells Sam that this will be her last week at the restaurant to allow her to focus on whatever is distracting her. Sam is at a crossroads. She does not know what to do. This internship, so far, has been a great learning opportunity for her, and she does not want to let the team at the internship down, but without a job she will not be able to pay for her car, gas, phone, food, or to help her family with bills.

Sam goes to her field director to explain her dilemma. Her field director reminds Sam of the policy that the internship takes priority. Sam tells her field director that she needs to work to be able to afford attending her internship and that if she starts working more, she is afraid that she will not be able to get enough hours for her internship. The field director tells her if she is worried about not getting enough hours, then she needs to work on her time management skills.

Feeling dejected after that conversation, Sam talks to her field supervisor. Her field supervisor seems empathetic at first, listening to Sam about her struggles through the internship. She suggests that Sam can do some of the aspects of her internship remotely, but she will still need to be in person for the bulk of it. She suggests to Sam that if she is unable to complete the internship for financial reasons, she can try again next semester and they would happily take her back as an intern. Sam does not like this idea. She has already put a lot of time and effort into this internship and does not want to quit now, but at the same time if she is unable to afford food, transportation, and other necessities, how can she afford to work for this organization for free?

Sam talks to others in her intern cohort. Most of them express that they are also struggling with finding a balance between internship and work. They brainstorm ways to support themselves financially through their internships, including student loans, moving in with their parents, and using public transportation, but ended up with more questions than answers. Why do we have to pay so much to work for free? What programs or policies should be put in place to assist students during their internships and why are they not already in place? What programs are in place at other schools? Other states? Other countries? In other fields? There must be a different way of doing things.

What Can Be Done

If our primary mission is to "enhance human well-being and help meet the basic human needs of all people, with particular attention to the needs and empowerment of people who are vulnerable, oppressed, and living in poverty" (National Association of Social Workers, 2017, Preamble section, para. 1), we need to start with our own students, like Sam. A safety net needs to be established to support those from economically disadvantaged backgrounds. In the United States, Federal Work-Study is designed to provide such a safety net for college students, and purportedly "encourages community service work and work related to the student's course of study" (U.S. Department of Education, n.d., para. 3), which is exactly what the social work practicum entails. However, a stipulation in the Federal Work-Study regulations states that if a student is receiving academic credit for their work, they may not be paid unless an employer would normally pay a person for that job (U.S. Department of Education, 2020). Therefore, it is argued that because it is legal and common not to pay practicum students, they can be excluded from Federal Work-Study benefits. Even though they may not be replacing a paid employee, interns are still providing un-remunerated labour for the benefit of the agency. If a student receives an internship opportunity that follows Work-Study guidelines, they should then be eligible to use their Work-Study benefits for that internship.

The Fair Labor Standards Act, on which the Federal Work-Study guidelines rely, operates on the "primary beneficiary test," which reduces the relationship between an intern and their practicum site to a transaction, and puts into question who benefits the most from it (U.S. Department of Labor & Wage and Hour Division, 2018, The Test section, para. 1). This leaves no room for the mutually beneficial nature of the social work practicum to exist. Viewing the relationship as inherently more beneficial to one party than the other and determining that the intern is the one that benefits more than the agency, is certainly not indisputable. Social workers need to make it a priority to advocate for the Federal Work-Study guidelines to be amended to allow this already-existing safety net of paid employment to easily and consistently be extended to low-income students in social work practicums.

The Interns Rights movement in Québec, led by students in female-majority "helping professions" such as social work, contended that student labour is exploited even more in fields where women represent the majority (Caldararu, 2019). Notably, majority does not translate to power in this case, as female social work students are essentially expected to care for others at their own expense (Hodge et al., 2020; Lewis, 2018). In 2019, this movement achieved a safety net in another way by successfully advocating for the provincial-level government to pay a wage for students completing their practicums (Ministère de l'Éducation, n.d.). In this way, the government systems that will directly benefit from well-trained social workers are also actively investing in their future. This model could potentially be replicated locally, as calls grow for municipalities to decrease police budgets and hire more social workers as an alternative approach to public safety. This could create room for cities and counties to invest in the support and expansion of the social work profession. For example, the city of Austin, Texas voted to redirect 45.1 million dollars from the police budget to create a fund to reimagine public safety (City of Austin, 2020). By spending $100,000, that is, less than 0.25% of that fund to create a stipend program for social work students, the city could pay for 20 semester-long internships at a rate of $5,000 per student. Social workers already work closely with all levels of government and they need to use their influence to enact programs such as these. These efforts can also be moved forward through community organizing, as was seen in the Intern's Rights movement.

Though paid practicums are rare, they are not nonexistent. Currently, some practicums are funded to promote interest in specific populations, like the Title IV-E stipend for work in the child welfare system. These programs acknowledge that funding students leads to better quality practitioners in the field. But since they are limited to specialty populations rather than needs-based, students may feel limited in their choice of practicum experience; they may even opt for paid placements out of necessity, rather than being able to pursue their personal interests (Hodge et al., 2021). Allowing social work students to explore their areas of passion will undoubtedly benefit our profession as well as society as a whole, and establishing a safety net would support this.

Students in paid practicums can benefit from their employment contributing to their education, thereby creating a synergy between work and learning (Hemy et al., 2016). Some agencies can offer stipends or full pay to practicum students. This shows that agencies can find room in their budgets if it is a priority. Additionally, disruptions to field education during the COVID-19 pandemic have led social work program administrators to rethink previous prohibitions against interning in places of employment. This is another tradition that should be reconsidered through an equity lens. Prohibiting students from being able to complete their practicum at their place of employment creates a barrier for students who have no choice but to continue working as they complete their practicum. Additionally, it adds to the stress of transportation and limited time within the student's schedule to move from location to location: students travel to campus for classes, to their place of employment, and to their field agency. This is an unnecessary stressor that could be easily eliminated should students be permitted to complete their field placement at their place of work.

Universities also need to step up and contribute to funding social work practicums. Through reallocation of current funds or seeking out new streams, schools need to ensure that their students have the support they need to successfully complete the requirements in their course of study. As the cost of tuition is increasing steadily, and far above the inflation rate, the economic barriers for students from low income families only become higher (Sherman, 2020). Universities themselves may be more reluctant to create funding avenues from within for social work students specifically. However, social work departments have the opportunity and ethical responsibility to push for change from within and to create avenues of compensation for their students. This could be done by evaluating the university budget and advocating for funds to be reallocated specifically for practicum students, assessing the budget within social work departments themselves to see where adjustments could be made to provide stipends, creating independent fundraising efforts to raise money to be distributed to practicum students, and so much more. In social work departments, collaboration between professors, administrators, and students presents the opportunity for vast creativity in finding an equitable and sustainable solution.

Providing an economic safety net for students will also increase diversity in the social work field, as students from underrepresented groups who previously could not afford an unpaid practicum will be able to pursue the profession. As social workers, we are currently less diverse than the general labour force and the populations we serve (Lewis, 2018); therefore, we need to make strides to live up to our commitment to promote equity and diversity within our own profession and to better represent and address the needs of the populations we work with (Warde, 2009). We can do this by adapting to the changing face of college students and addressing barriers that underserved students experience (Smith et al., 2021). With practicum remaining unpaid, the implication is that social work students, and thus social workers, do not come from economically oppressed communities. Through the amendment of the Federal Work-Study guidelines, collaboration with state or local government, agency and university investment, and other creative solutions, we need to demonstrate that we value the contribution of practicum students to organizations and to the profession by compensating them for their time and talent.

Conclusion

Across undergraduate and graduate students' experience, practicum is generally considered to be "the single most useful, significant, and powerful learning experience of their formal social work education" (Garthwait, 2005, p. 2). Notably, despite all that is stacked against them, students continue to demonstrate persistence and ingenuity in completing their practicums (Johnstone et al., 2016). As the signature pedagogy of social work education, field education has both an obligation to our students and a unique opportunity to demonstrate social justice values in action (Bhuyan et al., 2017). By addressing the oft-overlooked implications of requiring unpaid internships as a requirement for graduation, we can help level the playing field and promote inclusiveness in social work.

There is a need to adopt more innovative and sustainable models in social work field education, as the historical model that continues today has proven to only benefit those with economic means. Additionally, the lessons learned from the COVID-19 pandemic has opened our eyes to realities that need new understanding and approaches. Economic justice starts with us confronting our own critical issues within social work field education. As demonstrated, supporting students' material needs is imperative to their educational and professional success. There is an urgent need for social work education programs to reimagine how the profession prepares the next generation of social workers beyond what is learned in the classroom alone. As we aim to address an issue that has been overlooked for too long, we must welcome the opportunity to strengthen the field of social work by providing a more just experience to social work students and expanding the number of students who could potentially enter the field.

REFERENCES

Austin, D. M. (1983). The Flexner myth and the history of social work. *Social Service Review, 57*(3), 357–377. https://www.journals.uchicago.edu/doi/abs/10.1086/644113

Bacon, N. (2011). Unpaid internships: The history, policy, and future implications of "Fact Sheet #71." *Ohio State Entrepreneurial Business Law Journal, 6*(1), 67. https://kb.osu.edu/bitstream/handle/1811/78418/OSBLJ_V6N1_067.pdf

Bhuyan, R., Bejan, R., & Jeyapal, D. (2017). Social workers' perspectives on social justice in social work education: When mainstreaming social justice masks structural inequalities. *Social Work Education, 36*(4), 373–390. https://doi.org/10.1080/026154 79.2017.1298741

Boitel, C. R., & Fromm, L. R. (2014). Defining signature pedagogy in social work education: Learning theory and the learning contract. *Journal of Social Work Education, 50*(4), 608–622. https://doi.org/10.1080/10437797.2014.947161

Caldararu, A. (2019). "Class" is in session: Activism and adult learning in unpaid student practicums. *Canadian Journal for New Scholars in Education/Revue canadienne des jeunes chercheures et chercheurs en éducation*, *10*(1), 81–89. https://journalhosting. ucalgary.ca/index.php/cjnse/article/view/61767

City of Austin. (2020). *Police department budget.* https://austintexas.gov/page/apd-budget

Council on Social Work Education. (2014). *Internships, department of labor regulations, and social work field education: Setting the record straight.* https://www.cswe.org/ getattachment/Accreditation/2014-02-25AnnouncementreDOLandField-EF.pdf. aspx

Garthwait, C. (2005). *The social work practicum: A guidebook and workbook for students.* Pearson.

Hemy, M., Boddy, J., Chee, P., & Sauvage, D. (2016). Social work students 'juggling' field placement. *Social Work Education*, *35*(2), 215–228. https://doi.org/10.1080/0261547 9.2015.1125878

Hodge, L., Oke, N., McIntyre, H., & Turner, S. (2021). Lengthy unpaid placements in social work: exploring the impacts on student wellbeing. *Social Work Education*, *40*(6), 787. https://doi.org/10.1080/02615479.2020.1736542

Johnstone, E., Brough, M., Crane, P., Marston, G., & Correa-Velez, I. (2016). Field placement and the impact of financial stress on social work and human service students. *Australian Social Work*, *69*(4), 481–494. https://doi.org/10.1080/031240 7X.2016.1181769

Lager, P., & Hamann, B. (2010). History of social work practicum: Development of field education. In G. Thomas (Ed.), *Social work practicum and supervision* (pp. 23–44). Indira Ghandi National Open University. https://www.egyankosh.ac.in/ bitstream/123456789/52008/1/Block-1.pdf

Lewis, G. B. (2018). Diversity, pay equity, and pay in social work and other professions. *Affilia*, *33*(3), 286–299. https://doi.org/10.1177/0886109917747615

Ministère de l'Éducation. (n.d.). *Student internships.* http://www.education.gouv.qc.ca/en/ current-initiatives/student-internships/

National Association of Social Workers. (2017). *Code of ethics of the National Association of Social Workers.* https://www.socialworkers.org/About/Ethics/Code-of-Ethics/ Code-of-Ethics-English

Reisch, M. (2002). Defining social justice in a socially unjust world. *Families in Society*, *83*(4), 343–354. https://doi.org/10.1606/1044-3894.17

Royse, D., Dhooper, S. S., & Rompf, E. L. (2016). *Field instruction: A guide for social work students.* Waveland Press.

Sherman, E. (2020, August 31). *College tuition is rising at twice the inflation rate — while students learn at home.* Forbes. https://www.forbes.com/sites/ zengernews/2020/08/31/college-tuition-is-rising-at-twice-the-inflation-rate-while-students-learn-at-home/

Slaymaker, R. (2014). Are students' rights violated in field practicums? A review of the Fair Labor Standards Act in social work field education. *Field Educator*, *4*(2). https:// www.proquest.com/openview/fe06ed3b5e1ec5cb1e64e92728f386a5

Smith, D. S., Goins, A. M., & Savani, S. (2021). A look in the mirror: Unveiling human rights issues within social work education. *Journal of Human Rights and Social Work, 6*(1), 21–31. https://doi.org/10.1007/s41134-020-0057-7

United States Department of Education. (n.d.). *Federal work-study jobs help students earn money to pay for college or career school.* https://studentaid.gov/understand-aid/types/work-study

United States Department of Education. (2020). *Federal student aid handbook.* https://ifap.ed.gov/ilibrary/document-types/federal-student-aid-handbook?award_year=2020-2021&

United States Department of Labor & Wage and Hour Division. (2018). *Fact sheet #71: Internship programs under the Fair Labor Standards Act.* https://www.dol.gov/sites/dolgov/files/WHD/legacy/files/whdfs71.pdf

Warde, B. (2009). Why social work, and what does the future hold? The narratives of recently graduated Hispanic and African-American male BSW and MSW students. *Journal of Ethnic & Cultural Diversity in Social Work, 18*(1–2), 129–145. https://doi.org/10.1080/15313200802595369

Waxman, O. B. (2018). How internships replaced the entry-level job. *Time.* https://time.com/5342599/history-of-interns-internships/

Wiebe, M. (2010). Pushing the boundaries of the social work practicum: Rethinking sites and supervision toward radical practice. *Journal of Progressive Human Services, 21*(1), 66–82. https://doi.org/10.1080/10428231003782517

2

Social Work Field Education Experience with Non-Social Work Field Supervisors in Community Senior Service Setting

Karen Lok Yi Wong

There has been an ongoing debate over the years on whether social work students should be matched with non-social work field supervisors during their placements. This study contributes to the resolution of this debate for its findings should be significant to social work field education, especially during COVID-19, as this is one of the most challenging times to match a social work field student with a supervisor.

There are several reasons why a social work field student might be matched with a non-social work field supervisor. First, there are not enough social work field supervisors (Maynard et al., 2015; Strom, 1991). This has been a long challenge in social work field education. Moreover, this challenge has been exacerbated by the COVID-19 pandemic. Many social work field supervisors also have limited capacities to take field students as the impacts of COVID-19 have increased their workload or changed their practice, thus increasing the need to explore social work field placement opportunities with non-social work field supervisors. Second, social work field students may want to be placed in settings where there are no social workers (Maynard et al., 2015). Therefore, if they want to do their field placement in these settings, their supervisors will be non-social workers.

There are benefits for social work students to be matched with non-social work supervisors. The first advantage is that the field students can have richer and more varied education experiences by learning different approaches and perspectives from supervisors with backgrounds other than social work (Chipchase et al., 2012; Maynard et al., 2015; Strom, 1991). Another benefit may be that working with and learning from supervisors from multidisciplinary backgrounds stimulates field students to think outside the box and have more creative thinking (Maynard et al., 2015; Strom, 1991). Last but not least, some field students also consider that it is valuable to work with both a non-social work supervisor in the field agency and with an off-site social work supervisor (Maynard et al., 2015), which helps them build their confidence. There may be an additional benefit to the profession when social work is introduced to a student through a setting that has not traditionally employed social workers, for this may open the possibility for expansion in this area.

However, there are also concerns for social work field students if they are matched with non-social work field supervisors. The first concern is that students will have fewer, and possibly insufficient, opportunities to experience and be socialized within the profession (Chipchase et al., 2012; Maynard et al., 2015; Rogers & McDonald, 1989). A reason for this is that non-social work field supervisors may have a limited understanding of social work (Strom, 1991). They may also be less clear about the roles of a social worker and, therefore, they may not know how to support field students to develop their social work knowledge and skills (Maynard et al., 2015). Consequently, they may ask the social work students to do tasks unrelated to social work or outside the profession's scope of practice (Strom, 1991).

Generally, social work field students who are matched with non-social work field supervisors are provided some social work supervision support. For example, they may have as a secondary supervisor a social worker who is either in the field agency (Chipchase et al., 2012) or external to it, in the university setting or in a private social work supervision agency (Maynard et al., 2015). While this can help alleviate the issues just raised, there can also be problems that counteract that support. For example, the student and non-social work field supervisor are physically distant from the social work supervisor outside the field agency (Maynard et al., 2015).

As such, the social work supervisor may not have a complete picture of the field agency and how the student is doing in their field practice on a daily basis (Maynard et al., 2015). The student and social work supervisor outside the field agency may also be quite professionally distanced from the non-social work field supervisor due to different professional backgrounds. Specifically, they may lack shared theories and languages (Strom, 1991). This may impede communication and understanding between the student, non-social work field supervisor, and social work supervisor outside the field agency (Maynard et al., 2015). They may also be less clear about their own and each other's roles (Maynard et al., 2015; Strom, 1991). In some circumstances, there may also be a split between the two supervisors, creating a situation where the student is caught between the two (Maynard et al., 2015). This can be counterproductive to the student's learning. Further understanding about the dynamics of being supervised by a non-social worker may help address some of these concerns.

Research Methods

The research method used in this chapter is based on a case study from my Master of Social Work (MSW) program field placement. The field placement was a part of service enhancement study project on seniors' access to technology in a senior community service setting. Two non-social work field supervisors oversaw my work. The placement occurred between May and August 2020 during the COVID-19 pandemic. I will apply critical self-reflection to my field placement experience using the framework developed by Lay and McGuire (2010), which was specifically developed for social work education. At the core of the framework is a process of critical self-reflection using reflexivity. Reflexivity means that the person does not only reflect but also considers themselves and the people surrounding them, the power relationships, and the context within which they are operating. The goal is to challenge existing assumptions and/or think of alternative viewpoints. Although in traditional academic writing authors usually identify themselves by third-person pronouns (Tang & John, 1999), in this chapter I will use first-person pronouns "I," "me," and "mine" to identify myself, as this was my experience, instead of third-person pronouns "she," "her," and "hers;" I also want to bring myself into the chapter and thus engage with the readers more effectively (Tang & John, 1999).

A field placement refers to practical training for students in education to be prepared to work in the field after graduation (Egan et al., 2020; Gelman, 2004; Kanno & Koeske, 2010; Spector & Infante, 2020); it is also meant to serve as an opportunity to integrate classroom learning into practice. There are many different terms for this type of training and learning opportunity; however, to maintain consistency and reduce confusion, I will systematically use "field placement."

Research Context

My Field Placement

During the time spent in my placement, I consulted 28 participants from senior community services across British Columbia about their experience with information and referral services. I also attended, observed, and, when possible, participated in relevant service provision sessions, meetings, and conferences. I took field notes, critically reflected, and analyzed the data in the process. I wrote a report and an academic paper with my field supervisors to disseminate the findings. The report was aimed at service users, service providers, and the public audience, while the paper was written for academic users. Owing to social distancing guidelines during the pandemic, I did my field placement remotely. I consulted the participants and I attended, observed, and participated in sessions, meetings, and conferences via video calls, phone calls, and emails.

My Field Agencies

I found placement in two agencies. My primary field agency was a community senior service centre in Downtown Vancouver. It was established over 40 years ago and was well-known for its information and referral services in the province. The agency had a small staff, but a large volunteer population and many volunteers were also service users, aiming to promote senior-led service provision. I worked in this agency as a program coordinator from 2016 to 2017, so I knew my primary supervisor and many of the staff and volunteers before starting my field placement.

My secondary field agency was a university research institute on ageing and technology that had knowledge translation as one of its mandates. A primary goal of the institute was the transferring of research learnings to practice through active collaboration with community agencies. One of them was my primary field agency. My primary and secondary agencies had a few collaboration projects. One of these had the objective to understand information and referral services in the province, and how the services could be delivered at the community senior service centres and remotely by technology. I was the only social worker in either organization.

My Field Supervisors

My primary field supervisor was the executive director of my primary field agency, the community senior service centre. Although she did not have a social work degree, she had extensive community service experience. She provided regular supervision to me by emails and a one-on-one supervision session by phone or video call every week. She connected me with people who were from grassroots community senior services. She engaged me to think by way of concepts related to community services such as human rights, social justice, and intersectionality. She had previously worked with social workers, so she knew the strengths of social workers. She helped me understand how I could contribute as a social worker in this project-based placement. For example, she encouraged me to be a facilitator of intersectionality communication and collaboration based on my social work training.

My secondary field supervisor, a professor of gerontology specializing in ageing and technology, was the director of the institute. He provided me with regular supervision through emails and a one-on-one supervision session by video call every two months.

The two field supervisors worked closely together. The three of us met together by video call, when needed, regarding my work and progress.

My Field Education Coordinator

My field education coordinator at my school, a social worker, worked in the field education office. She collaborated with me, along with my primary and secondary field supervisors, before I started the field placement to see if we would be a good match and if the potential placement would contribute to my social work education. The school valued the extensive experience of non-social work supervisors and was open to match social work field students and non-social work field supervisors.

My Faculty Liaison

My faculty liaison, a professor at my school, was also a social worker. She was my social work supervisor outside my field agencies as well. As my faculty liaison, she made sure that I received appropriate and sufficient social work supervision. Once every two weeks, she provided by video call group supervision to me and other social work students doing their field placements with other field agencies. In addition, she provided me with individual supervision by emails and video calls. She reviewed every two weeks the reflective journals I kept on my field placement experience. In this capacity, she guided me to reflect on my roles and significance as a social worker in my field placement. My faculty liaison, my primary supervisor, and I met every two months by video call. They also jointly reviewed my field placement progress to see what I learned from my field placement.

Myself as the Field Placement Student

I had previously completed two field placements for my Bachelor of Social Work (BSW), and I had paid practice experience. After graduation from my BSW and before entering the MSW program, I practised for three years in senior community service and long-term care. I was already a social worker prior to starting my graduate degree and I had a strong social work identity. I felt ready to be supervised by non-social work supervisors because of my previous experience working in an interdisciplinary team with diverse professionals. Because of this experience, I knew how to access the social work support resources when necessary.

Additional Support

My primary field supervisor connected me with a provincial group promoting information and referral services to senior citizens in British Columbia. I was invited to observe their work in meetings. I was also connected with their members who were providers of information and referral services for senior communities. I was invited to be their trainee and I created an inventory about information and referral services across the province, which I completed alongside my field placement project.

My secondary field supervisor connected me with a national organization promoting technology supporting ageing in Canada and recommended me to be their trainee. The organization consisted of academics, professionals, service providers, seniors, and caregivers involved in a program that offered coaching and support to trainees on ageing and technology (e.g., mentorship, networking, scholarship, webinars, and courses.)

My school further connected me to a national organization promoting social work field education in Canada. It consists of academics and professionals interested in social work field education and it provides training to students in social work field education. For instance, I joined the digital storytelling program. I learned how to create a digital story of my experience being matched with my field placement. This project was showcased in a social work field education conference where I received positive feedback from the audience. It was an excellent opportunity to think about what I would like to get out of my field placement.

Discussion

Comparison with the Literature

I analyzed my field experience by comparing it with the literature on benefits and concerns in regards to matching social work field students with non-social work field supervisors.

Benefits of Having Non-Social Work Supervisors. Overall, my graduate placement experience echoes the literature that supports using non-social work supervisors. I found that I learned to collaborate with supervisors who come from non-social work backgrounds and I built confidence in such collaboration (Chipchase et al., 2012; Maynard et al., 2015; Strom, 1991).

Before my field placement, I had experience collaborating with professionals from disciplines other than social work, but their disciplines were still within the scope of healthcare and social services, such as nursing, occupational therapy, and counselling, which were closely related to social work. However, this field placement also provided me with an opportunity to collaborate with my secondary supervisor who came from a technology background. Because I had already collaborated with professionals from backgrounds other than social work before, this field placement strengthened my confidence in doing so.

I believe that my field supervisors also learned from my social work discipline. For example, there was an occasion when my supervisors and

I discussed technology as a necessary resource for seniors, and I called attention to the many discussions on access to and re-distribution of resources in the social work discipline. My secondary supervisor found this very interesting, and it helped me understand that my non-social work field supervisors and I learned from each other in the process, and the learning was mutual.

A topic less discussed in the literature is the necessity to raise awareness among field agencies to learn from and to collaborate with social workers. For example, being the first social worker at my secondary agency, I introduced the concepts of human rights on seniors' access to technology. The agency found the perspective of social work on ageing and technology inspiring. This raised their interest in listening to more social work perspectives in the future. As a social worker, I reflected upon the fact that an important part of my role was the social work perspective I brought to the table so that important social work values, such as social justice and human rights, could have a positive influence on the development of the agency.

Challenges of Having Non-Social Work Supervisors. I did not encounter the challenge of having fewer opportunities to engage in social work learning or socialization as suggested in the literature (Chipchase et al., 2012; Maynard et al., 2015; Rogers & McDonald, 1989). The main reason was that there was a close collaboration and frequent communication among all parties involved, including the field supervisors, field education coordinator, faculty liaison, and me, as the field student, to ensure that I had appropriate and sufficient social work education elements in this field placement. For example, and although she was not a social worker, my primary supervisor constantly guided me to consider social work concepts, such as social justice. My faculty liaison also guided me to think of my role as a social worker in this field placement. Finally, my field education coordinator ensured that my field placement was suited for my social work education.

I did not encounter any challenges either in clarifying my roles. All parties involved had numerous and thorough discussions about my roles in my field placement before I started it, and we set up a detailed plan based on these discussions. During my placement, my primary supervisor, faculty liaison, and I constantly had conversations about my roles. I reflected and put down my thoughts on my roles in my reflective journals for my faculty liaison to review and give feedback. I also had discussions about my roles in my placement with other social work students in my group supervision sessions through the university. I listened to other social work students sharing their roles in their placements. I compared the similarities and differences in our roles as social workers in our field placements, and this comparative process helped me understand and clarify further my roles in my placement.

I did not encounter communication challenges either (Maynard et al., 2015). I knew my primary supervisor before my placement. My primary and secondary supervisors also knew each other well before my placement. All parties involved in my placement constantly communicated prior to and during my field placement.

The last reason why I did not encounter the above challenges mentioned in the literature was because my supervisors, field education coordinator, and faculty liaison were all experienced and had knowledge and skills in interdisciplinary collaboration. For instance, although my supervisors were not social workers, my primary supervisor was experienced in community services and working with and supervising social workers. My secondary supervisor was also experienced in teaching and supervising students from diverse professional backgrounds. My field education coordinator and faculty liaison were experienced in supporting social work field students with non-social work field supervisors, as well as communicating and collaborating with their supervisors.

Things for Consideration

I am aware that my field placement was exceptionally time and resource intensive, and each party contributed a great deal to my education opportunities. All parties involved spent a lot of time meeting and communicating with each other. The communication was of such high quality that I did not encounter the types of challenges suggested in the literature. However, not every field placement could be as time and resource intensive as my field placement.

Also, I am aware that although my supervisors were not social workers, they were exceedingly experienced in supervising students or trainees from professional backgrounds different from their own. However, not every field supervisor is as experienced as my field supervisors. It could be a challenge for other non-social work field supervisors to supervise social work field students, and they might need additional training and support.

Myself

It has been noted that what the students brings to their placement plays a crucial part in the success of the field placement (Street, 2019). My previous field placement experience in BSW and my post-BSW practice experience helped me understand what I wanted to learn and achieve from my MSW field placement. Thus, I could define and discuss with people involved in my field placement my roles without anxiety. This accords with what has been noted in the literature: Students who have prior experience in social work field placements do not need a lot of hand-holding, and they can take responsibility for their learning and a suitable placement with non-social work supervisors (Maynard et al., 2015).

In my opinion, social work field students matching with non-social work supervisors should be more suitable for MSW than BSW field placement. As suggested, one challenge of having non-social work supervisors is that field students are not sure about their roles as social workers. This should not be a problem if the students are already BSW-level social workers. They do not need the same level of socialization into the profession and they already have a grounded understanding of their roles as social workers. Unfortunately, it would appear that field supervisors without a social work degree are more likely to supervise field students at an entry (BSW) level (Rogers & McDonald, 1989). We may need to re-think whether this is appropriate.

Implications for Social Work Field Research

There are a couple of outstanding questions that I think need to be addressed regarding this issue, and both of which are somehow interconnected. The first is how can we know whether a non-social work field supervisor is ready to supervise a social work field student? For example, we would like to know whether the non-social work field supervisor has a certain level of understanding of social work in order to supervise a social work field student. The second is how can we know whether a social work field student is ready to be supervised by a non-social work field supervisor? For instance, we would like to know whether the social work field student has a certain level of communication skills to communicate with supervisors whose backgrounds are not social work. Answering these questions before matching non-social work field supervisors and social work field students is important. Ideally, both sides should be ready. Future research may consider addressing these questions.

Conclusion

This study is a critical self-reflection of my graduate field placement. It is a single case example based on my personal experience, and as such it is not generalizable. I believe, however, that my example may be of benefit to others, at the very least, a starting point to weigh the benefits and challenges of using non-social workers as field supervisors.

REFERENCES

Chipchase, L., Allen, S., Eley, D., McAllister, L., & Strong, J. (2012). Interprofessional supervision in an intercultural context: A qualitative study. *Journal of Interprofessional Care, 26*(6), 465–471. https://doi.org/10.3109/13561820.2012.718813

Egan, R., Hill, N., Rollins, W., & Taylor & Francis eBooks A-Z. (2020). *Challenges, opportunities and innovations in social work field education.* Routledge.

Gelman, C. R. (2004). Anxiety experienced by foundation-year MSW students entering field placement: Implications for admissions, curriculum, and field education. *Journal of Social Work Education, 40*(1), 39–54. https://doi.org/10.1080/10437797.2004.10778478

Kanno, H., & Koeske, G. F. (2010). MSW Students' Satisfaction with their field placements: The role of preparedness and supervision quality. *Journal of Social Work Education, 46*(1), 23–38. https://doi.org/10.5175/JSWE.2010.200800066

Lay, K., & McGuire, L. (2010). Building a lens for critical reflection and reflexivity in social work education. *Social Work Education, 29*(5), 539–550. https://doi.org/10.1080/02615470903159125

Maynard, S. P., Mertz, L. K. P., & Fortune, A. E. (2015). Off-site supervision in social work education: What makes it work? *Journal of Social Work Education, 51*(3), 519–534. https://doi.org/10.1080/10437797.2015.1043201

Rogers, G., & McDonald, L. (1989). Field supervisors: Is a social work degree necessary? *Canadian Social Work Review, 6*(2), 203–221.

Spector, A. Y., & Infante, K. (2020). Community college field placement internships: Supervisors' perspectives and recommendations. *Social Work Education, 39*(4), 462–480. https://doi.org/10.1080/02615479.2019.1654990

Street, L. A. (2019). Field instructor perspectives on challenging behaviors in social work practicum. *Field Educator, 9*(1). https://fieldeducator.simmons.edu/article/field-instructor-perspectives-on-challenging-behaviors-in-social-work-practicum/

Strom, K. (1991). Should field instructors be social workers? *Journal of Social Work Education, 27*(2), 187–195. https://doi.org/10.1080/10437797.1991.10672188

Tang, R., & John, S. (1999). The 'I' in identity: Exploring writer identity in student academic writing through the first person pronoun. *English for Specific Purposes, 18*, S23–S39. https://doi.org/10.1016/S0889-4906(99)00009-5

Enhancing Equity and Accessibility in Field Education: Reflections on Mobilizing Local Research Findings in One School of Social Work

Alise de Bie, Janice Chaplin, and Jennie Vengris

In this chapter, we reflect on our experiences implementing locally-derived research findings and recommendations to our field education programme — with a focus on the beginning stages of setting-up and matching students to placements. In doing so, we contribute to several conversations in the social work education literature, including those pertaining to the field education "crisis," advancing equity and accessibility in field education, and equity-salient connections between placement learning and student employability after graduation.

As has been widely observed and analyzed, we are facing — in Canada and internationally — a scarcity of field learning opportunities for students (Ayala et al., 2018). Neoliberal policies are having a devastating impact on the social welfare sector, resulting in programme funding cuts and the elimination of social work positions which reduce the availability of placement sites and supervisors. These forces are also prompting academic institutions to expand enrollment in order to increase revenues, with a resultant expansion in the number of social work students seeking field placements (Ayala et al., 2018). This means that there has been an heightened competition for, and lack of choice in field placements. This is having a significant impact on student learning experiences, with students from equity-deserving groups (e.g., racialized, Indigenous, 2SLGBTQ+, and/or disabled students) facing particularly detrimental effects (e.g., Srikanthan, 2019). The aspirations of equity-deserving students are becoming increasingly difficult to support.

The situation is exacerbated with the understandable desire of students to have placements that will enhance their employability for preferred positions. As Ayala et al. (2018) report from their conversations with field education coordinators, students often request placements in particular sectors (e.g., hospitals and government) that they anticipate will prepare them well for secure and well-paid employment; placements in non-traditional settings are perceived as less beneficial to this goal. Hill et al. (2017) similarly found that faculty members report that students are not selecting macro concentrations due to perceptions of fewer jobs and lower salaries. This is notable in a context where many students enter social work with the hope that a professional degree will facilitate access to job security, career development, and upward mobility (Karki et al., 2018).

These decisions are especially weighty for students from equity-deserving groups who are looking for a route out of precarity, debt, and multigenerational poverty. Nashwan and Bowie (2018) found that Black social workers are more likely than white social workers to pursue a Master of Social Work (MSW) degree to increase their income. Limb and Organista (2006) found that racialized MSW students rank above-average earnings as a more important job characteristic than white students, with its overall importance increasing between their entry and exit from the program. Daniel (2011) similarly found that racialized MSW students, many of whom having grown up with financial difficulties which they still face, were attracted to the social work profession because of its focus on addressing poverty in communities and also its perceived flexibility as a career — making it possible to easily move from one job to another. At the same time, these students were concerned about supporting themselves and their families on an average social work salary and having their career mobility impeded by discrimination (also see Karki et al., 2018).

The evidence in support of students' fears, whereby macro placements or specializations indeed decrease access to well-paid employment, is limited and inconclusive. Choi et al. (2015) found that graduates with specializations in micro/direct practice were more likely to find a job matching this focus (91%), compared to graduates with a macro specialization matching related employment (64%). However, Zerden et al. (2016) report that while MSW students with a macro concentration were less likely to find a macro-oriented job directly after graduation, they continued to use macro-related skills 58% of the time, with no significant difference noted either in the time it took to find employment or the salary of graduates with micro and macro concentrations. Pritzker and Applewhite (2015) found supporting evidence that macro-trained social workers compete well for jobs and report higher salaries than the social work averages.

These findings may offer some reassurance to students pursuing macro or social justice-focused community placements that their decision may not negatively impact their career progression. However, research on the experiences of Canadian social work graduates transitioning into employment is limited (Newberry, 2011), and the literature, both Canadian and international, does not disaggregate their reporting for graduates with marginalized identities. While students from equity-deserving groups may be more likely to pursue macro practice to bring about systemic changes to the injustices they have faced (Apgar, 2020), there is limited research tracing — critically and in-depth — this decisional process (e.g., whether occurring through voluntary choice and/or discriminatory streaming to macro placements based on identity; Razack, 2002; Srikanthan, 2019) and their impact on future employment satisfaction and salaries. There is a need for further research into how racialized, Indigenous, 2SLGBTQ+, and/or disabled recent graduates and early career social workers fair in the workplace and how their placement experiences impact these trajectories.

The experiences of field instructors from equity-deserving groups are another important consideration with regards to enhancing accessibility and equity in field education, although to date there has been limited discussion in the social work literature in this area. It has been noted that marginalized social workers may not be perceived as suitable for practice education teaching; they may also be refused this opportunity for career advancement by their manager or agency (e.g., Healy et al., 2015; Stokes, 1996). Stokes (1996) reviews how Black social workers may face heavier workloads and demands (e.g., to work with Black clients, be the "race" experts) that leave little time, energy, or motivation to supervise student placements; alternately, their mentorship of Black students may go unrecognized. Singh (2004) describes how internalized racism among Black students can lead them to hold low expectations and regard for the abilities of a Black field instructor. Conversely, students may hold such high expectations of the person doing the supervision that, when unmet, lead them to disrespect a Black role model for "selling out." Black practice teachers have also reported racism from white student supervisees (Singh, 2004). While potentially challenging, field instruction opportunities are both desired and pursued by social workers from marginalized groups in order to empower, mentor, and act as role models for students — both those similarly located and from majority groups (Healy et al., 2015; Newman et al., 2008; Singh, 2004; Stokes, 1996).

Finally, it is important to note that, although the literature offers research-based recommendations for enhancing the field learning experiences of students from equity-deserving groups (e.g., Newman et al., 2008; Srikanthan, 2019), there are few examples (e.g., Razack, 2002, as one notable exception) of how Schools of Social Work have endeavoured to incorporate these recommendations into practice. This may be due to a gap between those conducting research into field education and those facilitating field education; or, an overall lack of mobilization and implementation of research findings; or, that many fields education teams do not have the dedicated time to publish about their work. Written by two members of our Field Education team at the School of Social Work at McMaster University and a postdoctoral fellow in our university's teaching and learning centre with field instructor responsibilities, this chapter offers an example of how one School of Social Work has sought to implement research findings to further support students from racialized, Indigenous, 2SLGBTQ+, and disability communities in placement learning.

Project Context and Methodology

McMaster University, a mid-size institution, is located in the urban centre of Hamilton, Canada, on the traditional territories of the Mississauga and Haudenosaunee nations. Our Field Education team (Janice Chaplin and Jennie Vengris) place approximately 150 undergraduate and six to 10 graduate social work students per year in local field settings, leading to the completion of two placements of 390 hours each for BSW students, and the completion of one placement of 450 hours for MSW students in our leadership stream. In addition, student organizing in the school, over its 50+ year history, has led to a number of important initiatives to advance equity and accessibility. Recent efforts have included the development/ re-activation of student-led caucus groups for racialized, Indigenous, queer/trans, and disabled students. These caucus groups have resulted in student-led research projects, reports, presentations, and events on 2SLGBTQ+ inclusiveness in field education, accessibility and disability inclusion in the social work program, and social work students' experiences of racism. All of this work has implications and recommendations for field education (de Bie, 2015; de Bie et al., 2020b; Watt et al., 2014). In 2016, our Field Education team applied for and received a two-year teaching fellowship from the Paul R. MacPherson Institute for Leadership, Innovation and Excellence in Teaching at McMaster to conduct research responsive to student recommendations for supporting greater equity and accessibility in field education.

The project team included Chaplin and Vengris, two student partners (de Bie, a PhD student at the time, and Dagnachew), and Dr. Randy Jackson, an Indigenous faculty member and researcher. Together, in 2017, we conducted an online survey and in-person focus groups and interviews with approximately 30 racialized, Indigenous, 2SLGBTQ+, and/or disabled students, and recent alumni to learn about their experiences of field education. In 2018, we sent an online survey to our field instructors, in which 40 people participated, 19 of whom identified as belonging to one or more equity-deserving group. This survey was administered to field instructors to understand practices they already had in place to support equity and to explore the resources they would need in relation to the themes identified in the research conducted with students. Both aspects of the project were reviewed by, and received clearance from our university's research ethics board.

While the rest of this chapter presents our efforts to implement these research findings in the chronological order of their impact on a student's trajectory through our field education processes, facilitating change has been an iterative, rather than linear, practice. For example, when conversations about and in response to our research prompted us to begin asking students explicitly about identities/experiences informing their placement preferences, we learned that some students were interested in being matched with a field instructor who shared a similar identity. This provoked a need to increase representation among our field instructors. We elaborate some of these complexities and contextual factors through our discussion of the research findings below.

Mobilizing Research Findings to Enhance Equity and Accessibility in Field Education

Getting Students Ready for Placement

We offer several orientation activities and documents to support students in entering the social work program. These include our *Important Considerations for BSW Students at McMaster* document on program structure, goals, and expectations that students read, ask questions about, and sign upon admission and initial academic advisement, as well as an orientation opportunity before classes start to meet faculty, staff, and fellow students and learn more about the School of Social Work. A second orientation session at the end of the first month of studies focuses on expectations specific to being in a professional program (e.g., professional communication and the importance of self-care). There is also an orientation to field placements at the end of first term.

Over the course of our research, a number of students challenged messages they were receiving that they should treat placement like a job; instead, they called for a greater emphasis on, prioritization of, and support for placements as "learning" experiences, not employment. At the same time, students expressed considerable worry about facing prejudice and inaccessibility in their placement that would impact their chances at obtaining social work employment. They were clearly very concerned about future career prospects (see de Bie et al., 2020a). For the students' sake, we want to treat placements as supportive and flexible learning opportunities rather than high pressure employment; yet, in our current context of significant competition for placements, particularly in Southern Ontario where the density of social work programs is high, students are required to treat placement matching seriously at the risk of losing placements to another school. Rather than expect students to navigate this context on their own, we have been supporting them through resume writing and interview preparation workshops facilitated by our university's career skills centre. We have also offered individual support to students from equity-deserving groups, encouraging them to highlight their community/activist work and skills in their resumes and interviews so that prospective field instructors can recognize students' unpaid work as valuable and significant preparation for competitive placements.

Additionally, in light of ongoing conversations with faculty and students about the impact of students' identities on their learning, we have recently been focused on having more explicit conversations about equity and accessibility in placement. During placement orientation sessions, we now highlight that sometimes students might prefer to be placed with a field instructor who shares a similar identity as a racialized, Indigenous, 2SLGBTQ+, and/or disabled person. Although we explain how this may not always be possible given historic underrepresentation of these groups in social work and amongst our field instructors, we invite students to share this optional information, if they so choose, so that we can best attempt to meet their needs. We also encourage students with disabilities to consider how any academic accommodations they receive for their coursework might translate into field placements, encouraging them to reach out to their accommodation advisor and/or the field education team for assistance.

Recruiting and Training Field Instructors

Recruiting Field Instructors. In our research, students from equity-deserving groups talked about the burden of "diversity work" they felt they were expected to perform within their placement — for example, to educate staff and speak as an expert on equity issues or to support service users from particular groups a student is perceived to belong to. Many others described feeling pathologized when they expressed concern with this type of work and coming to doubt their field instructor's ability to support them. They also faced significant "emotion work" as they sought to manage their worries about discrimination and inaccessibility in their field placement. Overall, 79% of student survey participants indicated that further recruitment of field instructors who identify as racialized, Indigenous, 2SLGBTQ+, and/or with disabilities would help to support them and their experiences (see de Bie et al., 2020a). Likewise, 75% felt that the creation of further placement opportunities explicitly focused on social justice issues affecting equity-deserving communities would be helpful to them.

In response to these students' concerns, we have been working more intentionally to increase the number of placements in these areas. This has been supported by the creation of a new faculty position with field education responsibilities to develop new macro, community, and justice-focused placement opportunities. Relationships are central to our approach to placement development, in accordance with an emphasis on relationality in field education scholarship (e.g., Asakura et al., 2018) and the six principles encouraged by our university's Office of Community Engagement (2021): Relationships build community, reciprocity, equity, continuity, openness to learning, and the commitment to act. We tapped into our existing relationships in the field while being explicit about our interest in increasing the number of placement offerings focused on equity. Additionally, over many years of discussions at faculty meetings and the School of Social Work Director's advisory council, we have kept the field program front and centre, encouraging the rest of the faculty group to consider field as applicable to them as well. We have specifically sought support to increase the number of placements focused on equity from our faculty colleagues who are connected to equity-deserving communities because of their own identities and affiliations. We know that a formal email to a generic address will not yield the kind of results that careful, relational approaches do — both in terms of the number of new field placements and the quality and connection of those placements.

While we have had some success developing new placement opportunities in organizations that do racial justice work and work with 2SLGBTQ+ communities and Indigenous community partners, some significant challenges remain. Many of the organizations involved in social justice work experience precarity in our neoliberal funding context, which can and often does result in high staff turnover because of under-resourcing. This means that our offerings within these more politicized spaces are often not secure and require ongoing connection and negotiation, as well as additional student supervision and support when staff in these settings do not hold a BSW or MSW degree (Mehrota et al., 2018). Finally, the challenge with our reliance on colleagues from equity-deserving groups to facilitate and establish new placement-generating connections is that they are already over-subscribed to represent and provide access to their communities within the university context. This work would benefit from increased representation of faculty from equity-deserving groups to share this labour more equitably.

Another challenge is that while we spend time fostering these new placement opportunities, some years we have no students interested in filling them. This upsets an organization that has started to imagine the projects they could complete with the support of a student and, in turn, this may disincentivize them from offering any placement in the future. There are complex reasons for this student disinterest in new placement options. We have heard from students — and the literature confirms this (Srikanthan, 2019) — that while students' politicized identities are central to who they are, the realities of job precarity mean that to secure future employment, many equity-deserving students want placements in "mainstream" organizations (e.g., hospitals, child welfare, school boards) that hire the greatest number of social workers and often pay higher salaries. Students, particularly those concerned about facing prejudice or discrimination in the hiring process, perceive that having more conventionally recognized placement experiences, referees/mentors, and clinical social work skills will facilitate a more successful school-to-work transition. One response might be to further encourage students from majority backgrounds, who benefit from existing social structures and may be less motivated to develop the macro-level skills needed to make systems-level change, to enter macro placements and practice settings (Apgar, 2020).

Another approach in our recruitment of field instructors is the recent development of a more robust alumni engagement strategy, an idea that was presented as part of a brainstorming session of field teams across the country at the 2019 Field Education Committee Meeting of the Canadian Association of Social Work Education (CASWE) Conference. We need to improve our ability to stay in touch with graduates from our BSW and MSW programs to facilitate their engagement as field instructors. Over the last several years, in addition to recruiting placements via email communications with our alumni, we have also begun attending 4th year practice seminars towards the end of the academic year to provide a brief interactive presentation on becoming a field instructor. We focus both on the reflective components of why they might want to be a field instructor and the technical components involved when the school begins to contact alumni about their interest in field instruction. Given our research findings, we are now explicit about our interest in finding mentors for social work learners from equity-deserving groups.

It is too early to make any claims about the effectiveness of this approach; we are unsure if it has resulted in any new field instructors — especially with respect to field instructors from equity-deserving groups — but it is a low resource, easy process with many possibilities for enhancement. Moving forward, requiring 4th year students to complete the CASWE field instructor training as part of their practice seminar might present a new opportunity to encourage their interest and prepare them to offer field instruction. We can also further support and resource our school's existing caucus/peer support groups (United in Colour, Indigenous Social Work Students Community, Social Work Queer Trans, and Disability Action Group) and work with them to develop and extend an intergenerational mentorship network of students and alumni.

Prior scholarship affirms the contribution of peer mentorship schemes to support racialized social work students in practice learning (e.g., Thomas et al., 2011), and the value of alumni engagement programs for strengthening connections between alumni and schools of social work (e.g., Skrzypek et al., 2020). There have also been calls to offer peer support groups for new social work graduates as they negotiate the challenging transition of bringing a critical perspective into the workplace (e.g., Gallop, 2018; Richards-Schuster et al., 2015). The limited social work literature on alumni engagement and early career professionals does not specifically focus on new graduates from equity-deserving groups. However, we suspect inter-cohort peer initiatives composed of current and former students from racialized, Indigenous, 2SLGBTQ+, and/or disabled communities may offer alumni valuable support and connection while also facilitating mentorship and placement opportunities for registered students.

Training Field Instructors to Provide Effective Supervision. As part of our online survey of field instructors, we asked them how their identities (e.g., race, sexuality, gender, age, disability status) and community affiliations impact the manner in which they offer field supervision and support to social work students. The vast majority (90%) of our respondents who identified as belonging to one or more equity-deserving groups provided a response to the question, in contrast to only 38% of respondents from majority backgrounds (e.g., white, heterosexual, nondisabled). This finding suggests that explicit discussions about identity (and associated power) in field instruction are important, particularly for the participants who did not see this question as relevant to them or were uncertain about how to reply. In response to these and other aspects of our research findings, we have revised and added several new equity-focused components to our 15-hour field instructor training, which is organized around the beginning, middle, and ending of field placements with an emphasis on teaching and supervision.

One addition is a module on the challenges we heard from student participants and the proposed recommendations for mediating them. In engaging with this content, attendees encouraged us to discuss early-on and explicitly how student experiences of discrimination, isolation, and witnessing oppression can manifest as behaviours that may be misperceived as a performance problem (e.g., lateness, not taking risks in meetings). We also developed an interactive group activity that invites participants to reflect on the complexity of power and how it flows between various roles in a field placement (e.g., student, field instructor, other staff, service users, organization management, community partners). We spend time debriefing dimensions that impact power — for example, what happens when a student is white and the field instructor is racialized. As well, we have had students from equity-deserving groups review the field training slides and provide feedback on how students are represented, the language used, and ideas for future modules.

There exist several challenges in providing training to current and potential field instructors. Finding 15-hours to complete training can be difficult and onerous for social workers who are already working in time- and resource-constrained settings and so, thus far, we have elected to integrate equity content into the existing training rather than add additional time. Moreover, while we ask field instructors to complete training within the first two years of supervising a student and add them to a distribution list to learn of upcoming opportunities, participation in any training is not presently mandatory. Other schools similarly grapple with this decision in a context of placement scarcity (Dalton et al., 2011), with the possibility that those who may most benefit from the training and its support to develop their equity analysis may not attend. As well, while we do ask attendees to evaluate the training to improve future iterations, we have not conducted research into how the training informs field instruction and whether those who complete training provide better field instruction and supervision. However, we have heard from a number of participants in our research that ensuring "that all field instructors have to take a training before being allowed to work with students" (S3 - disabled)[1] and setting and holding a "high standard" (FI35 - racialized) for field instruction are important strategies for supporting students from equity-deserving groups.

Finally, we have offered field forums once a year to stay connected with our field instructors and demonstrate reciprocity by providing workshops on topics relevant to their practice or field instruction. For the past couple of years, these sessions have focused on mobilizing themes and recommendations from our research (e.g., sessions discussing project findings, accessibility and accommodations for placement learners), which we intend to continue. Moving forward, many field instructor survey participants expressed an interest in online resources, the provision of which has become increasingly possible given the technological upskilling that has occurred in response to the global COVID-19 pandemic. Openness to engage with online formats will enable us to provide additional, more accessible training opportunities (e.g., webinars, lunch and learns, communities of practice) on equity-relevant topics and to link our field instructors with national field instruction training and resources.

Matching Students to Placements

While discussion of "matching" or finding a "fit" between students and placements has received little attention in the social work literature (Hay, 2020), we have found that spending time on matching students to placements and field instructors/agencies leads to more positive experiences for everyone involved. Teaching required courses in the social work program, as we both do, Chaplin and Vengris, in our roles as teaching faculty, helps us build relationships with students that become key when matching them to a placement. We get to know them, and they get to know us. In addition, we meet them individually for placement planning.

These 30-minute meetings allow us to deepen our understanding of the student's interests, needs, and concerns. Over time, and with intentional effort, we have also come to meet and know each field instructor (150 in any given year) and their practice contexts. We spend considerable time thinking and talking to each other about students' expressed needs and preferences with regards to practice context and supervision, as well as the knowledge we hold about students and potential agencies and field instructors.

Our research findings raise a number of considerations regarding potential opportunities and challenges of students from equity-deserving groups working with a similarly located field instructor, which has thus far received little attention in the social work literature (e.g., Black et al., 1997; Newman et al., 2008; Singh, 2004; Stokes, 1996). Ninety percent of field instructor survey respondents from equity-deserving groups indicated their willingness to supervise a student interested in being matched to an instructor with similar identities. Seventy-one percent of student survey respondents likewise affirmed interest in working with a field instructor who shared their identities (de Bie et al., 2020a).

We heard how helpful matching can be, if it is attentive to these considerations. For example, an "out" field instructor described their desire to mentor 2SLGBTQ+ students in navigating their identities in the workplace and facilitate opportunities to work with 2SLGBTQ+ service users and employees (FI11; see Newman et al., 2008). A field instructor with mental health disabilities described how it could be "helpful for students to be matched with someone who understands their experiences without them always having to explain or self-identify. ... It is good to see yourself reflected in someone with similar experience in a successful career" (FI8). As a racialized field instructor suggested, pairing similarly located students and field instructors can also mitigate the power differential between them, which "can be potentially empowering" for students, particularly racialized students, who may not see themselves reflected among their social work faculty/instructors (FI35). Matching in this way may also be "mutually supportive and beneficial" (FI33) and "provide opportunities for growth for both the instructor and the learner" (FI66).

We also heard that matching based on identity is complex. For example, some communities are small and identity-related matching might result in multi-faceted and complex navigation of relationships, such as when service users, providers, and students cross paths in social spaces (FI11). A field instructor with mental health disabilities also noted the potential for stigma at work and from the School of Social Work if they were to disclose their condition (FI31). As a racialized field instructor elaborated, working with a similarly located student may bring up reminders of the way the system discriminates, as well as cause field instructors to fear students' judgment with respect to the decisions the former may have made to survive the work landscape (e.g., following the status quo as a means of negotiating safety and emotional labour) (FI33). An additional limitation may be "that the student and instructor do not challenge each other's beliefs because they are too similar" (FI8). Lastly, a student "warn[ed] against identity matching unless the student wants it," given the potential negative impact on employment pathways (S8 – student identifying as racialized/pansexual).

In light of these research findings, and in consideration of both the potential opportunities and challenges of identity-based matching, all students complete a newly developed placement planning form, which invites them to optionally name aspects of their identity they would like to have considered as part of the matching process (Table 3.1). Given the range of reasons why students may be reluctant to talk about identity, we provide some context and rationale for the questions. In our trial of the form this year, equity-deserving students seem to be making use of the option to name preferences for field instructor matching.

Another consideration regarding identity-related matching pertains to different understandings and experiences of a seemingly shared identity — informed by generational differences, intersections of identity, forms of politicization, etc. We heard from one lesbian-identifying field instructor about their dislike of being grouped into a 2SLGBTQ+/queer movement or referred to as a member of an equity-deserving group, because they saw themselves as more than this and felt they had already achieved equity in their employment context (FI19). A disabled field instructor similarly contested identity-based pairing as a way of being "siloed": "[M]y disability is not my identity, and it does not define my needs. A person with a disability is no more able to 'understand' or 'relate' to me than any other person" (FI61) (for another example regarding this concern, see Healy et al., 2015).

Table 3.1: Equity/Identity-Focused Placement Planning Questions

- Is representation an important aspect of supervision for you? What does that look like? For example, if you identify as racialized, Indigenous, 2SLGBTQ+, and/or with disability, would you like us to try to find a field instructor who shares some aspects of your identity? We cannot ensure that you will always be matched with a field instructor with a similar representation due to availability, but we can try our best.

- From speaking with previous students, we know that placement experiences can include unique needs and barriers for equity-deserving individuals. If you identify as an equity-deserving student, what considerations should we take into account?

- Are there any other experiences or aspects about your identity that would be important for us to consider in terms of your placement?

- Are there any specific accommodations or equity measures that you may need in place to be successful through this placement process?

We thus recognize that any identity-related placement matching also needs to consider potentially significant differences between how any two people — student and field instructor — understand and experience their identities. For example, it is important to know which aspects of a social movement they may affiliate with, if any (e.g., disability movement efforts at desegregation; efforts to build disability-specific student community), and their relative experiences of precarity and discrimination. For this reason, it has become important for us to invite prospective field instructors to share, if they wish, their identities, backgrounds, and what these mean for them as a consideration during placement matching, as well as to recruit recent graduates from equity-deserving groups as field instructors who may share an understanding of students' politicized identities.

Pre-Placement Interviews. A critical step in the matching process is the pre-placement interview where a student and prospective field instructor meet to discuss whether the student's existing experience, desired learning objectives, and learning needs are a good fit for the placement opportunity. While students need to engage fully and professionally in this conversation to protect their chances of being offered the placement, we also suspect that if they can adequately assess the learning opportunity in this meeting, we will have fewer concerns and possible placement breakdowns later on.

Unfortunately, there is a significant power imbalance in this dialogue, further aggravated by the reality of placement shortages, and students often struggle to ask questions that allow them to adequately determine whether a placement will be a good fit. A majority (67%) of student survey participants worried about disclosing their identities/experiences in the context of placement or people at placement finding out. While some students expressed a preference to proactively disclose their needs early-on to best facilitate support for their learning, many others were fearful and held significant reservations about how disclosure might provoke prejudice with implications for placement success and future employment. Disclosure was especially difficult when students felt they did not have a choice, when they experienced regret after a disclosure, or when the disclosure did not result in desired changes or support.

Importantly, several field instructors valued and desired proactive disclosure as it facilitates their ability to provide effective supervision. Some described past experiences of student disclosure as "voluntarily shared" (FI18), "c[oming] up organically in conversation" (FI9), or as emerging when the student felt comfortable and trust was established (FIs 11, 29, 35, 36). The potential risk is that these perceptions may underreflect and overlook the significant worry and involuntariness that some students felt around disclosure, such as when they disclosed reluctantly or out of desperation and a need for support. As one field instructor explained, "I am now realizing my reliance on self-disclosure, as though this is an easy thing. I think I just realized how easy it makes supervision for me, but not necessarily for the student" (FI 58). Nolan et al. (2015) have noted a similar difference in perspective with field instructors wishing for disclosure to happen prior to placement and in a timely way as it makes arranging accommodations easier, while students delayed disclosure or did not disclose (disability and other obstacles) because they did not have an opportunity to discuss their needs or feared being judged or facing other negative consequences.

We heard from students that they wanted tools for engaging in conversations about their learning needs with field instructors, particularly in preparation for their first placement when, owing to limited experience, they could not anticipate what they might need. In our initial focus groups, 67% of our survey participants endorsed the recommendation proposed by students whereby we should develop a list of questions about accessibility, wellness, and learning needs that students might review during a pre-placement interview with a prospective field instructor. Having a school-developed and endorsed form where these questions were raised and discussed as standard practice really mattered to students, who felt it could reduce their worries about how they should disclose. Students additionally recommended that field instructors be encouraged to make gestures of openness to disclosures of equity/identity-related needs so that students could more easily assess and determine the relative safety of providing this information earlier in the placement process (see Newman et al., 2008, for similar recommendations). They also hoped for field instructors to proactively enhance the accessibility and flexibility of a placement rather than wait for students to disclose a need.

In our relationships with, and training of field instructors, we have likewise heard their uncertainty regarding what they should and should not ask in a pre-placement interview to assess for potential accommodation needs, and signal their openness to engage in conversations about identity and access. In response, we have engaged in additional consultation to develop two pre-placement interview guides, launching in the fall of 2022, one for students and the other for field instructors. We hired a student partner who consulted with other BSW students in equity-centred conversations about the kinds of questions they might want to ask or be asked. In addition, over the past four years, participants in field instructor training have engaged in a small group activity to identify what they would want to explain and ask in a pre-placement interview. We are also developing an evaluation strategy to see how these guides support conversations about student learning, equity, and access.

Conclusion

Since starting our research in 2016, we have moved the needle on equity in our field education program, implementing concrete strategies to open the conversation, while also recognizing how change processes are perhaps more complex than we anticipated. While our unique faculty positions do not require significant engagement in research, we have found this change-oriented project valuable. It became a way of holding time in our calendars for broader and deeper conversations on equity, beyond the hectic day-to-day of managing our local field education program amidst placement scarcity. Grant funding enabled us to collaborate with paid student partners from equity-deserving groups, and to gather and apply local research findings that confirmed and extended what we knew informally from our relationships with students and field instructors.

As is common in research, we are left with more questions than we have answered. Further research into how our social work graduates, particularly those from equity-deserving groups, are doing may prove vital to recruiting new field sites and supervisors, and to addressing students' concerns about employability and placement-to-workplace transitions. For example, research is needed to determine how students' placement experiences inform future career pathways and satisfaction, to understand the barriers they face in seeking employment, and to gauge the proportion of graduates who become field instructors for us. Additionally, while we have endeavoured to implement insights and recommendations from students and field instructors (e.g., integrating further equity content into field instructor training, inviting disclosures to facilitate identity-related matching when desired, and developing pre-placement interview guides), we have yet to formally evaluate whether and how these changes might enhance student and field instructor experiences. One significant implication of our work for field education, then, is recognition and promotion of the value of field education coordinators working in partnership with students and field instructors in ongoing change-oriented research and evaluation projects to enhance equity and accessibility in placement teaching and learning.

Acknowledgement: The research discussed in this chapter was funded by a 2016–2018 Leadership in Teaching and Learning Fellowship from the Paul R. MacPherson Institute for Leadership, Innovation and Excellence in Teaching, McMaster University. Thanks to Eminet Dagnachew and Randy Jackson for their contributions to the research team.

NOTE

1   Here and throughout, we use the code FI for a field instructor survey participant and S for a student survey participant.

REFERENCES

Apgar, D. (2020). Increasing social work students' participation in macro specializations: The impossible dream? *Advances in Social Work, 20*(3), 709–724. https://doi.org/10.18060/24045

Asakura, K., Todd, S., Eagle, B., & Morris, B. (2018). Strengthening the signature pedagogy of social work: Conceptualizing field coordination as a negotiated social work pedagogy. *Journal of Teaching in Social Work, 38*(2), 151–165. https://doi.org/10.1080/08841233.2018.1436635

Ayala, J., Drolet, J., Fulton, A., Hewson, J., Letkemann, L., Baynton, M., Elliot, G., Judge-Stasiak, A., Blaug, C., Gérard Tétreault, A., & Schweizer, E. (2018). Field education in crisis: Experiences of field education coordinators in Canada. *Social Work Education, 37*(3), 281–293. https://doi.org/10.1080/02615479.2017.1397109

Black, J. E., Maki, M. T., & Nunn, J. A. (1997). Does race affect the social work student-field? instructor relationship? *The Clinical Supervisor, 16*(1), 39–54.https://doi.org/10.1300/J001v16n01_03

Choi, M. J., Urbanski, P., Fortune, A. E., & Rogers, C. (2015). Early career patterns for social work graduates. *Journal of Social Work Education, 51*(3), 475–493. https://doi.org/10.1080/10437797.2015.1043198

Dalton, B., Stevens, L., & Maas-Brady, J. (2011). "How do you do it?": MSW field director survey. *Advances in Social Work, 12*(2), 276–288. https://doi.org/10.18060/599

Daniel, C. (2011). The path to social work: Contextual determinants of career choice among racial/ethnic minority students. *Social Work Education, 30*(8), 895–910. https://doi.org/10.1080/02615479.2010.520121

de Bie, A. (2015). *Enhancing accessibility and disability inclusion in the School of Social Work*. McMaster University, Hamilton. http://hdl.handle.net/11375/25050.

de Bie, A., Chaplin, J., Vengris, J., Dagnachew, E., & Jackson, R. (2020a). Not 'everything's a learning experience': Racialized, Indigenous, 2SLGBTQ, and disabled students in social work field placements. *Social Work Education*, 1–17. https://doi.org/10.1080/02615479.2020.1843614

de Bie, A., Kumbhare, S., Mantini, S., & Evans, J. (2020b). Disabled student advocacy to enhance accessibility and disability inclusion in one School of Social Work. *Critical and Radical Social Work*, 1–8. https://doi.org/10.1332/204986020X16031173597330

Gallop, C. (2018). Lost and finding: Experiences of newly graduated critical social workers. *Critical Social Work, 19*(1), 43–63. https://ojs.uwindsor.ca/index.php/csw/article/view/6027

Hay, K. (2020). "It's a whole orchestra": What are the instrumental elements in quality field education? *Social Work Education*, *39*(4), 417–429. https://doi.org/10.1080/02615479.2019.1651261

Healy, J., Tillotson, N., Short, M., & Hearn, C. (2015). Social work field education: Believing in supervisors who are living with disabilities. *Disability & Society, 30*(7), 1087–1102. https://doi.org/10.1080/09687599.2015.1076379

Hill, K., Erickson, C. L., Donaldson, L. P., Fogel, S. J., & Ferguson, S. M. (2017). Perceptions of macro social work education: An exploratory study of educators and practitioners. *Advances in Social Work, 18*(2), 522–542. https://doi.org/10.18060/21455

Karki, K. K., Chi, M., Gokani, R., Grosset, C., Vasic, J., & Kumsa, M. K. (2018). Entering precarious job markets in the era of austerity measures: The perceptions of Master of Social Work students. *Critical and Radical Social Work, 6*(3), 291–310. https://doi.org/10.1332/204986018X15388224539606

Limb, G. E., & Organista, K. C. (2006). Change between entry and graduation in MSW student views on social work's traditional mission, career motivations, and practice preferences: Caucasian, student of color, and American Indian group comparisons. *Journal of Social Work Education, 42*(2), 269–290. https://doi.org/10.5175/JSWE.2006.200400458

Mehrotra, G. R., Tecle, A. S., Ha, A. T., Ghneim, S., & Gringeri, C. (2018). Challenges to bridging field and classroom instruction: Exploring field instructors' perspectives on macro practice. *Journal of Social Work Education, 54*(1), 135–147. https://doi.org/10.1080/10437797.2017.1404522

Nashwan, A. J., & Bowie, S. L. (2018). Social work as a career: Comparative motivations of Black and White social workers. *Journal of Baccalaureate Social Work, 23*(1), 31–53. https://doi.org/10.18084/1084-7219.23.1.31

Newberry, A. M. (2011). Field experiences of newly qualified Canadian social workers. *Canadian Social Work, 13*(1), 74–92.

Newman, P. A., Bogo, M., & Daley, A. (2008). Self-disclosure of sexual orientation in social work field education: Field instructor and lesbian and gay student perspectives. *The Clinical Supervisor, 27*(2), 215–237. https://doi.org/10.1080/07325220802487881

Nolan, C., Gleeson, C., Treanor, D., & Madigan, S. (2015). Higher education students registered with disability services and practice educators: issues and concerns for professional placements. *International Journal of Inclusive Education, 19*(5), 487–502. https://doi.org/10.1080/13603116.2014.943306

Office of Community Engagement. (2021). *Principles of community engagement.* https://community.mcmaster.ca/about/strategic-priorities/principles-of-community-engagement/

Pritzker, S., & Applewhite, S. R. (2015). Going "macro": Exploring the careers of macro practitioners. *Social Work, 60*(3), 191–199. https://doi.org/10.1093/sw/swv019

Razack, N. (2002). *Transforming the field: Critical antiracist and anti-oppressive perspectives for the human services practicum.* Fernwood Books Limited.

Richards-Schuster, K., Ruffolo, M. C., Nicoll, K. L., Distelrath, C., Galura, J., & Mishkin, A. (2015). Exploring challenges faced by students as they transition to social justice work in the "real world": Implications for social work. *Advances in Social Work, 16*(2), 372–389. https://doi.org/10.18060/18526

Singh, G. (2004). *Anti-racist social work, context and development: Refracted through theexperiences of Black practice teachers* [Unpublished doctoral dissertation]. University of Warwick.

Skrzypek, C., Diebold, J., Kim, W., & Krause, D. (2020). Formalizing alumni mentoring in social work education: Lessons learned from a three-year program evaluation. *Journal of Social Work Education,* 1–14. https://doi.org/10.1080/104377 97.2020.1817820

Srikanthan, S. (2019). Keeping the boss happy: Black and minority ethnic students' accounts of the field education crisis. *The British Journal of Social Work, 49*(8), 2168–2186. https://doi.org/10.1093/bjsw/bcz016

Stokes, I. (1996). Black practice teachers: A review of some literature and its meaning for social work education and practice. *Social Work Education, 15*(2), 5–20. https://doi.org/10.1080/02615479611220101

Thomas, G. C., Howe, K., & Keen, S. (2010). Supporting Black and minority ethnic students in practice learning. *The Journal of Practice Teaching and Learning, 10*(3), 37–54. https://doi.org/10.1921/jpts.v10i3.251

Watt, L., Srikanthan, S., Adjekum, S., & Chambers, L. A. (2014). "United in Colour": Students of colour's response to racism in the university. *Canadian Association of Social Work Education Conference,* Brock University, St. Catherine's, Ontario, Canada.

Zerden, L. D. S., Sheely, A., & Despard, M. R. (2016). Debunking macro myths: Findings from recent graduates about jobs, salaries, and skills. *Social Work Education, 35*(7), 752–766. https://doi.org/10.1080/02615479.2016.1188915

The Current State of Developmental Social Work Theory and Field Education in Africa: A Scoping Review

Emmanuel Chilanga

Social work is an emerging and evolving scholarly discipline in many African countries, although it remains a field generally informed by Western social work theories and approaches (Mabvurira, 2020). Social workers apply the person-in-the-environment perspective in addressing human problems. They also engage the social, political, and natural systems to ameliorate people's distress conditions (Stoeffler, 2019). The main goal of social work in Africa is to enhance human well-being and to help individuals and communities meet their basic and complex needs; however, Afrocentric social work scholars have argued since the 1970s that the casework approach to social work does not adequately address the needs of people in Africa (Mupedziswa, 2001). They suggest that what is needed is the blending of casework and social development social work paradigms so as to align practice with socioeconomic context and objectives of the 2030 *Sustainable Development Goals* (Ibrahima & Mattaini, 2019). Consequently, there is a call for a major paradigm shift whereby social work educational institutions are encouraged to promote the incorporation of development models within the casework and field work pedagogies (Mathebane & Sekudu, 2018; Smith & Rasool, 2020).

The transforming from Eurocentric to Afrocentric social work pedagogies has the potential to influence Africa's social work theory, policy, and practice. A growing number of studies are exploring the various dimensions of development social work pedagogies and practice. For instance, some scholars are delving into the history of development social work practice in Africa (Mamphiswana & Noyoo, 2000). Other scholars are focusing on the conceptualization of developmental social work practice, while others draw attention to the relevance and conceptualization of developmental social work practice in Africa (Muleya, 2020). A growing number of studies are exploring ways in which development social work competencies are being promoted through social work theory and field education in African universities (Hochfeld et al., 2009).

Despite this overall progress, there has been to date no current study that has consolidated the literature on the status of developmental social work pedagogies in African tertiary education. A scoping review was conducted of the literature to address this gap in knowledge and to highlight the implementation of developmental social work pedagogies in Africa. This chapter reports the findings of that exercise and intends to stimulate debate and document the application of developmental social work pedagogies in African tertiary education.

Conceptualizing Clinical and Developmental Social Work

According to Goldstein (1996), clinical social work is the professional application of social work theories and approaches to the identification, treatment, and prevention of biopsychosocial problems usually focused on the individual, the family, or small-group level. In Africa, clinical social work has been criticized for its stance and overemphasis on the remedial approach, which medicalizes social problems that need socio-structural interventions (Muchacha & Matsika, 2018). These critiques are shaping and strengthening social work theory and field education pedagogies in order to develop competent professionals who can address the challenges that are unique to the continent. As such, the focus of developmental social work is social work practice at the mezzo- and macro-level and is primarily on the application of social development theories (Ibrahima & Mattaini, 2019). The result has been the conceptualization of a hybrid clinical-developmental social work model.

Clinical-developmental social work is the combination of the clinical and social developmental social work methods which aims to avert the incidences of diseases, diminish disease burden, and deal with socio-structural issues that impact clinical issues (Chigangaidze, 2021). Clinical-developmental social work includes valuing the drivers of human well-being within the micro, mezzo, and macro systems. The paradigm involves the analysis of the political, economic, social, technological, legal, and environmental factors that influence human well-being. It is argued that in Africa, clinical-developmental social work should be mainly concerned with addressing the biopsychosocial factors that predispose and exacerbate human poverty and disease burden (Kurevakwesu & Maushe, 2020). Therefore, it is indispensable that education institutions in Africa should also pay much attention to developmental social work practice that has the potential to empower social work professionals to address local community problems.

Situational Analysis of Challenges that Affect People in Africa

Africa is a continent with approximately 1.3 billion people across 54 countries (Dang & Dabalen, 2019). Most African nations experience severe social problems that undermine people's well-being. This section focuses on common problems that affect people in Africa, the theory and practice of social work pedagogies, and the study objectives.

Research has shown that poverty is one of the main drivers of social problems in Africa. According to the international poverty line whereby an individual disposes of less than US$1.25 per day for their livelihood (Crespo Cuaresma et al., 2018), it is estimated that about 490 million people (36% the African population) experience extreme poverty. Poverty in Africa is exacerbated by social factors such as corruption (Riley & Chilanga, 2018) and nepotism that are not checked due to poor governance structures, weak constitutions, and political instability. Other scholars suggest that neocolonial policies, such as structural adjustment programs, exploit economies in Africa and impoverish its citizens (Durokifa & Ijeoma, 2018). Consequently, there is a high level of poverty in Africa which is coupled with high and ever-increasing levels of unemployment

(Salecker et al., 2020). This means that to overcome the structural factors that perpetuate poverty among Africans, social workers need to have theory and field practice competencies that can support communities.

In Africa, food insecurity is recognized as one of the main predisposing factors of biopsychosocial challenges, particularly among vulnerable groups (Amungo, 2020). A significant number of people in Africa experience chronic starvation despite the continent being endowed with rich natural resources that could exponentially increase food production. It is suggested that food insecurity in Africa can be mitigated by addressing diverse environmental and socioeconomic factors. These include erratic weather conditions, poor food security policies, high costs of farm inputs, prohibitive transportation costs, lack of credit facilities for farmers, and competition for markets (Kerr et al., 2016). Hence, social work pedagogies in Africa should be tailored to equip students with clinical-development competencies that can address the underlying factors which drive food insecurity.

In addition, epidemics such as HIV/AIDS, malaria, and COVID-19 are either perennial or emerging threats that are affecting the socioeconomic well-being of many Africans (Chilanga et al., 2020; Dzimbiri et al., 2022). It is documented that Africa, mainly in the Sub-Sahara, has the highest HIV/AIDS infection rates in the world. The HIV/AIDS pandemic was intensified in Africa mainly owing to most African leaders' denial of the presence of the disease and their unwillingness to take urgent public health action. Millions of people have become infected and millions have died (McGee, 2020). Since the onset of COVID-19, the livelihood and well-being of many people in Africa have deteriorated. For instance, studies have shown that the pandemic has increased poor mental and physical health due to the infection itself and the negative impacts of preventative measures (Posel et al., 2021). Social work education in Africa should be geared to address diseases that affect the quality of life of many people on the continent.

Theory and Practice of Social Work Pedagogies

Social work is a practice-based profession that entails a combination of theoretical and practice learning. Field practicums provide an interactive context where students learn and demonstrate the knowledge, skills, and values of the social work profession (Boitel & Fromm, 2014). However, the field of social work is not well established on the African continent, partly because of its colonial heritage and the lack of unified social work regulatory bodies (Mwansa, 2011). The foundation of social work education in Africa is grounded in Eurocentrism that assumes a neoliberal value system of social control (Mwansa, 2011). Hence, many social work educational institutions in the region continue to apply Western-oriented social work pedagogies that are focused on casework to address social problems.

Of late, however, scholars are advocating that the indigenization of social work education in Africa would better address its social problems (Zvomuya, 2020). Clinical-developmental social work theory and practice education curriculum is regarded as an effective education model that can mitigate challenges that undermine the well-being of Africans (Muleya, 2020a). Developmental social work is a form of social work that departs from an entirely clinical social work (residual, service-oriented) model that is directed at specific groups of people in need, to broader development approaches that place people and human rights at the heart of social organizing. The theory and field education curriculum of developmental social work is designed to empower social workers to advocate for economic development and confront structural systems that perpetuate social problems. The practice focus is at the mezzo and macro levels where practitioners work with political actors to build a conducive environment for socioeconomic development (Rankopo & Diraditsile, 2020). The approach also equips students with critical social work skills, such as community organizing and empowerment. Hence, development social work practice is claimed to be aligned with the 2030 Agenda for *Sustainable Development Goals* (SDG), which aims to facilitate human development in Africa (Muleya, 2020).

Objectives

Despite compelling evidence that social work educational institutions in Africa should recast their curriculum towards social developmental pedagogy, there is no scoping review that has highlighted how the curriculum is being implemented through theory and practicum pedagogies. There is also a dearth of broader knowledge on factors that are enhancing or undermining the implementation of the curriculum in social work theory and field education (Manomano et al., 2020). Therefore, this study examines how social development pedagogy is being implemented in social work tertiary education on the African continent. This scoping review is guided by a set of questions that were used to explore approaches in which development social work pedagogies are promoted in theory and field education. The following questions guide the review of the literature:

- What criteria are used to assess the promotion of social development pedagogies in social work theory and field education in Africa?
- How are social development-oriented pedagogies taught in social work theory and field education in Africa?
- What are the common aspects of social development being promoted in social work theory and field education in Africa?
- What factors undermine the implementation of developmental social work pedagogies in social work theory and field education in Africa?

Methods

Systematic Scoping Review

This study adopted the Preferred Reporting Items for Systematic Reviews and Meta-Analyses — Extension for Scoping Reviews (PRISMA-ScR) checklist and guidelines to ensure a robust and replicable process (Tricco et al., 2018). The checklist contains 20 essential reporting items and two optional items to include when completing a scoping review. The goals of scoping reviews are many. They are used to examine the extent, range, and nature of the evidence on a topic or question. They are also used to determine the value of undertaking a systematic review on a given topic. In addition, scoping reviews are used to summarize findings from a body of knowledge that is heterogeneous in methods or discipline. Finally, they are used to identify gaps in the literature to facilitate the planning and commissioning of future research (Tricco et al., 2018). The protocol is presented in Figure 4.1.

Figure 4.1: The Study Protocol

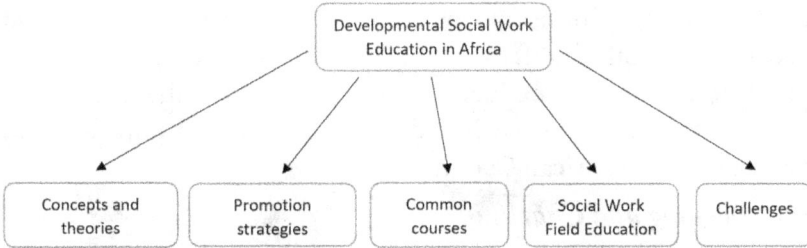

Data Collection

Search Strategy

The author conducted a systematic search of the following 10 Social Work electronic databases for articles published from 1980 up to June 2021: CINAHL PsycArticles (APA); PsycINFO 1987- (Ovid); Social Services Abstracts (ProQuest); Social Work Abstracts (Ovid); Ebsco; eScholarship@ McGill; MEDLINE(R) (OVID) ALL; 1946-, Social Sciences Citation Index (SSCI) (Web of Science); SocINDEX with full text (EBSCO); and Google Scholar. An iterative search using the combination of the following terms was conducted: "development* social work," "social development social work," "education," "field education*," "field practice*," "theory class," and "classroom lessons." Since the review focused on studies that were conducted in Africa, the following search terms were also included: "Africa," "Botswana," "Malawi," "South Afri* Zimbabwe," "Lesotho," "Namibia," "Zambia," "Tanzania," "Kenya," "Ghana," "Uganda," "Mozambique," "Nigeria," etc. The following Boolean operators 'OR' and 'AND' were used to connect the words. These terms were informed by a priori knowledge and were intended to capture the breadth of the nomenclature used in social work theory and practice research pedagogies. Restrictions were set based on language as only English journal papers were considered.

Inclusion and Exclusion Criteria

Inclusion criteria were based on studies and reviews that were presented in English. To include more papers with relevance-based evidence in regard to implementation of developmental social work pedagogies in theory and field education, both qualitative and quantitative studies were included in the search. Articles were excluded if they failed to fulfil the following two criteria: (1) to primarily delve into developmental social work; and (2) to feature at least one African Country.

Data Screening and Charting

All records were screened by the author using the eligibility criteria. After reading titles and abstracts for their relevance to this scoping review, full papers were retrieved and exported to Zotero (Kratochvíl, 2017) before being downloaded to a personal computer. This was followed by a screening of full text articles. Data charting was completed by the author with a focus on level of developmental social work pedagogy implementation in Africa, key concepts, challenges, and outcome variables. Methods were categorized as either qualitative or quantitative. The data charting form was piloted on a random sample of 11 articles.

Results

In total, 58 documents published between 1982 and June 2021, including journal articles, books, dissertation, and reports, were considered as shown in Figure 4.2.

Criteria Used to Assess the Promotion of Social Work Development Pedagogies in Africa

This scoping review has identified three papers that focused on developing a criterion for evaluating the degree to which social development pedagogies are promoted in social work theory and field education in Africa (Hochfeld et al., 2009; Mupedziswa, 2001; Mupedziswa & Sinkamba, 2014). The criterion is divided into two broad subcategories which are curriculum and extracurricular related activities (Mupedziswa, 2001). Five critical curriculum-related activities have been identified to adequately assess the extent to which developmental social work pedagogies are promoted in social work theory and field education in Africa.

Figure 4.2: Literature Search Results

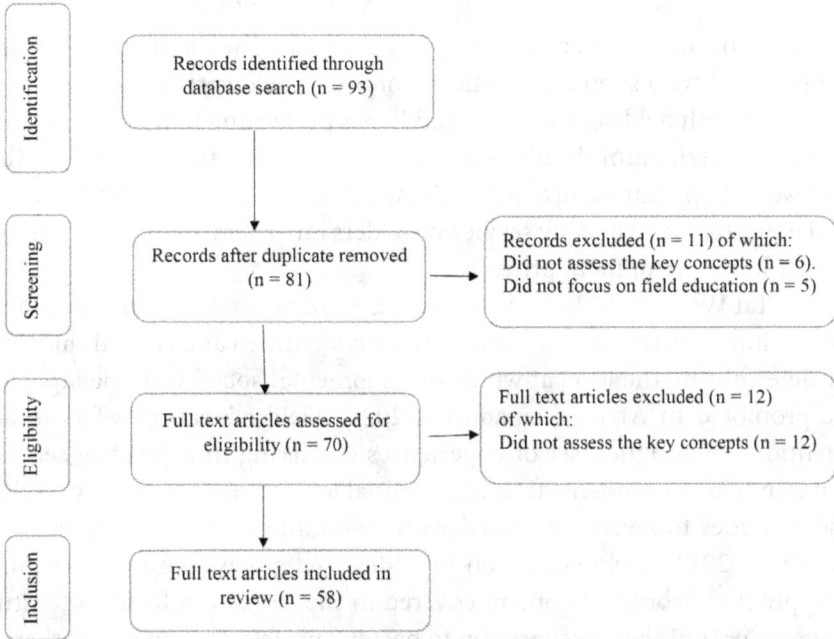

Curriculum-Related Activities

Continuous Curriculum Review Exercise. Continuous curriculum review exercise is the first category that has been documented for ensuring that social development competencies are incorporated in social work curriculum in African tertiary educational institutions. One article argued that if social work educators are engaged in rigorous developmentally focused curriculum review exercises, they can tailor social work theory and field education to address the challenges that confront people in Africa (Gray et al., 1996). It is advocated that the review process should ensure that courses are analyzed horizontally, with emphasis on the depth of the content of each course, and vertically, with the emphasis on each course linking in well with those at the levels below and above it. It is also acknowledged that there is a need for carrying out a rationalization exercise for the courses, and new additional courses should be introduced where necessary to make the education curriculum more sensitive to the needs of any given country (Ibrahima & Mattaini, 2019).

In addition, the literature suggests that social work curriculum developers in Africa should periodically organize fieldwork workshops during which both fieldwork matters and issues pertaining to the relevance of the entire curriculum should be discussed (Osei-Hwedie et al., 2006). The field workshops can ensure that social work stakeholders such as students, field educators, and agency service providers and users are involved in the curriculum development process.

Social Work Field Education. Social work field education is a second curriculum-related activity which has been identified as a critical category for determining the level at which developmental social work pedagogies are promoted in Africa (Amadasun, 2021). Field education refers to an intentionally designed set of experiences occurring in a practice setting that aim to move students from their initial level of comprehension, skills, and attitudes to levels associated with autonomous social work practice (Dhemba, 2012). Field education provides students with an opportunity to apply the theoretical content covered in the classroom to real life situations as part of their preparation to become professional social workers.

This review identified that social work training institutions in Africa use one of four forms of field education. These are concurrent, block, a combination of both concurrent and block, and in-service placements (Schmidt & Rautenbach, 2016). In-service field placements refers to a practice in which a serving lay trainee social worker participates in field education in their own work agency (Kagee, 2020). Each of the field education approaches has its own strengths and limitations.

The general agreement in the reviewed literature is that institutions should reorient field education to make it consistent with the developmental social work goals (Amadasun, 2021). One way of reorienting field education that is suggested is to place students in rural field agencies (where the majority of underprivileged population resides) that can equip them with development competencies (Thurlow et al., 2019). It is also recommended that students should be placed in some development-related urban placements when rural placements are not feasible. To make developmental pedagogies attainable, some scholars underscore that at least one rural field placement should be mandatory to students (Smith & Rasool, 2020). The aim is to introduce social work students to under-privilege areas where they can appreciate, from a social work perspective, the nature of the problems that most of the African marginalized population face.

Application of Social Development Themes, Perspectives, and Concepts. The reviewed literature suggests that the inclusion and application of specific social development themes, perspectives, and concepts is one of the curriculum-related approaches that are used to assess the promotion of social work developmental pedagogies in Africa (Patel & Hochfeld, 2013). There are several concepts that have gained popularity in this respect.

The reviewed literature shows that indigenization is one of concepts that African social work curriculum should inculcate in students. Indigenization refers to a worldview that states that the theories, values, and philosophies of social work practice must be influenced by local factors such as cultures, beliefs, cosmology, and social milieu (Ugiagbe, 2015). Therefore, indigenization aims to develop social work competencies among students that are appropriate to the needs of different communities in Africa.

Other notable concepts include the reconceptualization of social work concepts to more community-oriented approaches in order to empower marginalized groups in society (Raichelis & Bravo, 2021). This reconceptualization aims to make room for social workers to adapt and modify old ideas, knowledges, and processes of practice, as well as the emergence of new ones in a concerted efforts to develop competent social work professionals.

Authentication and recontextualization are also terms that are advocated in social development pedagogies (Hugman, 2009). These terms focus on the identification of genuine and authentic roots in the local system, which can then be used for guiding social development social work practice through a marked departure from the Eurocentric models in order to affect changes that consider existing local views, behaviours, and conditions.

Teaching Methods. The reviewed papers consider that an assessment of teaching methods is one of the ways to authenticate if a social work institution is committed to promoting developmental social work pedagogies (Hochfeld, 2009). The literature supports that, apart from commonly used teaching strategies such as seminars, role plays, guest lectures, field visits, and video films, actual classroom instruction must be characterized by dialogue, discovery, and exploration. These teaching and learning methods are known by different names in other parts of the world, such as self-directed learning, small group teaching, and use of small groups (de Bruijn & Leeman, 2011). To achieve discovery learning, some scholars suggest that social development-oriented classrooms should be organized in circular sitting patterns as opposed to conventional sitting patterns in which the teacher is at the front (Hochfeld, 2010). This sitting pattern can give room to a problem-posing teaching approach, a strategy which is more suitable for enhanced interaction and dialogue among students and a teacher.

Student Projects and Assignments. The nature of student projects and assignments is another common critical curriculum-related feature that is used to evaluate the degree to which an education institution is promoting developmental social work competencies (Mupedziswa, 2008). The reviewed papers emphasized that instructors should ensure that student projects reflect key areas of concern in the communities where the students will serve. Some scholars stressed that evaluation projects should focus on empowering students with skills to enable them to play a significant role in improving conditions of ordinary people in the community (Anucha, 2008). In particular, the reviewed papers noted that student projects should focus on broad issues such as unemployment and underemployment, hunger, inadequate shelter and homelessness, illiteracy, diseases, and local development.

Extracurricular Activities

Social work extracurricular activities have also been identified as a critical aspect in the promotion of a developmental approach in social work education in Africa (Mupedziswa, 2001). In the field of education, extracurricular activities are optional activities that are designed and carried out after classes to develop and enhance students social skillsets (Buckley & Lee, 2021). The reviewed literature indicates that there are eleven extracurricular activities that are documented to be used in gauging if social work in education institutions are promoting developmental social work competencies (Hochfeld et al., 2009). The following paragraphs delve into selected extracurricular activities that are promoted in social work education in Africa.

Generation and Use of Indigenous Teaching Materials. The reviewed literature suggests that developmental-oriented institutions should encourage educators and students to engage in extracurricular activities that generate and use Indigenous teaching materials such as clay models that can be used to represent ideas (Ugiagbe, 2015). The authors acknowledge that most students shy away from producing and utilizing Indigenous resources that can address local problems and needs, as the legacy of professional imperialism is claimed to undermine the use of local resources. As such, social work scholars are encouraged to sensitize African students to be proud of local resources (Mabvurira, 2020b).

Generation and Use of Relevant Local Research. Generation and use of relevant local research are among the extracurricular activities that are documented in the reviewed literature as a criterion for promoting developmental social work competencies in Africa (Canavera et al., 2020a). Notable scholars, such as Osei-Hwedie and Rankopo (2009), have argued that local research must be promoted to ensure that social work education is relevant in solving Africa's unique challenges. Scholars suggest that the focus of research efforts should be on aspects relating to societal values, social institutional arrangements, and major social problems affecting the majority of people in African countries (Sewpaul & Lombard, 2004). Therefore, they propose to draw attention to diverse areas of research that can promote developmental social work. These include informal sector activities, social security for the rural poor, survival strategies of the marginalized population, the role of non-governmental organizations (NGOs) in poverty alleviation, AIDS home care, the social impact of structural adjustment programmes, and issues pertaining to refugees and other displaced persons (Gilbert et al., 2009).

Networking with Other African Institutions. Development of strong linkages among public and private welfare stakeholders has also been proposed as an important aspect of the extra-curriculum that can promote developmental social work competencies among scholars and students in

Africa (Osei-Hwedie et al., 2006). It is suggested that this mission can be achieved if deliberate initiatives are put in place where there can be an exchange of literature on teaching materials as well as the exchange of faculty members and students. Nevertheless, it is also suggested that social work scholars and administrators in Africa should promote scholars to be engaged in professional publications, workshops, and conferences that share relevant themes to developmental social work (Canavera et al., 2020).

Localization of Staff Complement. The localization of a substantial percentage of social work instructors at a given institution is one way of ensuring that a social developmental social work approach is being promoted (Mwansa, 2011b). The claim is that an African institution cannot possibly assert that it is promoting relevant social work if most of its instructors are expatriates from outside the continent. It is assumed that the majority of expatriates lack comprehension and appreciation of the local situation and, hence, they are marginally equipped to address social problems that affect many Africans (Pellebon, 2012).

Common Approaches to Teaching Social Work Development Curriculum in Africa

The reviewed literature suggests that the development approach to social work practice is taught through mainstreaming, specialization, and ad hoc undergraduate curriculum (Canavera et al., 2020a).

Mainstreaming Curriculum

The first approach is that the social development pedagogy is mainstreamed throughout the social work degree programme roadmap. For example, a regional study in Africa (Eastern and Southern Africa) observed that 24 universities apply social development as a fundamental approach to social work (Nhapi & Dhemba, 2020). This means that the curriculum is designed in such a way that social development competencies are mainstreamed in the curriculum.

Specialized Developmental Social Work Curriculum

The second approach is that developmental social work is offered as one of the specialization areas of social work curriculum in African tertiary education (Hochfeld, 2009). In this case, students are registered in the developmental social work stream during the program application. Hence, they acquire broader development social work competencies upon satisfactory completion of curriculum milestones. In the Sub-Sahara African region, less than 25% of the tertiary education institutions offer specialized social development social work curriculum (Kurevakwesu & Maushe, 2020).

Ad Hoc Development Social Work Curriculum

The reviewed literature has shown that in some tertiary education institutions in Africa, developmental social work is taught on a more ad hoc basis where it is not specialized or mainstreamed (Hochfeld et al., 2009). In this approach, developmental social work concepts and skills are integrated and conveyed through certain core course syllabi. In this case, students attain the concepts of social development through teaching methods such as case studies, examples, or guest lectures.

Common Developmental Social Work Course Content in Africa

The reviewed literature indicates that there are common developmental course content offerings that are taught in the sampled 61 African tertiary educational institutions (Canavera et al., 2020; Hochfeld et al., 2009). The most common courses include community development, HIV/AIDS, gender studies, social development, and poverty. These courses are considered relevant as they can stimulate and enhance the socioeconomic development of people in Africa. Figure 4.3 illustrates the proportion of Schools of Social Work in Africa in which particular social development topics are taught.

Figure 4.3: Common Developmental Social Work Courses

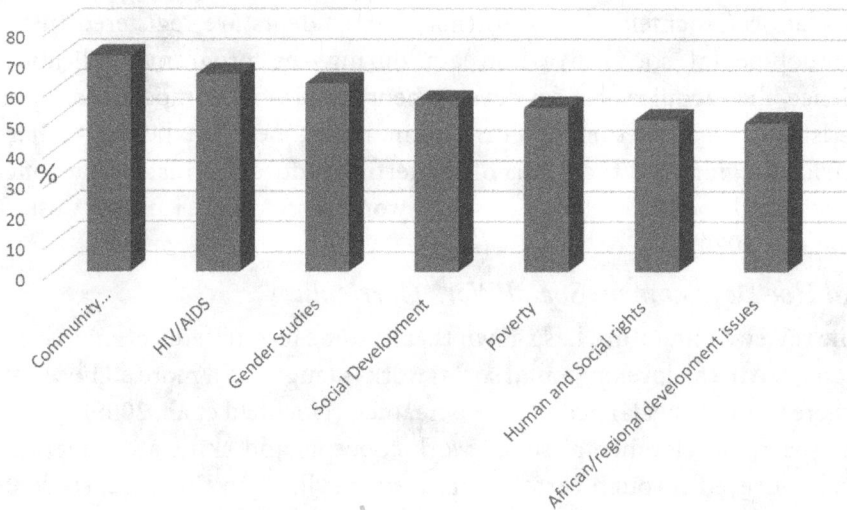

The Role of Field Education in Promoting Development Social Work Competencies in Africa

The reviewed papers suggest that field education is a mandatory component in many social work tertiary institutions (Canavera & Akesson, 2018). It has been observed that there are three models of supervising students during field practicum. The most common approach involves a shared supervision between the practitioners at the field agency and the school instructors. Almost 71% of the social work tertiary education in Africa follows this joint supervision model (Mathebane & Sekudu, 2018). The second approach involves field practitioners having sole responsibility for supervising students. About 26% of social work field curriculum in Africa follows this approach. Finally, supervision by field faculty from the school is the model whereby students are placed in an agency but are entirely supervised by the school supervisor who may be a professor or field practicum coordinator. This is a less common approach as only 3% of the programs follow it (Mathebane & Sekudu, 2018).

The literature suggests that in Africa, students and instructors agree that field education is a critical component of social work education as it provides opportunities for students to develop clinical and development social work skills (Dhemba, 2012). There are four common approaches that are effective in supporting students to acquire social work development competencies during field education. The first is when students are assigned to experienced social development practitioners who can mentor them. The second approach is when students are offered the chance to attend lectures that are related to social work skills during the field education. The third approach that enhances acquisition of social development field competencies is when students are involved in experiential field education program in small groups. The notable experiential programs include supervised role plays, simulations, and engagement with stakeholders. The fourth effective approach for acquiring developmental social work competencies during field education is when students are given opportunity to observe social work professionals during direct practice. This may include giving students opportunities to observe a counselling session, or getting students involved in development projects such as proposal writing and consciousness-raising campaigns.

Challenges Faced by Tertiary Institutions in Promoting Development Social Work in Africa

As shown in this review, many social work education and training institutions in Africa have heeded the call to move in the direction of developmental social work by incorporating developmental themes in their courses. Universities in South Africa, Lesotho, Ghana, Zimbabwe, Nigeria, and Malawi are among these institutions (Mathebane & Sekudu, 2018). Although this approach is indispensable in addressing African challenges, the reviewed literature suggests numerous obstacles that undermine the promotion of developmental theory and field education pedagogies in Africa. The following section illustrates common issues that have been documented in the literature, including inadequate local resources, limited research, field education challenges, and lack of social work regulatory bodies (Ioakimidis & Sookraj, 2021).

Lack of Indigenous Materials for Use in Schools of Social Work in Africa

There is a consensus that the lack of Indigenous materials is one of the main challenges that undermines the promotion of development social work theory and field education in Africa (Mogorosi, 2018). It is well documented that social work literature in many African institutions is imported from Europe, America, Australia, and other developed countries. Consequently, the literature used does not reflect African culture, its diversity, and socioeconomic realities (Almeida et al., 2019). Specifically, a study that was conducted in Lesotho illustrates that textbooks used in its social work tertiary education were written by British or American academics (Dhemba & Nhapi, 2020). It also observes that there was an overall shortage of books for social work students in comparison to students from other disciplines. This problem is not particular to Lesotho, as a study in Zimbabwe also indicates that the lack of local production of teaching resources affects the development of evidence-based and adaptable practice (Dhemba & Nhapi, 2020). Consequently, this challenge has hindered the effective learning and systematic indigenization of overseas social work knowledge, leaving Zimbabwe-trained social workers to rely on Western knowledge to support their professionalization process. Hence, there is a continuous call to synthesize the Western literature based on African values and culture to appropriately address African problems (Giliomee & Lombard, 2020). Curriculum that depends heavily on Western textbooks results in a lack of fitness-for-purpose between social work education and the service needs of the African population.

Limited Research to Inform Developmental Social Work Theory and Practice Pedagogies

The reviewed literature suggests that there is limited research that is carried out in African countries that can be used to inform development-oriented social work curriculum (Nhapi, 2021). As a result, the literature which is informed by Western research is used in teaching, despite the fact that study findings are not being replicated in Africa. A significant proportion of the social work assignments and case studies given to students are completely decontextualized from actual scenarios taking place in Africa (Hochfeld et al., 2009). It is noted that this often poses a great challenge when students are faced with real cases during practice, as some of the theories learned are not applicable in their local context. For instance, some scholars in Africa, including South Africa (Turton & Schmid, 2020), observed that social work training in the region is dominated by theories that are inherited from developed countries that have strong emphasis on academic subjects at the expense of local practical skills of intervention (Mathebane & Sekudu, 2018). There is a need to encourage social work scholars in Africa to be engaged in local research that can transform social work theory and practice pedagogies. Application of local research can reorient the curricular and teaching methods to be synthesize with indigenous information, so that social work education in Africa can be relevant to local needs (Osei-Hwedie & Boateng, 2018).

Challenges Related to Social Work Field Education

The reviewed literature suggests that there are some aspects of social work field education training on the African continent that affect the promotion of developmental social work practice. These include the demand for social work field placements that outstrips availability in most countries, due to the limited number of social work agencies (Chitereka, 2009). In addition, most field placement agencies do not have trained social workers to supervise all students, which undermines the acquisition of quality casework and the development of social work competencies. Limited funding for fieldwork supervision, combined to the lack of allowances for students on placement, also reduces the ability of social work tertiary institutions to send their students to remote areas where they are most needed. A study that was conducted in 16 social work programs in Southern African countries documented seven common field practicum challenges. The challenges are depicted in Table 4.1.

Another challenge related to field education focuses on the standard duration students can be placed at an agency to acquire experiential social work skills (Canavera et al., 2020). A limited number of studies in Africa suggest that there is great variation in the number of months for social work field placement. The minimum duration is three months, the mode is five months, while the maximum is six months. The literature agrees that it may be a challenge to prescribe the form and duration of field education as social work tertiary institutions are unique. This review has identified

Table 4.1: Common Challenges Facing Field Education in Africa

Challenge	Schools having the problem (n = 16)
Inadequately trained field supervisors	15
Shortage of relevant placement	14
Problem with timing of field placement	12
Poor quality of field supervision	9
Lack of field supervisors with social work education	8
Part-time students do not have time to fulfill the requirements	4
Experience gained by students does not reflect the reality of social work in the country	3
Other	2

a consensus among students and field supervisors that there is a need for field placement in Africa to be long enough for students to develop and consolidate their skills (Hochfeld et al., 2009).

Finally, the reviewed literature suggests that the lack of structured field education curriculum is another challenge that undermines the promotion of developmental social work education in Africa (Gray et al., 2017). Field placement curriculum is indispensable in social work education as the required competencies to be attained are shaped by the curriculum content. The field curriculum provides structure to students' learning process where simple skills are learned prior to complex skills. In addition, curriculum acts as a benchmark for student evaluation and, as such, it can be used to identify areas of student strength and shortfalls where field instructors can focus their remedial training. The reviewed literature suggests that fieldwork placement forms are the main course material documents that are used in many African field education curriculum. The forms include: background information forms of the students, assessment forms, guidelines for writing fieldwork reports, contract forms, and letters of introduction for students (Ross, 2018). The available literature suggests that many institutions did not have fieldwork manuals. Fieldwork manuals are necessary since they provide students, agency supervisors, and social work educators valuable reference material on emerging developmental competencies.

Social Work Regulation, Legislation, and Accreditation in Africa

In the reviewed literature, several scholars agree that the regulation of social work education and profession is critical as it can result in a wide array of benefits (Reyneke, 2020). These include improved public safety, higher standards of conduct and accountability, and improved professional development. In Africa, social workers operate in a wide range of settings. These include child protection agencies, refugee centres, and hospitals where social workers offer a wide range of services such as psychosocial support, assessments to clients, and community development mobilization. The nature of social work practice requires the establishment of long-term relationships based on trust, and the human costs of unsafe or unethical practice has been documented in many studies across the world (Farkas & Romaniuk, 2020). This must entail the integrity of the profession, whereby social work is upheld by a high standard of professionalism, safety, and accountability to ensure that members of the public are protected. The dangers of malpractices in social work practice can be alleviated through the institutionalization of regulatory systems, which benchmark and uphold standards of professionalism, and the introduction of formal mechanisms for oversight and accountability (Mthethwa, 2019).

Although social work is being regulated in many countries across the world, the current review suggests that a considerable number of countries in Africa do not have social work regulatory systems in place. It should be noted that some countries in Africa such as Zambia, Malawi, Tanzania, and Uganda are in the process of developing social work regulatory arrangements (Davies & Egbuchu, 2019). According to scholarly research, the process of creating regulatory bodies is facing challenges in the region as it does not have support from policy makers.

It is also of interest that some scholars agree that the mushrooming of unregistered social work colleges and training institutions in Africa poses a threat to the effectiveness of the profession (Mungai et al., 2014). This is because such institutions do not employ qualified social work trained staff, they do not invest in social work required resources, and are not regulated. The absence of these critical resources has generated a laissez-faire attitude towards social work in Africa. The consequences could be disastrous for human development, consumers, and the profession in general.

Conclusion and Way Forward

The reviewed literature suggests that social work education in Africa aspires to address emerging and perineal problems such as poverty, diseases, and food insecurity that are experienced by common people (Chilanga et al., 2020). The main goal of social work education is therefore to produce professionals that can assist countries to achieve human development. The literature suggests that the developmental social work approach is indispensable in Africa as it is tailored to equip students with knowledge, skills, relevant technologies, and an appreciation of local philosophy that can be applied in addressing local problems. There are diverse ways in which stakeholders evaluate the commitment of African tertiary education institutions to promoting developmental social work pedagogies. These approaches are categorized into curriculum and extra-curriculum. Curriculum-related indicators include continuous curriculum review, relevant field placement, the application of relevant concepts, development-related teaching methods, and assigning relevant projects to students. The extra-curriculum indicators include the production and use of local materials, local research, and local collaboration. The developmental social work competencies are integrated through mainstreaming and are offered as specialized course or through ad hoc approaches.

However, it is well documented that the education system is facing enormous challenges to produce social work professionals sufficiently equipped to address local problems such as corruption, disease burden, and poverty (Hochfeld et al., 2009). These constraints include shortage of local teaching resources such as books and research resources, inadequate and irrelevant field placements, and limited social work regulatory bodies.

This scoping review has indicated that the social work is an emerging, but a rapidly expanding profession in Africa. To effectively address African social problems, both social work professionals and social work educational institutions are called upon to adopt the developmental social work approach. To achieve this goal the following suggestions are made:

1. Social work professionals in Africa should prioritize developmental social work research to inform educational pedagogies that are appropriate and suited to the local context.

2. The onus should be put on the redesigning of the social work curriculum with alternative teaching methodologies that resonate with social development principles and local context in Africa.

3. Social work curriculum designers in Africa should pay attention to the specific skillset needs of field education supervisors to improve the overall quality of students' supervision.

4. Lastly, social work professionals should actively develop local teaching materials that contain case scenarios relevant to the needs of African communities.

REFERENCES

Almeida, R. V., Rozas, L. M. W., Cross-Denny, B., Lee, K. K., & Yamada, A.-M. (2019). Coloniality and intersectionality in social work education and practice. *Journal of Progressive Human Services*, *30*(2), 148–164. https://doi.org/10.1080/10428232.2019.1574195

Amadasun, S. (2021). COVID-19 pandemic in Africa: What lessons for social work education and practice? *International Social Work*, *64*(2), 246–250. https://doi.org/10.1177/0020872820949620

Amungo, E. (2020). Africa: A continent of shortages. In E. Amungo (Ed.), *The rise of the African multinational enterprise (AMNE): The lions accelerating the development of Africa* (pp. 47–59). Springer International Publishing. https://doi.org/10.1007/978-3-030-33096-5_4

Anucha, U. (2008). Exploring a new direction for social work education and training in Nigeria. *Social Work Education, 27*(3), 229–242. https://doi.org/10.1080/02615470701381459

Boitel, C. R., & Fromm, L. R. (2014). Defining signature pedagogy in social work education: Learning theory and the learning contract. *Journal of Social Work Education, 50*(4), 608–622. https://doi.org/10.1080/10437797.2014.947161

Buckley, P., & Lee, P. (2021). The impact of extra-curricular activity on the student experience. *Active Learning in Higher Education, 22*(1), 37–48. https://doi.org/10.1177/1469787418808988

Canavera, M., & Akesson, B. (2018). Supervision during social work education and training in Francophone West Africa: Conceptual frameworks and empirical evidence from Burkina Faso and Côte d'Ivoire. *European Journal of Social Work, 21*(3), 467–482. https://doi.org/10.1080/13691457.2018.1441131

Canavera, M., Akesson, B., Landis, D., Armstrong, M., & Meyer, E. (2020). Mapping social work education in the West Africa region: Movements toward indigenization in 12 countries' training programs. *International Journal of Social Welfare, 29*(1), 83–95. https://doi.org/10.1111/ijsw.12372

Chigangaidze, R. K. (2021). COVID-19 and the calls of humanistic social work: Exploring the developmental-clinical social work concerns of the pandemic. *International Social Work*, 00208728211007911. https://doi.org/10.1177/00208728211007911

Chilanga, E., Collin-Vézina, D., MacIntosh, H., Mitchell, C., & Cherney, K. (2020). Prevalence and determinants of malaria infection among children of local farmers in Central Malawi. *Malaria Journal, 19*(1), 308. https://doi.org/10.1186/s12936-020-03382-7

Chitereka, C. (2009). The challenges of social work training: The case of Lesotho. *International Social Work, 52*(6), 823–830. https://doi.org/10.1177/0020872809342660

Crespo Cuaresma, J., Fengler, W., Kharas, H., Bekhtiar, K., Brottrager, M., & Hofer, M. (2018). Will the Sustainable Development Goals be fulfilled? Assessing present and future global poverty. *Palgrave Communications, 4*(1), 1–8. https://doi.org/10.1057/s41599-018-0083-y

Dang, H.-A. H., & Dabalen, A. L. (2019). Is poverty in Africa mostly chronic or transient? Evidence from synthetic panel data. *The Journal of Development Studies, 55*(7), 1527–1547. https://doi.org/10.1080/00220388.2017.1417585

Davies, E. O., & Egbuchu, S. A. (2019). Ethics in the public service in Africa: A focus on the Nigerian public service. *KIU Journal of Social Sciences, 5*(2), 91–105. https://www.ijhumas.com/ojs/index.php/kiujoss/article/view/516

de Bruijn, E., & Leeman, Y. (2011). Authentic and self-directed learning in vocational education: Challenges to vocational educators. *Teaching and Teacher Education, 27*(4), 694–702. https://doi.org/10.1016/j.tate.2010.11.007

Dhemba, J. (2012). Fieldwork in social work education and training: Issues and challenges in the case of Eastern and Southern Africa. *Social Work & Society, 10*(1), Article 1. https://ejournals.bib.uni-wuppertal.de/index.php/sws/article/view/310

Dhemba, J., & Nhapi, T. G. (2020). Social work and poverty reduction in Southern Africa: The case of Eswatini, Lesotho, and Zimbabwe. *Social Work & Society, 18*(2), Article 2. https://ejournals.bib.uni-wuppertal.de/index.php/sws/article/view/609

Durokifa, A. A., & Ijeoma, E. C. (2018). Neo-colonialism and Millennium Development Goals (MDGs) in Africa: A blend of an old wine in a new bottle. *African Journal of Science, Technology, Innovation and Development, 10*(3), 355–366. https://doi.org/10.1080/20421338.2018.1463654

Dzimbiri, M. N., Mwanjawala, P., Chilanga, E., & Munthali, G. N. C. (2022). Perceived implications of COVID-19 policy measures on food insecurity among urban residents in Blantyre Malawi. *BMC Public Health, 22*(1), 522. https://doi.org/10.1186/s12889-022-12922-6

Dzinamarira, T., Dzobo, M., & Chitungo, I. (2020). COVID-19: A perspective on Africa's capacity and response. *Journal of Medical Virology, 92*(11), 2465–2472. https://doi.org/10.1002/jmv.26159

Farkas, K. J., & Romaniuk, R. (2020). Social work, ethics and vulnerable groups in the time of Coronavirus and COVID-19. *Society Register, 4*(2), 67–82. https://doi.org/10.14746/sr.2020.4.2.05

Gilbert, D. J., Harvey, A. R., & Belgrave, F. Z. (2009). Advancing the Africentric paradigm shift discourse: Building toward evidence-based Africentric interventions in social work practice with African Americans. *Social Work, 54*(3), 243–252. https://doi.org/10.1093/sw/54.3.243

Giliomee, C., & Lombard, A. (2020). Human rights education in social work in Africa. *Southern African Journal of Social Work and Social Development, 32*(1), 1–18. https://doi.org/10.25159/2415-5829/5582

Goldstein, E. G. (1996). What is clinical social work? Looking back to move ahead. *Clinical Social Work Journal, 24*(1), 89–104. https://doi.org/10.1007/BF02189944

Gray, M., Agllias, K., Mupedziswa, R., & Mugumbate, J. (2017). The role of social work field education programmes in the transmission of developmental social work knowledge in Southern and East Africa. *Social Work Education, 36*(6), 623–635. https://doi.org/10.1080/02615479.2017.1310833

Gray, M., Mazibuko, F., & O'Brien, F. (1996). Social work education for social development. *Journal of Social Development in Africa, 11*(1), 33–42.

Hochfeld, T. (2009). Social development and minimum standards in social work education in South Africa. *Social Work Education.* https://doi.org/10.1080/02615470903055463

Hochfeld, T. (2010). Social Development and Minimum Standards in Social Work Education in South Africa. *Social Work Education, 29*(4), 356–371. https://doi.org/10.1080/02615470903055463

Hochfeld, T., Selipsky, L., & Mupedziswa, R. (2009). *Developmental social work education in Southern and East Africa.* https://bettercarenetwork.org/library/social-welfare-systems/social-service-workforce-strengthening/developmental-social-work-education-in-southern-and-east-africa

Hugman, R. (2009). But is it social work? Some Reflections on mistaken identities. *The British Journal of Social Work*, *39*(6), 1138–1153. https://doi.org/10.1093/bjsw/bcm158

Ibrahima, A. B., & Mattaini, M. A. (2019). Social work in Africa: Decolonizing methodologies and approaches. *International Social Work*, *62*(2), 799–813. https://doi.org/10.1177/0020872817742702

Irurzun-Lopez, M., & Poku, N. (2005). Pursuing African AIDS governance: Consolidating the response and preparing for the future. In *The African State and the AIDS Crisis*. Routledge.

Kagee, A. (2020). Training lay counsellors in public health: Considerations for social workers, professional counsellors and psychologists. *Global Public Health*, *15*(6), 918–924. https://doi.org/10.1080/17441692.2020.1730931

Kerr, R. B., Chilanga, E., Nyantakyi-Frimpong, H., Luginaah, I., & Lupafya, E. (2016). Integrated agriculture programs to address malnutrition in northern Malawi. *BMC Public Health*, *16*(1), 1197. https://doi.org/10.1186/s12889-016-3840-0

Kratochvíl, J. (2017). Comparison of the accuracy of bibliographical references generated for medical citation styles by EndNote, Mendeley, RefWorks and Zotero. *The Journal of Academic Librarianship*, *43*(1), 57–66. https://doi.org/10.1016/j.acalib.2016.09.001

Kurevakwesu, W., & Maushe, F. (2020). Towards Afrocentric social work: Plotting a new path for social work theory and practice in Africa through ubuntu. *African Journal of Social Work*, *10*(1), 30–35. https://www.ajol.info/index.php/ajsw/article/view/194099

Mabvurira, V. (2020). Making sense of African thought in social work practice in Zimbabwe: Towards professional decolonisation. *International Social Work*, *63*(4), 419–430. https://doi.org/10.1177/0020872818797997

Mamphiswana, D., & Noyoo, N. (2000). Social work education in a changing socio-political and economic dispensation: Perspectives from South Africa. *International Social Work*, *43*(1), 21–32. https://doi.org/10.1177/a010518

Manomano, T., Nyanhoto, R., & Gutura, P. (2020). Prospects for and factors that militate against decolonising education in social work in South Africa. *Critical and Radical Social Work*, *8*(3), 357–370. https://doi.org/10.1332/204986020X16019188814624

Mathebane, M., & Sekudu, J. (2018). Decolonising the curriculum that underpins social work education in South Africa. *Southern African Journal of Social Work and Social Development*, *30*(1), 1–19. https://doi.org/10.25159/2415-5829/2360

McGee, C. (2020). The continuing impact of HIV/AIDS on development in Africa: A systematic analysis using the political systems and contagious disease theories. In K. T. Setiloane & A. K. Bangura (Eds.), *Africa and Globalization: Novel Multidisciplinary Perspectives* (pp. 171–187). Springer International Publishing. https://doi.org/10.1007/978-3-030-55351-7_9

Mogorosi, L. D. (2018). Social work and indigenisation: A South African perspective. *Southern African Journal of Social Work and Social Development*, *30*(1), 1–18. https://doi.org/10.25159/2415-5829/2393

Mthethwa, E. (2019). Trading the hard road: Social work ethics and the politicization of food distribution in Zimbabwe. In *The Routledge Handbook of Social Work Ethics and Values*. Routledge.

Muchacha, M., & Matsika, A. B. (2018). Developmental social work: A promising practice to address child marriage in Zimbabwe. *Journal of Human Rights and Social Work*, *3*(1), 3–10. https://doi.org/10.1007/s41134-017-0042-3

Muleya, E. (2020). Developmental social work and the sustainable development goals in South Africa: Opportunities and challenges. *The International Journal of Community and Social Development*, *2*(4), 470–486. https://doi.org/10.1177/2516602620975226

Mungai, N. W., Wairire, G. G., & Rush, E. (2014). The challenges of maintaining social work ethics in Kenya. *Ethics and Social Welfare*, *8*(2), 170–186. https://doi.org/10.1080/17496535.2014.895401

Mupedziswa, R. (2001). The quest for relevance: Towards a conceptual model of developmental social work education and training in Africa. *International Social Work*, *44*(3), 285–300. https://doi.org/10.1177/002087280104400302

Mupedziswa, R. (2008). Twenty-two years of training social work practitioners in Africa: Reflections on strategies and techniques. *Journal of Teaching in Social Work*, *28*(3–4), 343–354. https://doi.org/10.1080/08841230802160118

Mupedziswa, R., & Sinkamba, R. P. (2014). *Social work education and training in southern and east Africa: Yesterday, today and tomorrow*. https://ses.library.usyd.edu.au/handle/2123/18305

Mwansa, L.-K. (2011). Social work education in Africa: Whence and whither? *Social Work Education*, *30*(1), 4–16. https://doi.org/10.1080/02615471003753148

Nhapi, T. (2021). Social work decolonisation- forays into Zimbabwe experiences, challenges and prospects. *Social Work & Policy Studies: Social Justice, Practice and Theory*, *3*(2), Article 2. https://openjournals.library.sydney.edu.au/index.php/SWPS/article/view/14385

Nhapi, T. G., & Dhemba, J. (2020). Embedding the developmental approach in social work education and practice to overcome poverty: The case of Southern Africa. *Greenwich Social Work Review*, *1*(1), 11–20. https://doi.org/10.21100/gswr.v1i1.1103

Osei-Hwedie, K., & Boateng, D. A. (2018). "Do not Worry Your Head": The Impossibility of Indigenising Social Work Education and Practice in Africa. *Southern African Journal of Social Work and Social Development*, *30*(3), 12 pages-12 pages. https://doi.org/10.25159/2415-5829/3978

Osei-Hwedie, K., Ntseane, D., & Jacques, G. (2006). Searching for appropriateness in social work education in Botswana: The process of developing a master in social work (MSW) programme in a 'developing' country. *Social Work Education*, *25*(6), 569–590. https://doi.org/10.1080/02615470600833469

Osei-Hwedie, K., & Rankopo, M. J. (2009). Developing culturally relevant social work education in Africa: The case of Botswana. In *Indigenous Social Work around the World*. Routledge.

Patel, L., & Hochfeld, T. (2013). Developmental social work in South Africa: Translating policy into practice. *International Social Work*, *56*(5), 690–704. https://doi.org/10.1177/0020872812444481

Pellebon, D. (2012). Is Afrocentricity marginalized in social work education? A survey of HBSE instructors. *Journal of Human Behavior in the Social Environment*, *22*(1), 1–19. https://doi.org/10.1080/10911359.2011.588573

Posel, D., Oyenubi, A., & Kollamparambil, U. (2021). Job loss and mental health during the COVID-19 lockdown: Evidence from South Africa. *PLOS ONE*, *16*(3), e0249352. https://doi.org/10.1371/journal.pone.0249352

Raichelis, R., & Bravo, M. I. (2021). The social work reconceptualisation movement in Latin America and the renewal in Brazil: The protagonist role of the Latin American Social Work Centre. *Critical and Radical Social Work*, *9*(1), 31–45. https://doi.org/10.1332/204986020X16031175256697

Rankopo, J. M., & Diraditsile, K. (2020). The interface between Botho and social work practice in Botswana: Towards Afrocentric models. *African Journal of Social Work*, *10*(1), 1–4.

Reyneke, R. (2020). The legal and ethical obligations of school social workers. *Social Work*, *56*(2), 157–174. https://doi.org/10.15270/52-2-818

Riley, L., & Chilanga, E. (2018). 'Things are not working now': Poverty, food insecurity and perceptions of corruption in urban Malawi. *Journal of Contemporary African Studies*, *36*(4), 484–498. https://doi.org/10.1080/02589001.2018.1547373

Ross, E. (2018). Reimagining the South African social work curriculum: Aligning African and Western cosmologies. *Southern African Journal of Social Work and Social Development*, *30*(1), 1–16. https://doi.org/10.25159/2415-5829/2273

Salecker, L., Ahmadov, A. K., & Karimli, L. (2020). Contrasting monetary and multidimensional poverty measures in a low-income Sub-Saharan African country. *Social Indicators Research: An International and Interdisciplinary Journal for Quality-of-Life Measurement*, *151*(2), 547–574. https://link.springer.com/article/10.1007/s11205-020-02382-z

Schmidt, K., & Rautenbach, J. V. (2016). Field instruction: Is the heart of social work education still beating in the Eastern Cape? *Social Work*, *52*(4), 589–610. https://doi.org/10.15270/52-2-532

Sewpaul, V., & Lombard, A. (2004). Social work education, training and standards in Africa. *Social Work Education*, *23*(5), 537–554. https://doi.org/10.1080/0261547042000252271

Smith, L. H., & Rasool, S. (2020). Deep transformation toward decoloniality in social Work: Themes for change in a social work higher education program. *Journal of Progressive Human Services*, *31*(2), 144–164. https://doi.org/10.1080/10428232.2020.1762295

Stoeffler, S. W. (2019). Social work and poverty: A critical examination of intersecting theories. *Social Development Issues*, *41*(2), 21–32. https://drive.google.com/file/d/1Z07CAQ8NQSMa8RrLtLs9AjOtISZLj3Rn/view

Thurlow, J., Dorosh, P., & Davis, B. (2019). Chapter 3—Demographic change, agriculture, and rural poverty. In C. Campanhola & S. Pandey (Eds.), *Sustainable food and agriculture* (pp. 31–53). Academic Press. https://doi.org/10.1016/B978-0-12-812134-4.00003-0

Tricco, A. C., Lillie, E., Zarin, W., O'Brien, K. K., Colquhoun, H., Levac, D., Moher, D., Peters, M. D. J., Horsley, T., Weeks, L., Hempel, S., Akl, E. A., Chang, C., McGowan, J., Stewart, L., Hartling, L., Aldcroft, A., Wilson, M. G., Garritty, C., … Straus, S. E. (2018). PRISMA extension for scoping reviews (PRISMA-ScR): Checklist and explanation. *Annals of Internal Medicine, 169*(7), 467–473. https://doi.org/10.7326/M18-0850

Turton, Y., & Schmid, J. (2020). Transforming social work: Contextualised social work education in South Africa. *Social Work, 56*(4), 367–382. https://doi.org/10.15270/56-4-880

Ugiagbe, E. O. (2015). Social work is context-bound: The need for indigenization of social work practice in Nigeria. *International Social Work, 58*(6), 790–801. https://doi.org/10.1177/0020872813515013

Zvomuya, W. (2020). Utilization of ubuntu bowl in social work processes: The way to go towards attainment of social development in Africa. *African Journal of Social Work, 10*(1), 63–68. https://www.ajol.info/index.php/ajsw/article/view/194107

PART II:
Anti-racist and Indigenous Knowledges, Methodologies, and Perspectives

5

A Social Work Student in Search of an Anti-Racist Education: A Conversation with Myself

Zipporah Greenslade

Racism has, over the years, proven to be an almost insurmountable part of our lives. While we shy away from any suggestion that we may be racist, racism continues to affect everyday aspects of our lives. This has given rise to the concept of *racism without racists*, an avoidance that is reflected in the hesitancy to discuss race and racism for fear of arising tensions (Blake, 2014; Bonilla-Silva, 2013).

The year 2020 tested our humanity and our sense of community, as Canadians and as global citizens. As COVID-19 was spreading, another sinister element flared — racism. This was especially manifested in anti-Asian racism and in increased incidents of racially motivated harassment and attacks on visible minorities (Hango, 2020). George Floyd died on 25 May 2020 in the United States, with the arresting police officer's knee on his neck. In a video that was broadcast worldwide, the world watched in horror as Floyd's life ebbed away. This agonizing visual catapulted North America and Europe into racial justice movements — most notably, Black Lives Matter. Disturbing news of racial injustices grew by the day, and the unrest increased. A call to defund the police and invest in more social and mental health supports emerged.

While these sentiments originated in the United States, they were echoed in Canada. Social workers were called upon as leaders in anti-racism education and community mobilization. This is where I come in. In the summer of 2020, I was looking forward to the fourth and final year of my Master of Social Work (MSW) program. I was completing my final practicum, and I felt fairly grounded in my education and my potential as a social worker. As calls for racial justice and for social workers to step up were amplified, I found myself increasingly anxious about my readiness to practice. Soon I was reaching out to members of my cohort for support on how to engage in anti-racist conversations. Instead of answers, I found my angst echoed. Continued conversations with various groups of social work students, in and out of my university, emphasized this sense of unease. I began to notice a general sense of unpreparedness for anti-racist social work practice. While I was relieved to know that my apprehension was shared by other students, I began to question the role that social work education had played in preparing us for anti-racist social work. The need to understand the relationship between my sense of preparedness and my education became particularly salient as racial tensions intensified. Consequently, in November 2020, I embarked on an intentional anti-racist education research journey, both in the form of an autoethnography and an exploration of how transformative anti-racist education intersects with opportunities to engage.

While this chapter provides a review of literature focusing on anti-racist social work education, I highlight an ongoing gap in anti-racist education; I discuss critical race theory as a framework for engaging in race-based conversations; I locate myself as a researcher and I share a race-charged vignette from a practicum experience; then, I engage in a conversation with myself as I analyze the conflict that I encountered in an effort to move past my experience. In doing so, I bring forth the vital role of critical conversations in anti-racist education and the all-important role that social work field education plays in connecting theory to practice.

Anti-Racist Social Work Education

There is an assumption that social work students will automatically know how to engage in conversations about racism and how to provide support to racialized persons. This assumption can be linked to social work's connection to social justice, in so far as discussing the latter is expected to result in an understanding of anti-racism. However, becoming anti-racist is an intentional process that needs to be actively addressed within the curriculum and scaffolded through discussions, activities, and critical self-reflection (Ladhani & Sitter, 2020; Yee & Dumbrill, 2016).

Thus far, this intentionality has been sorely lacking in social work curricula. An even greater dearth of information is apparent in research focusing on anti-racist field education. This is partly attributed to a shift from anti-racism to an anti-oppressive approach. Additionally, terms and concepts, such as multiculturalism, equity, equality, ethnicity, cultural competency, prejudice, discrimination, anti-discriminatory, cultural sensitivity, and cross-cultural have taken over the social work curriculum as safer ways to talk about differences (Abrams & Moio, 2009; Constance-Huggins, 2012; Coxshall, 2020; Ladhani & Sitter, 2020; Pulliam, 2017; Singh, 2019; Yee & Wagner, 2013). This shift is of particular concern as it has resulted in students lacking foundational knowledge about systemic racism, let alone being prepared to dismantle it.

To this end, there is a growing body of literature that recognizes a multitude of challenges faced by social work educational programs. These include a lack of faculty professional development opportunities focused on race and racism; a fear and hesitancy to discuss Whiteness, power, privilege, race, and racism; varying needs and experiences of White versus racialized instructors and White versus racialized students; a Black/White binary approach to race; and a lack of clear expectations focused on anti-racist pedagogy (Almeida et al., 2019; Bubar et al., 2016; Fultz & Kondrat, 2019; McGuire & Lay, 2020; Nakaoka & Ortiz, 2018; Ortiz & Jani, 2010; Phillips, 2010; Varghese, 2016). With these obstacles to negotiate in the classroom, it is little wonder that anti-racism is barely discussed in field education. Up until now, far too little attention has been paid to the gap in anti-racist field education for social work students. This is evident in the scarcity of research resources available.

As is often the case with conversations about racism, much of the research has been descriptive of anti-racist social work education as an area of study defined by fear (Cox et al., 2021; Giwa & Mihalicz, 2019; Singh, 2019). This has served a silencing purpose whereby social work programs leave conversations about racism to the discretion of educators. In a field of study and a profession that is largely representative of White social work educators and practitioners, the silence in conversations regarding race, racism, and Whiteness brings into question the power structures within the profession and the educational setting.

Also of note is the sentiment that anti-racist education does not seem to be realistic or applicable because it does not outline specific proficiencies or acquisition of transferrable skills (Jeffery, 2005). Instead, students — and especially White students — continue to be torn between wanting to understand and dismantle systemic racism, while at the same time finding anti-racist education difficult to apply. In part, this is ascribed to the history of social work as a profession geared towards helping. To do that, we, as practitioners, feel the need to understand phenomena in ways that allow us to "wrestle them into submission" through "boxing them into solvable categories." Race and racism have continued to be a struggle for scholars, researchers, and practitioners. To assume that race and racism will be easy to understand or dismantle will presuppose a gross underestimation of these concepts' pervasiveness. To begin to grasp anti-racism, I propose adopting a critical race theory approach as an educational foundation.

A Critical Race Approach to Field Education

Critical race theory (CRT) is imperative as a theoretical framework in the context of anti-racist education, because it explicitly critiques race, racism, Whiteness, white supremacy, the construction of power, and the ways in which racism is sustained institutionally and systemically (Coxshall, 2020; Ortiz & Jani, 2010). The integration of CRT into anti-racist curriculum is essential in providing a framework to examine the social work profession and in analyzing power and oppression, with race at the epicentre. A stance in which race is central to the discussion is vital in all anti-racism efforts. To do otherwise would make a mockery of the enduring oppression borne out of racism.

One of the ways in which racism is sustained is by not being spoken about, which may be caused by the fear of not understanding, the fear of tensions that arise from its discussion, or the fear of saying the wrong thing. Yet, even as the silence persists, so too do incidents of racism and white supremacy in continuing to permeate all aspects of social work practice settings. This is evidenced by documented discrimination of racialized persons within health settings, education institutions, justice systems, housing and homelessness, employment opportunities, salary gaps, interactions with police, experiences of poverty, child and youth welfare systems, immigration and refugeeness, infant and adult mortality, and it is demonstrated in every social determinant of health (Fultz & Kondrat, 2019; Giwa & Mihalicz, 2019; Kolivoski et al., 2014; Weinberg & Fine, 2020). Given the prevalence of racism, it is safe to assume that social workers in any field of practice, knowingly or unknowingly, encounter persons affected by racism.

How, then, can social work graduates be prepared to identify and dismantle systemic racism? How can they be prepared to be anti-racist? To answer these questions, CRT as a theoretical framework becomes a foundational grounding for engaging in anti-racist social work education. CRT has its origins in law and was developed in the 1980s by law students and civil rights activists to challenge elite institutions that maintained notions of race neutrality (otherwise known as colour blindness) while engaging in exclusionary practices that ensured a status quo of racial power dynamics (Crenshaw, 2011). CRT was developed to directly address the ways in which racism was deeply rooted in the social fabric and to examine structural inequalities. Since then, the theory has been adopted by a variety of disciplines, including social work. Although various authors discuss between five and nine tenets, research and anti-racist education using CRT is guided by six consistent key tenets: (1) racism as ordinary and endemic; (2) the critique of liberalism and concepts of neutrality, fairness, and meritocracy; (3) race as a social construction; (4) Whiteness as ultimate property/normative; (5) interest convergence; and (6) the unique voice of colour and intersectionality (Abrams & Moio, 2009; Constance-Huggins, 2012; Pulliam, 2017; Kolivoski et al., 2014). These tenets encourage in-depth classroom and field education engagement in conversations about race and racism, while providing direction to challenge and dismantle systemic racism.

Locating My Voice and Experiences

In my anti-racist education research journey, I have been increasingly drawn to anti-colonial methodologies. This form of resistance provides different ways of knowing, being, doing, and sharing knowledge. In traditional research, the voice of the researcher is often silent, providing only "facts." This stance has often been credited with continuing to perpetuate Whiteness in research, silencing marginalized voices, and sustaining systems of coloniality (Carlson, 2016). As such, and in keeping with CRT, this chapter is personal and demonstrates the connectedness of everyday experiences to research, rather than presenting the two as separate entities.

Anti-racist education does not happen in a vacuum. Instead, it is a consistent reflection of everyday encounters, rife with the subtlety of racism and Whiteness that have become so much a part of our existence that we no longer question them. As Mason-Bish (2019) observed, researchers need to reflect on their positionality and their power, because these in turn affect how the researcher engages with participants and the research topic. The importance of locating oneself is further emphasized by Fook and Askeland (2007), noting that "critical reflection must incorporate an understanding of personal experiences within social, cultural, and structural contexts" (p. 522). With this in mind, I reflect on three central aspects of my position and identity that inform my engagement in this study.

The first reflection is on the power dynamic and my positionality as a graduate student. I find myself constantly trying to imagine how my research will be received by my faculty and by social work educators. What if my findings do not paint the current curriculum or field education in a good light? Will they receive my findings as a way forward or be "disappointed in me?" I acknowledge that my research was spurred on by the realization that, as a student, I did not feel prepared to skillfully engage in anti-racist practice. I remind myself that I need to be aware of these power and positionality concerns and, at the same time, maintain the integrity of the research.

The second intersecting identity involves me as a Black student. As I reviewed the literature and noted progress and gaps within anti-racist social work education, I found that I identified with the literature in a very personal way. I felt a desperate need to be understood and seen. I wanted the change to happen here and now. Some authors described experiences that could have been taken right out of my own academic life. Later in the chapter, I use an example from an experience I had as a Black student which, when I reflect upon it, I cannot help but focus on race.

The third aspect is that, in my professional capacity, I work with immigrants and refugees, wherein I am consistently exposed to the systemic racism experienced by racialized persons. I hold their stories within me, and I feel the urgency to advocate for stronger anti-racist knowledge and skills to address racism on a systemic level.

While these positions, identities, and experiences intentionally and/ or unintentionally shape how I enter into this research, naming them also empowers me. This interaction of personal and emotional experiences is crucial to name and make visible, because it ensures that knowledge is shared wholistically (Fook & Askeland, 2007). In this sense, I remain cognizant of the totality of the research, while honouring my experiences — which inform my research — and balancing it with mindful objectivity.

Vignette: "I Feel Like I Should Have Done Something Different … but I Don't Know What"

A Day in My Practicum

As a way to connect while working remotely, the team with whom I was completing my practicum met every Wednesday morning. Each week, one team member would pose a question as a way to "get to know you." This particular Wednesday, right after massive Black Lives Matter protests across Canada, the team leader was asking the question for the week. Their question was "how do you make considerations for systemic racism in the work we do?" All five team members answered before me, and each admitted that they really had not thought about how they could apply an anti-racist lens to their work. Then the leader turned to me and said, "I am sure as a social work student you likely have a better understanding, tell us what you think." I found myself giving a passionate talk about systemic racism, sharing personal experiences, and even sharing resources. When I was done, the leader responded with "Thanks. Now moving along…." And we did actually move on to other business.

A Conversation with Myself

Following the incident mentioned above, I found myself asking questions and rationalizing the experience with answers that continue to evolve and change. Below is an example of what I have continued to grapple with.

Q. Why Did They Ask Me to Share More?

A. This question raises more questions than it provides answers for me. There are so many things that, in retrospect, trouble me. The way in which the question was framed for me made it sound like more was expected of me. Was it because I am a "social work student" or because I am Black? Maybe both? To be honest, I think it is more because I am Black. I think that they assumed that, as a racialized person, I would know more about racism, more specifically, systemic racism (which was a term being discussed all over media).

The truth is that I had not really researched systemic racism. We had not discussed it in class either. Did we all assume that we know what it is? I, for sure, felt that I could "wing it," in a way that would make sense. I thought that I could explain things from my understanding and that would be enough. But what is enough? Is there ever enough in trying to explain or understand systemic racism? Should I know the answer as a Black person? Either way, I felt obligated to answer and, hopefully, get the team started on an anti-racist journey.

Q. Why Did I Feel Obligated to Answer?

A. As a student who had been engaging in a great deal of independent anti-racist education research, this seemed like a perfect "teachable moment." It felt like I finally was going to make a difference. Maybe I even wanted to look back and remember that moment as one when I really impacted people and made the world a better place. A "helper" moment of sorts? I automatically felt like there was no choice but to answer. I was a social work student and, after three years in the program, I should have been able to provide a well-constructed answer about how to employ an anti-racist lens in our work, right? Score one for the "good guys." Then I put my heart and soul into it, giving an impassioned plea for why anti-racism makes a difference.

As a Black person, I also felt obligated to add some personal experiences of racism and how these experiences had affected me. In my mind, I assumed that they would be "touched." How could they not? Now that I think about it, I realize that I often make this assumption — that if I tell my story enough and if I share what I know and how racism impacts people like me, perhaps enough people will be touched and want to do it differently. Should I have learned differently by now? Perhaps, but then again, I never stop long enough to reflect or put it in the context of research. I have a hard time deciding if it is just me, or if there is something bigger than me going on. I often think of it as a "one off" — better luck next time. Maybe this is why I always have the need to understand. I wonder how research explains this need.

Q. Did It Even Occur to Me That I Could Politely Decline?

A. Not really. I did not hesitate, even for a moment. In my mind, if they were asking me to help them understand racism, surely, they must be interested. How could I not heed such a call? This could have gone so well, if only they had been willing to engage a little more. Then again, I was a student in my practicum. Would I really say no when asked such an important question? How would that impact my practicum? But who am I kidding: as a curious anti-racist education enthusiast, there was no way I was going to miss this one.

I am only thinking about these other considerations as retrospective reflections. At the time, I genuinely thought that answering honestly was the only way to go. There is also the consideration that they were all White. A part of me (probably the one that sustains coloniality) felt flattered that these White people had trusted me enough to ask me such an important question! I mean, what could go wrong? All I had to do was play it cool and answer compassionately because they were, after all, making an effort to do things better. Plus, if I did not answer the question, would I have otherwise been disappointed in myself for failing to live up to a potential social justice education moment? I know without a doubt that I would have been disappointed in myself. In my "what ifs," I would have constructed a perfect scenario of what my answer would have been, how well it would have been received, and the enlightening discussion that would have followed. Instead, for having gone to the trouble of answering, the team was moving on. There was no follow up — no sense of a eureka moment.

Q. Why Did This Disturb Me So Much?

A. Again my answers are more questions. Did they actually move on? Maybe they just did not know how to respond to what I said? Did I engage in "too much disclosure?" But how much disclosure is too much or too little? Would that mean that I need to censor what I say? Well, if I did that, who would it benefit? Considering that they were all White, what was going on in their minds? Did they even think about the emotional burden that they put on me? Did the fact that I was a practicum student, while they all in positions of power, occur to them as a power imbalance? Who were these people? How dared they? These few weeks I had worked with them, I thought I knew them ... How could they not offer any feedback, even if they did not mean it? Now wait a minute, would I prefer that they say things that they did not mean, rather than sit in silence? Actually, at the time, yes!

In the backdrop of George Floyd's murder and the Black Lives Matter protests all around the world, how could they have nothing to say after a Black person answered their question about racism? I had an existential moment right there. Why did I even bother answering? Were they even interested in my answer or had they been asking the question because it seemed like the right thing to ask in light of the "political climate?" Afterwards, I also wondered whether they were afraid to speak in front of each other. After realizing that we were not going to engage in the conversation, I went into a "smile and act like nothing is going on" reaction. I may have overcompensated in later discussions, for a few weeks. I wanted them to not define me using that conversation. I also found myself wanting to be funnier, more eloquent, and to excel at my practicum tasks. In the end, I think what disturbed me was that they asked the question, but did not value the answer. They did not see or hear me. Would it have gone differently with a White student? I also felt disillusioned. How was I, as an emerging social worker, supposed to handle such a situation?

Q. What Did I Expect from the Follow Up?

A. My field instructor was not at this particular meeting, so they only heard about the conversation from me and, later, from the team leader. I now feel driven to mention that I had an amazing field instructor. I think this, in itself, is part of what I am beginning to recognize as a need to point out all the good, in order to cushion the not-so-good aspects of the conversation. I feel like I just cannot tell it as is. I cannot help but try to find the silver lining, even when I am deeply upset. Now I digress ... but do I, or is another thought to pin and reflect on?

Anyway, I requested a meeting with my field instructor, right away, and they were available. They could tell that I was upset as soon as I started talking. As I explained the situation to them, I found myself making an effort to relate what happened in such a way that I had no choice but to answer the question. I explained that I felt upset that I may have offended the team. We had a nice debrief. I call it a "nice" debrief because I did not tell them what was going on in my mind — what had disappointed me, what had hurt and frustrated me, or what I really wanted to say to the team. I found myself eager to reassure them that I was more worried about having said too much, which was a concern, but not one of my main ruminating thoughts.

Going back to the question, I do not know what I expected from the follow up. I just may have needed to vent or to be validated: I went with more of the latter for momentary comfort. We did speak about social justice and anti-racism. They asked me about them having a talk with the team, and I asked them not to do so. I did not want to draw attention to the fact that I was feeling troubled. While they did everything right, I found myself thinking that there could be more to unpack here. Maybe they could point out that I am Black, and that the whole team is White. They could ask me whether that played a role. Ask me deeper questions. I found myself unsure what to point at as the problem, so I made it out to not be a big deal.

Later, upon reflection, I knew in my heart that if my field instructor had been a racialized — and especially Black — social worker, I would have been more honest. I would have been more likely to assume that they would understand where I was coming from. It felt like a dirty secret that I could not voice, yet it remained sure at the back of my mind. I reflected on representation, and I wished that I had somebody to help me understand whether I had made a big deal out of an innocent question and discussion. I was convinced that there had been a teachable moment in there, but we missed it. In the end, I turned to research to better understand what may have happened and the ways in which it could have been different.

Q. What Does This Mean for Social Work Field Education?

A. It is easy to chalk this down to a one-off incident. Yet, as was earlier highlighted, research overwhelmingly indicates that the topic of racism is currently avoided in many schools of social work. Field education has the best potential for bringing anti-racist education to life (Razack, 2002). Perhaps the first step should be having conversations about the experiences of students, practitioners, and service users. We can explore questions about power, Whiteness, privilege, and systemic racism, and begin to articulate how these concepts operate in our societies.

Incidentally, it was while I was in the process of researching ways to engage in more race-based conversations in our social work classrooms and in field education that the 2021 Educational Policies and Accreditation Standards (EPAS) for Canadian social work education was approved (Canadian Association of Social Work Education [CASWE], 2021). The first thing I did, upon accessing the EPAS, was to search for the prefix "anti-." I was very encouraged to see the words anti-racism and anti-colonialism appear multiple times in the document (CASWE, 2021). Even more exciting was the fact that one of the core learning objectives was dedicated to "anti-racism" (p. 16). This, for me as a social work student, represented a new dawn as far as anti-racist pedagogy was concerned. It meant that soon we will be required to engage in conversations about race, racism, coloniality, anti-racism, and anti-coloniality. It meant that we will actively commit to dismantling systemic racism, instead of remaining silent, based on the false assumption that we are "non-racist and non-oppressive because the profession has a Code of Ethics to guide practice and because social work institutions proclaim they are committed to this ideology" (Sinclair, 2004, p. 52). There is hope. The road ahead is likely long and rough, but this does set the foundation for change.

Reflecting on the Conversation with Myself

The scholar in me wants to make the conversation with myself perfect, but that would defeat its purpose and the reflections within it. Like any discussion that seeks to analyze race, it is not meant to be complete and tidy. Neither is it meant to provide definitive answers. This chapter is by no means seeking to accomplish that. In fact, if it does anything, it should leave more questions than answers. It will also hopefully normalize questions and reflexivity with the self, for therein lies the crux of who we are as individuals and as social workers.

An essential tenet of CRT is giving voice to racialized persons and the counter-stories they share (Delgado & Stefancic, 2017; Einbinder, 2020). My reflective conversation is an effort to add to the voices of racialized persons needing to be heard, while learning through the process (Shumack, 2010). As a Black social work student, and like many Black scholars, I remain conflicted "over whether or not to view racism for what it is — how it actually exists in the world, or view racism through the lens of their hopes for a better tomorrow" (Curry, 2008, p. 43). For now, I engage in decolonial dreaming and I find ways to finally voice my experiences.

Moreover, with this reflection, I intend to add to social work field education literature, especially as pertains to student voices and anti-racist field education, a notably under-researched area. Student experiences represent an important source of information for shaping anti-racist field education (Tang et al., 2021). Further study is needed to broaden our understanding of student experiences in navigating anti-racism in field education, and especially as it relates to students' ability to apply CRT to practice (Einbinder, 2020). Such study will form an essential foundation for informing inclass preparation and field placement supports, both for students and field instructors.

The role of critical conversations cannot be overemphasized. The intentional engagement in questions and authentic responses that explore our conscious and subconscious reflections are key to embarking on an anti-racist education journey. It is important that social work education stakeholders, including classroom instructors, field educators, students, and practitioners, continuously question the power structures they encounter and sustain (Davis & Gentlewarrior, 2015; McGuire & Lay, 2020). These conversations will become building blocks in ending the fear and race-evasiveness that continue to cloud our desire to be anti-racist (Kendi, 2019).

Conclusion

As initiators in a profession committed to social justice, social work educators need to ensure that students are prepared for the realities they will face in their practice. The conversation that I had with myself is but one example of the many ways that race permeates our everyday field encounters as students and, later, as practitioners. It is through the conversations and reflections in which we engage, with ourselves and with others, that we begin to question and comprehend years of coloniality, white supremacy, and racist systems and structures that have gone unquestioned for so long that we hardly notice them anymore. Racism is much more than overt actions. Sometimes it is in the subtle ways we sustain it, which are harder to identify and thus dismantle. Even so, we must not despair. There is too much at stake. Instead, we must be brave and seek out ways to engage and to act. Owing to the continued pervasiveness of racism, intentional and explicit anti-racist social work education is long overdue, and it is imperative that these conversations start happening in field education. Failure to do so is to severely disadvantage social work students as they graduate to practice in environments and institutions plagued by racism.

REFERENCES

Abrams, L. S., & Moio, J. A. (2009). Critical race theory and the cultural competence dilemma in social work education. *Journal of Social Work Education*, 45(2), 245–261. https://doi.org/10.5175/JSWE.2009.200700109

Almeida, R. V., Werkmeister Rozas, L. M., Cross-Denny, B., Lee, K. K., & Yamada, A-M. (2019). Coloniality and intersectionality in social work education and practice. *Journal of Progressive Human Services*, 30(2), 148–164. https://doi.org/10.1080/10428232.2019.1574195

Blake, J. (2014, November 27). *The new threat: 'Racism without racists.'* CNN. https://www.cnn.com/2014/11/26/us/ferguson-racism-or-racial-bias/index.html

Bonilla-Silva, E. (2013). *Racism without racists: Color-blind racism and the persistence of racial inequality in America* (5th ed.). Rowman & Littlefield Publishers.

Bubar, R., Cespedes, K., & Bundy-Fazioli, K. (2016). Intersectionality and social work: Omissions of race, class, and sexuality in graduate school education. *Journal of Social Work Education*, 52(3), 283–296. https://doi.org/10.1080/10437797.2016.1174636

Canadian Association for Social Work Education (CASWE). (2021). *Educational Policies and Accreditation Standards for Canadian social work education.* https://caswe-acfts.ca/wp-content/uploads/2021/04/EPAS-2021.pdf

Carlson, E. (2016). Anti-colonial methodologies and practices for settler colonial studies. *Settler Colonial Studies*, 7(4), 496–517. https://doi.org/10.1080/2201473X.2016.1241213

Constance-Huggins, M. (2012). Critical race theory in social work education: A framework for addressing racial disparities. *Critical Social Work*, 13(2), 1–16. https://doi.org/10.22329/csw.v13i2.5861

Cox, D., Cleak, H., Bhathal, A., & Brophy, L. (2021). Theoretical frameworks in social work education: A scoping review. *Social Work Education, 40*(1), 18–43. https://doi.org/1 0.1080/02615479.2020.1745172

Coxshall, W. (2020). Applying critical race theory in social work education in Britain: Pedagogical reflections. *Social Work Education, 39*(5), 636–649. https://doi.org/10.1 080/02615479.2020.1716967

Curry, T. (2008). Saved by the bell: Derrick Bell's racial realism as pedagogy. *Philosophical Studies in Education, 39*, 35–46. https://eric.ed.gov/?id=EJ1071987

Davis, A., & Gentlewarrior, S. (2015). White privilege and clinical social work practice: Reflections and recommendations. *Journal of Progressive Human Services, 26*(3), 191–208. https://doi.org/10.1080/10428232.2015.1063361

Delgado, R., & Stefancic, J. (2017). *Critical race theory: An introduction* (3rd ed). New York University Press.

Einbinder, S. D. (2020). Reflections on importing critical race theory into social work: The state of social work literature and students' voices. *Journal of Social Work Education, 56*(2), 327–340. https://doi.org/10.1080/10437797.2019.1656574

Fook, J., & Askeland, G.A. (2007). Challenges of critical reflection: Nothing ventured, nothing gained. *Social Work Education, 26*(5), 520–533. https://doi. org/10.1080/02615470601118662

Fultz, A. J., & Kondrat, D. C. (2019). Privilege, white identity, and motivation: A call to action in social work. *Journal of Progressive Human Services, 30*(3), 260–277. https://doi.org/10.1080/10428232.2018.1525236

Giwa, S., & Mihalicz, M. G. (2019). What's all the fuss about social work syllabi? Action speaks louder than words in addressing the silence of whiteness in social work curriculum: A game theory perspective. *Journal of Sociology and Social Work, 7*(2), 46–63. https://doi.org/10.15640/jssw.v7n2a6

Hango, D. (2020). *Fear of COVID-19 related stigmatization*. Statistics Canada. https://www150.statcan.gc.ca/n1/pub/45-28-0001/2020001/article/00051-eng.htm

Jeffery, D. (2005). 'What good is anti-racist social work if you can't master it'?: Exploring a paradox in anti-racist social work education. *Race, Ethnicity and Education, 8*(4), 409–425. https://doi.org/10.1080/13613320500324011

Kendi, I. X. (2019). *How to be an antiracist*. One World.

Kolivoski, K. M., Weaver, A., & Constance-Huggins, M. (2014). Critical race theory: Opportunities for application in social work practice and policy. *Families in Society, 95*(4), 269–276. https://doi.org/10.1606/1044-3894.2014.95.36

Ladhani, S., & Sitter, K. S. (2020). The revival of anti-racism: Considerations for social work education. *Critical Social Work 21*(1), 55–65. https://doi.org/10.22329/csw. v21i1.6227

Mason-Bish, H. (2019). The elite delusion: Reflexivity, identity and positionality in qualitative research. *Qualitative Research, 19*(3), 263–276. https://doi. org/10.1177/1468794118770078

McGuire, L. E., & Lay, K. A. (2020). Reflective pedagogy for social work education: Integrating classroom and field for competency-based education. *Journal of Social Work Education*, *56*(3), 519–532. https://doi.org/10.1080/10437797.2019.1661898

Nakaoka, S., & Ortiz, L. (2018). Examining racial microaggressions as a tool for transforming social work education: The case for critical race pedagogy. *Journal of Ethnic & Cultural Diversity in Social Work*, *27*(1), 72–85. https://doi.org/10.1080/15313204.2017.1417947

Ortiz, L., & Jani, J. (2010). Critical race theory: A transformational model for teaching diversity. *Journal of Social Work Education*, *46*(2), 175–193. https://doi.org/10.5175/jswe.2010.200900070

Phillips, C. (2010). White, like who? Temporality, contextuality and anti-racist social work education and practice. *Critical Social Work*, *11*(2), 71–88. https://doi.org/10.22329/csw.v11i2.5825

Pulliam, R. M. (2017). Practical application of critical race theory: A social justice course design. *Journal of Social Work Education*, *53*(3), 414–423. https://doi.org/10.1080/10437797.2016.1275896

Razack, N. (2002). *Transforming the field: Critical antiracist and anti-oppressive perspectives for the human services practicum*. Fernwood Publishing.

Shumack, K. (2010). The conversational self: Structured reflection using journal writings. *Journal of Research Practice*, *6*(2), M17. http://jrp.icaap.org/index.php/jrp/article/view/195/192

Sinclair, R. (2004). Aboriginal social work education in Canada: Decolonizing pedagogy for the seventh generation. *First Peoples Child & Family Review*, *1*(1), 49–61. https://fpcfr.com/index.php/FPCFR/article/view/10/41

Singh, S. (2019). What do we know the experiences and outcomes of anti-racist social work education? An empirical case study evidencing contested engagement and transformative learning. *Social Work Education*, *38*(5), 631–653. https://doi.org/10.1080/02615479.2019.1592148

Tang Yan, C., Orlandimeje, R., Drucker, R., & Lang, A. J. (2021). Unsettling reflexivity and critical race pedagogy in social work education: Narratives from social work students. *Social Work Education*, 1–24. https://doi.org/10.1080/02615479.2021.1924665

Varghese, R. (2016). Teaching to transform? Addressing race and racism in the teaching of clinical social work practice. *Journal of Social Work Education*, *52*(S1), S134–S147. https://doi.org/10.1080/10437797.2016.1174646

Weinberg, M., & Fine, M. (2020). Racisms and microaggressions in social work: the experience of racialized practitioners in Canada. *Journal of Ethnic & Cultural Diversity in Social Work*, 1–12. https://doi.org/10.1080/15313204.2020.1839614

Yee, J. Y., & Dumbrill, G. C. (2016). Whiteout: Still looking for race in Canadian social work practice. In A. Al-Krenawi, J. R. Graham, & N. Habibov (Eds.), *Diversity and social work in Canada* (pp. 13–37). Oxford University Press.

Yee, J. Y., & Wagner, A. E. (2013). Is anti-oppression teaching in Canadian social work classrooms a form of neo-liberalism? *Social Work Education*, *32*(3), 331–348. https://doi.org/10.1080/02615479.2012.672557

6

Culturally Responsive Child Welfare Practices: An Integrative Review

Alexandra K. Mack

Disproportionality and Disparity Within the Modern-Day Child Welfare System

This chapter was written as an addendum to the author's field education experience while interning at a Child and Family Services Agency in the United States. According to Detlaff (2015), disproportionality refers to "the state of being out of proportion" (p. 4). Within the context of the child welfare system, disproportionality is described as a phenomenon wherein a racial group is overrepresented within the child welfare system's context compared to their representation within the general population (Dettlaff & Boyd, 2020). In the United States, African American children are overrepresented within the child welfare system; they make-up 14% of the general population, but 23% of the foster care population (Annie E. Casey Foundation, 2020). Additionally, children of Native/Alaskan descent also are disproportionately represented within the system (Annie E. Casey Foundation, 2020). Nationally, Latino children have typically been underrepresented within the welfare system; however, state trends have shown an increasing overrepresentation of these children (Dettlaff, 2015). LaLiberte et al. (2015) note that "disparity is typically used to describe unequal outcomes experienced by one racial/ethnic group when compared to another racial/ethnic group" (p. 5). Disparity in the child welfare system is evidenced by the fact that kids of colour are more likely to drift in care, less likely to be reunited with families, more likely to experience group care, less likely to find a permanent family, and more likely to have poor educational, social, behavioural, and other outcomes (The Annie E. Casey Foundation, 2011, p. 5).

There are two primary methods utilized to measure disproportionality. The U.S. Census Bureau and the U.S. Department of Health and Human Services uses the racial disproportionality index (RDI) to "compare the percentage of children by race in the general population to their percentage at various points in the child welfare continuum" (Child Welfare Information Gateway, 2016, p. 2). The second disproportionality measurement tool compares "a particular racial or ethnic population's representation in the child welfare system to its representation at the prior decision point" (Child Welfare Information Gateway, 2016, p. 4).

Racial Disproportionality and Disparity Theories

Understanding the existence of disparity and disproportionality within the child welfare system is writ large, but the theories that provide rationale for the disparity and disproportionality differ and overlap. Hines et al. (2004) provide that "parent and family-related risk factors, CWS [child welfare system] involvement, social factors related to poverty, neighborhood effects" are factors that contribute to disparity and disproportionality (p. 507). Hines et al. also (2007) hypothesize that racial disproportionality and disparity exist due to biased decision-making among child welfare agency staff. Community structures, poverty, and oppression further perpetuate involvement in the child welfare system among families of colour. These authors (2007) further note that the specific contexts of the child welfare system, such as agency structure, culture, resources, and management are contributing factors. Barth and colleagues (2005) propose three primary theories to explain racial disproportionality and disparity: (1) overwhelming needs of families of colour; (2) racial prejudice among child welfare agencies and staff; and (3) the multiplicative interaction between family risk and the child welfare service trajectory.

Culturally Responsive Practices Throughout Service Engagement

Cultural Responsiveness

The consideration of the current rates of disproportionality and disparity lead to the discussion regarding practices that child welfare organizations can utilize to actively address these concerns. Cultural competence, cultural humility, and cultural responsiveness are among the multiplicity of terms used to discuss cultural adeptness. For the purpose of this chapter, the term cultural responsiveness will be utilized. This term is conceptualized in various ways across disciplines and sectors. Within the context of the child welfare system, cultural responsiveness is a framework that "enables individuals and organizations to respond respectfully and effectively to people of all cultures, languages, classes, races, ethnic backgrounds, disabilities, religions, genders, sexual orientations, and other diversity factors in a manner that recognizes, affirms, and values their worth" (Child Welfare Information Gateway, n.d., Cultural Responsiveness section, para.1).

The embodiment of cultural responsiveness requires understanding culturally-based differences, recognizing personal bias, and looking beyond these differences to effectively work with families, children, and communities whose contexts differ from ours (Child Welfare Information Gateway, n.d.). The subsequent sections discuss culturally responsive child welfare practices to address both disproportionality and disparity.

Culturally Responsive Workforce Development. The implementation of cultural responsiveness throughout the stages of workforce development is essential. According to LaLiberte et al. (2015), child welfare agencies' infrastructure, ethnicity of caseworkers, minimal resources for families of colour, institutional racism, organizational culture, disconnection from the community, and value of services are all aspects that could explicate racial disproportionality and disparity. A cross-state study conducted by the Children's Bureau found that culturally responsive and effective child welfare practice "begins with staff diversity or a staff that reflects the population served by the agency" (Chibnall, 2003, p. 51).

Workforce diversity is defined as "the systematic and planned commitment by the organizations to recruit, retain, reward and promote a heterogeneous mix of employees" (Henry & Evans, 2007, p. 72). Within the context of the child welfare system, the pursuit of a diverse workforce is not merely a focus of diversification of cultures and ethnicities, but also of age, national origin, religion, disability, sexual orientation, values, ethnic culture, education, language, lifestyle, beliefs, physical appearance, and economic status (Wentling & Palma-Rivas, 2000).

Prior to making adjustments, it is necessary for an organization to assess their levels of cultural responsiveness regarding areas of strengths and areas for growth. The Institutional Analysis developed by The Center for the Study of Social Policy (CSSP) and Ellen Pence of Praxis International, LLC is specifically geared to conduct cultural organizational assessments. The Institutional Analysis tool is used to "uncover problematic policies and practices that define and constrain child welfare systems, with a focus on contributors to racial disparities in child welfare services and outcomes" (Center for the Study of Social Policy [CSSP], 2020, Institutional Analysis section, para. 1). The primary process of understanding systematic disparities is to ask questions "from the standpoint of children, youth, parents, and caregivers involved with child welfare systems" (CSSP, 2020, Institutional Analysis section, para. 2). The tool also focuses on asking how something comes about, rather than who does the action (CSSP, 2020). Other helpful tools include "A Guide to … Planning and Implementing Cultural Competence Organizational Self-Assessment," by Georgetown University (Goode et al., 2002) and the "Assessing Organizational Racism tool," by the Western States Center (Jones & Okun, 2003).

Cultural competence and anti-racism training have been essential tools in combating disparity and disproportionality within the child welfare system. Augmented cultural awareness and sensitivity tackle the issue of disproportionality by directly addressing workers' racial attitudes and biases which affect their decision-making regarding families of colour (Chibnall et al., 2003). At all points in the child welfare system, race represents a significant factor in decision-making by professionals (Hill, 2007). Hence, the necessity of cultural competence and anti-racism training.

The effectiveness of anti-racism training hinges on taking a self-assessment approach as opposed to a survey approach, which focuses primarily on external cultural factors and stereotypes. The self-assessment approach encourages professionals to self-reflect on the issues of race and culture (Johnson et al., 2009). Cultural responsiveness is an evolving process that depends largely "on self-reflection, self-awareness, and acceptance of differences, and is based on improved understanding as opposed to an increase in cultural knowledge" (Webb & Sergison, 2003, p. 291).

The child welfare system consists of social workers and staff and relies heavily on mandated reporters to initiate the referral and investigation process. Decision makers within the system are quite numerous, particularly in the early stage, including "teachers, healthcare staff, law enforcement, judges and mental health providers and even community members who report suspected maltreatment to child protective services" (Johnson, 2009, p. 688). This broad list of engaged professionals and community members highlights the necessity of ensuring that culturally responsive practices are standardized and implemented at every point of engagement. It is necessary that all professionals who are involved in the child welfare system and its processes attend culturally responsive training to effectively streamline culturally responsive practices.

Although a diverse workforce provides a multiplicity of benefits for organizations and their clients, the process of moving toward a more heterogeneous work force increases the likelihood of more friction and conflict (Henry et al., 2007). This increase in friction and conflict is the result of prejudice, ignorance, and derogatory comments, and requires managerial and organizational interventions to ensure that these behaviours and attitudes do not escalate to ethnocentrism, stereotyping, and culture clashes (White, 1999). The pursuit of diversity and inclusion within an organization typically follows a six-stage process: denial, recognition, acceptance, appreciation, valuing, and utilization (Porras & Silvers, 1991). The ability to assess where the organization is in this process is a necessary and helpful step in moving toward diversity.

Front Door

The Front Door pillar of the child welfare system concentrates on *how* children and families gain access to services. Commonly, the nature of the Front Door system is forensic, technocratic, and risk-averse, focusing primarily on reports and risk assessments (Lonne et al., 2021). Front Door-related procedures include hotline calls, referrals, investigations, and in-home services. Essentially, the Front Door is a culmination of engagements and decisions that influence whether a child will be removed from their home. There is increasing concern that many Front Door processes and systems have the effect of widening the net. The focus on "children at risk" as opposed to "children in need" has further contributed to the system's forensic nature. This focus decreases child welfare practitioners' ability to identify family strengths and engage thoroughly with the family; it also can limit clinical judgement and decrease consistent decision-making in reporting and assessing concerns (Lonne et al., 2021).

Data from the Fourth National Incidence Study of Child Abuse and Neglect (NIS-4), the National Child Abuse and Neglect Data System (NCANDS), and the State of California were utilized to assess the child welfare referral system, which operates under the Front Door pillar. According to Mumpower, the referral system is "less accurate for Blacks than for other racial or ethnic groups," as demonstrated through higher rates of false positives and false negatives, and more referrals that lead to unsubstantiated findings (2010, p. 364). The identification of disproportionality within the referral system has caused multiple states to implement processes to decrease disproportionality.

Among the variety of national-, state-, and county-level efforts, two counties in New York utilized culturally responsive practices to decrease disproportionality rates. Qualitative research was conducted to identify thematic patterns of factors that contributed to the decrease in disparity, including preventative measures and community resources. The counties also engaged other systems within the community that are correlated and connected with the child welfare system (e.g., Department of Juvenile Justice, Foster and Adoptive Parent Association, Office of Minority Affairs, Hispanic Counseling Center) to discuss potential strategies to eliminate racial disparity within the child welfare system. These gatherings involved discussion groups, community training, and school-based initiatives (Pryce et al., 2019).

One strategy is provided through Blind Removal meetings, which are intended to enable unbiased decision-making. Blind removal meetings "involve the presentation of cases to determine the need for removal without any information that may identify the family's race and socioeconomic status" (Cullen et al., 2021, p. 13). Data reveal that the blind removal process helps heighten practitioner awareness of "institutionalized racism and implicit bias" (Pryce et al., 2016, p. 17). Furthermore, evidence demonstrates that the blind removal process, along with related training, "increased staff awareness of institutionalized racism and implicit bias and reinforced the values of self-examination and cultural diversity" (Casey Family Programs, 2021, p. 3).

Temporary Safe Haven

The Temporary Safe Haven pillar involves a focus and a belief that foster care must be a temporary safe haven, with planning for permanence, which begins the day a child enters care (Child and Family Services Agency, 2019). Unfortunately, despite all efforts, some children need to be removed from their parents to provide them with the best protection. It is necessary that child welfare practitioners utilize culturally responsive approaches to mitigate against the harm that often results from removals.

Family-centered approaches are highly recommended as a means of decreasing racial disparity within the system. The American Humane Association (2010) notes that there are six core aspects in conducting a family group decision-making session. These include: (1) having an independent conference coordinator who supports respectful and honest interactions during the conference; (2) providing agency resources to convene the extended family group and prepare them for their role as "decision-making partners"; (3) ensuring that the family group has time to meet and discuss the plan privately; (4) giving preference to the plan developed by the family, once agency concerns have been addressed; (5) implementing follow-up processes to track progress and achievements; and (6) assisting family groups in carrying out their plans by connecting them to the resources and services that will best meet their needs (American Humane Association, 2010).

The Family Group Conferencing Model (FGC) was first legislated by New Zealand to lower reliance on legal and protective interventions, and to advance the principles of family responsibility, children's rights, cultural affirmation, and community-state partnerships. The FGC occurs prior to the case moving to court (Waites et al., 2004). Benefits of this model include built-in checks and balances, removal of power imbalance, and a focus on the authority of the family to solve their own problems. The social worker plays the role of coordinator and focuses on organizing the conference by inviting family members, preparing the family for participation, providing sufficient information without attempting to influence, allowing families to have time alone to deliberate, and assisting with negotiating the final plan (Waites et al., 2004).

Where children have been identified as needing to be removed from the care of their parent(s), kinship care is a culturally responsive practice with a myriad of inherent protective properties. Kinship care "enables important biological ties and can assist children with loss and grief issues, which can go unrecognized in the context of child welfare service delivery" (LaLiberte et al., 2015, p. 26). Children in kinship care also experience fewer home transitions, which is foundational to their overall emotional and psychological health (Winokur et al., 2008). Kinship care may provide a more conducive environment for positive ethnic identity perspectives than foster care. It is suggested that individuals who serve as kinship caregivers be paired with peer-to-peer support, which is a culturally responsive approach that increases child safety and caregiver's capacity to fulfill their responsibilities (Denby, 2011).

Well-Being

The Well-Being pillar is rooted in the belief that "every child has a right to a nurturing environment that supports healthy growth and development, good physical and mental health, and academic achievement" (Child and Family Services Agency [CFSA], Well Being Section, 2019, para. 4). Not only does every child have a right to nurturing environments, but children are expected to be better off after their stay in foster care. This pillar focuses on the services provided and engagement with families.

A case study was conducted on a New York County that utilized a system of care approach to provide culturally responsive practice during the well-being phase, which is offered through two primary modalities. The first modality focused on creating partnerships with local systems that serve children and youth, including "schools, mental health, juvenile justice, special education, foster care, and child welfare" (Pryce et al., 2019, p. 51). Hurlburt et al. (2004) found that increasing the connection between the child welfare system and local mental health services can decrease racial disparity outcomes within the system. This is especially true for African American children ages 6–10, who are more likely than their White counterparts to have unmet mental health needs (Burns et al., 2004).

Children within the child welfare system require a variety of assessments and health services. In response to this need, multi-agency collaboration helps to provide improved service access and outcomes (Hurlburt, 2004). The intent of this systems approach is to effectively streamline services to assist youth in the child welfare system. The second modality focuses on an access team consisting of frontline workers who help clients navigate the system. Instead of contacting multiple organizations or agencies for services, clients contact the access team, who is responsible for assisting clients in connecting with services. The county administration noted that the care approach system made it easier for families to access and remain connected to services (Pryce et al., 2019).

Another culturally responsive practice involves ensuring that families and children have access to care and that the services are culturally competent. It is recommended that child welfare agencies develop a diverse list of therapists, counselors, and other service providers so that they can readily refer families to providers who are culturally competent and, when possible, converse in the preferred language of the client (Child Welfare Information Gateway, 2011). Further, it is recommended that caseworkers also assume responsibility for identifying aspects of an individual's culture that may impact an individual's engagement with services (Child Welfare Information Gateway, 2011).

Exit to Permanence

The fourth pillar, Exit to Permanence, strives to have every child exit foster care as quickly as possible into "a safe, well-supported family environment or life-long connection" (CFSA, Exit to Permanence Section, 2019, para. 5). This pillar also focuses on providing older youth with the skills they need to succeed as adults. At the time of the study, research was not available regarding culturally responsive practices during the Exit to Permanence phase.

Implications for Social Work Field Education

Field education practicums provide opportunities for students "to integrate and apply theory to practice, and to examine, critique, and test out in action the knowledge, values, and principles studied in academic courses" (Bogo, 2006, p. 163). Furthermore, the quintessential relationship between the student and their field practicum places the student in a recipient position while the field practicum and supervisor are the primary providers of knowledge (Bogo, 2006). However, this research opportunity afforded the author with the experience of gathering and providing insight for institutional use. Research highlights that this form of student contribution is beneficial for two reasons. First, research findings note that students' satisfaction with their field education experience improves when they are given opportunities to increase their understanding of the population they are working with and the provided services (Alperin, 1998). In addition, Zlotnik (2002) notes that research conducted within the field education context can be beneficial to further institutionalize the relationship between social work education and public child welfare and ensure that quality services are provided for consumers.

Recommendations

This literature review provides an overview of culturally responsive practices within the context of child welfare agencies' programmatic implementation. The following recommendations are directed at American child welfare organizations for use in tandem with the implementation of the culturally responsive practices discussed in previous sections of this chapter. However, other jurisdictions may have parallel concerns and therefore may benefit from the following recommendations.

For many child welfare organizations, engaging in or increasing culturally responsive practices will require organizational change. It is recommended that organizations utilize a "phase model" to implement change (Packard et al., 2015). The Availability, Responsiveness, and Continuity (ARC) Organizational Intervention model "involves the use of trained change agents to help change culture, climate, and performance in human service programs" (Packard et al., 2015, p. 446). This model addresses the critical importance of the organizational context, and more specifically social, strategic, and technical factors that impact prospects for improving program operations and outcomes. The ARC model includes seven steps: (1) assessing the present state of the organization; (2) creating a sense of urgency; (3) clarifying the change imperative; (4) ensuring support and addressing resistance; (5) developing an action system; (6) implementing the change plan; and (7) evaluating, institutionalizing, and celebrating effective change (Fernandez & Rainey, 2006; Palmer et al., 2009; Proehl, 2001). It is recommended that child welfare agencies undertaking organizational change to enhance cultural responsiveness utilize the ARC model or a similar phase model.

According to Tilbury et al. (2010), "performance indicators are not neutral or merely technical — they represent viewpoints and values that may influence policy and practice" (p. 226). Performance indicators influence how issues are defined, how and where resources are allocated, what programs are funded, and the conceptualization of children and family outcomes (Grasso & Epstein, 1987; Martin & Kettner, 1997). Additionally, "child welfare performance indicators contain implicit values about what is important in practice and how best to intervene to meet the needs of vulnerable children and their families" (Tilbury et al., 2010, p. 226). In light of the influence of performance indicators on programmatic investment, it is recommended that, for the sake of accountability and vision casting, cultural responsiveness be implemented into child welfare organizational performance accountability measurements.

Regarding field education, the Council on Social Work Education (CSWE) notes that a primary competency of social work education is to prepare social workers to work in varied contexts with diverse populations (CSWE, 2008). Furthermore, social work education strives to assist students in acquiring adept awareness of the client's community and cultural context (Colvin, 2013).

Therefore, in alignment with these CSWE educational objectives, it is recommended that field education supervisors and students collaborate on ways to integrate opportunities for discussing, applying, and promoting culturally responsive practices within the field practicum setting. The particulars of the discussion and implementation will likely vary depending on the specific population served. Campinha-Bacote (2002) provides insightful recommendations such as increasing cultural awareness, engaging in skill-based interventions, seeking more profound cultural knowledge, participating in cultural encounters, cultivating cultural desire, and implementing action-oriented practices as beneficial modalities apt to enhance cultural responsiveness within the context of field education.

Conclusion

In contrast to historical rates of underrepresentation, the American child welfare systems, on a national and state level, experience high disproportionality and disparity rates for families and children of colour (Hill, 2007). As a result, researchers have engaged in robust discussions regarding theories exploring the rationale for racial disproportionality and disparity of child welfare, and they have identified specific practices to address these concerns. This literature review explores and categorizes culturally responsive practices within the structure of Washington, D.C.'s Child and Family Services Agency outcome-based plan, the Four Pillars.

Furthermore, the author provides recommendations for child welfare agencies interested in implementing or enhancing their cultural responsiveness. Owing to the influence of performance indicators on policy and practice, the author recommends that child welfare organizations seeking to become more culturally responsive include, as a performance measurement domain, cultural responsiveness by incorporating it in their state-specific performance measurement language and structure. It is further recommended that organizations utilize the Availability, Responsiveness, and Continuity (ARC) Organizational Intervention model, or similar phase models, to assist in the organizational change necessary to support cultural responsiveness (Packard et al., 2015).

Additionally, implications for field education are considered, particularly the integral role that field education plays in practitioner training and competency building. Within the context of field education, specific actions are recommended: providing opportunities for increasing cultural awareness, engaging in skill-based interventions, seeking more profound cultural knowledge, participating in cultural encounters, cultivating cultural desire, and implementing action-oriented practices Campinha-Bacote, 2002).

REFERENCES

Alperin, D. E. (1998). Factors related to student satisfaction with child welfare field placements. *Journal of Social Work Education, 34*(1), 43–54. https://doi.org/10.1080/10437797.1998.10778904

American Humane Association. (2010). FGDM committee guidelines for family group decision making in child welfare. http://www.pacwrc.pitt.edu/Curriculum/207 RemoteFGDMPart2/TableResources/TBLR01_GdlnsFrFmlyGrpDcsnMknginChld Wlfre.pdf

Annie E. Casey Foundation. (2011). *Disparities and Disproportionality in Child Welfare.* https://www.aecf.org/resources/disparities-and-d is proportionality-in-child-welfare/

Annie E. Casey Foundation. (2020). *Child population by race in the United States.* https:// datacenter.kidscount.org/data/tables/103-child-population-by-race

Barth, R. (2005). Child welfare and race: Models of disproportionality. In D. M. Derezotes, J. Poertner, & M. F. Testa (Eds.), *Race matters in child welfare: The overrepresentation of African American children in the system*, (pp. 25–46). The Child Welfare League of America, Inc.

Bogo, M. (2006). Field instruction in social work: A review of the research literature. *The Clinical Supervisor, 24*(1–2), 163–193. https://doi.org/10.1300/J001v24n01_09

Burns, B. J., Phillips, S. D., Wagner, H. R., Barth, R. P., Kolko, D. J., Campbell, Y., & Landsverk, J. (2004). Mental health need and access to mental health services by youths involved with child welfare: A national survey. *Journal of the American Academy of Child & Adolescent Psychiatry, 43*(8), 960–970. https://doi. org/10.1097/01.chi.0000127590.95585.65

Campinha-Bacote, J. (2002). The process of cultural competence in the delivery of healthcare services: A model of care. *Journal of Transcultural Nursing, 13*(3), 181–184. https://doi.org/10.1177%2F10459602013003003

Casey Family Programs (2021). Transforming the Child Welfare System. Retrieved November 27, 2021, from https://caseyfamilypro-wpengine.netdna-ssl.com/ media/21.07-QFF-TS-Blind-removals-Nassau.pdf

Center for the Study of Social Policy. (2020, March 4). *Institutional analysis: Unearthing institutional racism and other biases.* https://cssp.org/our-work/project/ institutional-analysis/

Chibnall, S., Dutch, N. M., Jones-Harden, B., Brown, A., Gourdine, R., Smith, J., ... & Snyder, S. (2003). Children of color in the child welfare system: Perspectives from the child welfare community. *Child Welfare Information Gateway.* https://www. childwelfare.gov/pubPDFs/children.pdf

Child and Family Services Agency [CFSA]. (2019). *Temporary safe haven.* cfsadashboard. https://cfsadashboard.dc.gov/page/temporary-safe-haven

Child Welfare Information Gateway. (n.d.). *Cultural responsiveness.* https://www. childwelfare.gov/topics/systemwide/cultural/

Child Welfare Information Gateway. (2011). *Addressing racial disproportionality in child welfare.* Department of Health and Human Services, Children's Bureau. https:// www.freestatesocialwork.com/articles/racial_disproportionality.pdf

Child Welfare Information Gateway. (2016). *Racial disproportionality and disparity in child welfare.* Washington, DC: U.S. Department of Health and Human Services, Children's Bureau. https://www.childwelfare.gov/pubs/issue-briefs/racial-disproportionality/

Child Welfare Information Gateway. (2021). *Child welfare practice to address racial disproportionality and disparity.* U.S. Department of Health and Human Services, Administration for Children and Families, Children's Bureau. https://www. childwelfare.gov/pubs/issue-briefs/racial-disproportionality/

Colvin, A. (2013). Building culturally competent social work field practicum students through the integration of Campinha-Bacote's cultural competence healthcare model. *Field Educator, 3*(1), 1–13. https://www.proquest.com/ openview/1689764eef9afd9e381a865146e415bb

Council on Social Work Education [CSWE]. (2008). *Educational policy and accreditation standards.* http://www.cswe.org/cswe/

Cullen, C., Alden, O., Arroyo, D., Froelich, A., Kasner, M., Kinney, C., Aburaad, A., Jacobs, R., Spognardi, A., & Kuenzli, A. (2021). Children and racial justice in the United States: A selective and annotated bibliography and call to action. *Children's Legal Rights Journal, 41(1),* 1–26. https://heinonline.org/HOL/P?h=hein.journals/ clrj41&i=6

Denby, R. W. (2011). Kinship liaisons: A peer-to-peer approach to supporting kinship caregivers. *Children and Youth Services Review, 33*(2), 217–225. https://doi. org/10.1016/j.childyouth.2010.09.004

Dettlaff, A. J. (2015, Winter). *Racial disproportionality and disparities in the child welfare system. CW360°.* http://cascw.umn.edu/wp-content/ uploads/2015/03/CW360-Winter2015.pdf#page=4

Dettlaff, A. J., & Boyd, R. (2020). Racial disproportionality and disparities in the child welfare system: Why do they exist, and what can be done to address them? *The ANNALS of the American Academy of Political and Social Science, 692*(1), 253–274. https://doi.org/10.1177%2F0002716220980329

Fernandez, S., & Rainey, H. (2006). Managing successful organizational change in the public sector online. *Public Administration Review, 66*(2), 168–176. https://doi. org/10.1111/puar.2006.66.issue-2

Goode, T., Jones, W., & Mason, J. (2002). A guide to planning and implementing cultural competence organizational self-assessment. *National Center for Cultural Competence.* https://nccc.georgetown.edu/documents/ncccorgselfassess.pdf

Grasso, A. J., & Epstein, I. (1988). Management by measurement: Organizational dilemmas and opportunities. *Administration in Social Work, 11*(3–4), 89–100. https://doi. org/10.1300/J147v11n03_08

Henry, O., & Evans, A. J. (2007). Critical review of literature on workforce diversity. *African Journal of Business Management, 1*(4). https://doi.org/10.5897/ AJBM.9000171

Hill, R. B. (2007). *An analysis of racial/ethnic disproportionality and disparity at the national, state, and county levels* (Vol. 27). Casey-CSSP Alliance for Racial Equity in Child Welfare. https://racialequity.issuelab.org/resources/8256/8256.pdf

Hines, A. M., Lemon, K., Wyatt, P., & Merdinger, J. (2004). Factors related to the disproportionate involvement of children of color in the child welfare system: A review and emerging themes. *Children and Youth Services Review, 26*(6), 507–527. https://doi.org/10.1016/j.childyouth.2004.01.007

Hurlburt, M. S., Leslie, L. K., Landsverk, J., Barth, R. P., Burns, B. J., Gibbons, R. D., ... & Zhang, J. (2004). Contextual predictors of mental health service use among children open to child welfare. *Archives of general psychiatry, 61*(12), 1217–1224. https://doi.org/10.1001/archpsyc.61.12.1217

Johnson, L. M., Antle, B. F., & Barbee, A. P. (2009). Addressing disproportionality and disparity in child welfare: Evaluation of an anti-racism training for community service providers. *Children and Youth Services Review, 31*(6), 688–696. https://doi.org/10.1016/j.childyouth.2009.01.004

Jones, K., & Okun, T. (2001). *Dismantling racism: A resource book for social change groups.* ChangeWork.

LaLiberte, T., Crudo, T., Ombisa Skallet, H., & Day, P. (Eds.). (2015). *CW360°: A comprehensive look at a prevalent child welfare issue.* Center for Advanced Studies in Child Welfare, University of Minnesota. https://cascw.umn.edu/portfolio-items/winter-2015-cw360/

Lonne, B., Russ, E., Harrison, C., Morley, L., Harries, M., Robertson, S., ... & Smith, J. (2021). The "front door" to child protection — Issues and innovations. *International Journal on Child Maltreatment: Research, Policy and Practice, 3*(4), 351–367. https://link.springer.com/article/10.1007/s42448-020-00051-9

Martin, L. L., & Kettner, P. M. (1997). Performance measurement: The new accountability. *Administration in Social Work, 21*(1), 17–29. https://doi.org/10.1300/J147v21n01_02

Mumpower, J. L. (2010). Disproportionality at the "front end" of the child welfare services system: An analysis of rates of referrals, "hits," "misses," and "false alarms." *Journal of Health and Human Services Administration,* 364–405. https://www.jstor.org/stable/25790786

Packard, T., McCrae, J., Phillips, J., & Scannapieco, M. (2015). Measuring organizational change tactics to improve child welfare programs: Experiences in 13 counties. *Human Service Organizations: Management, Leadership & Governance, 39*(5), 444–458. https://doi.org/10.1080/23303131.2015.1067268

Palmer, I., Dunford, R., & Buchanan, D. A. (2017). *Managing organizational change: A multiple perspectives approach.* McGraw-Hill Education.

Porras, J. I., & Silvers, R. C. (1991). Organization development and transformation. *Annual review of Psychology, 42*(1), 51–78. https://www.annualreviews.org/doi/abs/10.1146/annurev.ps.42.020191.000411

Proehl, R. A. (2001). *Organizational change in the human services.* Sage.

Pryce, J., Lee, W., Crowe, E., Park, D., McCarthy, M., & Owens, G. (2019). A case study in public child welfare: county-level practices that address racial disparity in foster care placement. *Journal of Public Child Welfare, 13*(1), 35–59. https://doi.org/10.1080/15548732.2018.1467354

Pryce, J. A., Lee, W., Sellati, Park, D., & McCarthy, M. (2016). *Race equity: Nassau and Onondaga County: Report.* Social Work Education Consortium, University of Albany.

Tilbury, C., Osmond, J., & Crawford, M. (2010). Measuring client satisfaction with child welfare services. *Journal of Public Child Welfare, 4*(1), 77–90. https://doi.org/10.1080/15548730903563160

Tsoukas, H., & Chia, R. (2002). On organizational becoming: Rethinking organizational change. *Organization Science, 13*(5), 567–582. http://dx.doi.org/10.1287/orsc.13.5.567.7810

Waites, C., Macgowan, M. J., Pennell, J., Carlton-LaNey, I., & Weil, M. (2004). Increasing the cultural responsiveness of family group conferencing. *Social Work, 49*(2), 291–300. https://doi.org/10.1093/sw/49.2.291

Webb, E., & Sergison, M. (2003). Evaluation of cultural competence and anti-racism in child health services. *Archives of Disease in Childhood, 88*(4), 291–294. https://doi.org/10.1136/adc.88.4.291

Wentling, R. M., & Palma-Rivas, N. (2000). Current status of diversity initiatives in selected multinational corporations. *Human Resource Development Quarterly, 11*(1), 35–60. https://doi.org/10.1002/1532-1096(200021)11:1%3C35::AID-HRDQ4%3E3.0.CO;2-%23

White, R. D. (1999). Managing the diverse organization: The imperative for a new multicultural paradigm. *Public Administration & Management: An Interactive Journal, 4*(4), 469–493. http://www2.aueb.gr/users/esaopa/courses/maniatis/99_4_4_4_w.pdf

Winokur, M. A., Crawford, G. A., Longobardi, R. C., & Valentine, D. P. (2008). Matched comparison of children in kinship care and foster care on child welfare outcomes. *Families in Society, 89*(3), 338–346. https://doi.org/10.1606%2F1044-3894.3759

Zlotnik, J. L. (2002). Preparing social workers for child welfare practice: Lessons from an historical review of the literature. *Journal of Health & Social Policy, 15*(3–4), 5–21. https://doi.org/10.1300/J045v15n03_02

Champions of Hurdles: A Multiple Case Study on the Experience and Meaning of Pursuing a Doctoral Degree for Ethiopian Women

Endalkachew Taye Shiferaw, Helen Asrate, and Afework Eyasu

In the Western world, one-fifth of master's degree graduate students pursue their doctoral education; of these students, 40%–60% of them do not graduate (Ivankova & Stick, 2007). Schmidt and Hansson (2018) also reported an attrition rate of up to 50% in doctoral studies depending on the discipline and country. Those who pursue their doctoral studies often experience high levels of anxiety, depression, physical symptoms of poor health condition, problems in maintaining relationships, and strains related to financial resources, quality of life, and well-being (Sverdlik et al., 2018). Factors such as lack of supervision, paucity of funds, demotivation of students, and family commitment are correlated to attrition from doctoral programs (Magano, 2013).

Internationally, the gender gap in higher education has been showing progress. However, in developing countries like Ethiopia, it is still a tangible problem. Ethiopia has one of the lowest literacy rates in the world, with 41% of women considered illiterate (Beyene, 2015). Girls in Ethiopia often are vulnerable to harmful traditional practices, including early marriage, genital mutilation, and expectations to manage domestic house-work at an early age, which affect their ability to attend school (Beyene, 2015). Moreover, it is estimated that one quarter of female students with-draw from higher education before graduation.

At each level in the pyramidic education system, the proportion of females is smaller than males and decreases progressively (Abraha, 2012). For instance, in the 1967–1968 academic year, the available data show that only 29.7% of primary school (grades 1–6) students, 26.7% of junior secondary (grades 7–8) students, and 18.3% of senior secondary (grades 9–12) students were female (Arts, 1968). Thirty years later, in the 1995–1996 academic year, female students were 38.2% in primary schools, 46.4% in junior secondary schools, 45.2% in senior secondary schools, and 13.9% in universities (Habtu, 2001). More recently, during the 2018–2019 academic year in Ethiopia, there were 1,255,569 students who sat for the grade 10 Ethiopian General Secondary Education Certificate Examination (EGSECE), and among them 572,997 (45.6%) were female. From the total number of students (854,893) who scored 2.0 and above — which is considered the passing grade — only 367,067 (43%) were female (Ministry of Education [MOE], 2018–2019). At the tertiary level of education in Ethiopia, women's enrollment increased from 27% to 35% between 2008–2009 and 2016–2017. Similarly, there was an increase in female undergraduates from 23.4% to 30.6% between 2009–2010 and 2016–2017 (Federal Democratic Republic of Ethiopia [FDRE], 2014; MOE, 2016–2017). At the post-graduate level, the proportion of females increased from 11.3% and 17.8% between 2008–2009 and 2016–2017 (FDRE, 2014). Although the data show that progress is incremental, there still remains a high gender gap in postgraduate programs (MOE, 2012–2013).

According to Abraha (2012), there are three fundamental reasons for the pervasive gender disparity in Ethiopian education: the challenge of translating policies into practice and gender factors, such as percep-tions about earning potential and male favouritism. Owing to tradition, Ethiopian society sees education as the exclusive preserve of men (Habtu, 2001). The socialization process determines gender roles by subjugating women, so that girls are perceived as holding an inferior position. Boys are expected to learn and become self-reliant household breadwinners, and girls are brought up to conform, be obedient and dependent, and specialize in indoor household activities. As a result, Ethiopian women, particularly in rural areas, hold higher illiteracy rates and lower educational attainment, which leads them to earn less wages and get married at younger ages (United Nations Population Fund [UNFPA], 2008). In recent years, the Ethiopian government has recognized the critical role that women's empowerment plays in achieving its development goals and has instituted various legal and policy reforms (Beyene, 2015). However, there is a tangible disparity in the implementation of laws and policies all over the nation. There still is a significant gap between regional states within the nation, and between urban and rural areas (Abraha, 2012).

In general, due to a multitude of factors, the relatively few Ethiopian women who join postgraduate programs face challenges including evaluation biases, added family responsibilities, sexual harassment, and strict, gender-based discriminatory policies (Beyene, 2015). Gao (2019) added that the double burden of domestic work and the domination of male desires and preferences, especially in love and marriage choices, influence women's decisions to withdraw from their education. However, by overcoming such challenges, some women have benefited from the opportunity to attend school. For example, we begin to see women as policymakers, activists, entrepreneurs, academics, and other successful activities in a variety of sectors.

However, a significant gender gap remains. To further highlight this, in 2016–2017 only 13.6% of all 28,761 academic staff in higher institutions were women. Among these women, only 7.7% were doctorate-level degree holders (MOE, 2016–2017). This relatively small group of women were able to overcome significant academic and social barriers to earn their doctoral degrees. To explore this gap, Ethiopian social work doctoral students from the University of Gondar were invited to remember former female professors in their prior studies: most were unable to recall any. The lack of female professors prompted the doctoral students to conduct a study on the experiences and meanings of pursuing doctoral studies by Ethiopian women holding a Doctor of Philosophy (PhD) degree. The research team authoring this chapter believe that sharing the experiences and meanings of women who have completed a doctoral degree can inform future generations of students regarding gender equality and justice in Ethiopian higher education.

This multiple case study aims to describe and examine three Ethiopian women's experiences and meanings of earning a PhD. The research team was composed of two male and one female social work PhD students from the University of Gondar in Ethiopia. As doctoral students ourselves, we witnessed and experienced the challenges associated with doctoral programs. We were curious about how Ethiopian women with a PhD recalled their unique challenges and perceived the meaning of earning this advanced degree.

The social work profession is known for its commitment to advancing social justice and women's rights as a necessary component of human rights. The profession also focuses on integrating the global gender equality and empowerment agendas in collaboration with international organizations such as the United Nations (International Federation of Social Workers [IFSW], 2012). Furthermore, the past Millennium Development Goals (MDGs) and the current Sustainable Development Goals (SDGs) provide social workers the opportunity to revisit and modify their empowering role in socio-economic development, human rights, and environmental issues (Jayasooria, 2016).

As mentioned above, the goal of this qualitative study is to understand the experiences of Ethiopian women who pursued a doctoral degree, and the factors that affected their academic and career endeavours in higher education institutions. The theoretical framework adopted for the study is situated in feminist theories, specifically intersectionality theory. Intersectionality theory advances that everyone has various multilayered identities based on social relationships, history, and the operation of power structures (Ferguson et al., 2014). According to Guittar and Guittar (2015), intersectionality is a framework that considers the analysis of people's experiences based on the interconnections of ethnicity, race, class, gender, nationality, religion, sexuality, and any social categories that situate one's experience of power in society. It provides a unique vantage point to consider a holistic understanding of the experiences of an individual within a society. Therefore, this study considers the participants' social identity factors, such as spirituality, family background, economic situation, culture, and personal values, in their educational and personal journey.

Methods

A multiple case study research design was used to gain an in-depth understanding of the three Ethiopian women's experience and meaning of earning a PhD. This approach helps comprehend the differences and similarities between the cases (Stake, 1995). Furthermore, grounded in empirical evidence, the suggestions obtained from multiple cases can also support convincing theories through strong and reliable information (Baxter & Jack, 2008).

A purposeful sampling strategy was used to select study participants to get thick information on the research problem and the central phenomenon of the study (Creswell & Poth, 2018). Purposeful sampling is a form of non-probability sampling in which researchers depend on their own judgment when choosing members of the population to participate in their study. The researchers' judgment relies on the premise of seeking out the best data for the study to address the research purpose and questions (Morse, 2010; Patton, 2015). Accordingly, in this study, the participants were selected based on the criterion identified by the researchers, that is, Ethiopian women who had earned a PhD.

An interview guide matrix was developed by the researchers to design the interview questions, using the biopsychosocial and spiritual model of social work. Biopsychosocial and spiritual assessments provide a holistic understanding of past and current circumstances, needs, risk and protective factors, and the environmental context (Gale, 2019). The interview guide was designed to gain information on the experiences of the participants' educational path from elementary school through their completion of a PhD.

After being informed of the purpose of the study, all participants voluntarily accepted and signed an informed consent form. The researchers assured the participants that their identity would be kept confidential. To maintain participants' confidentiality, researchers used pseudonyms and interviewed the women separately in different places and times. One participant was interviewed by phone and two were interviewed face-to-face in their offices. All interviews were conducted in Amharic, the working language of Ethiopia. These three interviews lasted between 1.5 to 3 hours in duration. All three participants allowed the researchers to audio-record the interviews.

After each interview, the data were transcribed into the English language and analyzed using within-cases analysis to compare themes across multiple cases. Cross-case analysis was also used to discern common and different themes among the participants (Creswell & Poth, 2018).

Findings (Within-Cases Analysis)

Kidist's Case

Kidist, born in 1971 in the northern rural part of Ethiopia, is the oldest daughter of her family. After the death of Kidist's father, when she was three months old, her mother remarried and gave birth to a son. Due to her mother's remarriage, when she was 1 year old, Kidist moved to live with her grandmother. Her grandmother was a nun and Kidist regularly attended church with her. Kidist was exposed to measles at age 3, when a measles epidemic hit the province, causing her to partially lose her vision. Her grandmother, who was unable to afford medical treatment, tried unsuccessfully through rituals to save her vision at the age of 7; Kidist had nonetheless the chance to attend a boarding school for visually impaired children. Kidist stayed at the boarding school for 3 years, where she completed grade 1–7. Because of her excellent academic performance, within one year, Kidist completed 5 grade levels (from 1–5).

> When I joined the boarding school it was the end of the academic year, so until the new academic year began, I was practicing reading and writing in braille. When I attended grade 1 class, my performance was excellent, and the school administration decided [that I] pass the next grades by taking each grade level exam. So due to this, within 1 year I reached grade 5.

Kidist had good social relationships with her classmates and teachers. She was also a leader in the church choir. However, living far from home made Kidist miss her family and feel lonely quite often. To manage her stress, she frequently went to church to pray for herself and her family. After completing grade 8, following the school's rules, she left, with a small amount of pocket money, to attend her remaining grade levels outside the boarding school, elsewhere in an urban area.

Kidist then moved to Addis Ababa, the capital city, with her aunt. However, while living with her aunt, she was expected to perform many domestic tasks that interfered with her education. It was by resisting domestic labour that Kidist managed to get a very good result on the regional exam for grade 8 students, enabling her to join a high school for special students in Addis Ababa. When she was in grade 10, Kidist's mother traveled to Addis Ababa to support Kidist. While there, Kidist's mother started a petty street vegetables vendor business with her daughter's pocket money to cover their living costs; when the boarding school had stopped providing financial support to Kidist, she had obtained from the Ministry of Education monthly pocket money for disabled students until she graduated. Life out of boarding school was difficult for Kidist, but her academic performance remained strong. At the end of her secondary education, she was able to achieve a very good score on the national exam.

In 1990, Kidist joined Addis Ababa University to study English language and literature. When Kidist was at the university in the early 1990s, there was minimal access to educational materials, such as books, for visually impaired students. To deal with her academic issues, she used the help of an assistant reader. However, finding an assistant reader who could convert notes to braille was a serious challenge. The students who served as voluntary assistant readers read books and gave her recorded tapes. She often used the recordings to write notes and complete her assignments. Meanwhile, Kidist became a member of *MahibereKidusan* (an association of orthodox Christian students). She found the association helpful in strengthening her spiritual life, providing both relief from stress and hope to face any challenges.

Immediately after graduation, in 1994, the government assigned Kidist to an English language teaching position in a high school. After starting her new job, Kidist married one of her colleagues at the school where she was teaching. Her husband was much older, and they had a son in 2002. Her husband had already two children from his previous marriage, but Kidist did not know about them before she married him. When Kidist decided to attend graduate school, her husband was not in favour of the idea. As a result, they separated until she completed her master's degree in TEFL (Teaching English as a Foreign Language). Without support at home, she took her son with her while studying at the university.

While she was in the master's program, one of her instructors discouraged her based on her visual impairment and tried to prevent her from attending his class. The instructor also told his other students that he did not want to have a blind student in his class: "I feel sick when I [see] a blind person in my class. You blind guy, it is shame on you and [it] is too much for you even attending class in BA, not only MA and PhD." He tried to get Kidist stop attending his class. Kidist did her best to convince him that she was capable, but he ignored her pleas. She was confused about whether to drop or continue his course. If she dropped out, she could not afford to retake the course with another instructor at a later stage, because her sponsor organization only allowed funding for 2 years. If she continued the class, her teacher would not willingly teach her. Finally, she decided to continue the class without his permission, even though she knew there were no blind students who had completed the course properly in the history of his teaching.

> I became confused because the time to add and drop the course had already passed and even if the time of graduation had been postponed, my salary would have terminated. Without a salary, I couldn't have continued my class and I would have faced a serious economic problem to support my mother and care for my son. Therefore, I decided to continue the class without my teacher's permission, and I was ready to take any risk that came from him.

At the end of the semester, in addition to the written exam, there was an oral presentation required to fulfill the course. At the time of her presentation, her teacher provided 16 questions only for her, while the other students got less than 5 questions. Kidst responded to those questions properly. Finally, for this course, Kidist earned a B+. "I don't know … whether my God covered his eye or not, [but he] finally he gave me B+."

Some of Kidist's classmates and faculty members used to assume that, owing to her visual impairment, she could not be successful in her studies or her future career. However, she overcame such problems through personal strength and the help of God.

> When people undermine me, I t[ell] … myself I should be strong and show them I can perform things. Most of the time I don't hate those persons who undermine me because I believe that they are the source of my strength. I always pray to gain a solution from God. And I also believe … He can manage things for me, and I stay in patience.

After earning her masters' degree, Kidist was hired as a lecturer at one of the public universities in Ethiopia. At that time, she reunited with her husband and started a new life in the new place. Kidist's husband's friends often mocked him on the basis of his wife's disability and he began to show shame for marrying a disabled woman. Finally, she decided to leave him without any official divorce and joined another university in a different province.

After 2 years, Kidist received a scholarship to undertake her PhD at Addis Ababa University. She was able to manage the academic pressure by giving priority to her education. However, the added role of taking care of her mentally ill brother as well as her son challenged her for quite some time.

> I was used to schedule my own activity and I gave priority [to] my education. At times, when I became overloaded, I hired a temporary servant to wash clothes and make injera [food]. My mother also helped me by [caring for] my brother even if [caring for] him was more challenging to her.

While dealing with this situation, Kidist began to experience economic hardship and she became diabetic. To manage her financial difficulties, she sold some of her educational equipment and household items and began to skip meals quite often.

> When I was attending the PhD program, I was faced with serious economic problems to print my dissertation and for

transportation fees to return from my working place. So, at that time, I decided to sell my braille [equipment] that I was awarded from boarding school. I know it is very important for me, but printing my dissertation also was a must, and to do it getting money by selling this braille was a solution. I always ate only twice (morning and night) a day because I couldn't afford to eat more than this. This situation was making my life very difficult when I attended my second and third degrees.

When Kidist wrote her dissertation proposal, she faced a serious challenge from one of her evaluators (or leaders) who, by not giving any comments, delayed the process for about 6 months. As a result, she was forced to extend her graduation.

After I submitted my dissertation proposal, the department distributed it to three individuals, who are called anonymous leaders, to evaluate my proposal. They read my proposal and returned it to the department within one month: their comments indicated that my proposal would be approved after I corrected it based on their comments. But the remaining anonymous leader did not give any response to the department and held it for 6 months. Finally, the department decided to give my proposal to another anonymous leader. Based on the new and the previous two anonymous leaders' comments, the proposal needed 3 months to correct. Therefore, the department again decided to submit my proposal by this extended time. Due to this, the date of completion of this PhD program was extended for about 6 months.

Despite this delay, for Kidist, earning a doctoral degree was like returning from death — like a resurrection and a miracle.

I considered it as I return from death. I also considered it a miracle. Because when I think about the uncountable challenges that I faced, I did not believe ... I could ... reach that goal. I ... believe that I did with] the help of my almighty God.

After returning to her university, in addition to teaching, Kidist competed for a different administrative position. However, the authorities were concerned and not willing to give her a chance to hold that position due to her visual impairment. They also assumed that she was awarded her PhD through affirmative action, not by her own efforts. Her colleagues considered their doctoral degrees superior to hers.

> To your surprise, the people who have a PhD, like me, considered ... their PhD as unique and better than mine, since they assumed or considered ... I hold my PhD through begging the name of Saint Mary or affirmative action, and not by my own effort. Now even the people who are educated considered me just like a person who can't survive in every position.

Jegnit's Case

Jegnit, who was born in 1974 in the northern highlands of Ethiopia to farmer parents, is the third daughter of the house. Even though her two elder sisters got married at the age of 8 or 9 years, her father decided to send her to school in their vicinity. Close to her neighbours and family members, Jegnit was also used to having a good relationship with both her teachers and classmates. Jegnit's religious life started when she was a child and, throughout her childhood, she used to carry "Sunday bread" baked by her grandmother to church.

To continue her junior high school education, Jegnit had to go to a nearby town. Her father took her to live with his relatives, who were closer to the school, and she stayed there until she completed junior high school. She started to miss her family, since it was the first time she was separated from them. She believed that "... being separated from my family posed the biggest challenge in my life."

In the new school, as a rural girl, she dressed like the "country/ rural" community. Other students stared and mocked her way of dressing, but later she began to dress like urban dwellers. Another challenge was the shift of instructional language from Amharic to English. In the new school, Jegnit felt alienated and confused. Her social relationships suffered, but later she took on the new habit of admiring the beauty of nature. Both in her elementary and junior high school surroundings, there was no electricity, so they used a gas-lamp to study at night. She believed that such difficulties contributed to her future strength.

To attend secondary school, Jegnit went to a bigger town, which was located 30km away from home. In the new town, Jegnit rented a room with three other female students. Her roommates were her only friends and her relationships with the teachers were good. Her goal in high school was to get strong enough grades to gain access to the university. Jegnit knew that if she failed at that point, the only option in life would be to get married and become a housewife. So, she often went to church to pray to God to make her wishes come true. After studying very hard, Jegnit became one of the top students from the school and she was admitted to Alemaya (now Haromaya) University in 1990. She chose to study agriculture to benefit her farming family and community.

After Jegit registered for the second semester, the socialist government ordered all university students to go to military training. At the time, Jegnit, who was 17, was sent to the Belate Military Training Camp in southern Ethiopia. The soldiers from the camp provided their uniforms and equipment, and they started the training. In the midst of the 2-month training period, President Mengistu Haile Mariam (1974–1991) left the country. At that time, the country was in the middle of a civil war between the government forces and the guerilla fighters. For security reasons, the soldiers took the trainees to Moyle, a border town with Kenya. The Kenyan soldiers then took them to a place called Odaa, and they later settled in a big refugee camp called Walda. Jegnit was registered as a refugee and stayed there for 3 years. Many students in the camp became ill with yellow fever, and some of them died. Likewise, Jegnit became ill for 3 months and nearly died. After recovering, she got a part-time job in the UN Refugee Agency (UNHCR) field office at Odaa and, through this opportunity, met a French pharmacist woman. The pharmacist helped Jegnit get a 3-month tourist visa and together they went to France. The "French lady's" parents became Jegnit's guardians. After receiving asylum, Jegnit entered a language school to learn French at the university.

Right after she finished French language class (within 2 years), Jegnit continued her studies at the *Université de Poitiers* and earned a Bachelor of Science (BSc) in 2000 and a Master of Science (MSc) in chemistry in 2001. She was awarded another scholarship and graduated with an MSc in environmental science in 2002 from the *Université de Mulhouse*. Jegnit reported she had good relationships with her professors in France at both levels.

In 2001, Jegnit returned to Ethiopia to see her biological parents and was happy to find that they were alive. After returning from Ethiopia, Jegnit wanted to start a job in France; however, there were no job opportunities that enabled her to fulfill her career vision, so she began to apply for scholarship programs. She was accepted at Kingston University in England. After 4 years, in 2008, she graduated with a PhD degree in organic chemistry. Jegnit published her research in journals and a book. She then moved to the University of Toronto in Canada to pursue a post-doctoral research position in biochemistry.

While Jegnit was in Canada, she married an Ethiopian man and had a son. Later Jegnit and her husband, who has a PhD in sociology, received an invitation to work at a higher education institution in Ethiopia. After accepting the invitation, Jegnit and her husband launched new graduate study programs in their respective disciplines in Ethiopia. Currently an associate professor, she is heavily engaged in research and advising students. Along with fellow institutional female PhDs, she sometimes makes motivational speeches at different universities. Dr. Jegnit believes that she is happy, and also wants to focus her work on rural education and environmental rehabilitation areas.

Jegnit attributes her earning a PhD to her father's positive attitude and motivation to continue her education since her elementary years. She believed that her spiritual connection with God also contributed to her successes because it kept her moving on, from the beginning of her education to the end.

... My life is the reflection of God's work. Now I don't think the whole thing is done by my power and my capacity. It is the power of God, and I do not want to boast about what I have done. I'm a person that has a lot to do, a lot more ... we all have a purpose with God, if we can pass anything it is with God ... and if we walk faithfully and work hard, we can achieve the thing that we wanted the most. I want people not to admire me, but to acknowledge God and to honor Him ... I succeed because of him. Without God, I wouldn't just sit down and talk to you right now.

The overall meaning of pursuing her education up to the doctoral level was about becoming a relevant contributor to her community. Having a doctoral degree provides her with the means to make a meaningful contribution for the betterment of her community and her nation at large. Earning a PhD made Jegnit realize the power she has to bring change for herself and others.

Abeba's Case

Since 2006, Abeba has been working as an assistant professor of Fisheries and Aquatic Science (Biology) at an Ethiopian university. She was born in 1982 and raised in a rural part of the Amhara region. She is the fifth of six children from an uneducated family. Four of the six children attended school, though, and were able to attend a university; the other two became a priest and a farmer.

Abeba started school in grade 1, since kindergarten was unavailable. She was among the top-ranking students and received a double promotion at one point. Her father passed away when she was 11 and later a marriage proposal came, but her elder brother saved her from early marriage. After finishing elementary school, she joined a secondary school. Since it was far from her village, Abeba had to rent a room in the nearby town and travel every weekend to get food at home. During the time she was living away from her family, some men approached her to engage in a relationship, and she told them that she had a dream to achieve. However, when she experienced tuberculosis, her academic competency began to decline. Abeba discussed this issue with her brother and came up with the solution of withdrawing from classes for a year until she fully recovered. After a year, she was reinstated in grade 11 and became successful. She earned a top score on the national exam and was admitted to study biology at a university.

At the university, Abeba devoted most of her time to her education and participated in church activities. During this time, she met her future husband while they were attending church education. After her graduation in 2004, Abeba was married in an orthodox religious ceremony, had two children, and was hired as a biology teacher in a secondary school. While working, she also started her master's program. However, she did not have a sponsor and she paid for the entire tuition fee. At the time she started her master's program, Abeba had a 2-month-old child. She convinced herself to manage her child, her career, and her education in order to achieve her goal. In the end, she became a top scorer in the department.

After finishing her masters' degree, Abeba had a chance to work as a university lecturer. After some years of service, she was awarded a scholarship from Addis Ababa University to earn her PhD. In the doctoral program, she was the only woman in her cohort of five students. Her PhD research project required her to get into sophisticated laboratory testing and seasonal data collection in a distant area. Also, some of the laboratory equipment was not available at the Addis Ababa University laboratory. Therefore, she went overseas for short term training and for further sample investigation, leaving her children with her husband.

> The scholarship helped me to access very necessary laboratory tools and experiences [knowledge] for my experiment. The university [where] I studied didn't have access to these lab tools. So, I went to Belgium, Korea, Japan, Germany, and China for short-term training.

In the meantime, Abeba spent copious amounts of time in the laboratory and became detached from her family. She also faced economic hardship because of a lack of funds for her research project. Her PhD advisors were very helpful to her. She described herself as a kind of self-deterministic woman and open to critique from her supervisors. "They supported me in all matters from the beginning up to the end of my dissertation."

Abeba's family, and especially her husband, who also has a doctoral degree, shouldered her throughout her education. She shared, "I am so lucky ... while doing my MSc and PhD education ... my husband had a lion share of my success." She completed her PhD in the allotted time, and developed good social skills, both at the university and in her community.

After Abeba returned to her university in Ethiopia, she became the Director of the Assessment Center and President of the Female Teachers Association, in addition to the usual duties of an assistant professor. She also mobilized other fellow female faculty members to work on gender issues, through planning conferences, organizing induction training for new female staff members, and motivating them to conduct action research on gender issues. Even though Abeba has been engaged in all of these activities, she explained that she is not satisfied with her current position. Due to the corrupt system, budget constraints, and the lack of laboratory facilities, she could not excel with her research projects.

Concerning the meaning of having a PhD, Abeba said it was an "enjoyable adventure." Despite the challenges, she had a great experience and explained that "... there were ups and downs, but I enjoyed it." Abeba elaborated, "the process of acquiring doctoral education was very tough. After we acquired it, we didn't give it value as such, but we should value it. You know, at the level of PhD, you do your new findings, mostly by yourself so it was challenging and enjoyable."

Cross-Case Analysis

All participants were born and grew up in the northern part of rural Ethiopia, which is characterized by a patriarchal community. All three were raised under the culture of the traditional Ethiopian orthodox Christianity. They also were required to travel away from their families to access education. Specifically, for Kidist, due to her visual impairment, it was difficult to get special needs education nearby, and she was forced to move to another region far away from her family. For Abeba and Jegnit, the threat of early marriage was a factor in their educational experiences.

Health concerns were experienced by both Kidist and Abeba. The measles epidemic outbreak in Kidist's vicinity exposed her to harm and led her to partially lose her vision. Her visual impairment deterred her from attending a formal school near her family. Likewise, Abeba's health problem (throat tuberculosis) and the stress of life changes contributed to her lower academic performance when she was in high school.

Concerning their academic journey, all three women were able to gain admission to university. Two studied science and one studied language. Two of the participants were able to graduate within the allotted time, while Jegnit was forced to drop out of university due to political reasons and became a refugee. Despite this experience, she was able to graduate overseas after being granted asylum.

After graduation, Abeba and Kidist became high school teachers and got married. Jegnit pursued her master's and doctoral education abroad right after finalizing her undergraduate classes and was married after her doctoral education. After working for some years, Abeba started her master's degree by paying the tuition on her own, while Kidist received sponsorship from the government. After accomplishing their master's degrees, both Abeba and Kidist became lecturers at a university. After a couple of years of service in their respective universities, both were awarded domestic scholarships to continue their doctoral education.

While attending their post-graduate programs, Abeba and Kidist were engaged in multiple responsibilities, including taking care of their children, helping their parents, managing their home affairs, and the like. They both experienced economic hardships. In the case of Kidist, her marital separation forced her to carry the whole burden of the family by herself. Abeba also had to work to generate income while also working on her master's degree. Because of Kidist's disability, she encountered discrimination at all levels, from her husband and his friends and from some of her instructors, classmates, and other faculty members.

With regard to support, the participants' parents, other family members, husband (for Abeba), and other individuals contributed significantly to their overall achievement. Their persistence towards their education also contributed to their success. Their personal strength, family support, and their spiritual affiliations contributed to their persistence towards their education and success. The meaning they gave to their academic endeavour varied based on their musings about their respective experiences. For Kidist it is all about "resurrection," for Abeba, it was an "enjoyable adventure," and for Jegnit, it was a path to become a relevant being for the community.

Discussion

This multiple case study reveals the experience and meaning of earning a doctoral degree for three Ethiopian women. The main finding of the study was that each participant encountered a host of hurdles to completing their education. However, the participants' strength, family support, and religious affiliation helped them to achieve their current professional status. As rural girls, all three experienced a lack of access to formal education at an early age, and their parents were forced to send their daughters far from their hometown to get educated. Similarly, Mergo (2007) identified that accessing formal education was difficult for girls in Ethiopia due to various societal and infrastructural challenges. The challenge of early marriage was evident for two of the participants; however, their family members refused to let them get married so that they could continue their education. Beyene (2015) also stated that vulnerability to harmful traditional practices such as early marriage, abductions, forced marriages, and female genital mutilation, as well as economic, physical, psychological, and sexual violence, hinders girls' education.

Additionally, the study also revealed that the participants' spirituality contributed significantly to successfully managing their life and academic stresses. All three women used their religious affiliations to cope with their stress. Likewise, Wood and Hilton (2012) found that spirituality can serve as a mechanism for students to overcome barriers. A spiritual base provides them with purpose, direction, focus, and a sense of fulfilling their destiny.

The measles epidemic outbreak led Kidist to partially lose her vision, which deterred her from attending a formal school near her family. Abeba's health problem (throat tuberculosis) and stress of life changes contributed to her lower academic performance at high school. Sverdlik et al. (2018) acknowledge that both the physical and psychological well-being of students can influence their performance and achievement.

While they were attending post-graduate education, the three participants had multiple or added responsibilities which posed challenges for them. Bireda (2015) reported that women who have the chance to engage in graduate and post-graduate studies often add the role of student to an already existing set of family, community, and partner-related responsibilities. The double burden of domestic work and the domination of male desires and preferences, especially in love and marriage choices, influences women's decision to withdraw from their education (Gao, 2019). Douglas (2014) also stated that overload and strain represent a challenge for women's performance in graduate school.

Two of the study participants experienced economic hardship during their postgraduate studies. In line with this, Bireda (2015) explained that women in post-graduate studies face a higher level of stress due to financial constraints. Furthermore, Douglas (2014) added that to overcome financial problems, female students often engaged in additional income-generating opportunities. To accomplish their doctoral program successfully, all participants were effectively managing their time and made their education a priority. Similarly, Mirick and Waldkowski (2019) indicated that students' time management, careful organization of responsibilities, and the desire to be a positive role model enabled them to complete all required doctoral tasks successfully.

In addition, negative experiences encountered from faculty and administrators motivate women to persist in their education (Mirick & Waldkowski, 2019). This is consistent with the findings of our study. For instance, one of our participants viewed people who undermined her as a source of strength, which motivated her to show her performance by disproving their expectations. In our study, the participants' meaning for having a PhD derived from their personal, social, and spiritual experiences. Their respective meanings of educational and life journeys ranged from a resurrection, an enjoyable adventure, and being relevant to one's community. Likewise, Burton (2016) described the meaning of earning her PhD as a redefinition of her identity.

Conclusion

Our chapter is entitled "Champions of Hurdles" because it is about the life and educational experiences of three Ethiopian women who overcame the odds to earn doctoral degrees. As women of color, citizens of one of the poorest countries in the world, and members of a religious community, their educational journeys were replete with difficulty. However, each of them was able to earn a doctoral degree and provide services for her nation.

This multiple case study explored the selected cases of three Ethiopian women who earned a PhD. Given the socioeconomic conditions and cultural attitudes towards girls in Ethiopia, the study revealed how difficult it is for Ethiopian girls to gain access to formal education. Moreover, the situation is much worse for girls with disabilities. Postgraduate study often poses challenges of economic insecurity and added responsibilities for women. However, family support, spirituality, and personal strength contributed to these women's accomplishments.

This study may not reflect the overall reality of Ethiopian women; nor does it assess the overall policy and strategies of Ethiopian higher institutions empowering or disempowering female postgraduate students. Therefore, we recommend further expansive research to shed more light on this issue.

The Ethiopian government needs to prioritize girls' education at all levels, particularly in rural areas as the majority (80%) of the population resides there. They also need to provide equal access to education for people with disabilities. The notion of "education for all" is about providing educational opportunities for children and young people. The educational system, in turn, could help the nation achieve the Millennium Development Goals (MDGs; United Nations Educational, Scientific, and Cultural Organization [UNESCO], 2010) and the Sustainable Development Goals (SDGs).

According to the International Labor Organization (2013), there are an estimated 15 million people with disabilities in Ethiopia, who represent 17.6 % of the population. The Ethiopian Ministry of Education estimates that only 4% of children with special needs are enrolled in primary education (Federal Democratic Republic of Ethiopia-Ministry of Education [FDRE-MOE], 2015). Minimizing this huge gap represents a great task for the Ethiopian government. The provision of economic support and other affirmative actions for girls and students with disabilities will contribute to their enrollment in higher education and participation in higher positions. This can encourage young people to advance their educational and career endeavours. Likewise, UNESCO (2010) supports affirmative action and other incentive programs for female students and other socially disadvantaged groups.

To reduce gender-based discrimination, higher education institutions need to create an empowering climate on the issues of gender and disability. They have to train their staff members and students on gender equity, and craft new policies to enhance women's involvement. Furthermore, universities need to share best practices of women educators in academia in the mainstream media and other social networks.

Local social workers, educators, and social development practitioners are required to address local realities regarding personal, social, and community challenges. We can use student practicum reports to gain a much wider understanding of local problems and solutions. In this regard, Ethiopian universities need to revisit their "business as usual" practicum trend, by focusing on communal settings in rural areas to address the gender gaps so evident in education and in other social institutions.

REFERENCES

Abraha, A. (2012). Gender inequalities in tertiary education in Ethiopia: Mediating the transition to university through the development of adaptive competencies. *Global Scholars Program Working Paper Series.* https://www.brookings.edu/wp-content/uploads/2018/03/gender-inequalities-in-tertiary-education-in-ethiopia.pdf

Arts, M. O. (1968). *School census for Ethiopia (part 1): 1967–68.* https://thedocs.worldbank.org/en/doc/342801595577842662-0240021969/render/WorldBankGroupArchivesFolder20015I.pdf

Baxter, P., & Jack, S. (2008). Qualitative case study methodology: Study design and implementation for novice researchers. *The Qualitative Report, 13*(4), 544–559. https://doi.org/10.46743/2160-3715/2008.1573

Beyene, H. (2015). *Final report national assessment: Ethiopia gender equality and the knowledge society.* Chestnut Ave.

Bireda, A. D. (2015). Challenges to the doctoral journey: A case of female doctoral students from Ethiopia. *Open Praxis, 7*(4), 287–297. https://search.informit.org/doi/abs/10.3316/INFORMIT.663785098517848

Burton, K. (2016, April 15). What I lost when I got my PhD. *The World University Ranking.* https://www.timeshighereducation.com/blog/what-i-lost-when-i-got-my-phd

Creswell, J. W., & Poth, C. N. (2018). *Qualitative inquiry & research design: Choosing among five approaches* (4th ed.). SAGE Publications, Inc.

Douglas, D. T. (2014). *Employed graduate student mothers: The benefits, challenges, and perspectives of women fulfilling student, family, and worker roles* [Doctoral dissertation, University of California]. https://alexandria.ucsb.edu/downloads/9w032326m

Federal Democratic Republic of Ethiopia [FDRE]. (2014). *The implementation of the Beijing Declaration and Platform for Action (1995) and the outcome of the 23rd special session of the United Nations General Assembly (2000).* https://

sustainabledevelopment.un.org/content/documents/13067Ethiopia_review_en_
Beijing20.pdf

Federal Democratic Republic of Ethiopia-Ministry of Education [FDRE-MOE]. (2015). *Education sector development programme v (ESDPV) 2015/16-2019/20.* https://www. unicef.org/ethiopia/reports/education-sector-development-programme-v-esdp-v

Ferguson, A. D., Carr, G., & Snitman, A. (2014). Intersections of race-ethnicity, gender, and sexual minority communities. In M. L. Miville & A. D. Ferguson (Eds.), *Handbook of race-ethnicity and gender in psychology* (pp. 45-63). Springer Science+Business Media.

Gale, L. (2019, June 14). *Biopsychosocial-spiritual assessment: An overview.* Retrieved June 5, 2021, https://www.ebsco.com/sites/g/files/nabnos191/files/acquiadam-assets/ Social-Work-Reference-Center-Skill-Biopsychosocial-Spiritual-Assessment.pdf

Gao, Y. (2019). Experiences of Chinese international doctoral students in Canada who withdrew: A narrative inquiry. *International Journal of Doctoral Studies, 14,* 260–276. https://doi.org/10.28945/4240

Guittar, S. G., & Guittar, N. A. (2015). Intersectionality. In J. D. Wright (Ed.), *The International Encyclopedia of Social and Behavioral Sciences* (2nd ed., pp. 657–662). https://doi.org/10.1016/B978-0-08-097086-8.32202-4

Habtu, A. (2001). Women's higher education in Ethiopia under three regimes, 1950–1997. *International Conference on African Development, 32.* http://homepages.wmich. edu/~asefa/Conference%20and%20Seminar/Papers/2001%20papers/PaperII3.pdf

International Federation of Social Workers. (2012, February 23). *Women.* Retrieved May 12, 2021, from https://www.ifsw.org/women/

International Labor Organization [ILO]. (2013). *Inclusion of people with disabilities in Ethiopia.* https://www.ilo.org/wcmsp5/groups/public/@ed_emp/@ifp_skills/ documents/publication/wcms_112299.pdf

Ivankova, N. V., & Stick, S. L. (2007). Students' persistence in a distributed doctoral program in educational leadership in higher education: A mixed methods study. *Research in Higher Education, 48,* 93–135. https://link.springer.com/ article/10.1007/s11162-006-9025-4

Jayasooria, D. (2016). Sustainable development goals and social work: Opportunities and challenges for social work practice in Malaysia. *Journal of Human Rights and Social Work, 1,* 19–29. https://link.springer.com/article/10.1007/s41134-016-0007-y

Magano, M. D. (2013). The lament of a female postgraduate PhD student at a South African University: An academic wellness perspective. *International Journal of Higher Education, 2*(2), 211–221. https://eric.ed.gov/?id=EJ1067487

Mergo, L. (2007). Gender disparity in higher education in Ethiopia: Quantitative and qualitative indicators from three selected universities. *Proceedings of the National Symposium on Establishing, Enhancing & Sustaining Quality Practices in Education, Jimma University,* 78–89. http://africainequalities.org/wp-content/ uploads/2016/07/Gender-Disparity-in-Higher-Education-in-Ethiopia.pdf

Ministry of Education [MOE]. (2012/13). *Education statistics annual abstract.* Addis Ababa.

Ministry of Education [MOE]. (2016/17). *Education statistics annual abstract.* Addis Ababa. https://aacaebc.files.wordpress.com/2018/06/2009-annual-abstract.pdf

Ministry of Education [MOE]. (2018/19). *Education statistics annual abstract.* Addis Ababa.

Mirick, R.G., & Waldkowski, S. (2019). Making it work: Pregnant and parenting doctoral students' attributions of persistence. *Advances in Social Work, 19*(2), 349–368. https://doi.org/10.18060/23220

Morse, J. M. (2010). Sampling in grounded theory. In A. Bryant & K. Charmaz (Eds.), *The SAGE handbook of grounded theory* (pp. 229–244). SAGE.

Patton, M. Q. (2015). *Qualitative research and evaluation methods* (4th ed.). SAGE.

Schmidt, M. & Hansson, E. (2018). Doctoral students' well-being: A literature review. *International Journal of Qualitative Studies on Health and Well-Being, 13*(1), 1508171. https://doi.org/10.1080/17482631.2018.1508171

Stake, R. (1995). *The art of case study research* (pp. 49–68). Sage.

Sverdlik, A., Hall, N. C., McAlpine, L. & Hubbard, K. (2018). The PhD experience: A review of the factors influencing doctoral students' completion achievement and well-being. *International Journal of Doctoral Studies, 13,* 361–388. http://ijds.org/Volume13/IJDSv13p361-388Sverdlik4134.pdf

United Nations Educational, Scientific, and Cultural Organization [UNESCO]. (2010). *Gender issues in higher education: Advocacy brief.* https://unesdoc.unesco.org/ark:/48223/pf0000189825

United Nations Population Fund [UNFPA]. (2008). *Gender inequality and women's empowerment; Ethiopian society of population studies.* https://www.yumpu.com/en/document/read/10622636/gender-inequality-and-womens-empowerment-unfpa-ethiopia

Wood, J. L., & Hilton, A. A. (2012). Spirituality and academic success: Perceptions of African American males in the community college. *Religion & Education, 39*(1), 28–47. https://doi.org/10.1080/15507394.2012.648576

Use of Self in Social Work: A Critical Race and Social Identity Perspective

Anita R. Gooding

In their latest analysis of social justice curricula from 27 social work programs in the United States, Mehrotra et al. (2019) found that a key assumption of Master of Social (MSW) diversity and social justice classes was that social workers were from dominant identity groups, and that their service users were not. For instance, course descriptions positioned marginalized groups as "other," and did not challenge or discuss dominant identities like Whiteness or maleness. Badwall (2015) also contends that Whiteness is so embedded within social work identity, values, and knowledges that many racialized social workers doubt their professional abilities, and/or experience others questioning their skills. This doubt begins in the classroom, where lessons on working with diverse clients assume that the practitioner is White, and do not explore or name what it means to experience racism while practicing social work as a racialized person (Badwall, 2015). In other words, because social work centres Whiteness, the profession struggles to accept that race and racism are central to the practice experience of BIPOC (Black, Indigenous, and People of Colour) social workers. Thus, when social work content erases the practice insights and knowledges held by marginalized groups — that race is a part of practice — it hides perspectives that may provide a more nuanced societal view.

In this current moment, where American society is continuing to grapple with the murder of Black and Brown bodies at the hands of police, alongside an increase in anti-Asian hate crimes, it comes as no surprise that bodies also factor into use of self, because they are often read through social scripts. Therefore, if use of self is truly about relationship, then there must be an understanding that relationships do not live outside of societal constructions of race, and that social worker bodies become a part of use of self. Critical Race Theory (CRT) and Social Identity Theory (SIT) help illustrate the need to discuss race as a component of use of self.

The social work literature has only a few articles that explore social work practice from the perspective of BIPOC social workers, and none that specifically examine how these practitioners use self. However, scholars have looked extensively at the student-field instructor dyad. Broadly speaking, students report that supportive relationships with their field instructors are associated with greater satisfaction in their field practicum (Fortune & Abramson, 1993) and are a critical component of their learning (Bogo, 1994, 2015). Moreover, students gave field instructors positive evaluations based on the frequency and amount of supervision they received (Knight, 2000; Lefevre, 2005). Clearly, students value time with, and attention from, their field instructors. Since field instruction is a role that is central to social work education, and students who have been supervised by BIPOC practitioners have reported feeling prepared to work with racial groups other than their own (Black et al., 1997), it is important to learn more about how the supervisory relationship and use of self are affected by racialization.

Race and Use of Self

Use of self describes social workers' intentional exercising of their "motivation and capacity to communicate and interact with others in ways that facilitate change" (Sheafor & Horejsi, 2003, p. 69). In other words, use of self is how social workers selectively use aspects of self in their work to facilitate client growth and student learning; these tools include personality, self-disclosure, and application of theory to practice (Reupert, 2007). Yet even though we know that race affects social work practice, it has not been considered a component of use of self.

In one of the few social work articles to consider the implications of race in professional social work practice from a non-dominant perspective, Ashley et al. (2016) shares their experiences doing transdisciplinary social work as women of colour. Despite their initial excitement, the transdisciplinary meetings quickly became tense, and one of the authors shared the rejection she felt when her 20+ years of practice insights were ignored around a particular client case. She states:

> I felt that my years of experience and recommendations were ignored by my teammates in lieu of others who seemed to have little insight into this case. My professional pride was bruised, and my personal self was hurt and enraged. Painful questions surfaced in the back of my mind. I wondered if my expertise was viewed as insignificant next to my White counterparts. While I knew I was the most competent one on the team to address these concerns, it seemed that the team didn't realize or respect that. I tried to rationalize that they were ignorant regarding the role of social workers, but their outright dismissal of my input gnawed at me (p.11).

The authors' experience highlights how race can affect the way one is perceived and, thus, the way they use self. As much as the authors tried to "communicate and interact with others in ways that facilitate change" (Sheafor & Horejsi, 2003, p. 69), race stood in the way. Since use of self is a tool for social work practice (Heydt & Sherman, 2005), an examination of use of self that engages both CRT and SIT offers an opening into how race may affect a practitioner's understanding of use of self, and their ability to use who they are to advance student learning.

Critical Race Theory

Several scholars apply CRT principles to social work's mission and values (see Kolivoski et al., 2014); CRT also has been used to frame conversations on equity, inclusion, and diversity within social work courses (see Abrams & Moio, 2009; Constance-Huggins, 2012; Ortiz & Jani, 2010) and social work pedagogy (see Razack & Jeffrey, 2002). They have made it clear that the principles of CRT align with the social work discipline's orientation toward social justice and advocacy. In addition, the authors indicate CRT's utility in all areas of social work practice.

CRT is an offshoot of Critical Legal Studies, which arose in the 1970s from the work of Derrick Bell and Alan Freeman (Ladson-Billings, 1998). As legal scholars, Bell and Freeman believed that for racial reform to occur, the legal system needed a radical shift. Critical legal scholars analyzed the law as an artifact that maintained the US class structure (Ladson-Billings, 1998), and noted that the legal system needed to centre the unique experiences of marginalized groups to change perspectives. As a related, but standalone concept to Critical Legal Studies, CRT has been used in various disciplines, from education to political science and social work, to examine the relationship between race, racism, and power (Taylor, 2009). Despite its wide application, there are some main tenets to CRT, five of which directly relate to my theoretical assumptions about race and use of self.

The first tenet of CRT is that racism is well established within customs, experiences, and structures, and is central to the human experience (Crenshaw et al., 1995; Solórzano & Bernai, 2001). At the same time, racism's ordinary presence makes it invisible to those who hold racial privilege and, therefore, it is difficult to correct. Ortiz and Jani (2010) go as far as to say that CRT recognizes race as a relational concept whose main goal is to stratify and separate. Through internalization of these racial categories, individuals evaluate themselves and others. Consequently, race becomes one way that society organizes itself, and one way that individuals organize self and other.

The second tenet of CRT is a critique of liberalism that rejects dominant narratives, which assume equal opportunity exists for all peoples. Liberalism as a political doctrine upholds unrealistic ideas of meritocracy, equal opportunity, and colourblindness (Razack & Jeffrey, 2002). Instead, CRT explains that race's ordinary presence in society makes it challenging for racialized peoples to gain access to power; they are often unable to completely step outside the racial categorizations and bias imposed upon them and achieve "equal" status. In addition, the critique of liberalism acknowledges that power has often been granted to dominant groups (Gotanda, 1995; Yosso et al., 2009). For instance, since the early years of the United States, cis men of European descent have been able to serve on juries, thus having power to sentence Black and Brown persons under the power of the law. CRT recognizes the institutionalized power granted to Whites and the struggles BIPOC communities face to obtain civil rights. Thus, CRT holds that liberalism ignores the historically slow process of extending rights to BIPOC communities (Yosso et al., 2009). Liberalist conversations of meritocracy, equal opportunity, and colourblindness benefit only those who already hold power (Gotanda, 1995; Kolivoski et al., 2014).

Third, CRT holds that race and races are socially constructed by dominant groups to protect their interests (Bell, 1979; Haney-Lopez, 1994). Through the creation of racial categories, dominant groups decide which groups have access to rights and which groups do not. As a system, race functions to categorize people based on their physical characteristics, even though race is a societal, not biological marker (Constance-Huggins, 2012).

The fourth tenet of CRT is anti-essentialism. One of the many downsides of racial categorization is that it ignores other forms of societal marginalization individuals can be subjected to. Anti-essentialism holds that an intersectional approach to identity is necessary to avoid further replication of oppressive structures (Crenshaw et. al, 1995; Hylton, 2012). Since everyone has intersectional identities that may overlap (Taylor, 2009), focusing on one identity replicates the idea that a person can be contained within one category. Thus, while CRT centres race, it also recognizes the effects of other kinds of oppression — for example, immigration status, gender, sexual orientation — on human life (Constance-Huggins, 2012; Ortiz & Jani, 2010). This intersectional approach acknowledges that one's experience is dependent on a myriad of factors.

Finally, the fifth tenet of CRT centres the viewpoints of racialized peoples to rebuild our flawed and racialized society (Calmore, 1995). Based on their varying histories and personal experience with race and racism, racial minority groups have unique insights (Bell, 1995). This is what Barnes (1990) calls "insight racial distinctiveness." Thus, to contrast master narratives, the final relevant tenet of CRT encourages BIPOC writers to share counternarratives (Taylor, 2009). Through sharing their stories, racialized peoples can teach about racial oppression and translate their struggles into social action (Yosso et al., 2009).

Advancing marginalized voices through counternarratives is a key principle of CRT, for it asks racialized peoples to reclaim their stories and experiences so social change can occur. Sharing counternarratives is one specific way critical race theorists enact social justice. It allows them not only to collect alternative histories of events, based on non-dominant experiences, but also to use storytelling to directly challenge liberalist notions of meritocracy, colourblindness, and equal opportunity. This paper serves as a counternarrative to colourblind discussions of social work supervision and use of self.

Critical Race Theory and Use of Self

When combined, these tenets of CRT illustrate the ways that race informs use of self in the supervisory relationship. Firstly, as noted by Lopez (1994), race is a relational concept because races exist in comparison to each other. For instance, the construct of Whiteness relies upon the construct of Blackness to exist. Following CRT's first tenet, it can be assumed that if race organizes society, then racial categorizations (and our internalization of them) also impact interpersonal relations; thus, the ways in which society categorizes race affects interactions between students and field instructors. Therefore, society's racial categorizations are not just abstract. Instead, these racial categories affect the ways in which social workers, particularly BIPOC social workers, engage with use of self in their work with students. In sum, if racism organizes society, then race also is present within the supervisory space.

Secondly, those in dominant positions often get to assess what should be considered knowledge and are viewed as knowledge generators by society-at-large (Collins, 2002; Janack, 1997). The same knowledge is then granted power socially and, in the academy, without acknowledgement of minoritized experiences. As a result, concepts such as use of self are understood through colourblind narratives, which assume that dominant narratives are the only narratives. Hence, the second tenet highlights another point — as we do not live in a colourblind society with equal opportunity for all, interpersonal relations and use of self are neither colourblind nor equal across racial groups.

Thirdly, CRT holds that race is socially constructed and, because it is an ordinary part of society, also may affect intra- and interracial relations. Therefore, the social construction of race could impact the supervisory experience of BIPOC social workers, both with members of their own communities and with members of dominant groups. Since race and its effects continue to shift over time, it is useful to note how current understandings of race affect the student-field instructor dyad. Not only will this benefit current social work practitioners and students, but it also may aid future BIPOC social workers as they compare today's sociocultural practice realities with their own.

Fourthly, while this chapter centres race and use of self, it is worth mentioning that race may be one of many components of use of self that is missing from the scholarly literature. Other identities such as religion, age, gender, and class may all intersect and overlap in BIPOC social workers' use of self. These identities may do so in both explicit and implicit ways. While this is the final tenet of CRT to be reviewed, advancing marginalized voices is at the heart of the theory and is crucial to include in conversations about use of self in social work. I believe social work can do more to uplift the subjugated knowledges of BIPOC social workers. In addition, social workers are called to uphold principles of social justice. The fact that counternarratives exist should be enough to indicate that solo narratives tend to favour those in power. In its stead, a consideration of both dominant and counternarratives will offer social workers a deeper understanding of social structures — the same social structures that the profession wants to change. Therefore, social workers can contribute to social change by paying attention to counternarratives. Through counternarratives, social work can better understand that race may impact use of self.

To conclude, Critical Race Theory is useful to conversations about use of self for multiple reasons: first, because race organizes society, it also presents within the supervisory space; second, since we do not live in a colourblind society with equal opportunity for all, interpersonal relations (like those between students and field instructors) and use of self are not colourblind either or equal across racial groups; third, the social construction of race could impact the supervisory experience of BIPOC social workers; and finally, solo narratives favour those in power, so it is important that social workers contribute to social change by paying attention to counternarratives.

The next section of this chapter explores the principles of SIT, which highlight additional assumptions around race and use of self. While CRT provides a macro view of society, SIT addresses a micro look at social life.

Social Identity Theory

SIT, considered a preeminent theory within social psychology (Brown, 2000), is well-respected worldwide for redefining intergroup relations (Hornsey, 2008). SIT was developed by social psychologist Henri Tajfel and his graduate student, John Turner, after a series of studies sought a deeper understanding of prejudice and conflict, particularly in the aftermath of the holocaust and WWII (Jenkins, 2008). Tajfel and Turner's research aimed to "establish minimal conditions in which an individual will, in his behaviour, distinguish between an ingroup and an outgroup" (Tajfel, 1974, p. 67). They found, through numerous social experiments, that participants favoured those in their social experimental group, and attempted to achieve maximum difference between their group and the other.

At its core, SIT is about inter- and intra-group relations: how people categorize their self-defined social group in relation to other groups (Brown, 2000). Arguably, the most central aspect of SIT relates to social categorization, which posits that humans organize their social environment into personally meaningful categories or groupings (Tajfel, 1982). Groups are loosely defined as individuals who share an identity — for example, a shared gender identity or shared profession. The consequence of these social categorizations is an accentuation of in-group similarities, alongside an accentuation of out-group differences (Stets & Burke, 2000). Within social categorization, it is important to note that groups do not exist in isolation, but rather interact with each other. Thus, when one category exists, it inherently creates another (Tajfel, 1974). For example, the gender binary forces the idea that the category male should only exist next to the category female.

In SIT, any characteristic can be used as a categorical tool (Cox & Gallois, 1996), from shared heritage to one's neighbourhood. Because SIT holds that the self is reflexive — meaning that it can position itself relative to social categories or classifications — individuals can elect (or not) to move through social categories. Hence, a person's social identity is not static, but may shift over time (Tajfel, 1974). For instance, at one point in time a social worker may be a student yet, at another time, a field instructor.

Most important to self in social identity is that social identity facilitates social categorization. By placing ourselves into groups, humans automatically create an in-group and an out-group, where the in-group belongs, and the out-group does not. Furthermore, social identity theorists note that individuals evaluate a group positively when they become a group member (Stets & Burke, 2000). The positive evaluation results in increased self-esteem, which validates one's self-understanding. In essence, SIT demonstrates that through upholding differences between groups — which may or may not exist — individuals gain a stronger understanding of where they fit into society (Tajfel, 1982).

> Social identity theory was the first social psychology theory to recognize that different groups occupy different levels of a hierarchy of status and power, and that intergroup behaviour is driven by people's ability to be critical of, and to see alternatives to, the status quo. (Hornsey, 2008, p. 207)

Therefore, racial prejudice and stereotypes are about individual desires to align themselves with social groups that appear superior to enhance their self-esteem. Consequently, members of one's racial in-group, for example, are evaluated positively, whereas out-groups, or those of other racial identities, are considered different and are therefore evaluated negatively (Nesdale, 1999). Hence, self-categorization allows individuals to develop social identities, and these social comparisons facilitate positive self-esteem (Cox & Gallois, 1996).

Because social categorization is motivated by self-esteem, one's social categorization depends on the assessment of which identity category is most salient to the specific context (Jenkins, 2008). In SIT, a salient identity is an activated identity (Stets & Burke, 2000). Thus, a person's context dictates which identity would be considered salient at what time. In this way, context becomes key to understanding social categorizations, as context shapes who we consider in-group and who we consider out-group. It allows people to "self-categorize themselves differently according to the contexts in which they find themselves and the contingencies with which they are faced" (Jenkins, 2008, p. 112). Notably, individuals with multiply marginalized identities (e.g., queer, Latinx, disabled) might find it harder to develop self-esteem through group membership because of negative reactions to their other identity categories. For instance, they may feel included in queer spaces, but excluded in Latinx spaces.

About race, Tajfel (1974) states "whatever its other uses may be, the notion of 'race' has become in its general social usage a shorthand expression which helps to create, reflect, enhance and perpetuate the perceived differences in 'worth' between human groups or individuals" (p. 75). He understood that race, although arbitrary, became a categorical tool that allowed one group to claim dominance over others, through evaluating their group positively and other groups negatively.

Social Identity Theory and Use of Self

Two components of SIT directly relate to race informing BIPOC social workers' use of self in the supervisory relationship. The first is racial categorization. Since humans cognitively categorize themselves and others into groups, and race is certainly a social grouping (per CRT), then it is possible for racial differentiation (out-group) and racial similarities (in-group) to impact a social worker's use of self. It also may affect how they are able to use self to affect student outcomes. A student's identity, as well as their perception of the racial group their field instructor belongs to, may change the ways in which a student and field instructor engage with each other. Therefore, racial categorizations may affect how social workers use self, both intra- and inter-racially. For instance, one may develop stronger relationships within their racial group, but struggle to engage cross-racially, or vice versa. Not always because of bias, this may be because of the discomfort of interacting with an unknown social group. Hence, race could impact use of self.

Second, context could influence student supervision when race is activated as a social identity. For instance, when working within a culturally specific agency, that is, with members of their own racial groups, a BIPOC social worker uses self in ways that could look different than if they worked at an agency with mostly White clients. Thus, a social worker of colour in a culturally specific agency may activate race in that context, while, in an alternative context (for example, religion), they may activate another social identity.

SIT offers a unique view into social relationships: namely how social groups relate to each other. As social workers are human beings who belong to social groups, it is worth exploring how these groupings, especially around race, factor into our practice realities. I believe that racial categorizations (in-group and out-group) could affect how the "self" of a social worker is perceived (insider or outsider). This, indeed, may influence field instructor engagement with use of self to advance student learning. In addition, context might affect when race is activated as a social identity; use of self is dependent on how both supervisor and student assess which identities are most salient to their interaction.

Intersections: Critical Race Theory and Social Identity Theory

It is useful to briefly note the similarities and differences between CRT and SIT, particularly as they relate to use of self. The primary area of divergence is that CRT provides a macro understanding of social relations, whereas SIT offers a more micro view. Although not inherently problematic, there may be additional mezzo-level factors, which are just as influential to the way BIPOC social workers use self, including agency structure and the communities in which they practice.

At the same time, CRT and SIT converge in very meaningful ways. First, both CRT and SIT acknowledge that race is one of the ways that society organizes individuals, as well as one of the ways that individuals organize themselves. Second, both theories are intersectional for they both recognize that race is one of many categories which organizes society. Third, both CRT and SIT acknowledge that social categories are defined by the societal context. Therefore, categories, such as race, are socially constructed and thus can change over time. Lastly, both CRT and SIT aim to expose power hierarchies within social groupings — hierarchies which influence individual experience and, potentially, influence social worker use of self. As theories, CRT and SIT portray race as a grouping that structures society and factors into micro-level social interaction. As a result, both theories contribute to the explanation of how race may impact use of self, which has implications for social work education, specifically the student-field instructor relationship.

Implications for Social Work Field Supervision

In their study on how difference is discussed within supervision, Maidment and Cooper (2002) found that students required prompting to think about issues of oppression in their practice. However, when field instructors utilized self-disclosure and questioned students around oppression and difference, many students gained awareness of their biases. Even more so, they were able to think through the ways that their experience informed their awareness of diversity and oppression in practice. Yet for some BIPOC field instructors, use of self is not something they have the agency to use because of societal understandings of what their race signifies. As a theory, CRT explains why race is pervasive. In its explanation, CRT opens the possibility for field instructors and students to explore non-dominant ways of social work practice during supervision. This includes conversations about how race informs and affects BIPOC use of self generally, both within the student-field instructor dyad and within the student-client relationship. When race is included in conversations about use of self, it gives social workers, BIPOC and otherwise, the freedom to bring race into the room explicitly because it informs social life.

Furthermore, the principles of SIT encourage field instructors to consider issues of structural and interpersonal power across difference, as well as within shared identities. Due to socialization within American culture, issues of white supremacy, dominance, and oppression can present themselves regardless of whether someone shares identity groups. While a great deal has been written about cross-cultural supervision (see Estrada et al., 2004; McRoy et al., 1986; Young, 2004), a major gap continues to exist in the ways oppression occurs intra-culturally and intra-racially, and in its differential impacts on historically marginalized groups. Discussing use of self, both within and across difference, will allow field supervisors to support and challenge students in their development as social workers and facilitate a critical praxis.

Conclusion

Critical Race Theory and Social Identity Theory help explain the ways in which race informs social life and thus social worker use of self. Naming race as a component of use of self rejects colourblind narratives about social work practice and acknowledges the real impacts of social identities on supervisory realities. Furthermore, this naming creates an opening for field instructors and students to engage in meaningful conversations about the social construction of race, its dimensions, and the ways a racialized identity informs one's ability to use self to build relationships with clients and to advance client goals.

REFERENCES

Abrams, L. S., & Moio, J. A. (2009). Critical race theory and the cultural competence dilemma in social work education. *Journal of Social Work Education, 45*(2), 245–261. https://doi.org/10.5175/JSWE.2009.200700109

Ashley, W., Santracruz-Cervantes, S., & Castro, T. K. (2016). Professional conflict in social worker development: Transdisciplinary challenges for women of color. *Reflections: Narratives of Professional Helping, 22*(1), 11–16. https://reflectionsnarrativesofprofessionalhelping.org/index.php/Reflections/article/view/1279

Badwall, H. K. (2015). Colonial encounters: Racialized social workers negotiating professional scripts of Whiteness. *Intersectionalities: A Global Journal of Social Work Analysis, Research, Polity, and Practice, 3*(1), 1–23. https://journals.library.mun.ca/ojs/index.php/IJ/article/view/996

Barnes, R. D. (1989). Race consciousness: The thematic content of racial distinctiveness in critical race scholarship. *Harvard Literature Review, 103*, 1864. https://heinonline.org/HOL/P?h=hein.journals/hlrl03&i=1882&a=dWNhbGdhcnkuY2E

Bell Jr, D. A. (1980). Brown v. Board of Education and the interest-convergence dilemma. *Harvard law review, 93*(3), 518–533. https://doi.org/10.2307/1340546

Black, J. E., Maki, M. T., & Nunn, J. A. (1997). Does race affect the social work student-field instructor relationship? *The Clinical Supervisor, 16*(1), 39–54. https://doi.org/10.1300/J001v16n01_03

Bogo, M. (2015). Field education for clinical social work practice: Best practices and contemporary challenges. *Clinical Social Work Journal, 43*(3), 317–324. https://doi.org/10.1007/s10615-015-0526-5

Bogo, M., Regehr, C., Power, R., & Regehr, G. (2007). When values collide: Field instructors' experiences of providing feedback and evaluating competence. *The Clinical Supervisor, 26*(1–2), 99–117. https://doi.org/10.1300/J001v26n01_08

Brown, R. (2000). Social identity theory: Past achievements, current problems and future challenges. *European Journal of Social Psychology, 30*(6), 745–778. https://doi.org/10.1002/1099-0992(200011/12)30:6%3C745::AID-EJSP24%3E3.0.CO;2-O

Calmore, J. O. (1991). Critical race theory, Archie Shepp, and fire music: Securing an authentic intellectual life in a multicultural world. *Southern California Law Review, 65*, 2129-2231. https://heinonline.org/HOL/P?h=hein.journals/scal65&i=2147&a=dWNhbGdhcnkuY2E

Crenshaw, K., Gotanda, N. Peller, G., & Thomas, K. (Eds.). (1995). *Critical race theory: Key writings that formed the movement*. The New Press.

Collins, P. H. (2002). *Black feminist thought: Knowledge, consciousness, and the politics of empowerment*. Routledge.

Constance-Huggins, M. (2012). Critical race theory in social work education: A framework for addressing racial disparities. *Critical Social Work, 13*(2), 1–16. https://doi.org/10.22329/csw.v13i2.5861

Cox, S., & Gallois, C. (1996). Gay and lesbian identity development: A social identity perspective. *Journal of Homosexuality, 30*(4), 1–30. https://doi.org/10.1300/J082v30n04_01

Estrada, D., Frame, M. W., & Williams, C. B. (2004). Cross-cultural supervision: Guiding the conversation toward race and ethnicity. *Journal of Multicultural Counseling and Development, 32*(1), 307–319. http://www.wyomingcounselingassociation.com/wp-content/uploads/Estrada-et-al-2004-Cross-Sultural-Supervision.pdf

Fortune, A. E., & Abramson, J. S. (1993). Predictors of satisfaction with field practicum among social work students. *The Clinical Supervisor, 11*(1), 95–110. https://doi.org/10.1300/J001v11n01_07

Gotanda, N. (1995). A critique of "our Constitution is color-blind." In Crenshaw, K., Gotanda, N. Peller, G. & Thomas, K., *Critical race theory: Key writings that formed the movement* (pp. 315–329). The New Press.

Heydt, M. J., & Sherman, N. E. (2005). Conscious use of self: Tuning the instrument of social work practice with cultural competence. *Journal of Baccalaureate Social Work, 10*(2), 25–40. https://doi.org/10.18084/1084-7219.10.2.25

Hornsey, M. J. (2008). Social identity theory and self-categorization theory: A historical review. *Social and Personality Psychology Compass, 2*(1), 204–222. https://doi.org/10.1111/j.1751-9004.2007.00066.x

Hylton, K. (2012). Talk the talk, walk the walk: Defining critical race theory in research. *Race Ethnicity and Education, 15*(1), 23–41. https://doi.org/10.1080/13613324.2012.638862

Janack, M. (1997). Standpoint epistemology without the "standpoint"?: An examination of epistemic privilege and epistemic authority. *Hypatia, 12*(2), 125–139. https://doi.org/10.1111/j.1527-2001.1997.tb00022.x

Jenkins, R. (2008). *Social identity* (3rd ed.). Routledge.

Knight, C. (2001). The process of field instruction: BSW and MSW students' views of effective field supervision. *Journal of Social Work Education, 37*(2), 357–379.

Kolivoski, K.M., Weaver A., & Constance-Huggins M. (2014). Critical race theory: Opportunities for application in social work practice and policy. *Families in Society: The Journal of Contemporary Social Services 95*(4), 269–276. https://doi.org/10.1080/10437797.2001.10779060

Ladson-Billings, G. (1998). Just what is critical race theory and what is it doing in a 'nice' field like education? *International Journal of Qualitative Studies in Education, 11*, 7–24. https://doi.org/10.1080/095183998236863

Lefevre, M. (2005). Facilitating practice learning and assessment: The influence of relationship. *Social Work Education, 24*(5), 565–583. https://doi.org/10.1080/02615470500132806

Lopez, I. F. H. (1994). The social construction of race: Some observations on illusion, fabrication, and choice. *Harv CR-CLL Rev., 29*, 1. https://heinonline.org/HOL/P?h=hein.journals/hcrcl29&i=11&a=dWNhbGdhcnkuY2E

Maidment, J., & Cooper, L. (2002). Acknowledgement of client diversity and oppression in social work student supervision. *The International Journal, 21*(4), 399–407. https://doi.org/10.1080/02615470220150366

McRoy, R. G., Freeman, E. M., Logan, S. L., & Blackmon, B. (1986). Cross-cultural field supervision: Implications for social work education. *Journal of Social Work Education, 22*(1), 50–56. https://doi.org/10.1080/10437797.1986.10671729

Mehrotra, G. R., Hudson, K. D., & Self, J. M. (2019). A critical examination of key assumptions underlying diversity and social justice courses in social work. *Journal of Progressive Human Services, 30*(2), 127–147. https://doi.org/10.1080/10428232.2018.1507590

Nesdale, D. (1999). Social identity and ethnic prejudice in children. *Psychology and Society*, 92–110. https://doi.org/10.4324/9780203391099

Ortiz, L., & Jani, J. (2010). Critical race theory: A transformational model for teaching diversity. *Journal of Social Work Education, 46*(2), 175–193. https://doi.org/10.5175/JSWE.2010.200900070

Reupert, A. (2007). Social worker's use of self. *Clinical Social Work Journal, 35*(2), 107–116. https://doi.org/10.1007/s10615-006-0062-4

Sheafor, B. W., & Horejsi, C. R. (2003). *Techniques and guidelines for social work practice* (6th ed.). Pearson Higher Ed.

Solórzano, D., & Bernai, D. (2001). Examining transformational resistance through critical race theory and LatCRIT theory framework: Chicana and Chicano students in an urban context. *Urban Education, 36*(3), 308–342. https://doi.org/10.1177/0042085901363002

Stets, J.E., & Burke, P.J. (2000). Identity theory and social identity theory. *Social Psychology Quarterly*, 224–237. https://www.jstor.org/stable/2695870

Tajfel, H. (1974). Social identity and intergroup behaviour. *Social Science Information, 13*(2), 65–93. https://doi.org/10.1177/053901847401300204

Tajfel, H. (1982). Social psychology of intergroup relations. *Annual Review of Psychology, 33*(1), 1–39. https://doi.org/10.1146/annurev.ps.33.020182.000245

Taylor, E., Gillborn, D., & Ladson-Billings, G. (2009). *Foundations of critical race theory in education.* Routledge.

Yosso, T., Smith, W., Ceja, M., & Solórzano, D. (2009). Critical race theory, racial microaggressions, and campus racial climate for Latina/o undergraduates. *Harvard Educational Review, 79*(4), 659–691. https://doi.org/10.17763/haer.79.4.m6867014157m7071

Young, R. (2004). Cross-cultural supervision. *Clinical Social Work Journal, 32*(1), 39–49. https://doi.org/10.1023/B:CSOW.0000017512.11072.6d

PART III:
Social Justice, Advocacy, and International Social Work

9

Field Education and Immigrant Serving Sector

Vibha Kaushik

Social work has a long history of serving immigrants in Canada by responding to their needs, and by engaging in settlement practices and integration programs for newcomers, immigrants, and refugees when they first arrive in the country. Social workers provide comprehensive responses not only to the predicaments and challenges facing immigrants and refugees, but also their families including their parents, grandparents, children, and grandchildren as they continue with their lives in this country (Dumbrill, 2008; Frideres & Biles, 2012; Lundy, 2010; Sethi, 2013). To assist them efficiently and to advocate for them effectively, it is very important for social workers to have an awareness of the challenges facing immigrants, refugees, and their families; to learn about their settlement and integration experiences; to develop an increased understanding of the needs of newcomers arriving through a variety of pathways; to become familiar with the services and support offered to immigrants and refugees; and to understand the policies and programs that govern Canada's newcomer intake, and their implications for newcomer settlement and integration in the Canadian society.

Newcomer settlement and integration is multidimensional and complex. Settlement is a process through which immigrants establish themselves in their new social environment. It captures distinct activities and processes as immigrants cross between cultures and socio-geographical locations (Valtonen, 2016). Integration, on the other hand, is a goal-oriented process through which immigrants seek full participation in the social, economic, cultural, and political life of the host society. It is also seen as the desirable outcome of a long-term process facilitated by initial settlement (Valtonen, 2016). Although certain aspects of settlement expectations and integration experiences are similar for most immigrants, there are subtle differences between different groups of immigrants. For instance, refugees are less likely to be proficient in English upon arrival, they may not always have the occupational background highly demanded in the Canadian labour market, and they are likely to have past experiences of trauma and violence. Therefore, they would expect compassionate support as they learn to build new lives against all odds. On the other hand, the immigrants within the skilled category are invited as permanent residents after a rigorous assessment of their skills, qualifications, and professional background to fulfill the labour shortage in high-demand professions in Canada. Therefore, skilled immigrants may prioritize insights and support for securing appropriate employment corresponding to their professional background in the shortest possible time (Bhayee, 2019; Drolet et al., 2017; Kaushik, 2020; Valtonen, 2016). Through this chapter, I invite attention of the social work profession to the preparation of the next generation of practitioners for addressing the complex issue of newcomer settlement and integration. Information from existing literature in the area of immigration and social work practice and education will be offered and relevant issues will be discussed. My goal in this chapter is to create a dialogue for developing immigration content in the education and training of social workers, including more field education and training opportunities in the immigrant serving sector, and to prepare future practitioners to respond to issues and challenges newcomers faced when they settle for a new life in Canada. For the sake of brevity in this chapter, I will use, henceforth, the terms "immigrants" and "immigrant" to include "refugees" and "refugee," unless a distinction needs to be made between the two groups.

The Realities of International Migration and History of Canadian Immigration

International migration, forced or voluntary, is an expression of globalization (Nash et al., 2006). Today, more people than ever live in a country other than the one in which they were born (United Nations, n.d.). Sometimes people move voluntarily in search of better economic opportunities, for personal and/or professional growth, to fulfill self-actualization needs or to rejoin their families. However, often times people are forced to migrate to escape conflict, persecution, terrorism, or human rights violations in their home countries. Many others are displaced due to the adverse effects of climate change, natural disasters, or other environmental factors (Becker & Ferrara, 2019; Dohlman et al., 2019; United Nations, n.d.). In recent years, the world has witnessed major migration and displacement events resulting in an overall increase in the scale of international migration. According to United Nation's *World Migration Report,* in 2019, the number of international migrants was estimated to be approximately 272 million globally, nearly two-thirds of whom were economic migrants. This was 51 million more than in 2010. In 2019, the estimated proportion of the global population who were international migrants was 3.5% compared to 2.8% in 2000, and 2.3% in 1980 (McAuliffe & Khadria, 2020).

Canada is a safe and welcoming destination for international migrants, including immigrants, refugees, and asylum seekers. Of all countries, Canada has the sixth highest number of immigrants per capita (Organization for Economic Cooperation and Development [OECD], 2022). Canada is globally recognized for its well-established immigration policies and public discourse that view immigrants and refugees as valuable resource for the country's local, provincial, and federal economic growth and social vitality (Sidney, 2014). According to historians, large scale immigration in Canada began in the 1860s; however, for almost a century, immigration in Canada continued to be highly restrictive as only people from United Kingdom, Europe, and America were truly welcomed to the country. In the post war years, Canada's immigration policy started demonstrating a humanitarian approach as it welcomed refugees, war brides, and displaced persons, but only from United Kingdom, Europe, and America (Knowles, 2016). Between 1947 and 1957, the immigration restrictions eased in order to admit refugees, displaced persons, and ordinary immigrants from a growing number of "white" Commonwealth countries (Knowles, 2016; Rawlyk, 1962). In 1957, facing a greater need for a much larger population (Rawlyk, 1962) and referring to the 1952 *Immigration Act*, then prime ministerial candidate John Diefenbaker famously announced, "We will overhaul the act's administration to ensure that humanity will be considered and put an end to the bureaucratic interpretations which keep out from Canada many potentially good citizens" (as cited in Knowles, 2016, p. 136). Later as prime minister, Diefenbaker declared, "Canada must populate or perish" (as cited in Knowles, 2016, p. 136) to encourage immigration to foster population growth in Canada.

By the 1960s, Canadian immigration policies began to change to offer solutions for several demographic challenges facing the country such as aging population; shrinking birth rates; declining ratio between the combined youth and senior populations (0 to 19 years and 65 years or older), and working-age people (20 to 64 years); and, skills shortages in a global, market-driven information-based economy (Boyd & Alboim, 2012; Elabor-Idemudia, 2005; Knowles, 2016). In the wake of the realization that restricting immigrant intake from the traditional source countries was insufficient to address the demographic challenges, or to meet the labour marker demands in Canada, the current points-based immigration system was established in 1967. The points-based system placed a higher emphasis on human capital and acknowledged the economic benefits of immigration. Under the points system, applicants were given points on nine factors: (1) education and training; (2) personal character; (3) occupational demand; (4) occupational skill; (5) age; (6) pre-arranged employment; (7) knowledge of French and English; (8) presence of a relative in Canada; and (9) employment opportunities in their area of destination. The points-based system was the first major step to provide explicit guidelines to the immigration officers and to limit their discretionary powers (Green & Green, 2004; Canadian Museum of Immigration at Pier 21, 2019). This shift in immigration policy facilitated intake of immigrants from developing countries in Asia, Africa, the Middle East, and Central and South America (Bhatta, 2017). Since then, in addition to continuing its global leadership in international refugee resettlement initiatives, Canada has adopted an immigration policy that emphasized immigration for "designated" occupations in order to attract highly skilled workers with advanced educational credentials and professional skills, and best address Canada's economic needs (Boyd & Alboim, 2012; Government of Canada, 2020; Green & Green, 2004; Henry & Tator, 2006; Reitz, 2007).

The provisions for immigration in Canada are regulated by the *Immigration and Refugee Protection Act* (IRPA), which came into force in 2002 to outline several basic economic, social, and cultural goals for Canada's immigration program (Government of Canada, 2021a). The major objectives of IRPA includes supplying regulations for (1) admitting skilled workers to Canada to support and develop a strong and prosperous economy; (2) fulfilling Canada's obligation to contribute to international efforts to provide protection to refugees and displaced persons; (3) reuniting families of immigrants; (4) offering settlement/resettlement assistance to all immigrants including refugees; (5) promoting successful integration of immigrants; and (6) facilitating the entry of visitors, international students, and temporary foreign workers (Government of Canada, 2021a). Since the introduction of IRPA until 2015, Canada welcomed an average of approximately 250,000 immigrants every year (Government of Canada, 2021b). This figure includes all classes of immigration such as economic class immigrants, family class immigrants, and refugees and protected persons. In subsequent years, with the increase in the intake of immigrants, the average immigration figure has gone up. For instance, in 2016, Canada accepted 296,346 immigrants while in 2019 the country welcomed 341,180 new immigrants. Between 2021 and 2023, Canada plans to admit over 1.2 million new immigrants to the country (Government of Canada, 2021b) or a number of immigrants equal to 1% of Canada's population each year (Government of Canada, 2018).

The Immigrant Serving Sector in Canada

Immigrants need efficient support as they establish themselves in the country and to overcome the challenges they face in the process (Kaushik, 2020). Cognizant of this need, the Immigration, Refugees, and Citizenship Canada (IRCC) funds the Settlement Program to offer a variety of services and supports that benefit immigrants and help them integrate into Canadian communities. Through the Settlement Program, IRCC works with several partners and community organizations across Canada and

Figure 9.1: Immigrant serving Sector at a Glance

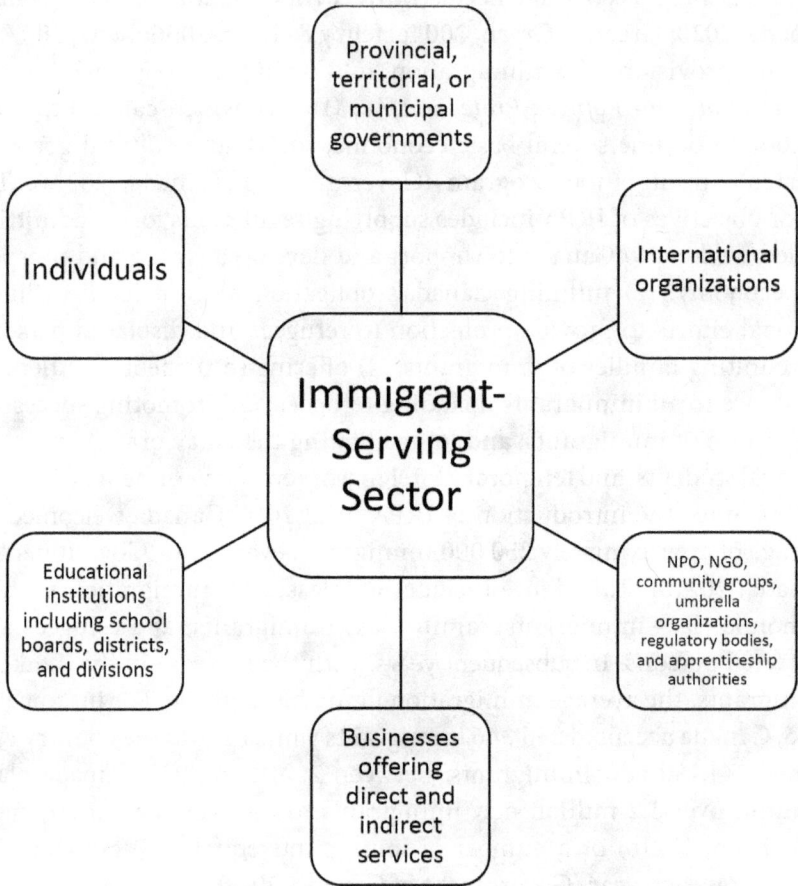

internationally to provide immigrants with the information they require to make informed decisions during the settlement process, with respect to language skills adequate for their settlement and integration goals, and the support they may need to build networks within their new communities. These organizations are mandated to support immigrants until they are able to fully participate in the Canadian economy and society (Government of Canada, 2021c; Praznik & Shields, 2018; Shields et al.,

2016). The first program of this kind in Canada was launched in 1974 as the Immigrant Settlement and Adaptation Program (ISAP). Since then, countless number of immigrants have been supported through a wide range of settlement programming and services as the sector has evolved tremendously (Bhatta, 2017). The settlement sector involves a network of not-for-profit organizations, community groups, various forms of associations, umbrella organizations, regulatory bodies, and local immigration partnership councils (see Figure 9.1). The primary purpose of these associations, organizations, and partnerships is to facilitate newcomer settlement and to enhance the knowledge and capacity in the settlement sector through research, networking, and training with the ultimate goal to improve newcomer outcomes. In addition, provincial, territorial, and municipal governments; school boards, districts, and divisions; and certain businesses that offer indirect services also play an active role in facilitating newcomer settlement (Government of Canada, 2019). According to IRCC, the planned settlement program expenditure in 2021–2022 amounted to around $894.6 million (Government of Canada, 2021b).

Social Work and the Immigrant Serving Sector

With the growing number of immigrants and refugees arriving in Canada and with the improved understanding of all types of predicaments and challenges they experience, social work has increasingly become interested in immigrants as a vulnerable and marginalized population group. Furthermore, social work has also become a regular human resource provider for the immigrant serving sector, particularly for supplying practitioners with high level of service expertise to fill key leadership positions in the sector organizations (Türegün, 2013). The high number of immigrants arriving annually affirms the ongoing need for immigrant services in Canada. To ensure necessary supports to new immigrants, the demand for services for immigrants has increased and, along with it, the need for well-equipped social workers trained and experienced in serving immigrants (Kaushik, 2020; Payne, 2014). Social work's focus on the "person-in-environment" perspective, along with anti-oppressive, culturally competent, ethical, and trauma-informed practice approaches, makes its practitioners ideally suited to play a central role in the interdisciplinary team of professionals who collaboratively respond to the needs of immigrants and their families. Social workers initiate coordinated and consolidated interventions with both the recognition and sophisticated understanding of complex issues of diversity, discrimination, exploitation, oppression, trauma, and a range of other social and emotional problems (see Chang-Muy & Congress, 2016; Kuttikat, 2012). However, the profession confronts some challenges related to education and training for its practitioners (Yan & Chan, 2010), which have been noticed and should be ironed out.

In the last several years, efforts have been made towards building capacity in the social work profession for working with immigrants in Canada; calls have also been made for considering social work with immigrants, refugees, and asylum seekers as a new field of practice within the profession (Nash et al., 2006; Yan & Chan, 2010). A decade ago, researchers noted that newcomer issues were rarely included in the curriculum of different levels of social work education and field training. A handful of social work programs offered courses that were specifically focused on working with immigrants and refugees; however, almost all of them were elective courses and did not constitute the core social work curricula. Topics relevant for practice with immigrants were usually explored within courses on cross-cultural, anti-racist, and anti-oppressive practices (Yan & Chan, 2010). A quick survey of the current online information available on the websites of social work institutions shows that social work programs in Canada have since made some progress. Currently, many accredited graduate and undergraduate programs offer one or more elective courses that consider issues of immigration and refugee resettlement. Likewise in the accreditation context, authors have been drawing attention to the fact that the Canadian Association of Social Work Education - L'Association canadienne pour la formation en travail social (CASWE-ACFTS) accreditation standards do not directly pinpoint materials and information related to practice with immigrants as a requirement for social work programs; they also argue that there is a need for new accreditation standards to better prepare social work students for working with immigrants and their families (Drolet, 2012; Yan & Chan, 2010). However, little has been done in this area and the status quo continues to remain. A quick search on the CASWE-ACFTS website (https://caswe-acfts.ca/) using the search tool returned no results that could suggest a specific mandate on the preparedness of social workers to serve immigrants and refugees or indicate CASWE-ACFTS's commitment to promote the inclusion of newcomer issues in social work education, scholarship, and practice. This lack of intentionality on the part of CASWE-ACFTS to enhance the profession's ability to deal with the changing demographic of the country, demands a critical examination of the existing focus of Canadian social work. Indeed, the new realities invite all stakeholders to both reflect on the current social work discourses that shape professional practice and begin a conversation in order to re-envision the goals and priorities of social work education in Canada.

Practice literature explicitly reveals that practitioners require specialized knowledge of the unique issues facing immigrants and refugees. Practitioners involved with this client group frequently agree that they should have sufficient information about immigration policies and regulations, laws and legal discourses surrounding immigrants, and labour market requirements and socioeconomic discourses to make informed decisions to support immigrants and to make necessary referrals. They must also have adequate knowledge of the range of factors that are of importance for immigrants such as human rights and social justice issues, local and international laws related to migrants and refugees, and service delivery systems specific to immigrants to get meaningfully engaged in advocacy and activism with and on behalf of this population. In addition, social work practitioners must also be culturally competent and informed about other key issues such as health, mental health, family dynamics, cultural diversity, language, and important socioeconomic factors including educational background and professional experience. Literature on practice with immigrants has and continues to emphasize both "knowing about policy" and "knowing about immigrants" because immigrant experiences are defined by the policy contexts. It has been argued that an understanding of immigrant experiences is important; yet, along with that, an understanding of macro-level contexts is also important because polices facilitate the nature and extent of services that social workers provide to immigrants (Düvell & Jordan, 2001; Kaushik, 2020; Kaushik & Walsh, 2018; Martinez-Brawley & Zorita, 2011; Padilla, 1997; Potocky-Tripodi, 2019; Sethi, 2013).

Social Work Field Education in the Immigrant Serving Sector

Field education has a critical role in social work education. It is considered a central component in social work training as it offers students a distinct perspective of the profession by integrating classroom knowledge with social work values and skills in the context of field. Specifically, CASWE-ACFTS (2020) outlines that "The purpose of field education is to connect the theoretical/conceptual contributions of the academic setting with the practice setting, enabling the student to acquire practice skills that reflect the learning objectives for students identified in the Standards" (para 7). It enables students to learn from experienced social workers in a variety of practice settings and gain practical knowledge and skills through experiential learning. Field education provides students with opportunities to develop skills beyond those obtained in a classroom-learning environment; therefore, students find their field education experience to be the most important element in becoming a competent practitioner. On the other hand, faculty and field instructors find it important as it allows them to evaluate students' suitability and preparedness for professional practice (Bogo, 2015; McConnell et al., 2013; Poulin et al., 2006).

Every year, a large number of social work students complete their field education placement in immigrant serving agencies and organizations that provide services to immigrants in Canada. Besides offering necessary support to immigrants, these immigrant serving agencies and organizations also provide an important learning site for social work students, specifically for those who plan to work with newcomer clients and client systems, as well as those who are interested in developing practice knowledge and skills in the related area of immigration practice (Drolet, 2012). As students complete their field placements, they learn about publicly-funded settlement services and programs; they understand the role of community-based partnerships in promoting immigrant settlement and integration at different levels; they gain first-hand experience of the challenges and struggles experienced by immigrants in their integration journeys; they receive opportunities to get engaged with social action and social justice for immigrants; and they improve their understanding of the historical, political, economic, and social factors associated with immigration, including both forced and voluntary international migration (Drolet, 2012).

The onsite experiential learning under the supervision of field instructors and mentors equips students to play a more central role in serving immigrants at the micro level in the direct practice arena, as they hone their problem-solving skills, case work, counselling, and therapeutic skills. At the mezzo level, the fieldwork experience offers students the opportunity to gain necessary knowledge to get productively engaged in community development to create welcoming and inclusive spaces where immigrants feel safe, develop a sense of belonging and connection, and can thrive and achieve their full potential. Last but not the least, the knowledge gained in the field also places students in a good position to foster deliberation and to influence the macro level discourse on human rights, social policy, social justice, and advocacy (Drolet et al., 2017; Martinez-Brawley & Zorita, 2010; Nash et al., 2006; Westoby, 2008).

In practice literature, we have evidence that in-person contact of students with marginalized and vulnerable populations on the one hand, predicts more understanding and favourable attitudes towards the people they serve and, on the other hand, reduces misinformation which leads to stereotypes and prejudices (see Bhuyan et al., 2012). Sometimes, while working with immigrants and being under the pressures and constraints of everyday practice, practitioners tend to make biased decisions which, potentially influenced by intersectional identities, culture-based stereotyping, and categorisation of service users, deeply affect the merits of casework (see Barberis & Boccagni, 2014; Bhuyan et al., 2012; Chang-Muy & Congress, 2016). However, students who receive field education practice with immigrant clientele or in immigration policies-related areas are found to significantly improve their attitudes towards immigrant service users. Through placements in the sector, they are given the opportunities of in-person contact which enhance their general knowledge of immigrants and immigration-related topics (Bhuyan et al., 2012). In the field, students begin not only to identify and challenge their personal biases, assumptions, views, and stereotypes about diversity, but they also learn how their personal circumstances and social locations may influence their practice with immigrant clients and communities. Students begin to understand that immigrants are not a homogenous group as they experience the diversity within the immigrant population. Students gain insight into how immigrant serving agencies respond to the needs of diverse immigrant clients and communities. The field experience helps students understand the role of social workers as immigrants navigate through the process of settlement and integration (Barberis & Boccagni, 2014; Drolet, 2012).

Competent Practice with Immigrant Clients and Communities

Two major learning objectives for social work students in today's highly globalized and diversified world is to develop practice competence with diversity and to learn to provide effective services to diverse service users. In relation to these objectives, the Canadian Association of Social Workers has made some broad references to social work principles such as cultural competence, cultural sensitivity and awareness, diversity and discrimination, social justice, and social action in their 2005 *Code of Ethics* and 2005 *Guidelines for Ethical Practice*. However, I would argue that those can hardly be regarded as sufficient or meaningful guidelines for practice with immigrants. Perhaps this is the reason why Yan and Chan (2010) stated that social workers are "less than fully prepared to serve newcomers effectively" (p. 16). In their British Columbia Association of Social Workers' (BCASW) organized survey-based exploratory study, only a handful of respondents (social workers registered with BCASW) reported that they had received education and training specific to working with immigrants in their academic programs; a vast majority additionally reported that they either had not heard about *Immigration and Refugee Protection Act* or knew nothing of the details it contained. Most respondents in the study suggested that if cross-cultural and anti-oppressive practice training is helpful, it is not sufficient for preparing students to work with immigrants. An overwhelming majority of respondents reported that their social work education and training lacked content on policies and programs unique to immigrants. They did not receive knowledge either about the specific needs of immigrants and the difficulties, challenges, and issues they face (see Yan & Chan, 2010).

Interestingly, this situation is not unique to social workers in Canada. Studies from other parts of the world such as the US, Italy, and Britain have concluded that practitioners in the immigrant serving sector learn by practice. They do not get the practice tools from their social work school training; instead, they train themselves through practice and in-person contact with immigrant service users, and by relying on other staff members. The literature reveals that at the grass roots level, the staff lack preparation and do not receive much guidance at work (Barberis & Boccagni, 2014; Duvel & Jordan, 2001; Martinez-Brawley & Zorita, 2010; Nash et al., 2006). This situation demands an expansive analysis and a comprehensive examination of the current state of preparedness of social workers for serving immigrants and their practice competence with immigrant service users. Furthermore, when the staff at the immigrant serving agencies, who also serve as field supervisors for student interns, themselves lack the necessary training, it invites a discussion on how we offer quality field training to social work students, in order for them to develop and enhance appropriate practice skills to service immigrants.

Conclusion

Immigrant service delivery is based on the fundamental criterion of addressing the needs experienced by immigrants in their immigration journey. Immigrant serving agencies often function as a bridge between immigrants and the host society. The availability of adequate services and professional support is critical for immigrants as they move through the stages of initial settlement to long-term integration. To provide appropriate services, it is important that practitioners are sufficiently equipped to work with, and work for immigrants at all levels of practice. As a profession, social work is diligent towards culturally sensitive and anti-oppressive practice. However, I would argue that the challenges and issues that immigrants face are often beyond cultural or ethnicity-based discrimination or racism, which social work education and training must consider. Owing to the rapid influx of immigrants, the changing demographic realities in Canada demand that the social work academic programs offer appropriate knowledge and experience on the range of issues experienced by the immigrants, and not just limit the focus on diversity and cultural competence.

The research completed for this chapter reveals that there is very limited to no scholarship or information available on this topic. As a social work researcher and academic who is highly interested in immigrant issues, I often come across the narrative that students want to complete their placements in the immigrant serving sector; however, there are not enough social workers in the sector to offer them field supervision. Is it just a narrative or a possibility backed by evidence? We must address this contention. We need updated research to establish whether we have appropriate capacity to offer field supervision to social work interns in the sector; if not, would receiving interdisciplinary supervision be a more effective strategy? We must also explore new models of field education so that the gap in field education is addressed. This chapter aims to draw attention of the profession to these important questions.

REFERENCES

Barberis, E., & Boccagni, P. (2014). Blurred rights, local practices: Social work and immigration in Italy. *British Journal of Social Work, 44,* i70-i87. https://doi.org/10.1093/bjsw/bcu041

Becker, S. O., & Ferrara, A. (2019). Consequences of forced migration: A survey of recent findings. *Labour Economics, 59,* 1–16. https://doi.org/10.1016/j.labeco.2019.02.007

Bhatta, S. (2017). *Professionalization of settlement work: understanding settlement work as a profession and its viability in the current immigration context.* https://welcomehome.to/project/whto-insights-professionalization-of-settlement-work-understanding-settlement-work-as-a-profession-and-its-viability-in-the-current-immigration-context/

Bhayee, S. (2019). *Perceptions of settlement workers on the needs and challenges of female Syrian Refugees* (Publication No. 6104) [Master's thesis, Western University]. Electronic thesis and dissertation repository. https://ir.lib.uwo.ca/cgi/viewcontent.cgi?article=8359&context=etd

Bhuyan, R., Park, Y., & Rundle, A. (2012). Linking practitioners' attitudes towards and basic knowledge of immigrants with their social work education. *Social Work Education, 31*(8), 973–994. https://doi.org/10.1080/02615479.2011.621081

Bogo, M. (2006). Field instruction in social work. *The Clinical Supervisor, 24*(1–2), 163–193. https://doi.org/10.1300.J001V24n01_09

Boyd, M., & Alboim, N. (2012). Managing international migration: The Canadian case. In D. Rodriguez-Garcia (Ed.). *Managing immigration and diversity in Canada: A transatlantic dialogue in the new age of migration* (pp. 123–50). McGill-Queens University Press.

Canadian Association of Social Work Education – L'Association canadienne pour la formation en travail social (CASWE-ACFTS). (2020). *Statement on the critical role of field education in social work education.* https://caswe-acfts.ca/statement-on-the-critical-role-of-field-education-in-social-work-education/

Canadian Museum of Immigration at Pier 21. (2019). *Immigration regulations, order-in council PC 1967-1616, 1967.* https://pier21.ca/research/immigration-history/immigration-regulations-order-in-council-pc-1967-1616-1967

Chang-Muy, F., & Congress, E. P. (Eds.). (2016). *Social work with immigrants and refugees: legal issues, clinical skills, and advocacy* (2nd ed.). Springer Publishing Company.

Dohlman, L., DiMeglio, M., Hajj, J., & Laudanski, K. (2019). Global brain drain: How can the Maslow theory of motivation improve our understanding of physician migration? *International journal of environmental research and public health, 16*(7), 1182. https://doi.org/10.3390/ijerph16071182

Drolet, J. (2012). Reflecting on field education partnerships on migration and immigration: A Canadian perspective. *Reflections: Narratives of Professional Helping, 18*(2), 87–91. https://reflectionsnarrativesofprofessionalhelping.org/index.php/Reflections/article/view/103

Drolet, J., Enns, R., Kreitzer, L., Shankar, J., & McLaughlin, A.-M. (2017). Supporting the resettlement of a Syrian family in Canada: The social work resettlement practice experience of Social Justice Matters. *International Social Work, 61*(5), 627–633. https://doi.org/10.1177/0020872817725143

Dumbrill, G. C. (2008). Your policies, our children: Messages from refugee parents to child welfare workers and policymakers. *Child Welfare, 88*(3), 145–168. https://refugeeresearch.net/wp-content/uploads/2016/05/Drumbill-2009-Refugee-parents-speak-to-child-welfare-workers-policymakers.pdf

Düvell, F., & Jordan, B. (2001). How low can you go? Dilemmas of social work with asylum seekers in London. Exeter. Department of Exeter University, Exeter.

Elabor-Idemudia, P. (2005). Immigrant integration in Canada: Policies, programs and challenges. In C. E. James (Ed.), *Possibilities and limitations: Multicultural policies and programs in Canada* (pp. 58–75). Fernwood Publishing.

Frideres, J., & Biles, J. (2012). *International perspectives: Integration and inclusion.* McGill-Queen's University Press.

Government of Canada. (2018). *Notice – Supplementary information 2019–2021 immigration levels plan.* https://www.canada.ca/en/immigration-refugees-citizenship/news/notices/supplementary-immigration-levels-2019.html

Government of Canada. (2019). *Settlement program.* https://www.canada.ca/en/immigration-refugees-citizenship/corporate/transparency/program-terms-conditions/settlement.html

Government of Canada. (2020). *2020 Annual report to parliament on immigration.* https://www.canada.ca/en/immigration-refugees-citizenship/corporate/publications-manuals/annual-report-parliament-immigration-2020.html

Government of Canada. (2021a). *Immigration and refugee protection act, S.C. 2001, c. 27.* Justice Laws Website. https://laws-lois.justice.gc.ca/eng/acts/I-2.5/FullText.html

Government of Canada. (2021b). *Immigration, refugees, and citizenship Canada departmental plan 2021–2022.* https://www.canada.ca/en/immigration-refugees-citizenship/corporate/publications-manuals/departmental-plan-2021-2022/departmental-plan.html

Government of Canada. (2021c). *IRCC settlement program initiatives*. https://www.canada.ca/en/immigration-refugees-citizenship/corporate/partners-service-providers/settlement-program-initiatives.html

Green, A. G., & Green, D. (2004). The goal of Canada's immigration policy: A historical perspective. *Canadian Journal of Urban Research, 13*(1), 102–139. https://www.jstor.org/stable/44320798

Henry, F., & Tator, C. (2006). *The colour of democracy: Racism in Canadian society* (3rd ed.). Thomson/Nelson.

Kaushik, V. (2020). *Settlement and integration needs of skilled immigrants in Calgary: A mixed methods study* [Unpublished doctoral dissertation]. University of Calgary. http://dx.doi.org/10.11575/PRISM/38349

Kaushik, V., & Walsh, C. A. (2018). A critical analysis of the use of intersectionality theory to understand the settlement and integration needs of skilled immigrants to Canada. *Canadian Ethnic Studies, 50*(3), 27–47. https://doi.org/10.1353/ces.2018.0021

Knowles, V. (2016). *Strangers at our gates*. Dundurn Press.

Kuttikat, M. (2012). Migration traumatic experiences and refugee distress: Implications for social work practice. *Clinical Social Work Journal, 40*(4), 429–437. https://doi.org/10.1007/s10615-012-0397-y

Lundy, C. (2010). Social work and migration: Immigrant and refugee settlement and integration. *Canadian Social Work, 12*(1), 224. http://www.casw-acts.ca/sites/default/files/csw10special_e.pdf

Martinez-Brawley, E. E., & Zorita, P. M.-B. (2011). Immigration and social work: Contrasting practice and education. *Social Work Education, 30*(1), 17–28. https://doi.org/10.1080/02615479.2010.481791

McAuliffe, M., & Khadria, B. (2020). *IOM UN Migration: World migration report 2020*. https://publications.iom.int/system/files/pdf/wmr_2020.pdf

McConnell, S., Sammon, S., & Pike, N. (2013, August 13). *Background document*. Document submitted to the CASWE-ACFTS Deans' and Directors' meeting with the Field Education Committee.

Nash, M., Wong, J., & Trlin, A. (2006). Civic and social integration: A new field of social work practice with immigrants, refugees, and asylum seekers. *International Social Work, 49*(3), 345–363. https://doi.org/10.1177/0020872806063407

Organization for Economic Cooperation and Development [OECD]. (2022). *Foreign-born population (indicator)*. https://doi.org/10.1787/5a368e1b-en

Padilla, Y. C. (1997). Immigrant policy: Social work practice. *Social Work, 42*(6), 595–606. https://doi.org/10.1093/sw/42.6.595

Payne, J. D. (2014). *Strangers next door: Immigration, migration and mission*. IVP Books.

Potocky-Tripodi, M. (2019). *Best practices for social work with refugees and migrants* (2nd ed). Columbia University Press.

Poulin, J., Silver, P., & Kauffman, S. (2006). Serving the community and training social workers: Service outputs and student outcomes. *Journal of Social Work Education, 42*(1), 171–184. https://doi.org/10.5175/JSWE.2006.200400486

Praznik, J., & Shields, J. (2018). *An anatomy of settlement services in Canada: A guide.* Ryerson University. https://bmrc-irmu.info.yorku.ca/files/2018/07/An-Anatomy-of-Settlement-Services-in-Canada_BMRCIRMU.pdf

Rawlyk, G. A. (1962). Canada's immigration policy, 1945–1962. *Dalhousie Review, 42*(3), 287–300. http://hdl.handle.net/10222/58908

Reitz, J. G. (2007). Immigrant employment success in Canada, part I: Individual and contextual causes. *Journal of International Migration and Integration, 8*(1), 11–36. https://link.springer.com/article/10.1007/s12134-007-0001-4

Sethi, B. (2013). Newcomer resettlement in a globalized world: The role of social workers in building inclusive societies. *Critical Social Work, 14*(1). http://www1.uwindsor.ca/criticalsocialwork/newcomerresettlementglobalizedSW

Shields, J., Drolet, J., & Valenzuela, K. (2016). *Immigrant settlement and integration services and the role of nonprofit service providers: A cross-national perspective on trends, issues and evidence.* Ryerson Centre for Immigration and Settlement. https://www.ryerson.ca/centre-for-immigration-and-settlement/publications/working-papers/

Sidney, M. (2014). Settling in: A comparison of local immigrant organizations in the United States and Canada. *International Journal of Canadian Studies, 49,* 105–133. https://doi.org/10.3138/ijcs.49.105

Türegün, A. (2013). Immigrant settlement work in Canada: Limits and possibilities for professionalization. *The Canadian Review of Sociology, 50*(4), 387–411. https://doi.org/10.1111/cars.12025

United Nations (n.d.). *Global issues: Migration.* https://www.un.org/en/global-issues/migration

Valtonen, K. (2016). *Social work and migration: Immigrant and refugee settlement and integration* (e-book ed.). Routledge.

Westoby, P. (2008) Developing a community-development approach through engaging resettling Southern Sudanese refugees within Australia. *Community Development Journal, 43*(4), 483–95. https://doi.org/10.1093/cdj/bsm017

Yan, M. C., & Chan, S. (2010). Are social workers ready to work with newcomers? *Canadian Social Work, 12*(1), 16–23. https://www.mosaicbc.org/wp-content/uploads/2017/01/Are-SW-ready-to-work-with-newcomers.pdf

Social Justice, Systems, and International Social Work in Field Education

Kelemua Zenebe Ayele and Ermias Kebede

Field education is a site for the intersection of social justice, systems, and international social work. To explore these intersections, we consider our own lived experiences in coordinating students for field placements when we were assigned field education courses in our doctoral studies, in addition to the relevant literature in social work practice and field education. As doctoral students at the University of Gondar in Ethiopia, our practice context informs our understanding of the strengths, lessons learned, strategies, and techniques both to address and overcome challenges in field education. We consider the gaps between theory and practice in Ethiopia, and we explore how these could be addressed in order to bring about social change in systems to promote social justice in international social work. This chapter deals with the realities of social work practice in Ethiopia that present challenges for organizations providing field placements for students, also known as field works or social work practices. It highlights the important role of field education in addressing visible gaps while also engaging in social work research, evaluation of programs or projects, and planning social work interventions at various levels. Our study further discusses the implications of integrating social justice, systems, and international social work within field education. Field education is an important platform through which international social work is the venue for Indigenous and local, context-specific social work practice. Finally, readers will be invited to use their privileged position as social work academics, researchers, and practitioners to advocate for social justice initiatives when they place students in field education, provide liaison with social work students, write reports, and engage as practitioners.

Context of Social Work Education in Ethiopia

Shawky (1968) stated that tracing the origin of the social work education in Africa was challenging because it was shared with other disciplines such as social administration, social welfare, and community and social development. There is a generalized consensus among scholars that Western colonial powers played a fundamental role in introducing social work education in Africa (Shawky, 1968; Ibrahima & Mattiani 2019; Mwansa, 2011). After independence in many African countries, there were attempts to redefine the focus of social work education to attend to the actual service needs and priorities of African people; however, social work training was informed by Western curriculum (Shawky, 1968).

The social work profession has a relatively brief history in Ethiopia. There is a dearth of research on the historical roots of social work education and practice in Ethiopia. Ethiopia is Africa's oldest independent country, and apart from a 5-year occupation by Mussolini's Italy, it has never been colonized (British Broadcasting Corporation [BBC], 2022). Kebede (2019) reported that the development of social work education in Ethiopia can be framed in two important historical trajectories: pre-2004 and post-2004. Social work as an academic discipline was first introduced in Ethiopia around 1959 (Mwansa, 2011; Tesfaye, 1987) as part of the imperial regime's desire to reform the entire social welfare service delivery system (Tesfaye, 1987). Accordingly, as Tesfaye (1987) noted, the major emphasis was to produce trained professionals who could lead the provision of social welfare services. Hence, Haile Selassie I University (the present-day Addis Ababa University) started to enroll students in social work with a 2-year diploma program in 1959.

Stout (2009) reported that efforts to provide social work education in Ethiopia were soon paralyzed when the socialist regime came into power in 1974. Given the regime's suspicion that social work, as a profession, was a "tool of imperialism," consequently social work ceased to exist as an academic discipline (Kebede, 2014, p.161). Beyond closing the school of social work, the socialist regime openly discouraged anything related to the social work profession, including methodological approaches and reference materials (Kebede, 2014). As a result, the social work profession was placed at the margins of academic disciplines and many social work professionals were forced to flee the country (Hagos Baynesagn et al., 2021).

After almost three decades of silence, social work education resumed in 2004 when Addis Ababa University reopened the School of Social Work (Kebede, 2019). Several factors contributed to the reinstitution of social work as an independent academic discipline at Addis Ababa University. The downfall of the socialist regime facilitated the rebirth of social work in Ethiopia, which was coupled with the new government's goals to liberalize the economy and to expand the number of higher education programs (Hagos Baynesagn et al., 2021). Changes in government policy also paved the way for Ethiopian social workers trained abroad to establish partnerships with foreign universities, which supported efforts to reinstall the schools in the country. Other factors that fueled the resurgence of social work education in Ethiopia include increasing demands from governmental and non-governmental organizations for social work training (Kebede, 2014).

Social work education in Ethiopia has long been influenced by several factors. It is evident that government's ideology and political orientation have influenced the status of social work education in the country. Government policies had a direct implication on social work education during the Marxist era (1974–1991). The return of social work education in Ethiopia was initiated within the context of Western social work with the support of United States-based universities and foreign-educated Ethiopian social work professionals. There is no doubt that social work education in Ethiopia is evolving to respond to local concerns. However, there remains a great deal of work to ensure the interface between social work education and addressing the major social problems in the country (Northcut et al., 2020).

Despite many ups and downs, the social work profession is currently flourishing in Ethiopia. With about 115 million people, Ethiopia is the second most populous nation in Africa after Nigeria (World Bank, 2020).

Currently, there are 13 universities delivering social work education programs in the country at the undergraduate, graduate, and doctoral levels (Kebede, 2019). As the Ministry of Education (MoE) is harmonizing the curriculum, whereby students at different public and private universities are expected to receive a similar level of education in terms of content and programs, all schools of social work in the country ought to deliver similar courses accordingly.

Field Education in Ethiopia

Field education is a partnership established between the social work profession, agencies, academic institutions, and students to enhance the professional competency of students and strengthen the theory to practice linkage (Australian Association of Social Workers [AASW], 2017). Field education, as a crucial element in the social work education, is essential to equip students with the relevant skills and knowledge for social work practice (Council on Social Work Education [CSWE], 2008; Parker, 2007). Moreover, Lemieux and Allen (2007) stated that field education enhances critical thinking and innovative problem solving among social work students. Field education provides students with insightful exposure to critically analyze the interface between theoretical discussions in the classroom and the actual application of theories and models in solving practical problems (Bellinger, 2010, Wayne et al., 2010; Zeira & Schiff, 2014). Additionally, field education may also play a vital role in identifying and intervening in unjust and oppressive practices at the individual, group, and community level. Hence, field education has long been integrated in the curriculum and pedagogy of social work education (Bogo, 2006; Papouli, 2014).

Despite the lack of empirical evidence on the status of field education in Ethiopia, it is possible to contend that field practicum is an integral component of social work education in the country's harmonized curriculum. Accordingly, Bachelor of Social Work (BSW) and Master of Social Work (MSW) students are expected to complete a specific number of hours in the field in order to earn their degree in social work. For instance, BSW students must complete three field practicums, each weighing four credit hours. A student who is enrolled in a 4-year BSW program is to complete a minimum of 200 field hours per placement, for a total of

600 field practicum hours in the BSW program. Similarly, MSW students are to complete a total of 900 field hours in two field placements (450 field hours each) to meet the requirements for a master's degree in social work.

Field education, particularly at the BSW level, aims to graduate students for generalist social work practice, whereas field education at the MSW level is primarily focused on developing students as competent professionals who could function as specialists in specific social work fields. Field education in social work is implemented in collaboration with various agencies that are working on a host of social issues. Northcut et al. (2020) reported that social work field education at the University of Gondar has been carried out in partnership with several agencies working in the areas of substance abuse, HIV/AIDS, or with elderly people and children who are experiencing homelessness. Moreover, social work students are deployed to different government sector offices such as police departments, courts, and hospitals (Northcut et al., 2020). In many instances, social work departments secure written agreements or develop a memorandum of understanding with agencies to facilitate formal engagements of students.

Schools of social work in Ethiopia have developed a field education manual to guide the overall performance of the program. The manual provides a detailed account of the program, including the aim and purpose of field education, and the responsibilities of the parties involved such as the department, students, field instructors, and faculty liaisons. Furthermore, ethical standards, engagement protocols, student evaluation parameters, and reporting are also included in the field education manual.

Hay et al. (2016) stated that field instructors are important sources of mentorship, education, and evaluation. Ayala et al. (2018) further noted that field education also helps field instructors learn new skills in the process of mentoring and teaching students. Several stakeholders are involved in the process of implementing social work field education. Field instructors are also among the essential elements in social work field education in Ethiopia, although, due to insufficient empirical data, it is difficult to provide a conclusive statement concerning their role and responsibilities. Therefore, in the implications section of this chapter, we draw from our personal experience as social work educators and students. Accordingly, field instructors play an important role in field education by providing students with the skills needed to apply theories into practice. In many instances, field instructors are tasked to help students learn how to solve practical problems by encouraging them to work collaboratively with agency social workers and staff. Moreover, field instructors are mandated to educate, mentor, and supervise the performance of practicum students. Finally, field instructors are expected to submit a conclusive evaluation of each student to the school or department of social work based on the student's overall engagement and activities in the field placement.

Field coordinators, commonly referred in Ethiopia as faculty liaisons, are another important stakeholder in field education in Ethiopia. Field coordinators assume a leadership role in planning, implementing, and evaluating the performance of the entire field practicum program (Robertson, 2013). Several schools of social work in Ethiopia have established a separate unit responsible to coordinate and supervise the implementation of field education programs. For instance, a field education coordinator or faculty liaison at the University of Gondar is mandated to consult both students and field instructors concerning the field practicum programs. Faculty liaisons are also in charge of assigning students to different agencies, providing guidance and counseling services to students in need, and assessing opportunities and major challenges for the field education programs. Evaluations of the field practicum program in general and, specifically, the performances of students are also included in the job description of field coordinators or faculty liaisons across many social work programs in the country.

Absence of National Regulatory Body in Social Work Education

Social work is a practice-based and professional academic discipline, and hence requires regulatory bodies that monitor the educational and practical dimensions of the profession. There is no doubt that social work education is flourishing in Ethiopia. However, there still exists no regulatory body at the national level to control and evaluate the quality of social work education. The absence of a regulatory body in social work education has been among the major factors that compromise the quality of social work education in general, and specifically in field education. Since many social work educators likely lack the necessary professional framework that guides education, they may provide education and training which deviate from the values and principles of the profession. In the absence of regulatory bodies, different social work education programs cannot graduate social work professionals with similar levels of professional competence. Therefore, it is difficult to ensure the quality of social work education at the national level. Social work educators are challenged by the fact that they do not share a common platform to evaluate the actual performance of the profession and its ability to address social issues — old and new — that demand the attention of social workers.

The absence of an independent national body that exclusively regulates social work education in Ethiopia has hindered efforts to harmonize social work education across the country. This is apparent in the lack of uniform policy and approach in social work field education. For instance, Kebede (2019) noted that some schools of social work have developed a field education manual that guides students' engagement in field education, whereas others deploy students to field practicum without any field manuals. Moreover, the absence of a regulatory body in social work education has also resulted in the lack of a national code of conduct that governs the professional behaviour of social work educators. Kebede (2019) asserted that this reality blurs the boundary between the social work profession and other disciplines in the country. In sum, despite the potential of field education to promote social justice at different levels, the lack of relevant regulatory institution has crippled social work's commitment and ability in challenging unjust practices.

Challenges Facing Social Work Educators and Practitioners

The social work profession has dramatically expanded over the past two decades in Ethiopia. The number of public and private universities providing social work education has grown from two in 2004 to thirteen in 2019 (Kebede, 2019). Beyond the expansion of social work education in Ethiopia, there are noticeable attempts to enhance the influence of the profession in the country. Field education is serving as an important avenue to promote the profession across a wide spectrum of governmental and non-governmental organizations.

Despite its importance to enhance the problem-solving skills of students, field education in Ethiopia is passing through a series of challenges that have crippled the promises enshrined in the profession. Furthermore, as indicated in the previous section, field education is a highly marginalized concept in social work research in Ethiopia. There is an urgent need to foster field research scholarship in Ethiopia. Our discussion in this section, thus, is mainly based on the review of the few available empirical contributions, as well as our professional and personal experience and communications with field educators.

Agency-Related Challenges

Lack of Trained Field Instructors. The social work profession in Ethiopia has long been portrayed as "a grey discipline" that can be performed by anyone with a university degree. This may be partly related to the brief history of social work (Liu et al., 2021) in Ethiopia. Moreover, the absence of a strong professional association that enforces practice standards is a contributing factor. Above all, the tendency to confuse the social work profession with adjacent disciplines, such as philanthropy and sociology, has attracted individuals from other disciplines to assume the role of social worker in different agencies with very limited or no training in social work. In this regard, Northcut et al. (2020) reported that field instructors at different governmental and non-governmental agencies in Gondar have very limited knowledge about social work method and practice. Kebede (2019) noted that the absence of field instructors with a social work background is belittling all efforts to equip students with practical knowledge. Similarly, Liu et al. (2013) revealed that the lack of well-trained field instructors is among the major factors compromising the quality of field education in mainland China. We have learned from our experience as MSW students that individuals with a remote relationship to social work (such as geography and economics) have been assigned as "social worker" in court and school settings. The lack of trained social work field instructors is a key challenge in social work field education in Ethiopia.

Lack of Sufficient Agencies for Placement. Field education programs are essentially planned and implemented in collaboration with agencies having direct relevance to the promotion of social work profession. Many field coordinators face challenges trying to find appropriate agencies for students' field placement. According to Ayala et al. (2018), the lack of placements may be partly related to the discrepancy in the increasing number of social work programs and students on one side, and the absence of sufficient placement agencies to accommodate students on the other side. Demonstrating this, Schmidt and Rautenbach (2016) reported a high mismatch of student/placement agencies as a major problem in Cape Town, South Africa, which results in the failure of field education programs to expose students to experiential knowledge.

Currently, the number of schools offering social work programs in Ethiopia is increasing rapidly. However, the number of agencies that can offer student placements is not keeping pace with this increased enrollment. This in turn overwhelms not only the existing field placement agencies, but also compromises the quality of field education programs. Moreover, as Northcut et al. (2020) reported, some placement agencies have doubted the importance of field education programs in social work due to the lack of sufficient inputs and supply to efficiently manage the field education programs. Most field placement agencies are not equipped with adequate office supplies such as stationery materials, desks, computers, and other essential equipment inputs to facilitate the field education program (Northcut et al, 2020). Accordingly, several agencies are now declining to accept students for field practicum. Even worse, some placement agencies have ceased to exist for an array of reasons, including shortage of funding and termination of projects. There is a need for future research in field education to better understand the situation.

University Related Challenges

Insufficient Attention for Field Education. Despite field education's integration in the curriculum of social work education, field placement is still one of the most marginalized areas in social work education. Kebede (2019) in this regard reported that the existing structure across many social work schools does not allow permanent assignment of faculty members in the position of field coordinator or faculty liaison. Faculty members who are assigned as field coordinator are not provided with additional resources or privileges, and share similar teaching loads as other faculty members. The high workload and the increased administrative and coordination functions of the field coordinator position, along with teaching responsibilities, contribute to deter faculty members to serve in this role. Faculty members are not motivated to support field education, and this also compromises the quality of field education programs.

Ayala et al. (2018) indicated that field coordinators face many complex tasks in matching students for placement. Many schools of social work in Ethiopia lack a separate unit in charge of coordinating, supervising, and evaluating field education programs, a situation that further compromises the quality of programs (Kebede, 2019). Furthermore, social work educators pay little or no attention to inviting faculty members, students, and agencies to critically reflect on the performance of field education programs in the form of seminars and research projects. Inadequate planning on the part of faculty liaisons is causing role confusion among students and agency social workers placed in different agencies. While the field education manual provides a generalized framework for the field education program, faculty liaisons are still expected to present students with background information about the nature of their engagement in the agencies. In many instances, students are simply deployed to the field with little or no clear information about their role in the organizations. Consequently, social work students are sometimes required to assume clerical responsibilities that essentially depart from the purpose of field education programs. There is potential, however, for field education programs to develop a monitoring and evaluation component in order to solicit feedback from stakeholders to improve field education experiences.

Misfits Between Field Education Programs and Actual Problems. In many instances, social work curriculums in Ethiopia are highly informed by Western-oriented theories and intervention models that need further refinement to apply adequately to the Ethiopian social and cultural context (Northcut et al., 2020). Since field education programs are similarly designed to be in line with theoretical discussions in the classroom, little has been done to establish the link between field education programs and major problems in the community. Liu et al. (2013) also argued that field education programs usually exhibit the deficiency in social work curriculums to sufficiently integrate social work theories and practice. Kebede (2019) argued that the existing social work curriculums (including field education program) have often ignored the experiences of vulnerable communities in rural parts of the country. In many cases, field education programs are designed based on a one-time assessment (if any) and assessments are not recurrently updated to incorporate emerging social problems.

Student Related Challenges

Failure to Suspend Personal Beliefs. Field experiences may be planned in such a manner as to challenge the personal beliefs and values of students (Lay & McGuire, 2010). Social workers are expected to detach themselves from commonsense and practice good sense in delivering services to clients (Sewpaul, 2013). Commonsense, according to Sewpaul (2013), refers to our general assumptions and what we have internalized without having any evidence on a given issue. Good sense, on the other hand, refers to one's understanding of the sources of oppression and undoing sources of privilege (Sewpaul, 2013). Henceforth, social workers are expected to suspend their beliefs and apply reflexivity in service provision to ensure that the voices of the oppressed are heard. Similarly, Tam et al. (2018) noted that students in field practice sometimes tend to violate the clients' own agency by exercising excessive power, and this usually constitutes a violation of ethical standards of the profession.

Implications of Social Work Field Education for Social Justice

Social justice can be broadly understood as the fair and compassionate distribution of the fruits of economic growth (United Nations [UN], 2016). Social justice is among the most pressing global social issues influencing global agendas in today's world. The ratification of the Universal Declaration of Human Rights (UDHR) has long been regarded as the first global initiative that signaled cooperation among nation-states towards the promotion of social justice. Many institutions, laws, and policies have been ratified at regional, national, and international levels to promote fair and equitable distribution of social, economic, and political resources. However, ensuring social justice remains a major challenge in the face of growing inequality and the violation of individual and group rights. The rights of individuals or groups continue to be denied by social systems and structures that operate in the widely accepted system called government. It is within these systems and structures that social work interventions are needed to advocate for social justice by social work researchers, educators, evaluators, and interventionists. This is particularly important in Ethiopia given the current context of civil strife during the global COVID-19 pandemic, which has exacerbated inequalities and social injustices.

Social justice is situated at the heart of the social work profession. For instance, the International Federation of Social Workers (IFSW; 2014) defined social work as follows:

> Social work is a practice-based profession and an academic discipline that promotes social change and development, social cohesion, and the empowerment and liberation of people. Principles of social justice, human rights, collective responsibility and respect for diversities are central to social work. (Global Definition of the Social Work Profession section, para. 1)

The global definition of the social work profession clearly indicates that the principle of social justice is central to the social work profession. Moreover, the notion of social justice is conceptualized broadly in a manner that promotes the social work profession's special commitment to the empowerment of the poor and vulnerable. Accordingly, IFSW (2018) noted that promoting social justice in social work includes challenging structural discrimination and institutional oppression, respecting diversity, ensuring access to equitable resources, challenging unjust policies and practices, and promoting solidarity with fellow professionals and service recipients.

Field education programs, as a critical element in social work education, could play vital roles in promoting social justice on several fronts. First, field education programs provide social work students with the opportunity to witness and challenge unjust policies and practices directly. In field practicum, students are set to work with experienced agency practitioners who have been working with vulnerable and marginalized segments of the population. This, in turn, encourages students to critically reflect on theories and methods of social work in the course of identifying and addressing unjust practices.

Second, field education programs enable social work students to realize how multiple factors in the social structure establish a mutually reinforcing circle of oppression that leaves individuals and/or groups vulnerable and marginalized. Field education programs are essential to learn more about how different systems and subsystems continually interact to produce and/or reproduce operation and injustice at different level. For example, while working with women living with HIV and AIDS, we have observed how age, gender, and patriarchy were intersecting to leave a young 14-year-old girl in an oppressed state when she was raped by her close relative, contracted HIV, and faced discrimination from her family members. In simple terms, field education can promote the application of the person-in-environment (PIE) context in this scenario. It also promotes students' capacity to comprehend the systemic and/or structural nature of social problems.

Promotion of the indigenization process is another potential implication of field education for social justice. It is widely reported that social work theories and methods have been dominated by Western-oriented perspectives and this can be portrayed as "unjust" practice in the social work profession. Field education programs, hence, can serve as a springboard to critically examine the applicability of theories and models of social work in the context of the Global South. In other words, field education may provide an essential platform to begin the decolonization process.

Conclusion

Social work is a relatively young profession in Ethiopia. However, the profession has been growing in prominence within the past two decades, following the increasing number of public and private universities providing social work education. Field education has long been integrated in the curriculum of social work education and almost all schools with social work programs have developed a manual that guides the implementation of field education. Furthermore, several stakeholders take part in implementing field education such as field instructors, faculty liaison, or field coordinators.

In Ethiopia, there are several factors that are impeding the successful implementation of field education. Lack of trained field instructors, inadequate number of placement agencies, poor attention from schools managing social work programs, and mismatches between field practicum and community needs are all identified as major challenges in field education. Above all, the absence of an independent regulatory body or council responsible to oversee the quality of social work education has been a major barrier to social work field education. Field education programs, if designed and implemented carefully, could play a significant role in promoting social justice. Field placement enhances social work students' capacity to identify and address unjust policies and practices. Finally, we recommend that field education programs in Ethiopia promote the indigenization process by challenging the conventional knowledge production processes in social work.

REFERENCES

Australian Association of Social Work [AASW]. (2017). *Australian social work education and accreditation standards (ASWEAS)*. https://www.aasw.asn.au/careers-study/asweas-2017-launch

Ayala, J., Drolet, J., Fulton, A., Hewson, J., Letkemann, L., Baynton, M., & Schweizer, E. (2018). Field education in crisis: Experiences of field education coordinators in Canada. *Social Work Education, 37*(3), 281–293. https://doi.org/10.1080/02615479.2017.1397109

Bellinger, A. (2010). Talking about (re)generation: Practice learning as a site of renewal for social work. *British Journal of Social Work, 40*(8), 2450–2466. https://doi.org/10.1093/bjsw/bcq072

Bogo, M. (2006). Field instruction in social work: A review of the research literature. *The Clinical Supervisor, 24*(1–2), 163–193. https://doi.org/10.1300/J001v24n01_09

British Broadcasting Corporation [BBC]. (2022). *Ethiopia country profile*. https://www.bbc.com/news/world-africa-13349398

Council on Social Work Education [CSWE]. (2008). *Educational policy and accreditation standards*. https://www.wcsu.edu/sw/wp-content/uploads/sites/124/2016/11/Appendix-A-EPAS-Standards-2008.pdf

Hagos Baynesagn, A., Abye, T., Mulugeta, E., & Berhanu, Z. (2021). Strengthened by challenges: the path of the social work education in Ethiopia. *Social Work Education, 40*(1), 95–110. https://doi.org/10.1080/02615479.2020.1858044

Hay, K., Dale, M., & Yeung, P. (2016). Influencing the future generation of social workers: Field educator perspectives on social work field education. *Advances in Social Work and Welfare Education, 18*(1), 39–54. https://search.informit.org/doi/abs/10.3316/aeipt.214681

Ibrahima, A. B., & Mattaini, M. A. (2019). Social work in Africa: Decolonizing methodologies and approaches. *International Social Work, 62*(2), 799–813. https://doi.org/10.1177%2F0020872817742702

International Federation of Social Workers [IFSW]. (2014). *Global definition of social work*. https://www.ifsw.org/what-is-social-work/global-definition-of-social-work/

International Federation of Social Workers [IFSW]. (2018). Global social work statement of ethical principles. https://www.ifsw.org/global-social-work-statement-of-ethical-principles/

Kebede, W. (2014). Social work education in Ethiopia: Celebrating the rebirth of the profession. In H. Spitzer, J. Twikirize, & G. G. Wairire (Eds.), *Professional social work in East Africa: Towards social development, poverty reduction and gender equality* (pp. 161–172). Fountain Publishers Ltd.

Kebede, W. (2019). Social work education in Ethiopia: past, present and future. *International Journal of Social Work, 6*(1), 1–17. https://doi.org/10.5296/ijsw.v6i1.14175

Lay, K., & McGuire, L. (2010). Building a lens for critical reflection and reflexivity in social work education. *Social Work Education, 29*(5), 539–550. https://doi.org/10.1080/02615470903159125

Lemieux, C. M., & Allen, P. D. (2007). Service learning in social work education: The state of knowledge, pedagogical practicalities, and practice conundrums. *Journal of Social Work Education, 43*(2), 309–326. https://doi.org/10.5175/JSWE.2007.200500548

Liu, M., Sun, F., & Anderson, S. G. (2013). Challenges in social work field education in China: Lessons from the western experience. *Social work education, 32*(2), 179–196. https://doi.org/10.1080/02615479.2012.723682

Liu, M., Sun, F., Zhang, Z., Jiang, G., Marsiglia, F. F., & Pantovich, T. (2021). Enhancing field education of social work in Mainland China: perspectives from students and faculty members. *China Journal of Social Work, 14*(3), 1–18. https://doi.org/10.1080/17525098.2021.1923402

Mwansa, L. K. (2011). Social work education in Africa: Whence and whither? *Social Work Education, 30*(1), 4–16. https://doi.org/10.1080/02615471003753148

Northcut, T. B., Getachew, A., Kebede, E., Zenbe, K., & Abebe, A. (2021). Clinical social work in Ethiopia: A field study in Gondar. *Clinical Social Work Journal, 49*(3), 312–324. https://link.springer.com/article/10.1007/s10615-020-00757-w

Papouli, E. (2014). Field learning in social work education: Implications for educators and instructors. *Field Educator, 4*(2), 1–16. https://fieldeducator.simmons.edu/article/field-learning-in-social-work-education-implications-for-educators-and-instructors/

Parker, J. (2007). Developing effective practice learning for tomorrow's social workers. *Social Work Education, 26*(8), 763–779. https://doi.org/10.1080/02615470601140476

Robertson, J. S. (2013). Addressing professional suitability in social work education. *The Journal of Practice Teaching and Learning, 11*(3), 98–117. https://doi.org/10.1921/jpts.v11i3.278

Schmidt, K., & Rautenbach, J. V. (2016). Field instruction: Is the heart of social work education still beating in the Eastern Cape? *Social work, 52*(4), 589–610. http://dx.doi.org/10.15270/52-2-532

Sewpaul, V. (2013). Neoliberalism and social work in South Africa. *Critical and Radical Social Work, 1*(1), 15–30. https://doi.org/10.1332/204986013X665947

Shawky, A. H. (1968). Training needs and problems in social welfare services in eastern and central Africa. *International Social Work, 11*(4), 35–42. https://doi.org/10.1177%2F002087286801100405

Stout, C. E. (Ed.). (2009). *The new humanitarians: Inspiration, innovations, and blueprints for visionaries, Vol. 2. Changing education and relief.* Praeger Publishers/Greenwood Publishing Group.

Tam, D. M., Brown, A., Paz, E., Birnbaum, R., & Kwok, S. M. (2018). Challenges faced by Canadian social work field instructors in baccalaureate field supervision. *Journal of Teaching in Social Work, 38*(4), 398–416. https://doi.org/10.1080/08841233.2018.1502228

Tesfaye, A. (1987). Social welfare programmes and social work education in Ethiopia. *Indian Journal of Social Work, 47*, 363–377. https://journals.tiss.edu/archive/index.php/ijswarchive/article/view/2043

United Nations [UN]. (2016). *Leaving no one behind – The imperative of inclusive development.* www.un.org/esa/socdev/rwss/2016/full-report.pdf

Wayne, J., Bogo, M., & Raskin, M. (2010). Field education as the signature pedagogy of social work education. *Journal of social work education, 46*(3), 327–339. https://doi.org/10.5175/JSWE.2010.200900043

World Bank. (2020). *The World Bank in Ethiopia.* https://www.worldbank.org/en/country/ethiopia/overview#1

Zeira, A., & Schiff, M. (2014). Field education: A comparison of students' and novice social workers' perspectives. *British Journal of Social Work, 44*(7), 1950–1966. https://doi.org/10.1093/bjsw/bct038

11

Advancing Community Development Field Placements in Pakistan: A Case Study on Community Drinking Water

Wasif Ali

Developing countries are increasingly adopting community development approaches to achieve their national development goals to enhance the living standards of the population. The community development approach has made remarkable improvements in the developing world in many ways and has been proven to be exceptionally successful in enhancing community well-being (Green, 2016; Iqbal & Khan, 2020; Islam, 2017; Nel, 2018). The role of social work is critical in delivering these community development practices and, therefore, quality field education is essential for social workers to succeed in their professional journey.

Community development practices have been implemented in Pakistan for several decades and have contributed significantly to the country's growth. These practices have been particularly successful in empowering the most vulnerable sections of society as millions of people in Pakistan live in underdeveloped areas without basic facilities (Seemab & Tahmina, 2019). The majority of the population lives below the poverty line, children are malnourished, mothers give birth without the support of trained nurses, health and hygiene standards are poor, infectious diseases are common, and women are subject to domestic violence (Ahmad & Talib, 2015). The country is also facing a serious climate challenge and ranks fifth on the list of most vulnerable nations (Saleet, 2019). A large portion of society, especially those from lower socioeconomic status, are experiencing a water crisis due to its scarcity and poor quality (Ahmed et al., 2020).

As a professional and academic discipline, social work is critical in helping to address these challenges. Social workers are implementing community development interventions, for example, by providing the general public with information about their basic human rights and giving them the necessary training to exercise those rights (Mehmood et al., 2016). Community development models have been introduced by numerous local and international development agencies working in diverse sectors. Many of these initiatives have been highly successful and have gained international recognition. Some examples include the Orangi Pilot Project, the Agha Khan Rural Support Program, the National Rural Support Program, and the Punjab Community Water Supply and Sanitation Program (Nazuk, 2019). These local and international development agencies are highly engaged with social work schools across the country in terms of research and training, and their relationships are playing a vital role in the development of the profession in Pakistan.

Gaining experience in the field, referred to as field education or practicum, is a vital component of social work education for students. Success stories and reports emerging from the field have informed the modernization of social work curriculums and community development (Ahmed & Ahsan, 2014). Opportunities for students to gain training and hands-on field experience have been created through partnerships between social work schools and development agencies. Internships at active project sites are the most popular form of field education in Pakistan. Following the completion of their practicum, students are often hired by these agencies on a permanent basis (Asrar-ul-Haq, 2015).

To illustrate the importance of social work field education in community development, this chapter describes on-site training and practicum opportunities for students in community development programs in Pakistan. A case study of a Pakistani community drinking water project provides insights into the field education model that trains practicum students in need assessment, community mobilization, participatory action research, capacity building, monitoring, evaluation, and long-term sustainability of the project.

Insights Into Social Work in Pakistan

In 1953, the Government of Pakistan trained its first cohort of 65 social workers with the assistance of the United Nations (UN). It was an 8-month training certificate for in-service government officers to support the social welfare services sector. This short course provided a foundation for social work discipline in the country. Consequently, in 1956, the University of Punjab initiated a 2-year diploma in social work by building upon the idea and content from UN training resources. A social work department was later established at the University of Punjab and a master's degree in social work program was introduced (Graham et al., 2007).

In Pakistan, social welfare and community development are two important features of practice where the role of social workers has been established and widely accepted. Federal and provincial governments allocate budgets in their annual plans to hire social workers and, as a result, many graduates are hired in service areas. Additionally, schools of social work have curriculums and field education which align with both sectors (Shah, 2015). There are defined programs and job structures for social work graduates (Riaz, 2016), particularly within governments. Lastly, social work students can get internships in federal and provincial social welfare departments.

Social Work, Community Development Practice, and Field Education

Pakistan is the world's fifth most populated country with a population of 229,488,994 (World Population Review, 2022). Governments and public sector organizations in the developing world face a lack of resources and capacity to provide social services. To address these challenges, there are international frameworks and arrangements to support developing countries (Lub, 2019). International developing agencies, such as the UN, have been providing resources and training, as well as introducing innovative best practices through capacity building arrangements and establishing support units to assist with social development programs in government organizations (Ahmad & Talib, 2015).

The community development approach has been used as a key strategy to uplift the vulnerable communities; it is built upon the idea that engagement initiatives can be used to empower the end-users (community). Community development as a method of social work practice is well established in Pakistan (Raza, 2021). Social workers play a key role in these initiatives by leading and coordinating the development process in the provision of basic human services such as water, food, health, and safety.

To respond to the need for leadership and coordination in these initiatives, social work schools focus on community development practice in their curriculums. Independent certificate courses and specialization in community development have been commonly offered in social work schools across the country (Bashir & Shah, 2017). Finally, practicum students have internship opportunities in several community development projects.

Internships in Pakistan: Field Work/Field Education/Practicum

While social work students take part in internships in community development initiatives in the areas of health, education, poverty reduction, and sustainable development, social work is not an established discipline like other social sciences in Pakistan, despite the significant increase in the number of social work programs in the last two decades (Ansari, 2015). Social work must compete for placements with other social sciences that also offer internships in their degree programs, such as sociology, anthropology, gender studies, and development studies. Furthermore, in the job market there is an overlap around the subject-specific jobs (Riaz, 2017). The other academic disciplines mentioned above get the majority of the placements that are supposed to be the domain of social work (Ahmad & Bano, 2021). The same holds true for the number of internships available in government and non-governmental organizations. Thus, when social work students serve in their practicums and professional settings, it is hard for them to distinguish themselves from the students and professionals from other social science disciplines (Naqvi & Ibrar, 2017).

Social work also faces two other challenges in terms of field education. While most social work students envision their future in the social development sector, there is stigmatization attached to social work practice and training. Local communities consider social workers as the representatives of Western culture and values in society. This can be discouraging to students, especially when these sentiments and attitudes are expressed by the population while students are doing their internships (Jamal & Baldwin, 2019).

The second challenge is that there are no formal supervisory arrangements through field educators or coordinators to facilitate field education and practicums. This has an influence on the development of internships as the arrangement of placements are not done in a systematic way. Agencies contact schools directly based on internship vacancies available, and conversely students can also obtain internships by directly contacting agencies (Ali & Rafi, 2013).

Case Study on Community Development Initiatives in the Water Sector

Background and Context

There is considerable concern in the social work literature about global environmental and climate change issues. Since the most vulnerable and poor segments of society are also the most impacted by environmental degradation, these issues have a social and environmental justice dimension (Chase, 2015). As noted earlier, Pakistan is the fifth most populous nation in the world and ranks among the top five countries facing global climate change and environmental threats (Hussain et al., 2020). Water quantity and water quality related issues are prevalent throughout the country, and they particularly affect vulnerable communities. Overall, 75% of the population is directly or indirectly dependent on agriculture to earn its livelihood. Water scarcity has affected this sector at a massive scale. This water crisis has implications for food production and overall financial security of poor people (Khalid & Khan, 2020).

Although the provision of clean drinking water is a basic human right, it is not being met in Pakistan. Large cities like Lahore, which has a population of more than 15 million, are facing a severe water crisis. Most of the country's urban centres rely on underground water for their drinking needs, but this resource is becoming scarce (Ahmed, 2016). There is not enough water available in the cities for many poor people, so they migrate seasonally to procure enough water for their family to survive during the hot summer season (Ali & Ali, 2019). The quality of the available water is another imperative issue. As a result of environmental changes and industrial activities, drinking water is often unsafe to consume. The poor often cannot afford to buy potable, clean water. Furthermore, some areas are at high risk of arsenic contamination. Arsenic is a poison that is tasteless, colorless, and odorless, and it becomes even more harmful when boiled (Rabbani & Fatmi, 2020).

Community Water Supply Initiative by the Punjab Public Health Engineering Department

The Punjab Community Water Supply project is a prominent community development initiative in the Punjab region of Pakistan. The Public Health Engineering Department (PHED) is planning, designing, and executing the water services activities with the financial support of government and international donors. The main objectives of this initiative are to provide clean drinking water and health hygiene education in the region. This project has been so effective that it has a presence across the Punjab province, which is demonstrated by the fact that every city and town in the region is represented in this project by community-based organizations (Padawangi, 2010). The Punjab Community Water Supply Project is the largest project of its kind in Pakistan. It provides internships and practicums for students of social work and other disciplines, and serves as a great learning platform for the students, researchers, and practitioners (Nabi et al., 2019)

In the past, drinking water delivery has been the role of traditional engineering-focused organizations. Until 2001, the Public Health Engineering Department (PHED) was mainly an engineering-focused entity and was responsible to provide the water services to the communities. This department has always controlled a significant portion of the project in terms of its size and areas of operation. Engineers have held the key positions at all levels of the project (Jabeen et al., 2015). However, various evaluation reports have highlighted the weaknesses of this traditional model. Despite spending more than 500 billion Pakistani rupee of public money in the last two decades of the 20th century, PHED was unable to serve at a large enough scale to reach across the region, resulting in many communities continuing to have unsafe and insufficient drinking water (Azizullah et al., 2011). Consequently, the government began to explore other options with the assistance of the UN and other agencies. Ultimately, a community development model of water governance was adopted, encouraging the engineers to step down from their traditional leading role in water management initiatives.

Subsequently, social workers were assigned the primary role in decision making, and to ensure community participation in all phases of development, social workers needed to directly engage with communities (Adam & Zulu, 2020). A community development unit was introduced in the organizational structure of PHED, within which social workers and sociologists were recruited through a competitive process. Following intensive training in community development practice with the support of UN agencies, community development staff were appointed to all offices throughout the province. As a government organization with a large converging area, the PHED currently employs more than 5,000 people in over 200 offices across the country to carry out the Community Water Supply Initiative (Tariq et al., 2020). The initiative includes activities such as needs assessment, community mobilization, training, capacity building, monitoring, and evaluation, as well as sustainable development.

Students are also engaged through internships. They are able to gain skills and experiences while participating in the project (Khalid & Rashid, 2020). Project leadership is well-connected with the academic community and includes personnel who have graduated from local universities. The intensive training program is facilitated by social work schools through seminars, workshops, and conferences (Ashiq et al., 2020). Master's students also conduct research on the different aspects of this project. The project team cooperates to facilitate this process. Several master's theses and doctoral dissertations highlight reflections on the field experience, as well as learning and project outcomes (Bashir, 2016).

Prominent Project Features and Learning Opportunities for Practicum Students

As highlighted earlier, the Community Water Supply Initiative is community-focused and has a large coverage area and presence throughout the province. Offices and active sites are available even in small towns and remote areas. The range of locations makes it convenient for social work schools to identify internships for the practicum students. Additionally, this type of practicum is also preferred by students, as they can complete a field placement close to their homes (Ahmad & Talib, 2010).

As part of the supervision model, trained social workers and sociologists oversee students in their practicum work and engage them in project activities. Formal documentation, such as learning agreements and contracts for practicum students, does not seem to exist in this water service initiative because in Pakistan, unlike in Western countries, social work schools and institutions are not aligned with the formal field education arrangements (Norrka, 2011). However, after completing their practicum, students need to submit a fieldwork report which is endorsed by the supervisor from the faculty and the agency where the practicum was completed (Shah & Baporikar, 2012).

Practicum students are provided a seat in the corresponding PHED office and travel to field sites using agency transportation. Students' learning and participation in the project are based on the ongoing activities in the field at the time of their placement (Anwar et al., 2020). It is worth mentioning that, owing to the on-going activities at the project's sites, students have the opportunity to understand its cycle and participate in field activities such as baseline surveys, needs assessments, community mobilisation, community-based organization (CBO) formation, on-site capacity building activities, office-based training of community leaders, monitoring and evaluations, operations and maintenance, and socio-economic sustainability measures in the project process (Khan & Bibi, 2011). Some of these unique features of the water service community development initiative and implications of the field education are discussed below.

Baseline Surveys. As the very first activity in the project cycle, the baseline survey is where practicum students begin their learning journey. Supervisors in the agency encourage students to participate in baseline surveys and walk them through the process. Basic information such as population data, number of households, tribes, castes, literacy rate, schools, hospitals, and distance from other public facilities have been collected in the baseline surveys. The initial training is conducted for the field visit at the relevant office, and questionnaire templates and relevant data collection tools are provided. There are standard operating procedures for the field visits: they include information to the relevant government authorities, transportation, and security arrangements (Luqman et al., 2021). Following the training sessions, students join field staff to visit the target community (village or town) to plan the project. Students actively participate in all of the activities associated with the baseline survey and facilitate the project process (Khan & Jan, 2015).

Needs Assessment. Once the baseline data has been collected, the next step in the project cycle is a needs assessment to help better plan a community development project. Project team members visit the community and engage in a dialog to determine the community needs. A community may have different groups, and their preferences may not be the same as those of other community members (Rana & Routray, 2018). In this case, needs assessment procedures are the most appropriate method for identifying the issues and problems the community is facing. The procedure aids in identifying the needs of various groups in a community — such as women — which have different needs with respect to water usage.

Identifying the social structure of a community and its needs is crucial (Amin & Afzal, 2019). Different tribes, castes, and clans may live in the community, but they will not want to share the same water source with each other, and this could lead to conflict. The needs assessment procedure facilitates decision-making in this case. This process helps promote reflection by the students about their social work practice. They share their field reflections and stories with their fellows, supervisors, and faculty. Students often incorporate these field reflections into their final reports and conduct seminars to share their experiences after the completion of their practicums (Asim et al., 2016).

Community Mobilization. High-level skills are needed to mobilize and engage communities to achieve the project goals, because when it comes to the immediate needs of people, their varying preferences emerge or become manifest. The severity of the problem is not always clear to them. For example, it can be hard for people to believe they are drinking polluted water since they have been using a water source for generations. In some cases, people oppose development and prefer their local water service arrangement, even if it is unsafe (Malik et al., 2020). If this is the case, instead of a development project on the ground, the government can allocate funds to other projects. As a result, social workers use several strategies to mobilize the people, including awareness campaigns, media campaigns, and consultations with the community (Shafique & Warren, 2015). Gaining support from local schoolteachers and educated groups within society is one effective method of mobilizing communities.

Another way to mobilize communities is through local religious institutions. Every community has a different strategy depending on the types of barriers that may surface in the development process. As part of their training, social work students engage themselves with these types of interventions (Khan & Irfan, 2018; Shah, 2018).

Formation of Community-Based Organization. Forming a community-based organization (CBO) is a crucial element of a successful community development program, because all future developments and decision-making in the selected community rest on a community organization's active role (Kafle, 2017). The CBO must ensure that each and every segment of the community is adequately represented. However, this is difficult to achieve in rural and tribal communities. It is often difficult for social workers to identify key community members and to ensure the participation of the youth, women, and marginalized groups in a community organization (Ahmad, 2020).

Communities sometimes experience major conflicts regarding the organization's structure and roles. Social workers are responsible for overcoming these conflicts, organizing community meetings and dialogues, and using this as an opportunity to ensure a sustainable future for the initiative. A CBO that has the support of the community and was formed with consensus can play a key supportive role throughout the development process (Rafique & Khoo, 2018). Participation in the formation of CBOs are important educational opportunities for social work students and their future professional journey, as it helps them to learn more about the community organization. In many cases, practicum students played an important role in engaging women and the youth in the CBOs formation process (Raza, 2020).

Capacity Building and Training. Capacity building and training of the community and CBO members are an important part of development activity. In the Community-Based Water Project, trainings are primarily focused on water quality, availability, conservation, health and hygiene, resource mobilization, and use of financial resources. Professional trainers, who are part of the PHED team, lead these learning activities. They utilize pedagogical resources such as cartoons, videos, field success stories, and training modules to assist in this task, and they are available as PHED resources (Wahid et al., 2017). Two types of training are offered in the water supply initiative. The first type is on-site training with a large number of participants. In the training program, the participants are motivated by success stories from around the world, and they learn about health and hygiene and how to combat waterborne diseases (Azhar & Choudhry, 2016). In the second type of training, many communities also mobilize their resources and bring positive changes to their local settings by participating in capacity building activities and in CBOs' work. An example of this is the vocational training that contributed to the economic well-being of people (Birkinshaw et al., 2021). Training activities provide a unique opportunity for social work students. They participate and organize these activities with the responsible PHED staff members. Some social work and sociology schools participate in these activities and facilitate the PHED to deliver better trainings. Some selected training happens in the PHED offices. Designated community members and CBO office bearers attend these trainings, which are usually donor funded (Malik & Rana, 2020).

Monitoring and Evaluation. A strong monitoring and evaluation framework is necessary for community and social development. Thus, a dedicated monitoring and evaluation unit is part of PHED's organisational structure. This unit is responsible for monitoring project tasks, milestones, and outcomes. Mostly, this unit's work involves data collection and analysis (Nibbering, 2019). Social workers and sociologists are part of this unit, and they work in conjunction with other staff members who have skills in information technology. They assist in the use of informational communication technology tools. Also, the unit serves as a data and resource bank for the project and supports the decision-making process with the daily data coming from the field (Khan, 2018). This unit has substantial involvement in outcome assessments and socioeconomic impact assessments in order to meet provincial government and donors' requirements about project outcomes.

Students with strong research skills often secure practicums/internships in the monitoring and evaluation unit. They are mostly engaged in organizing and reporting data, and they use a variety of software applications to help in the process. These students receive training and are given opportunities to learn how to use the software during their practicums. Students completing report writing or thesis work seek support from monitoring and evaluation staff about the latest information and data pertaining to the project. Social work schools encourage their doctoral students to engage with the monitoring and evaluation unit in PHED, in order to receive advanced training in data collection and analysis (Khan & Anjum, 2016).

Sustainability (Operations and Maintenance). It is the community's responsibility to operate and maintain the water supply project. Whenever major damage or failure occurs, the government is responsible for technical and financial support. However, the community is responsible for daily and monthly expenses. Water is viewed as a commodity, and convincing people to pay for it is an ongoing challenge, especially in the initial stages of this development process. A billing mechanism is imperative to ensure the sustainability of water infrastructure (Memon, 2004). However, by implementing project interventions and analyzing field assessments, it has become apparent to community members that collective arrangements are cheaper than solutions provided individually at the household level. This community development initiative contributed up to a 50% reduction in the costs of monthly electricity bills at the household level. The operation and maintenance mechanisms represent a major aspect in the overall sustainability of the project (Haq et al., 2014).

While studying the operation and maintenance mechanisms in the project areas, students gain an understanding of the environmental sustainability aspect of community development projects. The future priorities of the profession and global sustainability debates make this an excellent learning opportunity for social work students (Jamshed et al., 2018).

Conclusion

In summary, this chapter described the successful evolution of the Community Water Supply Project and the unique features of this project, as well as how social work students can take advantage of numerous learning opportunities in their field practicums through this initiative. The elaboration on students' training at active field sites and in collaboration with schools during their practicum, provides an inside glimpse at how the university and community development agency are connected in the development process. Stories that emerge from field practicums motivate and inspire students to pursue social work practice. Students integrate these stories into their field reflections in their final report and often conduct seminars to share their experience with their fellow students, supervisors, and faculty.

Over the years, community development techniques have remained dynamic while they evolved, but in the future more knowledge resources will be required in this sector to address multiple challenges, which include climate change, environmental degradation, population growth, and poverty (Agyeman et al., 2016). Community development is recognized as an essential component of social development by global development agencies such as the United Nations, World Bank, and Asian Development Bank. This chapter demonstrates the importance of collaboration between social work schools and social development agencies. In the future, even more collaboration is needed to address the multidimensional challenges related to social and environmental justice. Through their internships, students can play a critical role in this process while learning how to be effective members of our profession.

REFERENCES

Aashiq, U., Khalid, A., Alam, M., & Hassan, S. S. (2020). Community-based management strategies in sustainability of rural water supply schemes. *Review of Applied Management and Social Sciences*, 3(2), 271–278. https://doi.org/10.47067/ramss.v3i2.63

Aasim, M., Mahmood, B., & Sohail, M. M. (2016). Sociological analysis of community participation in sustainable water supply in rural areas of Punjab, Pakistan. *Mediterranean Journal of Social Sciences*, 7(2 S1), 448–448. https://doi.org/1010.5901/mjss.2016.v7n2s1p448

Adams, E. A., Zulu, L., & Ouellette-Kray, Q. (2020). Community water governance for urban water security in the Global South: Status, lessons, and prospects. *Wiley Interdisciplinary Reviews: Water*, 7(5). https://doi.org/10.1002/wat2.1466

Agyeman, J., Schlosberg, D., Craven, L., & Matthews, C. (2016). Trends and directions in environmental justice: From inequity to everyday life, community, and just sustainabilities. *Annual Review of Environment and Resources*, 41, 321–340. https://doi.org/10.1146/annurev-environ-110615-090052

Ahmad, A. (2020). *Inception report: Final evaluation of district governance and community development program under the Government of Khyber Pakhtunkhwa community driven local development policy*. Faculty of Graduate School, Cornell University.

https://ecommons.cornell.edu/bitstream/handle/1813/72661/Ashfaq_Ahmad_MPS_Capstone.pdf?sequence=1

Ahmad, B. (2011). Water management: A solution to water scarcity in Pakistan. *Journal of Independent Studies and Research, 9*, 111–125. https://doi.org/10.31384/JISRMSSE%2F2011.09.2.9

Ahmad, M. S., & Talib, N. B. A. (2010). Decentralization initiatives, economic and community development in Pakistan. *International Journal of Trade, Economics and Finance, 1*(4), 380–386. https://doi.org/10.7763/IJTEF.2010.V1.67

Ahmad, M. S., & Talib, N. B. A. (2015). Empowering local communities: decentralization, empowerment and community driven development. *Quality & Quantity, 49*(2), 827–838. https://doi.org/10.1007/s11135-014-0025-8

Ahmed, M. (2016). Contemporary built form in Pakistan: An analysis of residences and urban areas of Lahore. *Journal of Research in Architecture and Planning, 20*(1), 21–29. https://jrap.neduet.edu.pk/arch-journal/JRAP_2016(FirstIssue)/03.pdf

Ahmed, W., Tan, Q., Shaikh, G. M., Waqas, H., Kanasro, N. A., Ali, S., & Solangi, Y. A. (2020). Assessing and prioritizing the climate change policy objectives for sustainable development in Pakistan. *Symmetry, 12*(8), 1203. http://dx.doi.org/10.3390/sym12081203

Ali, M., & Rafi, S. (2013). Medical social work in Pakistan: A multi-model approach to collaborative practice in health care settings. *Academic Research International, 4*(4), 355. http://www.savap.org.pk/journals/ARInt./Vol.4%284%29/2013%284.4-38%29.pdf

Ali, T., Ali, W., & Shahnaz. (2019). Water scarcity and social well-being of people in Makran. *Indian Journal of Public Administration, 65*(3), 679–686. https://doi.org/10.1177%2F0019556119844578

Amin, M. A., & Afzal, M. K. (2018). Poverty assessment of farming community in rice wheat zone of Punjab, Pakistan. *Agricultural and Resource Economics: International Scientific E-Journal, 4*(3), 5–13. https://doi.org/10.22004/ag.econ.281746

Anwar, M., Khattak, M. S., Popp, J., Meyer, D. F., & Máté, D. (2020). The nexus of government incentives and sustainable development goals: is the management of resources the solution to non-profit organisations? *Technological and Economic Development of Economy, 26*(6), 1284–1310. https://doi.org/10.3846/tede.2020.13404

Asrar-ul-Haq, M. (2015). Human resource development in Pakistan: evolution, trends and challenges. *Human Resource Development International, 18*(1), 97–104. https://doi.org/10.1080/13678868.2014.979004

Azhar, S., & Choudhry, R. M. (2016). Capacity building in construction health and safety research, education, and practice in Pakistan. *Built Environment Project and Asset Management, 6*(1), 92–105. http://dx.doi.org/10.1108/BEPAM-09-2014-0044

Aziz, J. A. (2005). Management of source and drinking-water quality in Pakistan. *EMHJ-Eastern Mediterranean Health Journal, 11*(5–6), 1087–1098. https://apps.who.int/iris/handle/10665/117042

Azizullah, A., Khattak, M. N. K., Richter, P., & Häder, D. P. (2011). Water pollution in Pakistan and its impact on public health — a review. *Environment International*, *37*(2), 479–497. https://doi.org/10.1016/j.envint.2010.10.007

Birkinshaw, M., Grieser, A., & Tan, J. (2021). How does community-managed infrastructure scale up from rural to urban? An example of co-production in community water projects in Northern Pakistan. *Environment and Urbanization*, *33*(2), 496–518. DOI: 10.1177/09562478211034853

Bashir, S. (2016). The role of NGOs in community development in Balochistan. *Pakistan Journal of Applied Social Sciences*, *4*(1), 123–135. https://doi.org/10.46568/pjass. v4i1.300

Chase, Y. E. (2015). Professional ethics: Complex issues for the social work profession. *Journal of Human Behavior in the Social Environment*, *25*(7), 766–773. https://doi. org/10.1080/10911359.2015.1032654

Green, J. J. (2016). Community development and social development: Informing concepts of place and intentional social change in a globalizing world. https://doi. org/10.1177/1049731515627194

Haq, M. A., Hassan, S. M., & Ahmad, K. (2014). Community participation and sustainability of water supply program in district Faisalabad, Pakistan. *Journal of Quality and Technology Management*, *10*(2), 125–137. https://www. researchgate.net/publication/281434917_COMMUNITY_PARTICIPATION_ AND_SUSTAINABILITY_OF_WATER_SUPPLY_PROGRAM_IN_DISTRICT_ FAISALABAD_PAKISTAN

Hussain, M., Butt, A. R., Uzma, F., Ahmed, R., Irshad, S., Rehman, A., & Yousaf, B. (2020). A comprehensive review of climate change impacts, adaptation, and mitigation on environmental and natural calamities in Pakistan. *Environmental Monitoring and Assessment*, *192*(1), 1–20. https://doi.org/10.1007/s10661-019-7956-4

Iqbal, A., & Khan, A. A. (2020, May). Inclusive and sustainable community development and poverty reduction: An empirical study of Sindh, Pakistan. *IOP Conference Series: Earth and Environmental Science*, *511*, 012005.http://dx.doi.org/10.1051/ e3sconf/202021101019

Islam, M. R. (2017). Non-governmental organizations and community development in Bangladesh. International Social Work, *60*(2), 479–493. https://doi. org/10.1177/0020872815574133

Jabeen, A., Huang, X., & Aamir, M. (2015). The challenges of water pollution, threat to public health, flaws of water laws and policies in Pakistan. *Journal of Water Resource and Protection*, *7*(17), 1516. http://creativecommons.org/licenses/by/4.0/

Jamal, A., & Baldwin, C. (2019). Angels of mercy or smiling western invaders? Community's perception of NGOs in northwest Pakistan. *International Social Work*, *62*(1), 89–104. https://doi.org/10.1177/0020872817711239

Jamshed, A., Rana, I. A., Khan, M. A., Agarwal, N., Ali, A., & Ostwal, M. (2018). Community participation framework for post-disaster resettlement and its practical application in Pakistan. *Disaster Prevention and Management: An International Journal*, *27*(5). https://doi.org/10.1108/DPM-05-2018-0161

Kanta Kafle, S. (2017). Does integration matter? A holistic model for building community resilience in Pakistan. *Journal of Business Continuity & Emergency Planning*, *11*(1), 37–51. https://pubmed.ncbi.nlm.nih.gov/28903811/

Khalid, P. D. I., & Khan, M. A. (2020). Water scarcity: A major human security challenge to Pakistan. *South Asian Studies*, *31*(2). http://journals.pu.edu.pk/journals/index.php/IJSAS/article/view/3066

Khan, A. N., & Jan, M. A. (2015). Community based disaster risk management in Pakistan. In A. Rahman, A. N. Khan & R. Shaw (Eds.), *Disaster risk reduction approaches in Pakistan* (pp. 361–377). Springer. https://doi.org/10.1007/978-4-431-55369-4

Khan, A. R., & Bibi, Z. (2011). Women's socio-economic empowerment through participatory approach: a critical assessment. *Pakistan Economic and Social Review*, *49*(1), 133–148. https://www.jstor.org/stable/41762427

Khan, D., & Rashid, M. (2020). Crucial water issues between Pakistan and India, CBMs, and the role of media. *South Asian Studies*, *28*(1), 165–183. https://www.researchgate.net/publication/335259424_Issues_and_Challenges_of_Peace_Building_in_South_Asia

Khan, K. M. J. I., & Irfan, M. (2018). Climate governance: implementing water sector adaptation strategies in Pakistan. *Policy Perspectives*, *15*(3), 139–155. https://www.jstor.org/stable/10.13169/polipers.15.3.0139

Khan, M., Kasmi, J., Saboor, A., & Ali, I. (2020). A comparative analysis of the government and ngos in delivering quality services for the rural people of Pakistan: Community Perspectives. *Asia-Pacific Journal of Rural Development*, *30*(1–2), 203–225. https://doi.org/10.1177/10185291209772

Khan, S., & Anjum, G.A. (2016). Role of citizen community boards in promoting participatory development in Muzaffargarh District, Pakistan. *Pakistan Journal of Engineering and Applied Sciences*, *12*, 43–59. https://journal.uet.edu.pk/ojs_old/index.php/pjeas/article/view/130

Khwaja, A. I. (2004). Is increasing community participation always a good thing? *Journal of the European Economic Association*, *2*(2–3), 427–436. https://academic.oup.com/jeea/article/2/2-3/427/21949

Lub, V. (2019). Theory, social work methods and participation. *Journal of Social Work*, *19*(1), 3–19. http://dx.doi.org/10.1177/1468017318757297

Luqman, M., Mehmood, M. U., Farooq, M., Mehmood, T., Waqar, M., Yaseen, M., & Tahir, M. A. (2021). Critical analysis of rural development initiatives in Pakistan. *Journal of Economic Impact*, *3*(2), 121–129. https://doi.org/10.52223/jei30221038

Malik, M. N., Awan, M. S., & Saleem, T. (2020). Social mobilization campaign to tackle immunization hesitancy in Sargodha and Khushab districts of Pakistan. *Journal of Global Health*, *10*(2). https://dx.doi.org/10.7189%2Fjogh.10.021302

Malik, N., & Rana, A. (2020). Civil society in Pakistan: an exclusive discourse of projectization. *Dialectical Anthropology*, *44*(1), 41–56. https://doi.org/10.1007/s10624-020-09581-7

Mehmood, T., Ch, A.H., & Saeed A. (2016). Community development through open learning and distance education. *Bulletin of Education and Research, 38*(1), 183–196. https://files.eric.ed.gov/fulltext/EJ1210333.pdf

Nabi, G., Ali, M., Khan, S., & Kumar, S. (2019). The crisis of water shortage and pollution in Pakistan: Risk to public health, biodiversity, and ecosystem. *Environmental Science and Pollution Research, 26*(11), 10443–10445. https://doi.org/10.1007/s11356-019-04483-w

Nazuk, A. (2019). *Social Sector Organizations in Pakistan and Assessment of their E-Accountability Practices* (Doctoral dissertation, Quaid-i-Azam University, Islamabad.). http://173.208.131.244:9060/xmlui/handle/123456789/6092

Nibbering, J. W. (2019). *Evaluation in natural resource. Monitoring and evaluation of soil conservation and watershed development projects.* CRC Press.

Noorka, I. R. (2011). Sustainable rural development and participatory approach by on-farm water management techniques. In *Sustainable Agricultural Development* (pp. 139–146). Springer, Dordrecht. https://doi.org/10.1007/978-94-007-0519-7

Rabbani, U., & Fatmi, Z. (2020). Arsenic contamination of drinking water and mitigation in Pakistan: a case of Indus river basin. *Arsenic Water Resources Contamination, *273–296. https://doi.org/10.1007/978-3-030-21258-2

Rafique, Z., & Khoo, S. L. (2018). Role of community-based organizations (CBOs) in promoting citizen participation: A survey study of local government institutions of Punjab, Pakistan. *International Journal of Sociology and Social Policy.* https://doi.org/10.1108/IJSSP-02-2017-0008

Rana, I. A., & Routray, J. K. (2018). Multidimensional model for vulnerability assessment of urban flooding: an empirical study in Pakistan. *International Journal of Disaster Risk Science, 9*(3), 359–375. https://doi.org/10.1007/s13753-018-0179-4

Rauniyar, G., Orbeta Jr, A., & Sugiyarto, G. (2011). Impact of water supply and sanitation assistance on human welfare in rural Pakistan. *Journal of Development Effectiveness, 3*(1), 62–102. https://doi.org/10.1080/19439342.2010.549947

Raza, H. (2020). The role of reflexivity in participatory action research to empower culturally diverse communities in Pakistan. *Journal of Rural and Community Development, 15*(1), 71–88. https://journals.brandonu.ca/jrcd/article/view/1671

Seemab, K., & Tahmina, R. (2019). Inclusive community development: The one village one product program in Pakistan. *Development Bulletin* (81), 90–95. https://crawford.anu.edu.au/rmap/devnet/devnet/Electronic%2081%20amended.pdf

Shafique, K., & Warren, C. M. (2015). Significance of community participation in success of post natural disaster reconstruction project–Evidence from developing country. In *5th International Conference on Building Resilience.* https://understandrisk.org/wp-content/uploads/androiddoctoralschoolproceedin.pdf

Shah, A. A. (2018). Leadership and community mobilization for education access to marginalized communities: The case of an NGO in Sindh, Pakistan [Unpublished master's thesis. Aga Khan University, Karachi, Pakistan.

Shah, I. A., & Baporikar, N. (2012). Participatory approach to development in Pakistan. *Journal of Economic & Social Studies (JECOSS), 2*(1). https://doi.org/10.14706/JECOSS11216

Sleet, P. (2019). Water resources in Pakistan: scarce, polluted and poorly governed. *Independent Strategic Analysis of Australia's Global Interest. Nedlands, 2.*

Sumra, K., Mumtaz, M., & Khan, K. (2020). National water policy of Pakistan: A critical analysis. *Journal of Managerial Sciences, 14.* https://www.researchgate.net/publication/347968071_National_Water_Policy_of_Pakistan_A_Critical_Analysis

Tariq, M. A. U. R., van de Giesen, N., Janjua, S., Shahid, M. L. U. R., & Farooq, R. (2020). An engineering perspective of water sharing issues in Pakistan. *Water, 12*(2), 477. http://dx.doi.org/10.3390/w12020477

Tayler, W. K. (2007). Options for private sector involvement in rural water supply provision in Pakistan. *Journal of International Development: The Journal of the Development Studies Association, 19*(6), 829–839. https://doi.org/10.1002/jid.1404

Wahid, A., Ahmad, M. S., Talib, N. B. A., Shah, I. A., Tahir, M., Jan, F. A., & Saleem, M. Q. (2017). Barriers to empowerment: Assessment of community-led local development organizations in Pakistan. *Renewable and Sustainable Energy Reviews, 74,* 1361–1370. https://doi.org/10.1016/j.rser.2016.11.163

Using an Advocacy Practicum to Establish a Framework for Virtual Community Consultations in the Ottawa Adult Autism Community

Margaret Janse van Rensburg, Courtney Weaver, Christine Jenkins, Morgan Banister, Edward King, Sheila Bell, and The Ottawa Adult Autism Initiative

It has been established by autistic advocates and authors (Arnold, 2013; Douglas et al., 2021; Milton, 2014; O'Dell et al., 2016; Woods et al., 2018) that autistic persons are experts in their experiences and are therefore valuable sources of information when seeking information about their needs. While guidance on conducting interviews and focus groups with autistic adults in research settings exists (Harrington et al., 2014; Johnson, 2014; McEvenue, 2013; Tager-Flushberg et al., 2017), little has been written on how to establish favourable practices for consulting with autistic adults outside of a formal research environment. Consulting the public is an important step in social work community practice (Hardcastle et al., 2004) and is necessary to provide services, supports, and funding that is appropriate for targeted communities.

The Ottawa Adult Autism Initiative (OAAI) is a grassroots organization that was founded in Ottawa, Canada. It is committed to using a community-driven approach in adult autism community development.

The organization identified the need to consult with the adult autism community in Ottawa in order to build a strong knowledge base and gather information about the community. However, prior to consulting the adult autism community, it was important to pilot a consultation process with autistic steering committee members.

This chapter outlines the processes where members of the OAAI were joined by an advocacy practicum student to establish a strategy to host virtual consultations with the adult autism community in Ottawa. Informed by critical autism studies, which centre autistic persons as experts in autism (Douglas et al., 2021; Milton, 2014; O'Dell et al., 2016), and critical pedagogy, which emphasizes critical consciousness as a means for political participation (Giroux, 2010), they created together an *Instructions and Guidance Document* and a set of recommendations which engage the adult autism community in virtual consultations.

On a note about language, the term *autistic* is used in line with autism terminology guidelines published by *Autism: The International Journal of Research and Practice* (n.d.), which advises authors to be informed by the critical autism studies literature and to use personal preferences of autistic people actively involved in authorship.

Conducting Research with Autistic People

Previous autism research offers guidance on gathering information *about* autistic persons, which has been criticized by critical, feminist, and autistic scholars as perpetuating power imbalances (Bumiller, 2008; Douglas et al., 2021; O'Dell et al., 2016; Woods et al., 2018). Traditional autism research focuses on seeking a cause, cure, or techniques for coping with something that is perceived as not desirable (Arnold, 2013; McGuire, 2016; Verhoeff, 2012). This approach can perpetuate potentially ableist discourses (Bottema-Beutel et al., 2021).

When seeking information about the needs of autistic persons, some literature indicates that information about autism can be obtained from people who, although not autistic themselves, may be close to autistic persons such as service providers and family members (Dickie et al., 2009; Nealy et al., 2012; Shepherd & Waddell, 2015; Woodgate et al., 2008). While literature on consulting with autistic persons holds valuable knowledge about encouragement, support needs, and tools that can be of assistance, as well as consent and communication needs (Harrington et al., 2014; Johnson, 2014; McEvenue, 2013; Pellicano et al., 2014; Shepherd & Waddell, 2015; Tager-Flushberg et al., 2017), this research does not seek to create a dialogic relationship or partnerships with participants; instead, it focuses on research in academic spaces. Working from a critical autism studies and critical pedagogy lens, the members of the OAAI sought to establish a way to consult in an inclusive and accessible way with autistic adults in a community setting.

Conceptual Lens

Critical autism studies centres autistic persons as experts in autism (Douglas et al., 2021; Milton, 2014; O'Dell et al., 2016). The emerging field of critical autism studies is offering a scholastic perspective which seeks to explore and challenge power narratives surrounding autism (Milton, 2014; O'Dell et al., 2016), allowing autistic people to "reclaim autism narratives" (Woods et al., 2018, p. 977). The concept of critical autism studies has been in existence since at least 2010, when Orsini and Davidson introduced the term during a workshop at the University of Ottawa (Breen, 2017). It developed further in Laurence Arnold's introduction of *Autonomy, the Critical Journal of Autism Studies* (Woods et al., 2013). While critical autism studies literature is not widely apparent within social work, focusing on in-dividual and group empowerment is in line with social work's overarching goals (Bishop-Fitzpatrick et al., 2018; Carter, 2010; Carter & Wilson, 2013; Haney, 2018; Haney & Cullen, 2018; Mogro-Wilson et al., 2014).

Critical autism studies pair well with the participatory and collab-orative approach of critical pedagogy. As a perspective, critical pedagogy works towards "education that is concerned with questions of justice, democracy, and ethical claims" (Kincheloe, 2008, p. 7). It is grounded in Paulo Freire's concept of radical pedagogy (Carroll, 2013) in his ground-breaking book *Pedagogy of the Oppressed* (2018). Critical pedagogy chal-lenges mainstream educational assumptions that a learner is a blank slate who learns through deposits of information. Through a dialogical approach where power is shared, critical thinking, self-reflection, and im-agination are fostered. Rather than identifying practices and methods of instruction, critical pedagogy aims to prepare individuals to use know-ledge, skills, and social relations, regardless of their social location, in order to be critical thinkers (Giroux, 2010). In this way, critical pedagogy emphasizes critical consciousness as a means for political participation by acknowledging historic precedent, one's own and others' experiences, and the future (Giroux, 2010). Of central concern in critical pedagogy is understanding how education and knowledge are constructed in society by the powerful, in order to gain awareness of the impacts of how this knowledge is used and to challenge the structures that maintain societal power imbalances (Kincheloe, 2008). Informed by critical pedagogy, we were focused not only on knowledge construction, but also on co-developing knowledge that would be used in the future to engage the adult autism community in virtual consultations.

Therefore, the members of the OAAI engaged in a dialogical, problem-posing, participatory process which seeks to emphasize the knowledges of autistic adults in creating safe, equitable, and engaged spaces when being consulted. Using critical consciousness, developing a deeper understanding the social and cultural world, and applying this knowledge in actions was a goal for each person involved within this process (Freire, 2018). Therefore, acknowledging societal hegemony and being actively engaged in personal and social change through equitable knowledge generation was necessary (Barak, 2016).

Framed by critical and emancipatory theories, the OAAI was aware that the typical virtual consultation setting was not accessible to, or inclusive of, the adult autism community. By informing future virtual consultations with autistic persons' experiences, the OAAI could create a way to prepare members of the Ottawa adult autism community to engage in accessible and inclusive virtual consultations.

Situating the Practicum

The project was situated in Ottawa, Canada's capital region, where neoliberalism influences the social welfare services and supports available (Braedley & Luxton, 2010). Ideologically, neoliberalism prioritizes a free market and promotes privatization in the provision of welfare supports and services (Fanelli & Thomas, 2011). Past political and advocacy activity has resulted in limited social welfare supports pertaining to autistic children (Perry, 2002), while the needs of autistic children are being addressed under provincial legislation (see Janse van Rensburg, 2020). However, specific autism funding is removed at age 18 (Ministry of Children, Community and Social Services, 2021) and disability supports are insufficient to assist autistic persons accessing and securing economic and social inclusion (Canadian Autism Spectrum Disorder Alliance [CASDA], 2020; Canadian Academy of Health Sciences [CAHS], 2021). Therefore, a key concern for persons affected by autism in Ottawa, Ontario, is the inadequate supports, services, and funding for autistic adults.

In 2008, Autism Ontario published *Forgotten: Ontario Adults with Autism and Adults with Aspergers*, which specifically recommended a policy framework to assist autistic adults with financial supports external to existing programs: day supports which work towards social and economic inclusion; programs ensuring safety and well-being for autistic adults; options for supported housing; and professional supports. This policy framework was based on standard eligibility criteria and designed to provide a centre that connects autistic adults and their families with services, support, and information (Autism Ontario, 2008). Twelve years after the publication of this report, there has been little development with respect to municipal, provincial, or federal action towards meeting the goal of establishing a network to assist autistic adults in accessing services, supports, and funding (Ottawa Adult Autism Initiative [OAAI], 2021). To meet this gap, the OAAI, which was created in 2017 with the goal of assessing the needs of autistic adults in Ottawa, aims to establish a network that meets the services and support needs for autistic adults.

Organization: The Ottawa Adult Autism Initiative (OAAI)

The OAAI is a volunteer grassroots organization comprised of members that include autistic adults, family members, and allies. In 2019, the OAAI received a seed grant from the Ontario Trillium Foundation, in partnership with Autism Ontario, to help adults on the autism spectrum and their families to find the supports and services they need. As a grassroots organization, the OAAI is an organization still in its infancy that is led by a volunteer steering committee of autistic people, family members of autistic adults, services providers, and professionals in the field of autism. While the organization currently does not have a governance structure, members of the steering committee pursue goals of acquiring funding community outreach, volunteer co-ordination, and maintaining group resilience.

To ease the access to supports and services needed by adults on the autism spectrum and their families, the OAAI's first step was to conduct a community needs assessment. However, it was necessary to find an approach that was accessible and inclusive. A team was established that brought together members of the steering committee to develop and pilot a virtual community consultation process. This pilot project would establish a framework for hosting wider virtual community consultations with the adult autism community in Ottawa. Members of the steering committee included Christine Jenkins, Courtney Weaver, Edward King, and Morgan Banister.

Participants in the Pilot Consultation

Christine Jenkins, Courtney Weaver, Edward King, and Morgan Banister were integral in the process of developing guidance for hosting community consultations with the adult autism community. As autistic steering committee members, they acted as participants in the pilot consultation. Each member brought their own expertise: Christine, diagnosed at aged 48, is co-author of *Spectrum Women: Walking to the Beat of Autism* (2018). Courtney, diagnosed with Asperger's Syndrome at age 4, works four jobs within accessibility. Edward, diagnosed at age 3 with language delays, gives talks at schools and workshops about autism, bullying, and overcoming challenges. Finally, Morgan is an autistic adult who is engaged in Autism Ontario's Ottawa Chapter and is a dedicated member of two autistic adult social support groups. Working in collaboration with the rest of the OAAI team, these participants co-constructed knowledge in a dialogical, problem-posing, participatory process seeking critical consciousness with an advocacy student who emphasized their knowledge in creating safe, equitable, and engaged spaces for the adult autism community to be consulted.

Advocacy Practicum

Carleton University's School of Social Work requires doctoral students in social work to complete an advocacy practicum as a pass/fail course (Carleton University, n.d.). Differing from a traditional placement or practicum which is offered at the Bachelor or Masters' level, the advocacy practicum is proposed by the student and approved by their graduate supervisor. The practicum allows for 130 hours of work during the term when the practicum takes place.

Margaret Janse van Rensburg was a first-year Social Work PhD student who had recently completed their Master of Social Work, when, in the summer of 2020, she became a non-autistic ally and steering committee member of the OAAI. She became aware that the advocacy practicum provided an opportunity to contribute more to the OAAI; this was an opportune moment for her to build community connections for future practical work and research with the autistic community. Furthermore, the OAAI recognized that it would be beneficial to have a practicum student, in the fall of 2020, to contribute towards the OAAI's work through three major facets: (1) resources for sustainability; (2) building capacity and engagement; and (3) supporting collaboration.

As a practicum student, Margaret was overseen by three supervisors: a social worker with expertise in working with autistic older youth, autistic adults, and their families; a speech-language pathologist with expertise in non-verbal/non-vocal autism; and a psychotherapist transition specialist with expertise in working with autistic adults in academic settings. These three supervisors were co-founders of the organization. Sheila Bell directly supervised the co-development of the *Instructions and Guidance Document,* bringing her expertise in working with autistic people for more than 30 years.

Methodology

Problem-posing education is a concept developed by Paulo Freire (2018) which focuses on developing critical thinking skills. It is a liberating alternative to the banking model of education, which seeks to *deposit* factoids and information into a person, upholding power imbalances between a teacher and a learner and colonizing the mind of the recipient. Engaging in a methodology of problem-posing education requires dialogue. Since all are learners, power imbalances are challenged and restructured.

We applied the concept of problem-posing education by establishing a four-phase process in which all members of the consultation team could learn through dialogue, which would inform our future virtual community consultations with the Ottawa adult autism community. Inspired by *Pedagogy of the Oppressed* (Freire, 2018), this four-phase methodology developed through collaboration and participation of all authors. Positivism, scientism, and rigour were not aims in our work; rather, we were informed by flexible, subjective, narrative, and autistic-informed methods. Each of the phases, outlined below, included different questions for different members.

Members were invited to take part in the pilot consultation, and a date and time for the pilot consultation was decided based on consensus. The student and her supervisor collected data collaboratively through detailed notetaking during the virtual consultation, and by engaging with participants through email correspondence. The data were verified by each participant when they collaboratively participated in making a filmed and video-recorded presentation. This process allowed the authors to co-develop a way to consult with members of the adult autism community in an accessible and inclusive fashion.

Carleton University's Research Ethics Board was informed of the pilot consultation. The processes covered in this chapter fall under the scope of the Tri-Council Policy Statement 2 (2018) Article 2.5 "Quality Assurance and Quality Improvement Studies."

It is of key importance to note that all authors are white, cisgender, and vocal. The experiences and recommendations that were identified, however, were based on each author's understanding of their identity in reflection to others; thus, the team was, as a whole, able to identify support needs for virtual community consultations outside of their own experiences.

Four-Phase Process

The four-phase process included different questions for each phase in order to generate dialogue and feedback. Dialogue and mutual respect were necessary throughout the process, as critical consciousness was a goal for each person involved in this process (Freire, 2018). These phases resulted in a final set of instructions and guidance for our future virtual consultations.

Phase 1: Problem Posing to the Student

Phase one consisted of problem posing to the student. Sheila, as practicum supervisor, posed the problem to Margaret, that is, the needed requirement to create guidelines for an accessible and inclusive space to conduct community virtual consultations. To address this problem, a task was created to pilot our virtual consultation process by securing a space where we could learn from Christine, Courtney, Edward, and Morgan. The goal was to develop virtual consultation strategies while Margaret would facilitate a pilot virtual consultation.

Creating an online space that was inclusive and accessible for autistic steering committee members represented a challenge for Margaret. Autistic people interpret the world differently (Milton & Bracher, 2013). Some autistic people have communication difficulties, both in terms of hearing and speaking, and by way of social communication, such as reading other people's cues, being comfortable in a group setting, or negotiating a social situation (Anderson et al., 2018; Ward & Webster, 2018). While some autistics have praised zoom for its accessibility (Lawrence, 2021), a virtual setting could increase barriers in social communication because many social cues are removed when one is looking through a screen instead of being in a live room. It can make reading the body language and facial expressions in real time extremely difficult (Bailenson, 2021; Wolf, 2020).

Inspired by the work of Carol Gray (2010), a speech-language pathologist who conceptualized social stories, and the business environment's Standard Operating Procedure, the problem posed to the student was addressed by creating an *Instructions and Guidance Document* for the pilot virtual consultation. This document was designed to give detailed information to Christine, Courtney, Edward, and Edward, so that when they began the virtual consultation, they had a guiding document and a troubleshooting guide for whatever might happen during the meeting. This was meant to promote comfort, coping, and increased communication, especially when talking about difficult topics such as support requirements and needs.

Phase 2: Student Problem Solving

Phase two consisted of student problem solving. Margaret researched the process of facilitating virtual consultations and focus groups with autistic adults and created the first draft of an *Instructions and Guidance Document* surrounding four guiding questions for the virtual consultation. Margaret knew that this was a two-part task: first, to create the document, second, to facilitate a discussion guided by the document. To complete the first task, research was required surrounding how to best prepare for and run virtual consultations in non-overwhelming ways. Margaret considered the following aspects:

Technology. While technology offers many alternative and creative ways of collecting information and fostering engagement, it also comes with some challenges. It had to be considered that everybody's comfort levels with technology differed, and therefore it was necessary to identify how to enter a Zoom meeting for the virtual consultation session. We opted to keep technological features simple during the session. A Zoom meeting was chosen as a means of virtual communication (Zoom Video Communications, Inc., 2020), because this broadly popular technology had been previously used for steering committee meetings (Iqbal, 2020; Richter, 2021). No special features, such as polling or word cloud creation, were used for members to access the virtual consultation through Zoom's dial-in phone option (Zoom Video Communications, Inc., 2020).

Confidentiality and Privacy. While a virtual consultation may be able to create an environment where people bounce ideas off one another and share experiences, they might disclose issues that they do not want others to know or tell. Therefore, setting ground rules for the virtual consultation was important to ensure safety for each person in this environment.

Ground rules included acknowledging that discussion at a Zoom meeting is public (other people may hear your opinions and perspectives); getting meeting participants to agree that information about the group discussion can be shared, but names and/or identifying details of individual group members must not be shared; asking all in attendance not to name or give identifying details of friends or others they wish to share information/feedback with (protecting other's privacy and confidentiality); acknowledging that facilitators write down details from the group discussion, while names of the individuals who make comments are not to be recorded; and assurance that no audio or video recording of the session is allowed.

Accommodations. Disability-related accommodations are a human right (Canadian Human Rights Act, RSC 1985, c H-6). It was therefore necessary to be willing to accommodate our participants during the virtual consultation process. Each participant could request accommodations. Furthermore, there were alternative opportunities for accommodations to be provided. These were called "tips" on the Instructions and Guidance Document. Tips included having someone to contact prior to the virtual consultation to talk through technological, social, or other issues that could arise; ensuring that each participant is aware that there were no "right" or "wrong" answers; providing a contact email for participants to follow up if they do not have time to give a complete answer, or if they have more information to share after the virtual consultation; giving reminders to the facilitator to repeat the question in different ways in case a participant is unsure about the meaning of the question; allowing people to take breaks as needed; and providing contacts for support during and after the meeting.

Sharing Space. Considering that there may be certain times when people may dominate discussions, or times when people may ramble, it was important to identify that space needed to be shared. Therefore, a certain time and order for people to speak was presented in the preparation document. This could foster an environment where everyone could contribute.

Taking a Break. In the past, members of the steering committee had advocated the need to take breaks during meetings. Therefore, a planned break was presented and any conversations during that time was put on pause. No conversations could happen during that break so people would know that they were not missing out on anything critical. During this time, all were instructed to turn off their microphones and cameras.

Lateness. Finally, considering what would happen if a person was late or did not show up, and whether this would disrupt the virtual consultation process was important. It can be disruptive to a consultation setting, and disrespectful to the members being consulted, when a member shows up late. Therefore, in this setting, instructions requested that participants acknowledge if they were going to be late or miss the session to let the facilitators know prior to the session. While no members were late for the pilot virtual consultation, having two facilitators present during virtual community consultations proved useful for letting in people who were late in joining, and sending them a message to help them catch up on what they may have missed.

Phase 3: Problem Posing to the Community

Considering the universal design for learning (Meyer et al., 2014) to optimize choice and autonomy during the session, Margaret drafted the *Instructions and Guidance Document* based on accessibility, while recognizing different needs for different people. As a speech-language pathologist, Sheila then ensured that the document was written in an accessible, plain English script. In the end, we had a document, a guiding virtual consultation script, and a post-virtual consultation feedback email.

While Margaret developed a draft of the *Instructions and Guidance Document* under the specific guidance and support of her supervisor Sheila, the utility of this document was unknown. Therefore, it was necessary to pose the problem to the community by hosting a pilot consultation which applied the *Instructions and Guidance Document*.

Led by Margaret and co-facilitated by Sheila, the pilot virtual consultation began by welcoming participants Christine, Courtney, Edward, and Morgan. The purpose of the virtual consultation was identified as to "test run" one of the virtual consultation meetings that would be held in the future by the OAAI. This meeting was hosted on 15 October 2020.

Prior to getting started with the virtual consultation, Margaret overviewed the key information from the *Instructions and Guidance Document* (see Table 12.1). The problem of how to create an accessible and inclusive virtual consultation setting was then introduced to the community by engaging them in a discussion.

At the beginning, each participant introduced themselves briefly. Prior to having a five-minute break, two questions aiming at improving our goals as an organization were discussed. The first question was "how do you think we can advertise our consultations to autistic adults?" The second question was "what is important to consider in the selection of participants for the consultation sessions?" A third question, asked after a short break, was "how can we make sure that the ASD perspective stays at the centre of the OAAI project?" The last question was "do you have any suggestions for changing/improving the structure of our regular steering committee meetings?"

The consultation was one-hour long (11:30 AM to 12:30 PM), allowing for a break half-way through the meeting (12:00 to 12:05). Approximately ten minutes were spent on each question. Each person was called upon

Table 12.1: Final Instructions and Guidance Document Revised by All Authors

Instructions and Guidance Document
Goal of the virtual consultation session
Why your attendance is important
Accommodations and accessibility, and how to request
How to join the virtual consultation
Who to contact if you have trouble
Who will be at the virtual consultation
Familiar/unfamiliar faces (may or may not include names)
Confidentiality and privacy
Any ethics considerations
Agenda
Questions discussed & break
Any activities that may happen & any technological needs
How to contribute in vocal ways (leadership and structure of consulting)
How to contribute in non-vocal ways
How to contribute after the virtual consultation
Break
How to take one outside of the formal break
When the break will happen
Support during and after the meeting

twice per question to ensure that everyone had a chance to speak. After the break, the discussion was more in-depth. At this point, participants may have felt comfortable building off one another's ideas. The pilot virtual consultation concluded with a thank-you, a reminder that people could continue to contribute through email, and a reminder that people could reach out for support if needed after the virtual consultation. After the virtual consultation, an email sent to all participants repeated this information and asked them to identify ways in which the virtual consultation process could have improved.

Phase 4: Community Problem Solving

From the pilot virtual consultation, the participants identified the ways in which the *Instructions and Guidance Document* could be improved, while confirming that this document was useful and successful for guiding people through a community virtual consultation. Furthermore, they noted that this document was helpful for guiding people through the beginning of the meeting — which included the purpose of the consultation; the confidentiality and privacy protocol; the limited length for answers; the expectation for introductions; overviews of differing community guidelines regarding sharing space and how to share more information; a following-through with a break; and knowing when and how the consultation would end.

During the virtual pilot consultation, Christine, Courtney, Edward, and Morgan identified that autistic adults would like to see more autistic leadership, more autistic people "on board" and in central positions, and more agency given to autistic persons; they also mentioned a need for public education around autism and regularity surrounding OAAI meeting structures. After the virtual consultation, each participant contributed to the creation of a collaborative presentation to reflect on the process. This fourth and final step, the finalization of the *Instructions and Guidance Document* and the collaborative presentation, was a community solution to the problem of creating accessible and inclusive virtual consultation settings for the adult autism community.

Discussion and Recommendations

Reflecting about favorable practices for virtual consultations with autistic adults, Morgan, Edward, Christine, and Courtney identified several key considerations: preparing for the virtual consultation through information sharing and checking in; emphasizing leadership and organization; and using facilitation strategies that foster accessibility through breaks and positive attitudes.

Preparation for the Virtual Consultation

It is necessary to give information prior to a virtual consultation session about why attendance is important. This is because autistic adults may wonder about whether the virtual consultation is meaningful for the participant, and if they feel that they can contribute to the goals of the virtual consultation. By providing in the *Instructions and Guidance Document* clear reasons for the virtual consultation and the importance of its attendance, autistic adults may be more willing to attend and participate in virtual consultation sessions.

Furthermore, knowing who would be at the virtual consultation session helps with preparing autistic adults for understanding what the virtual consultation setting would look like, especially when this involves people they know — although there may be risks when participants already know one another. This provides them with an opportunity to consider whether there would be new or familiar faces, adding to increased comfort in the virtual consultation setting.

Checking in 24 hours prior to the session as a reminder of the upcoming virtual consultation and ensuring the emotional well-being of autistic adults during virtual consultations is very important, especially when touching on more sensitive topics such as housing and service needs. A pre-check-in would allow the participants to identify the time, the date, the topics covered in the session, and how to access the virtual consultation; a pre-check-in would also provide the opportunity to ask the participants how they are feeling about joining the virtual consultation setting. During the session, checking-in should focus on bringing attention to the topic of discussion to ensure that participants understand the questions being asked, while inquiring whether additional resources and support can be provided to meet the emotional needs of the autistic adults being consulted.

Leadership

Leadership is important in consulting autistic adults. Having organized leaders who can address potential confusion, unite persons, and make those being consulted feel like a team is necessary. This can be achieved by having a common goal. When consulting with autistic adults, however, allowing for autonomy is of priority: therefore, greater autistic-led consultation is better. If the virtual consultation leader is not autistic, having a co-leader who is autistic could be helpful as they can identify ways to structure the virtual consultation which consider autistic neurodiversity requirements, provide support with how to manage political discussions that may arise, and model autistic self-determination and self-advocacy for virtual consultation with participants. This was a learning experience in our virtual consultation process, as the leader was not autistic and therefore faced additional hurdles in ensuring accessibility.

Leaders should structure virtual consultations in an organized fashion, as autistic persons may prefer routine and structure. In a virtual setting, having everyone on mute while the host primarily leads the discussion, identifies who speaks in an order, and gives everyone a chance to speak can be helpful. This is providing that everyone knows this procedure prior to the beginning of the virtual consultation. If there is a point in the virtual consultation when it is clear that someone wants to say something or has something to say, the host then tries to find an occasion for them to mention it there, and then adjusts accordingly, or they can identify an alternative way for them to provide this information such as through email or through a chat function. This prevents interruptions and confusion, which should be avoided in the virtual consultation environment.

Facilitation Strategies

Consultations with autistic adults should not only focus on vocal data collection strategies, otherwise known as spoken word. They should also provide an opportunity to type on a tablet/computer/phone, use art, use sign language, and have other representatives support their virtual consultation input such as a support worker or parent. Those consulting with autistic adults will need to be aware that not all autistic people speak, and some selectively speak. The use of multiple modalities thus engages autistic persons, not only a certain sub-population. Subtitles, captioning, and translation are other types of accommodation that not only help autistic persons but can help everyone else. While it can be challenging to always provide all accommodations and accessibility features when checking in with autistic participants prior to consulting with them, it is a priority to identify any accessibility features which may facilitate the participant's engagement in the virtual consultation process. Accessibility is not a hurdle: it is a commitment.

Additionally, when hosting virtual consultations, it is important to give participants an opportunity to contribute after the virtual consultation has ended. Everyone's processing speeds differ, and therefore giving an opportunity for post hoc contributions can identify differing perspectives that were part of virtual consultation conversations. Furthermore, giving an opportunity to communicate further thoughts after the virtual consultation has ended provides participants with a way to give feedback on the virtual consultation process. Through this, facilitators can identify ways to improve future virtual consultations, while gathering information that contributes to the goals of the virtual consultations.

Foster Positive Attitudes and Atmospheres

As facilitators, we are often unaware of what is happening in a participant's life prior to the virtual consultation or their previous history with virtual consultation processes. People may have different attitudes and agendas in joining a virtual consultation. It is important for those creating virtual consultation environments to be aware of the multiplicity of experiences of participants, and to aim towards creating an environment that is welcoming. Facilitators must aim to foster an environment whereby people feel that it will be interesting to learn something new, where their presence is important, and that the environment will be calm and relaxing. All this information can be provided in the instructions and guidance given to participants prior to the beginning of the virtual consultation.

One such way to create an environment which is calm, welcoming, and open, is to implement breaks as these can promote a positive virtual consultation atmosphere. Sometimes, the virtual consultation environment can become overwhelming, and the amount of information being presented and asked about can begin to confuse the participants. Providing a planned break can allow for body and mind to rest, and for participants to come back feeling refreshed and ready to contribute again. Furthermore, letting participants know they can take their own breaks as needed, and that they can request one or take one themselves can foster a safe, engaging, and comfortable virtual consultation environment for autistic adults.

Through the four-phase process, we established the *Instructions and Guidance Document* to serve as guidelines for consulting a diverse sample of the Ottawa adult autism community "to voice opinions and provide input on needed services/supports" (Autism Ontario, 2021, n.d.). The results of the broader virtual consultations can be found on the OAAI's website: https://ottawaadultautism.com/. Furthermore, recommendations in preparation, leadership, and facilitation were established. These guidelines and recommendations promote dialogic discussions, equitable environments, and engagement among those involved, allowing for a positive atmosphere which provides multiple avenues for autistic adult participation.

Conclusion

This chapter has presented a four-phase pedagogical process that has led to the development of a strategy to engage the adult autism community in virtual consultations. As a result, an *Instructions and Guidance Document* and key recommendations, informed by problem-posing education and critical reflection, were developed, proposed, and created. This offers a way for the OAAI to continue future work with the adult autism community in Ottawa.

A strategy was developed and refined. In virtual consultations, it is useful to have an *Instructions and Guidance Document* to assist participant well-being; to instruct how to join the virtual consultation; to ensure confidentiality and privacy ground rules; to present the agenda and provide explanation for when to plan for a break during the consultation; and to demonstrate how to access support during or after the consultation. It is of utmost importance to set up participants for success in virtual consultations prior to engaging in the consultation proper. Additionally, the significance of leadership in facilitating virtual consultations and the impact of attitude and atmosphere on participants were noted.

Overall, an advocacy practicum environment provided the PhD student with an avenue to develop virtual consultation skills in fostering engaged and inclusive environments for autistic adults. In the four-phase process, she learned about the development of community problem-solving skills through the problem-posing education model. Future community field placements can assist grassroots organizations in establishing practices for broader community consultations through co-learning with steering committee members. By running a pilot consultation, students gain valuable knowledge in identifying community resources and opportunities for organizational growth, and in discovering avenues for future work of the organization.

Author Note

The virtual consultations run by the Ottawa Adult Autism Initiative, which adopted the framework referenced in this chapter, were funded by the Ontario Trillium Foundation. Findings from the virtual consultations can be found at https://ottawaaadultautism.com/project-reports/. Some of these reflections were presented at the Canadian Association of Social Work Education (CASWE) 2021 conference. There are no conflicts of interest to disclose.

REFERENCES

Anderson, A. H., Carter, M., & Stephenson, J. (2018). Perspectives of university students with autism spectrum disorder. *Journal of Autism and Developmental Disorders*, 48(3), 651–666. https://doi.org/10.1007/s10803-017-3257-3

Arnold, L. (2013). Introduction to the second edition. *Autonomy, the Critical Journal of Interdisciplinary Autism Studies*, 1(2), Article 2. http://www.larry-arnold.net/Autonomy/index.php/autonomy/article/view/ED2

Autism Ontario. (2008). OTF grant helps Autism Ontario and OAAI launch report led by autistic adults, caregivers and allies on service gaps and needs in Ottawa. https://www.autismontario.com/news/otf-grant-helps-autism-ontario-and-oaai-launch-report-led-autistic-adults-caregivers-and

Autism Ontario. (2021). *Forgotten: Ontario adults with autism and adults with Asperger's*. https://www.autismontario.com/sites/default/files/2019-01/Forgotten%2BReport%2BAutism%2BOntario.pdf

Autism: The International Journal of Research and Practice. (n.d.). *Terminology guidance*. Retrieved August 14, 2021, from https://journals-sagepub-com/pb-assets/cmscontent/AUT/Autism-terminology-guidance-2021-1626860796.pdf

Bailenson, J. N. (2021). Nonverbal overload: A theoretical argument for the causes of Zoom fatigue.. *Technology, Mind, and Behavior*, 2(1). https://doi.org/10.1037/tmb0000030

Barak, A. (2016). Critical consciousness in critical social work: Learning from the theatre of the oppressed. *The British Journal of Social Work*, 46(6), 1776–1792. https://doi.org/10.1093/bjsw/bcv102

Bishop-Fitzpatrick, L., Dababnah, S., Baker-Ericzén, M. J., Smith, M. J., & Magaña, S. M. (2019). Autism spectrum disorder and the science of social work: A grand challenge for social work research. *Social Work in Mental Health*, 17(1), 73–92. http://doi.org/10.1080/15332985.2018.1509411

Bottema-Beutel, K., Kapp, S. K., Lester, J. N., Sasson, N. J., & Hand, B. N. (2021). Avoiding ableist language: Suggestions for autism researchers. *Autism in Adulthood*, 3(1), 18–29. https://doi.org/10.1089/aut.2020.0014

Braedley, S., & Luxton, M. (2010). *Neoliberalism and everyday life* (1st ed.). McGill-Queen's University Press.

Breen, T. (2017). *Critical Autism Studies: Making a positive difference*. https://www.altogetherautism.org.nz/critical-autism-studies-making-a-positive-difference/

Bumiller, K. (2008). Quirky citizens: Autism, gender, and reimagining disability. *Signs: Journal of Women in Culture and Society, 33*, 967–991. https://doi.org/10.1086/528848

Canadian Academy of Health Sciences [CAHS]. (2021). *Community conversations on autism*. Ottawa, Ontario. CAHS. Retrieved August 15, 2021, from https://cahs-acss.ca/community-conversations/

Canadian Autism Spectrum Disorder Alliance [CASDA]. (2020). *Roadmap to a national autism strategy*. CASDA. https://www.casda.ca/roadmap/

Canadian Human Rights Act, RSC 1985, c H-6. Government of Canada. https://canlii.ca/t/5432c

Canadian Institutes of Health Research, Natural Sciences and Engineering Research Council of Canada, and Social Sciences and Humanities Research Council of Canada. (2018). *Tri-council policy statement: Ethical conduct for research involving humans*. https://ethics.gc.ca/eng/documents/tcps2-2018-en-interactive-final.pdf

Carleton University. (n.d.). *PhD program*. https://carleton.ca/socialwork/phd-program/

Carroll, W. K. (2013). Playdough capitalism: An adventure in critical pedagogy. *Socialist Studies/Études Socialistes*. https://doi.org/10.18740/S4B88R

Carter, I. (2010). Perceptions of professional intervention by parental advocates for autistic children: A need to improve practice with self-help groups and those with developmental disabilities. *Professional Development: The International Journal of Continuing Social Work Education, 13*(3), 4–15. http://www.profdevjournal.org/articles/133004.pdf

Carter, I., & Wilson, A. (2013). Reflecting on the need for social workers to consider various models of disability when working with parents of children with autism. *Professional Development, 16*(2), 5–18.

Dickie, V. A., Baranek, G. T., Schultz, B., Watson, L. R., & McComish, C. S. (2009). Parent reports of sensory experiences of preschool children with and without autism: A qualitative study. *American Journal of Occupational Therapy, 63*(2), 172–181. https://doi.org/10.5014/ajot.63.2.172

Douglas, P., Rice, C., Runswick-Cole, K., Easton, A., Gibson, M. F., Gruson-Wood, J., Klar, E., & Shields, R. (2021). Re-storying autism: A body becoming disability studies in education approach. *International Journal of Inclusive Education, 25*(5), 605–622. https://doi.org/10.1080/13603116.2018.1563835

Fanelli, C., & Thomas, M. P. (2011) Austerity, competitiveness, and neoliberalism redux: Ontario responds to the great recession. *Socialist Studies, 7*(1/2), 141–170. https://core.ac.uk/download/pdf/267827711.pdf

Freire, P. (2018). *Pedagogy of the Oppressed*. Bloomsbury Publishing USA.

Giroux, H. (2010). Rethinking education as the practice of freedom: Paulo Freire and the promise of critical pedagogy. *Policy Futures in Education, 8*(6), 715–721. https://doi.org/10.2304/pfie.2010.8.6.715

Gray, C. (2010). *The new social story book.* Jenison Public Schools and Future Horizons INC. Arlington.

Haney, J. L. (2018). Reconceptualizing autism: An alternative paradigm for social work practice. *Journal of Progressive Human Services, 29*(1), 61–80. http:// doi.org/10.108 0/10428232.2017.1394689

Haney, J. L., & Cullen, J. A. (2018). An exploratory investigation of social workers' knowledge and attitudes about autism. *Social Work in Mental Health, 16*(2), 201–222. https://doi.org/10.1080/15332985.2017.1373265

Hardcastle, D., Powers, P., & Wenocur, S. (2004). *Community practice theories and skills for social workers* (2nd ed.). Oxford University Press. USA.

Harrington, C., Foster, M., Rodger, S., & Ashburner, J. (2014). Engaging young people with Autistic Spectrum Disorder in research interviews. *British Journal of Learning Disabilities, 42*(2), 153–161. https://doi.org/10.1111/bld.12037

Iqbal, M. (2020, April 9). *Zoom revenue and usage statistics (2021).* Business of Apps. https://www.businessofapps.com/data/zoom-statistics/

Janse van Rensburg, M. (2020). *Autistics perspectives of autism funding in Ontario.* [Doctoral Dissertation, Carleton University]. Ottawa, Canada. https://doi.org/10.22215/etd/2020-14124

Johnson, J. (2014). *Exploring the social experiences of adults on the autism spectrum: Views on friendships, dating and partnerships.* [Doctoral dissertation, Carleton University]. Ottawa. https://doi.org/10.22215/etd/2014-10342

Kincheloe, J. L. (2008). *Knowledge and critical pedagogy: An introduction.* Springer Netherlands.

Lawrence, A. (2021). How Zoom helped the neurotypical world hear my autistic voice. *Nature.* https://doi.org/10.1038/d41586-021-02325-9

McEvenue, T. (2013). Reading, seeing and hearing voices: What can autistic people teach social work? [Unpublished Masters' Research Paper]. Toronto: Ryerson University.

McGuire, A. (2016). *War on autism: On the cultural logic of normative violence* (Illustrated edition). University of Michigan Press.

Meyer, A., Rose, D. H., & Gordon, D. (2014). *Universal design for learning: Theory and practice.* CAST.

Milton, D. E. (2014). Autistic expertise: A critical reflection on the production of knowledge in autism studies. *Autism, 18*(7), 794–802. https://doi.org/10.1177/1362361314525281

Milton, D.E.M., & Bracher, M. (2013). Autistics speak but are they heard? *Medical Sociology Online, 7*(2). https://kar.kent.ac.uk/id/eprint/62635

Ministry of Children, Community and Social Services. (2021). *Ontario autism program.* https://www.ontario.ca/page/ontario-autism-program

Mogro-Wilson, C., Davidson, K., & Bruder, M. B. (2014). An empowerment approach in teaching a class about autism for social work students. *Social Work Education, 33*(1), 61–76. https://doi.org/10.1080/02615479.2012.734802

Nealy, C. E., O'Hare, L., Powers, J. D., & Swick, D. C. (2012). The impact of autism spectrum disorders on the family: A qualitative study of mothers' perspectives. *Journal of Family Social Work, 15*(3), 187–201. https://doi.org/10.1080/10522158.2012.675624

O'Dell, L., Bertilsdotter Rosqvist, H., Ortega, F., Brownlow, C., & Orsini, M. (2016). Critical autism studies: Exploring epistemic dialogues and intersections, challenging dominant understandings of autism. *Disability & Society, 31*(2), 166–179. https://doi.org/10.1080/09687599.2016.1164026

Ottawa Adult Autism Initiative [OAAI]. (2021). *Ottawa Adult Autism Initiative.* https://ottawaadultautism.com/

Pellicano, E., Dinsmore, A., & Charman, T. (2014). What should autism research focus upon? Community views and priorities from the United Kingdom. *Autism, 18*(7), 756–770. https://doi.org/10.1177/1362361314529627

Perry, A. (2002). Intensive early intervention program for children with autism: Background and design of the Ontario preschool autism initiative. *Journal on Developmental Disabilities 9*(2), 121–128. https://oadd.org/wp-content/uploads/2016/12/art11Perry.pdf

Richter, F. (2021). *Zoom keeps momentum as workers stay at home.* https://www.statista.com/chart/21906/zoom-revenue/

Shepherd, C. A., & Waddell, C. (2015). A qualitative study of autism policy in Canada: Seeking consensus on Children's Services. *Journal of Autism and Developmental Disorders, 45*(11), 3550–3564. https://doi.org/10.1007/s10803-015-2502-x

Tager-Flushberg, H. Plesa Skwerer, D. Joseph, R. M. Brukilacchio, B. Decker, J. Eggleston, B. Meyer, S., & Yoder A. (2017). Conducting research with minimally verbal participants with autism spectrum disorder. *Autism, 21*(7), 852–861. https://doi.org/10.1177%2F1362361316654605

Verhoeff, B. (2012). What is this thing called autism? A critical analysis of the tenacious search for autism's essence. *BioSocieties, 7*(4), 410–432. https://doi.org/10.1057/biosoc.2012.23

Ward, D., & Webster, A. (2018). Understanding the lived experiences of university students with autism spectrum disorder (ASD): A phenomenological study. *International Journal of Disability, Development and Education, 65*(4), 373–392. https://doi.org/10.1080/1034912X.2017.1403573

Wolf, J. (2020). *The importance of nonverbal communication in virtual meetings.* https://www.smartbrief.com/original/2020/06/importance-nonverbal-communication-virtual-meetings

Woodgate, R. L., Ateah, C., & Secco, L. (2008). Living in a world of our own: The experience of parents who have a child with autism. *Qualitative Health Research, 18*(8), 1075–1083. https://doi.org/10.1177/1049732308320112

Woods, R., Milton, D., Arnold, L., & Graby, S. (2018). Redefining critical autism studies: A more inclusive interpretation. *Disability & Society, 33*(6), 974–979. https://doi.org/1 0.1080/09687599.2018.1454380

Zoom Video Communications, Inc. (2020). *Zoom.* https://zoom.us/

The Service Provider's Dilemma: Confronting the Challenges of Service Delivery for Undocumented Victims of Intimate Partner Violence

Nicole Balbuena

Social service providers, such as social workers, often confront challenges in the delivery of services. However, there is a better need to understand these challenges for undocumented people. Although intimate partner violence (IPV) agencies claim to offer services to all demographics — race, sexuality, gender, and most importantly, legal status — institutional policies and practices can impose restrictions on how service providers deliver support and services.

IPV is defined as physical, emotional, economic, verbal, and spiritual abuse that occurs within an intimate relationship — regardless of one's racial, income, cultural, socioeconomic status, or sexual orientation — where one partner asserts his/her/their power and control over the other partner (Marrs Fuchsel & Brummett, 2020). Prior research has revealed that immigrants who are victims of IPV have limited access to resources such as social and health care (Marrs Fuchsel & Brummett, 2020; Reina & Lohman, 2015). But there is limited research addressing the limitations and experiences of IPV service providers when delivering services to undocumented victims of IPV. It is critically important to understand the perspectives of IPV service providers, for they can inform state policy that culturally responsive practices and policies need to be implemented to remove structural and institutional barriers impeding IPV services providers — such as social workers — from delivering services to the undocumented populations.

Drawing on twelve in-depth interviews with IPV service providers, the study was conducted to examine how the legal status of the victim influences the way providers deliver their (in)formal services and resources. The snowballing sampling method was used to recruit participants from eight IPV agencies in Orange County (OC), California. OC was an ideal location because it has a relatively high number of undocumented people (289,000), who represent 9.6% of the total undocumented population in the United States (Public Policy Institute of California [PPIC], 2011).

Findings reveal that IPV service providers encounter social and structural barriers when delivering IPV services to the undocumented population, despite those services being "openly" accessible to them. Specifically, IPV service providers face various obstacles such as immigration policies (e.g., public charge), which limit them from providing formal support to undocumented clients; they are further restricted by the politics of the IPV agency (i.e., how funding is being allocated); and they also lack cultural humility.

This study explores the limitations of the IPV service providers when delivering formal resources to undocumented people before, during, and after an abusive relationship. Three key findings were made manifest in this study: (1) restrictive eligibility and selection process; (2) fear of deportation while accessing services; and (3) lack of valid social security number. Overall, the findings suggested that a restrictive process aimed to eliminate undesirable (prospective) clients creates structural barriers and politics within the IPV agency, which, in turn, inform how the agency provides services to undocumented victims of IPV.

Literature Review

A large body of literature demonstrates that the immigrant population in the US has limited access to formal resources such as social, legal, and health services, as well as basic human and social capital resources (Fuchsel & Murphy, 2012; O'Neal & Beckman, 2016; Runner et al., 2009).

While institutional systems in society are, in part, instruments of oppression that exclude vulnerable populations from accessing services and resources in various sectors, the undocumented status of an individual can add another layer of exclusion and social marginalization.

The legal status of immigrant women could influence how they understand and perceive their IPV, how they access resources in the US, and how they should respond to law enforcement regarding the nature and severity of their abuse (Erez et al., 2017). The persistent lack of formal and material resources leads them to find informal alternatives to seek assistance through their immigrant community organizations that offer a sense of "physical security, social standing, and legal stability" (Erez et al., 2017, p. 50). Their inability to seek external support, such as government and social service agencies, is influenced by their negative experiences with the legal system in the US, which produces a lack of trust in the law enforcement agency, government authorities, and immigration policies (Erez et al., 2017). Ingram et al. (2010) found similar responses from immigrant victims of IPV claiming that they fear and mistrust the legal system, especially when applying for legal services (e.g., restraining order), regardless of their eligibility.

Likewise, immigration status can cause complex situations immigrants have to face in their daily lives, especially when they encounter the criminal justice system (Erez et al., 2017). Just like US native-born citizens, noncitizens have basic constitutional rights such as freedom of religion and speech, equal protection, and the right to due process (American Civil Liberties Union [ACLU], 2018). However, noncitizens remain a vulnerable population as they face deportation at the federal and state level. With the increase of mass deportation throughout the years, immigrant women are reluctant to seek IPV services and report their abuse to the criminal justice system due to the fear of deportation for themselves, their family, or their partner (Real, 2018). Beyond the fear of deportation and the lack of resources that victims may encounter, the process of obtaining assistance from service providers to apply for legal protection and other legal documentation can be restricting and challenging, and thus, it can place the victim in a state of uncertainty (Ingram et al., 2010).

While undocumented immigrants often receive helpful support from the legal and social service providers, they also encounter "humiliation and frustration at the hand of police officers, legal services personnel, and social service providers" when seeking assistance for filing and processing their legal documents (e.g., Violence Against Women Act petition; Ingram et al., 2010, p. 869). In other words, service providers in the law and social service sectors instill stereotypes and — implicit and explicit — biases in their line of work when assisting immigrant victims of IPV (Ingram et al., 2010; Runner et al., 2009). According to Reina and Lohman (2015), public service provider's attitudes and behaviours toward immigrants of IPV "reflect our society's perceptions of domestic violence and the status of women in U.S. society" (p. 484). Notably, state and federal policies that provide economic support to women are reinforced with the notion of who is "deserving" versus who is "underserving" of public assistance. Here, women who are single, poor, of immigrant status, who lack healthcare, and who have little to no education are viewed as "underserving" (Clark et al., 2014). Beyond the legal and social challenges that undocumented immigrants may encounter, IPV services providers, like undocumented immigrant clients, can confront cultural barriers.

Cultural barriers are not only hampering the immigrant population when seeking services, but they can also manifest themselves within the IPV agencies. IPV agencies, like legal and social service agencies, often fail to incorporate "immigrant-related cultural and linguistic competencies" (Erez et al., 2017, p. 51). Scholars have considered how race/ethnicity, culture, and legal status influence immigrant victims' ability to access IPV services (Ingram et al., 2010). Linguistic and cultural barriers are major obstacles that prevent victims from seeking governmental, medical, and social assistance due to their incapacity to understand and communicate in English (O'Neal & Beckman, 2016). Most importantly, the lack of cultural sensitivity and therefore humility among service providers may prevent undocumented women from seeking formal assistance.

Moreover, IPV agencies conflate the meaning of IPV as a "homogenous" problem, where IPV service providers assume that every victim of IPV experiences similar challenges in terms of abuse, services, and needs (Burman et al., 2004; Faria, 2020). The implication of homogenizing an IPV population is that agencies ignore the cultural needs and socioeconomic position of minorities and people of colour, and this produces structural inequalities based on sexism, racism, and classism within the IPV agency

(Burman et al., 2004; Faria, 2020). Essentially, previous scholarship has demonstrated the plight of immigrant victims of IPV experiences, but it still lacks understanding on how IPV service providers encounter structural and cultural barriers within the agency when they deliver services to undocumented victims.

Methods

The present study used a qualitative design and conducted 12 in-depth interviews with IPV service providers in OC to analyze the experiences of delivering services to undocumented victims of IPV. The research ethic approval was obtained from the Institutional Review Board. Participants had to be 18 years of age or older, and an employee/volunteer from an IPV agency who worked for more than six months and directly with undocumented victims of IPV.

The recruitment of participants began with one IPV agency in OC. The other participants were recruited from other agencies using snowball sampling method, both in-person or email. For the in-person recruitment, the verbal recruitment script was used to inform potential participants about the study, ask for their participation, as well as collect their contact information to follow up and schedule an interview. Google Forms were used for the email recruitment as a method to collect their name, email, phone number, the name of the site they currently volunteer or work for, and finally the location and time they wanted to meet.

Each interview was approximately 45 minutes to an hour and verbal consent was requested before each interview. The interview guide included open-ended questions that were translated into English and Spanish based on the linguistic preference of the participant: seven interviews were conducted in English and two in Spanish. One interview was conducted in code-switching language using both English and Spanish. All participants received $30 in cash to compensate them for their participation time at the end of the interview. All interviews were audio recorded with the verbal consent of the participant, and each interview recording was transcribed verbatim for analysis. At the end of the interview, all participants completed a 3-minute demographic and characteristic profession questionnaire that asked about their education, race, age, and other characteristics.

Table 13.1: Participants' Demographics

Provider's pseudonym	Gender	Age	Ethnicity/ Race	Highest Level of Education	First Language	Job Title	Type of Practice	Years of Experience at Current Site
Janet	Woman	25	Mexican-American	College	Spanish	Legal Department Manager	Non-profit	2 years
Tiffany	Woman	24	Vietnamese-American	College	Vietnamese	Legal Advocate	Non-profit	2.5 years
Emily	Woman	26	Mexican-American	College	Spanish	Legal Advocate	Non-profit	2 years
Brenda	Woman	30	Mexican-American	College	Spanish	Housing Navigator/ Case Manager	Non-profit	3 years
Rosa	Woman	40	Mexican	College	English	Volunteer	Non-profit	2 years
Alexandra	Woman	40	Mexican	Some College	Spanish	Volunteer	Community clinic or health care	13.5 years
Maria	Woman	31	Mexican-American	College	Spanish	Confidential Campus Advocate	College (Women's Centre)	1.5 years
Rochelle	Woman	35	Egyptian-American	Grad/Prof School	Spanish	Prevention & Education Manager	Non-profit	5.5 years
Sofia	Woman	42	Mexican	College	English	Volunteer	Non-profit	1.5 years
Vicky	Woman	51	Mexican	High School	N/A	Founder/ President	Non-profit	10 years

N = 10

Note. These stages can vary across IPV agencies and does not represent all the services and programs they offer.

Braun and Clarke's (2006) coding technique was used to analyze the verbatim transcripts of the audio recordings through thematic analysis. Thematic analysis is a process that identifies themes and patterns by re-reading the raw data through line-by-line coding, examining the codes to identify significant broader patterns or themes, re-reviewing themes, and then developing a detailed analysis of each theme (Braun & Clarke, 2006). HyperRESEARCH, a software program, was also used to conduct selective coding for each participant's responses into key themes. There were two guiding research questions: (1) how do IPV agencies provide access to resources for undocumented victims of IPV; and (2) what types of barriers do undocumented victims of IPV face when trying to access resources before, during, and after the abusive relationship?

The demographic data of the participants included in the study are illustrated in Table 13.1. The participants' age ranged from 24 (the youngest) to 51 (the oldest) years old, with a mean age of 34.4 years. All participants self-identified as women; most were born in the US, with three participants who were born in Mexico and immigrated to the US between the ages of 17 and 25. However, those who were born in the US were overwhelmingly of Mexican origin (four participants), one was of Vietnamese descent, and another one was of Egyptian origin. One participant had a high school degree, one had some college education, seven obtained a college degree, and one completed her graduate program in social work. All participants but one spoke a second language. Occupation title varied across participants: three volunteers, two legal advocates, one legal department manager, one housing navigator/case manager, one confidential campus advocate, one prevention and education manager, and one founder/president. Most participants worked in a non-profit organizational setting, while one participant volunteered in a community clinic and another one worked at a university. Their number of years of experience at the site ranged from 2 to 13.5 years.

Findings

Victims of IPV go through various stages of development to successfully become a self-sufficient, independent person. Findings revealed three re-occurring themes: (1) restrictive eligibility and selection process among service providers; (2) fear of deportation while accessing services; and (3) lack of a valid social security number.

Figure 13.1: Stages of Development

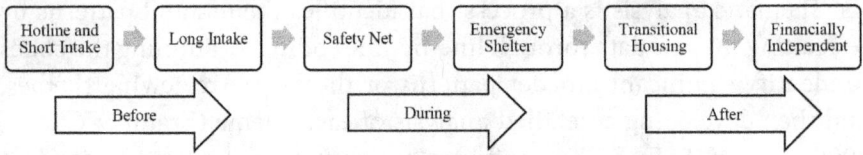

```
┌──────────┐   ┌──────────┐   ┌──────────┐   ┌──────────┐   ┌──────────┐   ┌──────────┐
│Hotline and│⇨ │Long Intake│⇨ │Safety Net │⇨ │Emergency │⇨ │Transitional│⇨ │Financially│
│Short Intake│  │          │  │          │  │ Shelter  │  │ Housing  │  │Independent│
└──────────┘   └──────────┘   └──────────┘   └──────────┘   └──────────┘   └──────────┘

    ┌──────────────────┐        ┌──────────────────┐        ┌──────────────────┐
    │      Before       ⟩       │      During       ⟩       │       After       ⟩
    └──────────────────┘        └──────────────────┘        └──────────────────┘
```

Note. These stages can vary across IPV agencies and do not represent all the services and programs they offer.

Figure 13.1 indicates the victim's journey when being accepted into the agency's program(s). The *before* stage consists of how restrictive the eligibility and selection process can be when a victim of IPV calls the IPV hotline and completes an intake. The *during* stage is when a victim of IPV is accessing services and enters the safety net (e.g., hotel) or emergency shelter. The *after* stage includes the victim moving into a transitional home and finally becoming financially independent. However, undocumented victims of IPV generally do not complete the last stage of development because they do not have a social security number.

Eligibility and Selection Process

IPV agencies have a mission to provide services and resources to anyone experiencing IPV, regardless of the victim's religion, gender identity, race, age, sexuality, disability, or legal status. However, these services are not tailored to accommodate every victim's individual needs, including un-documented victims of IPV. The selection and eligibility process of IPV for undocumented victims has become intentionally rigid and challenging to limit potential clients from accessing social and health services. The first stages of this restrictive process begin with the intake assessment process.

Depending on the agency's procedures, victims of IPV go through a lengthy "assessment" process and two short intakes that can last more than one hour. Rigid assessment measures consist of various questions that IPV hotline advocates ask potential clients before they can access the agency specific services such as therapeutic care, emergency shelter, temporary housing, advocacy services, and legal assistance. Questions include the client's mental health background, whether they consumed or smoked any illegal substances (e.g., marijuana), or if they have been arrested in the past.

The intake and assessment process negatively affects the ability of undocumented victims of IPV to access services. Essentially, IPV agencies, as one participant explained, are seeking "perfect candidates." A perfect candidate has no prior criminal record, has no drug abuse history, has the physical and mental capacity to work, and has legal status in the US. Such candidate supports the agency's reputation to obtain a higher success rate (e.g., participants completing the program). Completing the program is a form of success measurement that allows agencies, in order to obtain funding, to calculate how effective their programs are in helping their clients recover from their abusive relationships.

Domestic violence agencies need to report monthly and annually to both the federal and state governments regarding the services and resources they have provided toward the population they currently serve, and the overall outcomes of each intervention and educational programs the agency offers. Such results depend on how much funding and resources are allocated to the respective non-profit organizations. One participant urgently stated, "We have to show them [the government] how much progress we made to receive additional funding and grants because if not, our programs get cut." Non-profit organizations heavily rely on federal and state funding for the programs to function and keep running.

Essentially, the success rate is measured in two ways. The first is financial. Here, the funding is secured by philanthropists and the government, and for the most part, the measure of success is proven by and tied to numbers, such as "how many clients do you successfully serve? How many [victims] receive restraining orders, [and] how many presentations did you give." The second marker of success is determined by the actual client (e.g., victim). One participant clarified,

> We would basically set up what success looks like for them.
> Success for them may not be leaving the relationship. Like
> success for them is getting a job and making their own
> money. Or success could mean going to a shelter and then
> getting their own housing.

Thus, searching for the "perfect candidate" to successfully fulfill the program could potentially guarantee future funding. The eligibility process of IPV agencies opens doors for "perfect candidates" who have the required qualifications — legal status, no criminal background, or employment — while weeding out those who would harm the IPV agencies' success rate, respective reputation, and future funding.

Fear of Deportation While Accessing Services

During the process of receiving services, the fear of deportation was paramount for IPV service providers when supporting undocumented victims of IPV. Being undocumented can cause vulnerabilities such as experiencing isolation, violence, limited accessibility to resources, social, legal, and economic marginalization, and most importantly, immigration arrest and deportation.

Interviewed participants voiced concerns among the undocumented clientele who sought services and then left the IPV centre or program due to the fear of deportation. Immigrant women with and without legal status lack knowledge of their legal rights and services that are available to them. The undocumented victim has no way of knowing what type of services are safe to apply and receive, without experiencing legal and social consequences. Therefore, owing to the fear of deportation, in addition to sheer ignorance, undocumented victims are more likely to refuse the services to avoid legal prosecution and possible deportation. For instance, one participant expressed frustration on how undocumented victims seemingly and voluntarily refuse to receive support from the agency:

> We cannot help them because sometimes the victim does not stop being afraid of being deported. They arrive [at the agency] and ask for help, and they say they are undocumented. Then, they do not return. Even if you contact them, they do not want help.

The testimony demonstrates the inability for IPV agencies to provide services to undocumented clients, who are avoiding uncertain legal or social consequences. However, there are instances where the victim does seek services but faces another type of barrier: the U.S. Immigration and

Customs Enforcement agency (ICE). Since President Donald Trump took office in 2017, ICE has become prevalent in criminal and civil courts — including family law court — according to most participants. Some participants indicated that there has been an increase of immigration arrests in courthouses and a decrease of reporting crimes (e.g., IPV, sexual assault, etc.) and attending court hearings by immigrants, given the immigration and legal consequences they might encounter when coming forward to the police. Undocumented victims of IPV who do not qualify or apply for U nonimmigrant status (U-visa) and T nonimmigrant status (T-visa) visas — which legally provides immigration relief — are more vulnerable for deportation (ACLU, 2018). The U-visa is given to victims of criminal activity (e.g., mental or physical abuse), while T-visa is provided to victims of human trafficking (U.S. Citizenship and Immigration Services [USCIS], 2018).

Moreover, the process of filing a restraining order and Violence Against Women Act (VAWA) visa or the U-visa consists of undocumented clients "being inside of the legal system," as one participant explains it, where their legal and social identity can be shared with the immigration authorities by the court or legal system; thus, these undocumented clients are running a significant risk of being located and detained. In essence, according to one participant, undocumented victims are taking the risk to trade off their personal identity to obtain a protection order against their abusers.

Although the U-visa, T-visa, and VAWA offer relief from deportation, one participant clarified that once the undocumented victim applies for one of these visas, the victims "just handed over all of [their] information to immigration services" as ICE is responsible for receiving and approving the visa applications. As for the restraining orders, the participant further revealed that there have been cases in California where police departments (and even the abuser) have cooperated with ICE by sharing the court hearing dates, home addresses, and personal information of the undocumented victims who are pursuing a case against their abuser. Depending on the state, police departments are often told by police unions to cooperate with federal immigration agents to conduct arrest in courthouses, because "some law enforcement agencies [are] now refus[ing] to carry out immigration holds ('detainers') on noncitizens with whom they come into contact" (ACLU, 2018, p. 9).

Such compromise consists of ICE agents waiting outside the courthouse to potentially detain undocumented immigrants, a situation that increases their state of vulnerability even when the client is trying to "lay low." This process of entering their name into the court system deters potential undocumented clients from seeking support and services, with the significant implication of forcing the victims to return to their perpetrators. This creates more difficulty for undocumented women who have children, because they are more likely to fear that ICE agents will deport them back to their home country while leaving their children with an abusive father.

Sanctuary states and cities represent a space where immigration laws "aim to provide a measure of protection for unauthorized residents" from being questioned about their immigration status (Villazor, 2008). For instance, one participant expressed that sanctuary cities are a form of protection that bars police officers from detaining undocumented victims of IPV to interrogate them about their immigration status. She depicted a scenario that reveals the unintended consequences of a city that does not offer sanctuary, such as Los Alamitos in OC, which caused social unrest in the city, as well as jeopardizing lives of undocumented victims. For undocumented victims, the outcome of a city not being a sanctuary is the separation of family members, especially in mixed-status families or couples where the victim is undocumented and the partner is a legal resident or a natural-born citizen. There are also other types of legal administrative requirements that the undocumented victim must go through, such as completing immigration paperwork for the federal VAWA visa or the U-visa. Another participant also indicated that the legal court system is currently requiring that their clients show concrete and physical evidence of abuse in order to avoid deportation:

> It's really important for them [bruises] to be visible. Immigration courts are denying application very easily and if it does get denied, they [victims] are more likely to get an order of deportation. We're encouraging clients to have as much information, and physical [abuse] is the most

common type of abuse. If everything [is] emotional abuse, the case won't make it compared to a physical one. It's more likely that they might take the other one [physical case] just because it depends on the type of abuse.

The overall consequences of not establishing a strong case when filing for the VAWA visa or U-visa can result in the undocumented victim to discontinue seeking further services from the agency. The USCIS (2018) implemented the 28 June 2018 *Policy Memorandum* that altered the procedures in which courts operate on its basis of public safety with regards to immigration applications that are submitted for the purpose of seeking legal status.

Currently, the US Immigration courts are persistently denying applications that do not present evidence of physical harm from the abuse. Such violence must be conveyed in a physical manner for the judges to declare that the victim suffered abuse, which is part of the evidence that undocumented victims need to submit when seeking lawful permanent residence. Overall, this weeding-out process could prevent victims from seeking legal status; but this policy also becomes a powerful tool to minimize the pool of undocumented victims seeking legal status in the US, despite the ample support of the IPV service providers.

Lack of a Valid Social Security Number

All IPV service providers identified that the lack of a valid social security number was a significant barrier for undocumented victims to overcome, after the partial completion of their respective IPV programs. Being undocumented in the US brings social stigma, isolation, and a lack of government assistance, in addition to the inability to obtain a valid social security number. Without a valid social security number, undocumented immigrants are not able to obtain legal employment. Nevertheless, some of them work informally for employers who do not request a social security number; however, the unauthorized worker is often paid low wages, experiences unsafe working conditions, and suffers labour exploitation in exchange for a source of income (Enriquez, 2019).

The IPV service providers found that undocumented clients were unable to transition to the next step of the IPV program, because they were unable to obtain a job to secure financial stability and independence. Participants explained that there was an ethical dilemma within the IPV agencies. Questions arose whether advocates should discontinue providing IPV services, stop providing protection after clients leave the agency, or allow undocumented victims in the transitional housing program, even when 70% of rent funding came from the government. One participant elaborated:

> The ethical dilemma lies within the agency. [D]o you collect the funds from work that's under the table? Because if you do that, you are putting this person at risk…. You're having them work under the table, but they are not awarded those same protections that they had in your [emergency] shelter. You're forcing them to work under the table. They're being put at risk because now they must go and secure an income somehow when they legally don't have the ability to do that. They're risking deportation.

The participant conveyed concerns beyond an ethical and moral issue, by underscoring a systemic problem within an agency that is designed to support only certain victims to succeed. Conversely, another participant stated that the most significant barrier was the difficulty to get a job, although this was not an insurmountable problem.

> Part of my job was working with participants who were coming into emergency shelters and then, finding out where they're going to go in 45 days. Is it a bigger barrier when you have a mother who doesn't have status [and] is not able to work? Yea, it is a bigger barrier, but it's not impossible and yet right now for transitional it's a little bit different depending on the program that you're trying to transition [in] to. Their requirements might be that you become employed within 30 days or that you are already employed so that you can sustain your transitional housing.

However, the participant also pointed out that there are programs that require clients to satisfy certain "requirements," such as having a current job or becoming employed within a specific time frame. Such requirements could be challenging for some or all clients who are undocumented, because they cannot find an employer who can hire them without work authorization or a green card. Nevertheless, the percentage of undocumented victims transitioning to the next step, that is, transitional housing, was unknown.

Although it is difficult to gauge how many undocumented victims successfully transitioned into the last step in the program, other IPV service providers expressed distress when undocumented clients were unable to receive assistance from the IPV shelter during their transition process. Instead, the IPV shelter personnel would refer the undocumented client to another IPV shelter/agency. However, the referred IPV agency could not guarantee transitional shelter, causing the undocumented client to be in a state of uncertainty. For example, another participant stated,

> For us to be able to give them the proper referrals because I know a lot of the times these clients do want to file [the referral] but I feel that's where our services just like kind of cut out and it's like here I [give] you the resources on what you can potentially apply for, what you could do, and some safety planning. Yeah, that's it.

There is no support system in place after the transition from emergency shelter to transitional housing. Essentially, there is a stopping point that ends at the "referral" stage. This stage holds limited opportunity and mobility to access needed resources. As the participant stated, the services are "cut out" and the undocumented clients must fend for themselves and see what other resources are best for their health and financial and social stability by seeking informal support (e.g., community, friends, etc.). Therefore, the victim must obtain a job to maintain their place in the shelter. Essentially, having a job would make them independent and self-reliable. But, if the client failed to complete the program, there is limited access to alternative shelters. Similarly, another advocate expressed,

The reality is that most IPV survivors never get to step into a shelter. It is ok if we put an undocumented survivor in 30-day emergency shelter, but what happen[s] after? They don't have a job, or they don't have a social security [number]. Even if they do have a job, they are vulnerable to be fired at any given point. Some transitional shelters … do require their clients to have [legal] status because these agencies require that the victim pays some kind of rent. [T]o pay rent you have to be able to have a source of income and if you are undocumented and you have a job, it's like they are enabling you to break the law. Those type of services are great for some people, but it won't work for undocumented immigrants.

The consequences of not obtaining formal employment are factors that explain why many undocumented victims do not transition to the shelter. The risk of having a job causes undocumented victims to break the law and face legal and immigration repercussions such as deportation. In contrast, a victim who is not employed would be potentially barred from completing the final stages of the IPV program, that is, becoming financially independent. Overall, the IPV agencies (in)directly adopt a bureaucratic system that imposes barriers on undocumented victims throughout the program and, thereby, hinders their ability to recover from abuse. This structure not only limits clients' welfare but contradicts IPV organizational mission to serve all demographics regardless of legal status and state of condition.

Discussion

In this chapter, the experiences of IPV service providers show that IPV services are not accessible to undocumented victims of IPV due to the agency's structural — both internal and external — and political barriers. The structural barriers that IPV service providers experience include rigid agency protocols and restrictive eligibility criteria when admitting clients, which, in turn, contribute to undocumented clients' exclusion and inaccessibility of services and resources. Meanwhile, political barriers are driven by punitive immigration policies that directly influence how IPV service providers decide to serve undocumented clients. The study identified three themes: (1) restrictive eligibility and selection processes; (2) agency and client fear of deportation while accessing services; and (3) lack of valid social security number. The restrictive eligibility and selection process occurs before the IPV agency allows clients to access their services. Often, the agency is searching for the "perfect candidate" who has no prior criminal record, no drug abuse, and is a US citizen or a permanent resident in the US. This allows the victim to work legally without facing prosecution from the law. This ideal candidate enables the agency to obtain a high success rate with respect to clients completing the program, which then translates into receiving further funding from the state and the federal government.

Moreover, the fear of deportation was a paramount concern for IPV service providers when offering services to undocumented clients. IPV service providers experience the effects of immigration policies that prevent them from delivering services. Undocumented victims are reluctant to apply for specific legal protection, such as a VAWA visa or a restraining order, due to the fear of deportation. As a result, IPV service providers are very cautious about the type of services they are promoting and delivering for fear of causing legal harm to their clients. Finally, the absence of a valid social security number is a significant impediment that IPV service providers face when clients are transferred to transitional housing after completing their terms in the emergency shelter. Various shelters require their clients to work, but undocumented clients are unable to do so without a valid social security number. Often, the undocumented clients are then referred to other IPV agencies or are cut from the program since they are unable to become lawful employees. These findings supplement the gaps in literature and raise important questions for social work practice and field education.

The research findings suggest that social work service providers must become aware of their service delivery and cultural responsiveness to diverse groups of undocumented immigrants who are economically, socially, and politically marginalized. In theory, social work practice promotes services to all clients regardless of one's legal status as defined by the National Association Social Worker (NASW) *Code of Ethics* (2022). However, there needs to be attention to uncertain legal and ethical challenges arising (e.g., public charge) from oppressive systems that shape the experiences of how undocumented immigrants receive and respond to services, while the same systems hinder social workers' ability and practice to provide formal support to the undocumented population. Further research and continued discussion about unjust immigration policies and discriminatory ideologies from institutionalized systems are necessary for social workers to assist undocumented immigrants to overcome political, social, and legal barriers when accessing IPV services and other social services. Although the study captured new insights on the scarcity of resources, there are some limitations that need to be discussed.

Limitations

One limitation of this study is the lack of diverse study participants with respect to race, gender, and location of the IPV agencies in the OC area. Most of the participants came from a Latinx background, specifically from Mexico. However, the Latinx participants in this study were able to provide an "insider" perspective since some participants were once undocumented, and one participant was an IPV survivor with close ties to an immigrant community. Moreover, the location of the IPV agency is not representative of all agencies in California or throughout the US. The demographic location of other agencies might have different approaches in serving the undocumented population. Nevertheless, OC is an excellent location to conduct research as it is one of the counties with a large immigrant population. While the results are not generalizable due to the small sample, new insights on the lived realities of service providers who work with undocumented clients are provided.

Conclusion

This chapter provides insight into the perspective of IPV service providers on offering accessible services to the undocumented individuals who face abuse by a former or current partner; it also exposes the limitations these providers encountered in and outside of their agency that hindered them from delivering services. The IPV agencies should acknowledge societal factors that may affect the lives of undocumented clientele and consider their cultural and racial background when delivering IPV services. It is important to understand how the client's immigration status influences the choices and decision making of IPV service providers and, consequently, affects how resources are distributed to clients without legal status. Overall, the data collected can be used as an entry point, for future research, to better understand the lived experiences of undocumented migrants as a vulnerable population. There is a need for social work field education programs to acknowledge the importance of immigration status as a component of diversity.

REFERENCES

American Civil Liberties Union [ACLU]. (2018). How immigration arrests at courthouses are undermining the justice system. *Human Rights Documents Online.* https://doi.org/10.1163/2210-7975_hrd-9970-20180238

Braun, V., & Clarke, V. (2006). Using thematic analysis in psychology. *Qualitative Research in Psychology, 3*(2), 77–101. https://doi.org/10.1091/1478088706qp063oa

De Faria, L. (2020). Intimate partner violence in Hispanic communities. *Intimate Partner Violence,* 37–40. https://doi.org/10.1007/978-3-030-55864-2_6

Del Real, D. (2018). Toxic ties: The reproduction of legal violence within mixed-status intimate partners, relatives, and friends. *International Migration Review, 53*(2), 548–570. https://doi.org/10.1177/0197918318769313

Enriquez, L. E. (2019). Border-hopping Mexicans, law-abiding Asians, and racialized illegality. *Relational Formations of Race,* 257–277. https://doi.org/10.2307/j.ctvcwp0dz.21

Erez, E., Adelman, M., & Gregory, C. (2017). Intersections of immigration and domestic violence. *Feminist Theories of Crime,* 293–317. https://doi.org/10.4324/9781315094113-14

Fuchsel, C. L., Murphy, S. B., & Dufresne, R. (2012). Domestic violence, culture, and relationship dynamics among immigrant Mexican women. *Affilia, 27*(3), 263–274. https://doi.org/10.1177/0886109912452403

Ingram, M., McClelland, D. J., Martin, J., Caballero, M. F., Mayorga, M. T., & Gillespie, K. (2010). Experiences of immigrant women who self-petition under the Violence Against Women Act. *Violence Against Women, 16*(8), 858–880. https://doi.org/10.1177/1077801210376889

Marrs Fuchsel, C. L., & Brummett, A. (2020). Intimate partner violence prevention and intervention group-format programs for immigrant Latinas: A systematic review. *Journal of Family Violence, 36*(2), 209–221. https://doi.org/10.1007/s10896-020-00160-6

National Association of Social Workers [NASW]. (2022). *Read the Code of Ethics.* https://www.socialworkers.org/About/Ethics/Code-of-Ethics/Code-of-Ethics-English

O'Neal, E. N., & Beckman, L. O. (2016). Intersections of race, ethnicity, and gender. *Violence Against Women, 23*(5), 643–665. https://doi.org/10.1177/1077801216646223

Public Policy Institute of California [PPIC]. (2011, July). *Unauthorized immigrants in California estimates for counties*. https://www.ppic.org/wp-content/uploads/content/pubs/report/R_711LHR.pdf

Reina, A. S., & Lohman, B. J. (2015). Barriers preventing Latina immigrants from seeking advocacy services for domestic violence victims: A qualitative analysis. *Journal of Family Violence, 30*(4), 479–488. https://doi.org/10.1007/s10896-015-9696-8

Runner, M., Yoshihama, M., & Novick, S. (2009). Intimate partner violence in immigrant and refugee communities: Challenges, promising practices and recommendations. *PsycEXTRA Dataset*. https://doi.org/10.1037/e601452012-001

U.S. Citizenship and Immigration Services [USCIS]. (2017, August 25). *Victims of human trafficking and other crimes*. USCIS. https://www.uscis.gov/humanitarian/victims-human-trafficking-other-crimes/victims-criminal-activity-u-nonimmigrant-status/victims-criminal-activity-u-nonimmigrant-status

U.S. Citizenship and Immigration Services [USCIS]. (2018, June 28). *Policy memorandum*. https://www.uscis.gov/sites/default/files/document/memos/2018-06-28-PM-602-0050.1-Guidance-for-Referral-of-Cases-and-Issuance-of-NTA.pdf

Villazor, R. C. (2008). What is sanctuary. *SMU Law Review, 61*(1), 133–158. https://scholar.smu.edu/smulr/vol61/iss1/8

PART IV:
New Developments and Approaches in Field Education

Field Education, Disability, and COVID-19: Navigating a Virtual World

Kaltrina Kusari

In the last year, we have seen immense shifts in our local communities, as well as globally, due to the COVID-19 pandemic. In Canada, the first case of COVID-19 was recorded in Ontario on 25 January 2020, and the World Health Organization declared a pandemic on 11 March 2020 (CTV, 2021). Following this, Ontario and Alberta were the first two provinces in Canada to declare a "State of Emergency" (CTV, 2021). Attempting to "flatten the curve," governments asked people to practice physical distancing to stop the spread of the virus. In Alberta, 571,806 COVID-19 cases and 4,321 deaths have been recorded as of May 2022 (Alberta, 2022). In addition to loss of life, COVID-19 has also had social and economic impacts as many people lost their jobs and had to isolate from their natural support systems.

Among all aspects of society impacted by the COVID-19 measures was higher education (Archer-Kuhn et al., 2020; Day et al., 2021). Schools and Faculties of Social Work had to adjust course delivery to respect public health restrictions (Canadian Association for Social Work Education [CASWE], 2020; Tortotelli et al., 2020). This posed unique challenges for field education as many students had to cancel their practicum placements and/or find ways to complete their hours through remote work. Effective 20 March 2020, the Canadian Association for Social Work Education

(CASWE) asked that all "field education placements be suspended and/or moved to Remote Learning Plans (RLP)" (2020, n.p.). In addition, they noted that "students who have completed 75% of the required placement hours to a satisfactory level will be evaluated as having met the field placement requirements" (n.p.). This decision offered uniform guidelines for Schools/Faculties of Social Work to follow.

Although data from Canadian Social Work programs do not exist, at the very beginning of the pandemic, the US Council on Social Work Education (2020) administered a survey to the deans and directors of MSW and BSW programs (N = 197) and field directors (N = 235). Key findings suggest that only 3% of student placements were unaffected by the pandemic, thus most students had to modify their placements and/or cancel them altogether. To this end, 72.8% of deans and directors and 67.5% of field directors communicated that they had a continuity plan if further disruptions to field placements were to occur (Council on Social Work Education [CSWE], 2020).

Studies that examine the impact of COVID-19 on field education in Canada give us a glimpse into both the challenges and opportunities brought about by the shift to virtual course delivery (Day et al., 2021; Drolet et al., 2020; Kourgjantakis & Lee, 2020). In this chapter, I contribute to this body of scholarship by offering key insights I gained while supervising two social work practicum students during the 2020 winter and the fall terms. Considering that social work field education is varied, my reflections offer specific insights into the impact of COVID-19 within the disability sector. I write these reflections to centre social justice goals during a period of uncertainty that was brought on by COVID-19. To do this, I begin by grounding myself in critical disability theories. I will then provide an overview of the importance of field education in social work and discuss the impact of COVID-19 on field education. Lastly, I will share key insights related to my experience of COVID-19 as a field supervisor, the construction of disability, and the use of Information and Communication Technologies to facilitate practicum placements.

Critical Disability Studies

Critical disability studies (CDS) refer to a varied set of approaches which seek to engage with disability as a cultural, political, and social phenomenon (Goodley, 2013; Schalk, 2017). CDS holds that "disability is *the* space from which we think through a host of political, theoretical, and practical issues that are relevant to all" (Goodley et al., 2012, p.3, emphasis in original text). As such, CDS seeks to scrutinize "not bodily or mental impairments but the social norms that define particular attributes as impairments, as well as the social conditions that concentrate stigmatized attributes in particular populations" (Minich, 2016, p. 3).

CDS is largely informed by Foucault, who highlighted how relations of power impact the way a given society constructs disability (Carlson, 2001; Tremain, 2017). Grounded in this, critical disability scholars note that the sociopolitical construction of disability has historical roots and is shaped by the context in which we live. Goodley (2013) recognizes

> that we are living in a time of complex identity politics, of
> huge debates around the ethics of care, political and theo-
> retical appeals to the significance of the body, in a climate
> of economic downturn that is leading yet again to reformu-
> lations of what counts as disabled. (p. 632)

Therefore, CDS recognize that disability is not a fixed identity category because anyone can acquire a disability during their lifetime (Garland-Thomson, 2002). In addition, rather than merely acknowledging how people with disabilities are constructed, CDS scholars seek to transform the conditions which oppress people with disabilities. They do this through relying on an interdisciplinary approach, often drawing links to other critical theories such as critical race theory, postcolonial theory, and queer theory (Hall & Zalta, 2019; Sleeter 2010).

CDS is an important framework to use within social work because, despite their commitment to social justice, social workers are often critiqued for their reliance on medical models of disability (Hughes, 2017; Shakespeare, 2006). The medical model of disability views disability as an individualized, medical concern, thus directing attention to diagnosis, treatment, cure, and recovery while neglecting the potential of people with disabilities (Hughes, 2017; Shakespeare, 2006). In addition, many scholars have called for "a critical renewal of the profession" (Morley & Clark, 2020, p. 1049), which focuses on challenging neoliberal practices in order to depoliticize social work practice and encourage managerialism within social work agencies (Hanesworth, 2017; Morley & Clark, 2021). Indeed, Ayala et al. (2018) note that even prior to COVID-19, field education within social work was in "crisis" because of budget cuts, increased enrollments, and fewer practicum opportunities (Ayala et al., 2018). Thus, being grounded in CDS, which questions neoliberal practices, was especially useful for both myself and the students as we experienced the shift to a virtual format and the changes that occurred to funding schemes.

Importance of Field Education

Field education is an important aspect of the social work degree in Canada, and internationally. In 2008, the Council on Social Work Education in the US recognized field education as a signature pedagogy for social work (CSWE, 2008). First coined by Shulman (2005), signature pedagogies refer to unique ways of teaching and learning used in a particular profession. Within the Canadian context, CASWE does not construct field education as a signature pedagogy but promotes "field education as a central component of social work education" (CASWE, 2021, n.p.). Field education is central to social work because it helps students develop their professional identities by allowing them to experience frontline work and interaction with clients (Archer-Kuhn et al., 2021; Wayne et al., 2013). For this reason, field education has received significant attention within social work, with most studies reinforcing the transformative role that field education can play in student learning (Barlow & Hall, 2007; Didham et al., 2011; Lam et al., 2007; Pooler et al., 2012; Svoboda et al., 2013).

Current studies also highlight limitations to current models of field education in social work (Archer-Kuhn, 2021; Boitel & Fromm, 2014). For example, Wayne et al. (2010) examined Shulman's criteria for signature pedagogy and argue that there are both congruence and disparities in how field education fits as a social work signature pedagogy. For example, there is congruence with social work students' requirement to complete field placements, but disparities with students' public performance and peer-to-peer accountability (Wayne et al., 2010). Similarly, Archer-Kuhn et al. (2021), in a mixed-methods study which explored the understanding of students, field education staff, and faculty members, suggest that while these stakeholders understand the importance of field education, they do not always agree as to what is signature pedagogy for social work.

Commenting on current limitations, scholars also suggest that many field placements are more concerned with risk-management than creating an environment where practicum students can engage in reflective practice (Hay et al., 2019). Student supervision, therefore, may often "be viewed as an ancillary activity when agencies are stretched thin" (Davis & Mirick, 2021, p. 3). Thus, social work students have expressed that many field placements lack a social justice lens (Archer-Kuhn et al., 2021). In addition, and most relevant to this paper, another critique is that there are certain fields of practice which are not integrated well within field education. In particular, a limited number of students complete field placements in the disability sector (Moyle, 2016; Roulstone, 2012). Scholars suggest that this could be because social work education and training continue to maintain an "us versus them" approach, which tasks social workers with fixing clients rather than working with them to challenge ableism (Meekosha & Soldatic, 2013; Roulstone, 2012). In addition, social work curriculum, more generally, lacks a focus on disability (Morgan, 2012; Moyle, 2016) which often leads social workers to perpetuate ableist practices and discourses (El-Lahib, 2020). As ableism was something obvious during COVID-19, it is important to consider the role of field education in challenging ableism perceptions.

Impact of COVID-19

Field education, like social work practice, is impacted by the contexts in which it occurs, and must respond accordingly. To respond to COVID-19, most social work placements had to transition to a virtual format, thus leading to new challenges for all those involved in this process (Dempsey et al., 2021). Studies suggest that field education is, under normal circumstances, a stressful encounter for students as they experience anxieties related to their decision-making abilities, establishing and maintaining boundaries, and the quality of relationship with the field supervisor (Baird, 2016; Goodyear, 2014; Knight, 2018). These stressors were heightened during the COVID-19 pandemic because of the disruption caused to field education and the public health crisis, which asked social workers to serve others while ensuring their own health and safety (Dempsey et al., 2021; Davis & Mirick, 2021; Farkas & Romaniuk, 2020).

Emerging research offers insights into the impact of COVID-19 measures on social work field education. Within the Canadian context, Schools/Faculties of Social Work were able to respond to the pandemic in innovative ways. Offering an overview of the impact of COVID-19 on social work education, Archer-Kuhn et al. (2020) recognize that relationships were impacted because of the uncertainty brought about by COVID-19. In addition, they note both challenges and opportunities that emerged with regard to pedagogy and collaboration. They highlight that clear and accurate communication with students, which was at times missing because of the chaos caused by COVID-19, was necessary to help students navigate the fear and uncertainty caused by the virus (Archer-Kuhn et al., 2020). Regarding field education, they discovered that a virtual self-directed practicum placement, which the faculty had started to pilot, "is a viable option to help support both student learning and relieve some of the pressures experienced by the field staff in trying to find enough agency placements" (Archer-Kuhn et al., 2020, p. 1016).

Drolet et al. (2020) also comment on the innovative approaches that emerged as field education transitioned to a virtual format. Specifically, they share how the Transforming the Field Education Landscape (TFEL) partnership, which was established in 2019, responded to the pandemic. TFEL is a project that aims to bring together various local and international stakeholders interested in exploring social work field education. During COVID-19, TFEL offered remote field education opportunities for students, allowing many faculty members and students to find innovative ways to carry out TFEL activities (Drolet et al., 2020). These activities included virtual partnership among collaborators of the program, networking opportunities for students, and mentorship opportunities. Importantly, Indigenous participants point to the emergence of an "Indigisphere" that allowed individuals to continue practicing Indigenous ways of knowing and doing in virtual format, whereas racialized students highlighted that those virtual spaces offered a safe space for them to engage in discussions around social work field education.

Kourgjantakis and Lee (2020) and Tortorelli et al. (2020) explain that among the opportunities created by the shift to a virtual format was the increasing use of simulation in field education. Tortorelli et al. (2020) offer findings from a scoping review of studies that examine the use of simulation in social work education. They note that simulation is fitting for practice education as it allows students to bring their own experiences into the classroom and offers them a chance to experiment with new ideas and activities (Tortorelli et al., 2020). In addition, simulation is an important way to integrate theory and practice, suggesting that the successful use of simulation during COVID-19 warrants exploring it as an alternate field placement option, even after the pandemic (Tortorelli et al., 2020).

Offering a more specific elaboration of simulation, Kourgjantakis and Lee (2020) describe "Practice Friday" as a useful tool for Master of Social Work students whose practicum placements were disrupted. Two groups of 10 MSW students met for 3.5 hours each Friday to engage in case formulation, assessments, intervention, and termination stages of a given case study. These cases were situated within the COVID-19 pandemic and the global anti-racist movement, thus their discussion helped "students enhance meta competence, including self-awareness, self-reflection, emotion regulation, and professional judgment" (p. 763).

All these studies highlight the importance of clear guidelines and communication among stakeholders involved in the field education process (Archer-Kuhn et al., 2020; Kourgjantakis & Lee, 2020; Tortotelli et al, 2020). Indeed, literature coming from outside of Canada also emphasizes the importance of clear communication. Dempsey et al. (2021), for example, relied on the concept of shared trauma to review how the Field Learning and Community Partnerships (FLCP) at New York University addressed challenges related to COVID-19. Among the key learnings for the FLCP, their paper suggests, was the importance of "providing clear and consistent communication to students in a timely manner" (p. 7). To this end, Morley and Clark (2020), with a focus on Australia, share that timely communication allowed Queensland University of Technology to continue offering placements with critical pedagogic approaches.

Reflections on Supervising Students During COVID-19

To add to the existing literature, I share in this chapter insights into the shifts that occurred in field education within a disability agency in Alberta, Canda. During the COVID-19 pandemic I supervised two BSW social work practicum students. Ari (pseudonym) was completing her practicum during the winter 2020 term and had to transition to a remote placement while Kaitlyn (pseudonym) completed her entire practicum remotely during the fall 2020 term. The activities that students completed were: calling clients for mental-health check-ins; attending and co-facilitating a parent-support group for parents of children with disabilities; co-facilitating a support and social group for adults (18+) with disabilities; and participating in advocacy work for people with disabilities who experience poverty. The agency where I worked had offices in two of the largest cities in Alberta — Calgary and Edmonton. While before the pandemic the offices worked mostly independently of each other, the move to online service delivery required us to coordinate more closely in order to offer streamlined services.

In general, transitioning to an online format was not difficult for me because I was familiar with both of the programs we used to make this transition, Zoom and Microsoft Teams. My experience as a supervisor, however, had its challenges. This is because in addition to keeping up to date and being familiar with the guidelines that our agency created, I had to remain updated of the guidelines set by the university. This meant that I spent hours outside of my usually work-time to make sure that I was being fair to Ari and that she had all the supports that she needed. While doing this, I had to ensure that I was still offering the necessary services to our clients on the one hand, and that I was taking care of myself and supporting my family, on the other, as we dealt with the uncertainty of the pandemic. I felt validated when I read about these tensions in emerging literature:

> As educators, we had to facilitate teaching and learning around crisis response, appropriate termination, and self-regulation as part of holistic competence in social work practice. As trained clinicians, we were pained by the loss of service to clients and the meaning of that loss for students and agency partners. (Dempsey et al., 2021, p. 2)

To balance my commitments to clients, students, my family, and myself, I chose to write about the dilemmas I was experiencing. Journaling is a key aspect of my commitment to reflexive practice, as it allows me to make sense of my feelings and thoughts and become aware of how my own biases and ways of being exacerbated or helped me cope with stressful situations. Indeed, existing literature points to the benefits of journaling, highlighting that writing about difficult situations we experience can facilitate cognitive processing (Ullrich & Lutgendorf, 2002). Studies also suggest that journaling can support the development of reflective practice for helping professionals as it allows them to dialogue with themselves (Billings, 2006; Woodbridge & O'Brian, 2017). Being aware of this, I committed to write about how I was feeling at the end of each workday. Knowing that I would have some time, at the end of the day, to reflect on the sudden shifts that were happening to my workspace, helped me navigate the rapidly changing reality of social work practice. These reflections, in particular, made me aware of how I relate to practicum students, which allowed me to foster meaningful supervision relationships in an online format.

I often feel the pressure of acting like a role model for the students I supervise, yet, at the same time, I tend to treat them as colleagues. This means that, like Archer-Kuhn et al. (2020), I found myself oscillating between (1) ensuring that Ari completes all her learning agreement tasks, and (2) telling myself that, when dealing with a pandemic, other things were more important than the learning agreement. As I dealt with these dilemmas, I was also acutely aware that "research has consistently shown that a supportive field instructor relationship is crucial to student learning. Indeed, student satisfaction has been directly linked to their perception of the quality of supervision being provided" (Dempsey et al., 2020, p. 4). Since I had already established a relationship with Ari, I decided to discuss these dilemmas with her and let her know why I thought completing the learning agreements was important while also recognizing the strain caused by COVID-19.

Establishing a relationship with Kaitlyn felt different because we had never met her in person. I had to be more intentional about the questions I asked, especially when it came to how she imagined her practicum and how COVID-19 had impacted her. In addition, establishing a relationship with her was complicated because of the tensions between the priorities of the leadership team at our agency and Kaitlyn's learning needs. Kaitlyn started her practicum in September, and the agency was awarded a grant around the same time. As part of this grant, the social services team were required to call all our clients (around 1,000) to ensure they were doing well and had their needs met. The families that were struggling with food insecurity and/or did not have access to technology were supported through food boxes and computers. The grant covered an important need, but the leadership team at the agency applied for it without asking the social services team if we had the capacity to cover such a need. This happened partly because there was fear that if we did not apply for all the grants available, we might not make it as an agency. When they realized that both social workers and community program coordinators were extremely busy with offering one-on-one support and facilitating online programs, they bypassed me and directly asked the student to make these calls. While Kaitlyn enjoyed making these calls because she was in direct touch with the clients, she expressed concern that this activity was not allowing her to engage in other aspects of her practicum.

Having read the literature which examines the role of funders in social service agencies (Harlow et al., 2013; Preston et al., 2019), I was aware that while the leadership team wanted to respond to funder needs, my role was to respond to the needs of the student. Thus, in addition to reaching out to my manager to state that such practices hinder student engagement in their practicum, this situation gave me a chance to ask Kaitlyn about how she balanced her own needs (in this case her learning needs) with the priorities set by the agency. I felt this was an important discussion because social workers often must navigate social service agencies which might not have the same values as they do (Harlow et al., 2013; Rogowski, 2011). Social service agencies are increasingly led by business-minded people whose first aim is to fulfill donor criteria, often to the detriment of field education (Preston et al., 2019). Indeed, the majority of those in the leadership team at our agency did not have a background in social work or a related profession.

Previous studies have recognized the impact of managerialism in field education. Within the Alberta context, Archer-Kuhn et al. (2020) note that "prior to COVID-19, due to our provincial economic cutbacks (Government of Alberta, 2020), we were seeing diminished community capacity and struggled with sufficient and adequate student field education opportunities" (p. 1012). In addition, some have argued that practicum students are often used as free labour and asked to respond to the priorities of agencies rather than their own learning needs. Considering this, Asakura et al., (2018) considered field educators as having to navigate "new managerial institutions and the values and daily practice of the profession" (p. 152). For me, this was the first time I was dealing with a huge discrepancy between what we had promised the student and what the leadership team was doing. This offered me a chance to reflect on how I could best navigate this situation while ensuring that I was responding to agency needs and student needs. Ultimately, other team members offered to make some of the calls that Kaitlyn was asked to make, so she could return to her other practicum activities.

The Construction of People with Disabilities

COVID-19 measures showcased that governments rarely considered the impact of such measures on people with disabilities. For example,

> when individuals are expected to use face masks and physically distance, people with hearing loss who cannot lip read or people with visual impairment who use guide dogs can find it difficult to follow these rules and as a result they might be stigmatised. (Shakespeare et al., 2021, p. 1332)

In Alberta, only those who need assistance with using a mask and/or are unable to wear a facemask due to a physical or mental limitation were exempt from wearing masks (Alberta Health Services [AHS], 2021). While other countries had specific guidelines for those who are deaf and/or hard of hearing, the Government of Alberta did not have such guidelines (AHS, 2021). In addition, there was a lack of public awareness about the exemption made for people with disabilities, often leading to stigma (Koshek et al., 2020).

As these measures came into effect, students became aware of how Alberta's government constructs people with disabilities. During this time, relying on CDS when supervising students was a key aspect of my work. During her practicum, Ari had been involved with initiatives seeking to advocate for the rights of people with disabilities; this gave her a chance to see the innovative ways through which disability agencies had responded to the challenges faced by people with disabilities. However, once the pandemic was announced, she noticed incongruences between the government's statements about the importance of inclusion of people with disabilities and their lack of attention to the needs of people with disabilities during COVID-19. Indeed, a report released by the Alberta Council of Disability Services notes that the Alberta Health Services lacked an understanding of disability services and was, therefore, not able to respond to the emerging needs of this sector (Alberta Council of Disability Services [ACDS], 2020).

Grounded in the intersectional lens adopted by CDS, Ari recognized that while people with disabilities were more vulnerable to COVID-19, this was not always because of their impairment, but because of the challenges that are associated with having a disability. That is, due to the stigma and discrimination that people with disabilities face, they are more likely to experience poverty and lack access to health and social services (Shakespeare et al., 2021). Interestingly, Ari was struck by how quickly clients adjusted to social distancing measures. Relying on CDS, however, helped her realize that people with disabilities adjusted well to COVID-19 measures because isolation is something that they experience on a daily basis. As such, they had coping mechanisms in place which enabled them to navigate the beginning of the pandemic a lot better than able-bodied people. Similarly to Ari's experience, Davis and Mirick (2021) report that students in the US who completed their practicums during the pandemic were better able to identify systemic issues. They conducted a survey with 1,522 BSW and MSW students in universities across the US, 565 of whom commented on completing their field placement remotely (Davis & Mirick, 2021). The key themes emerging from the survey suggest that students became aware of systemic issues social workers need to challenge. While students in existing studies highlighted the increased vulnerability experienced by those living in poverty, students under my supervision remarked on the disparities affecting people with disabilities.

I also noticed a difference between how Ari and Kaitlyn engaged with respect to the impact that COVID-19 had on the communities they live in: the pandemic allowed them both to discuss the importance of context in one's experiences. However, while Ari — whom I only had contact with during the first month of COVID-19 — believed that both service providers and clients were sharing the same experience, Kaitlyn was able to see how, although we were all impacted by COVID-19, those who were marginalized were more negatively impacted. Kaitlyn noted that while she was able to continue her education, for example, this was not the case for many people with disabilities who lacked access to adequate technology. I felt that she was able to see this partly because, as the pandemic went on, it became apparent that those who enjoy certain privileges in our society had more access to protective equipment and were more likely to work from home — both elements that shielded them from the pandemic (Allen, 2020; Chandler et al., 2021).

Although Ari and Kaitlyn had different understandings of how the pandemic impacted us, both students appreciated the use of a critical disability lens when working and advocating with people with disabilities. How critical disability studies engage with creating systemic change was an eye opener to them. At the beginning of her practicum, Ari had been more interested in direct practice because she found macro practice daunting; towards the end of her practicum, she was more interested in better understanding the role of policies in shaping social work practice. The shift that happened for Ari is addressed by McGuire and Lay (2018), who note the transformative power of field placements:

> In social work education, the learning process must both challenge previous inaccurate meanings as well as integrate new knowledge for competent social work practice. Educators must understand how knowledge is applied and what happens when new learning conflicts with previous knowledge or personal beliefs. (p. 523)

The Role of ICT in Field Education

A transition to an online format meant that Ari had to cut her practicum short and could not finish all the tasks that she had started to work on. For Kaitlyn, who completed her entire practicum online, remote delivery of services did not give her a chance to meet people with disabilities in person. I have found, as a supervisor, that the reluctance of social work students to work in the disability field is often lessened once they interact with people with disabilities. In-person interactions seem to be the best way to challenge some of the misconceptions that exist with regard to what social work within the disability field looks like. Yet, as has been recognized by other scholars, the transition to remote delivery of field education came with opportunities for innovation (Archer-Kuhn, 2020; Mian & Khan, 2020).

For the disability sector, transition to online service delivery meant that some of our services became more accessible for people with disabilities. Because I was most familiar with Zoom, one of the programs that I facilitated was the first one to transition to an online format. This was a weekly program which offered adults with disabilities the chance to socialize and attend workshops on topics that interested them. Before the pandemic, the program included social dinners, visits to museums and galleries, and volunteer opportunities. In addition, once a month, I offered personal development workshops with topics including unlearning negative behaviour, challenging ableism, and adapting yoga for people with mobility limitations. The week after we had started to work from home, I asked my own supervisor if I could facilitate this program through Zoom. Zoom was still a new concept at the time, but I was given permission to give it a try. The clients showed adaptability and quickly learned how to use Zoom as well as navigate other virtual supports. They also asked if they could invite friends who did not live in Calgary to join. A month after we started offering this program online, the group had become so large that we had to split it in two.

The increase in attendance pointed to two important factors. First, the fact that people with disabilities not only adapted quickly to virtual supports, but also found ways to engage others in programs was a testament to their adaptability and resourcefulness. This is in contrast to dominant discourses which merely construct people with disabilities as vulnerable. Second, those who attended this program suggested that a virtual format of programs and service delivery would be something that people with disabilities might benefit from, even after the pandemic. For example, program attendance was low during winter months in Calgary because sidewalks were not always cleared, thus making it difficult for those who use wheelchairs to get to the bus/office. In addition, those who used Calgary Transit Access, a public transportation service for people with disabilities

(Calgary Transit, 2021), noted that trips often took as long as two hours to get them from their homes to our office. Lastly, some of our past clients who had moved to areas which did not offer disability services were able to join our programs. For example, we had a family who had moved to a rural area in Nova Scotia join our weekly programs regularly. While we initially thought of virtual service delivery as a barrier, it turned out to be an innovative approach to service delivery. Other studies share similar insights. For example, an MSW student in Davis and Mirick's (2021) study shared that

> I believe we need to move toward having telehealth services more available for everyone's safety and well-being. ... [N] ot only is telehealth incredibly helpful during a time like this pandemic, but it would be beneficial in general for clients who feel sick or for clients with transportation or childcare concerns. (p. 11)

In addition to increased program attendance, using Information and Communication Technologies (ICT) made certain aspects of advocating for change easier during COVID-19. Rather than relying solely on support from local agencies, as it was the case before the pandemic, online advocacy campaigns included anyone in the province, and beyond. Indeed, the ACDS organized several town halls between September and December 2020 (ACDS, 2021), making it easier for people with limited mobility to attend, thus increasing the inclusion of people with disabilities. Many of the agencies I collaborated with when supporting clients also noted that reliance on ICT facilitated collaboration as it cut down travel time between agencies, and it helped service providers learn more about available resources. Similarly, Archer-Kuhn et al. (2020), when commenting on collaboration among field education staff, note that online meetings allowed their team to discover their "strength and confidence as we gravitated and clung to one another like magnets in a force field moving forward together, growing in shape and size with each passing hour, day and week" (p. 1013). In addition, Morley and Clark (2020) share that working from home allowed students to get involved in a broader range of practicum placements, including international social campaigns.

A virtual format gave Kaitlyn the chance to join the parent support group. The parent support group consisted of parents who had children with disabilities and met once a week, during the evening. In the year before the pandemic, attendance in the parent support group was low, with many parents sharing that while they felt the need for such a group, they could not find the time to attend. Many of them noted that although the meeting place rotated in order to include each quadrant of the city, with Calgary being so widespread, getting to the parent support group from one part of the city to the other took a long time. In addition, most parents who attended the in-person group did not feel comfortable having a student join their group. This was understandable since it had taken the group time to establish trust and feel safe enough to share their stories. In addition, even when parents felt comfortable to have students join for certain sessions, the students were often not able to join because the parent support group met in the evenings and that conflicted with the students' own schedules.

During the pandemic, a few factors came together to enable students to join the parent support group. First, the fact that Alberta was on a lockdown meant that everyone was at home during the evening, thus timing was not an issue. In addition, there was a shift that happened when the group moved online that allowed parents to feel comfortable having a student join their weekly meetings. While I am not sure what led to this shift, this was highly beneficial for Kaitlyn as she had a chance to learn directly from parents. Kaitlyn noted that being part of the parent support group allowed her to better understand the intricacies of living with a disability, and the fact that disability does not only impact the individual who experiences it, but their families as well. In addition, meeting virtually also meant that parents who joined the group were from various places in Alberta, and this gave Kaitlyn a chance to see the difference in service provision across the province. Among the key insights that she gained, was the fact that services offered in rural versus urban settings vary. Many parents who lived in rural areas noted the difficulties in finding caregivers for their children, realizing that many caregivers did not want to travel to rural areas.

Listening to parents' stories about their struggles and resilience highlighted for Kaitlyn the fact that funding offered for people with disabilities is often not enough to cover their basic needs. Hearing this directly from parents, whom she got to know over the four-month practicum, made a larger impact than simply reading about the difficulties that parents of children with disabilities face. Indeed, previous research suggests that students enjoy learning directly from those they serve, as evidenced in a recent study which examined the experiences of social work practicum students in Canada (Archer-Kuhn et al., 2021). When noting the importance of aligning social work knowledge, skills, and values "some participants identified service users as influencing and co-creating an effective learning environment in social work education" (Archer-Kuhn et al., 2021, p. 390). One of the students in a focus group shared that "I learn social work best when I'm learning from the people that we work with because the people that we work with are the closest, they know the best about our services because they are receiving them" (Archer-Kuhn, 2021, p. 391).

In addition to benefiting student learning, having Kaitlyn as part of the parent group was helpful for parents as well. Experiencing first-hand the dedication with which social work students approached their work, parents expressed their confidence in the next generation of social workers. Indeed, Kaitlyn would often do research on subjects that parents discussed, and then would come to the next meetings with information about new government decisions on the kind of support that people with disabilities were offered in the context of COVID-19. At other times, Kaitlyn would look up information on key issues while parents were discussing such issues, so she could offer information to parents right away. Doing this in person, which would require her to be on her phone or computer, would have most likely been frowned upon because it would have seemed that she was not present. However, the fact that, during the virtual meetings, she could use discretely her computer gave her the chance to engage in double tasking without appearing as rude.

Conclusion

The disruptions that COVID-19 caused to field education provided both challenges and opportunities for innovation. Within the disability field, COVID-19 allowed students to engage with how people with disabilities are constructed, and the shift to a virtual format created opportunities which previous practicum students did not have. As a supervisor, this allowed me to see how students navigated power dynamics within the agency and gave me a chance to reflect on the impact that neo-liberal practices have on my experience. Despite the challenges it presented, COVID-19 also offered a space to experiment with field education opportunities which were conceptualized as unconventional. Fortunately, the transition toward a virtual format was successful as it offered students access to a wider range of experiences, while allowing them to complete their field education requirements. This helped ease the uncertainty and stress that COVID-19 caused. In fact, both students and clients at our agency highlighted that virtual service delivery might be something that would be helpful in the future as well.

REFERENCES

Alberta. (2022). *Case Breakdown.* Retrieved from https://www.alberta.ca/covid-19-alberta-data.aspx

Alberta Council of Disability Services [ACDS]. (2020, October). *Impact and insights: COVID-19 and Alberta's community disability services sector.* https://acds.ca/files/Resources/pandemic_planning/COVID-19-Impact-and-Insights-Executive-Summary.pdf

Alberta Health Services [AHS]. (2021). *COVID-19 scientific advisory group rapid evidence report.* https://www.albertahealthservices.ca/assets/info/ppih/if-ppih-covid-19-sag-evidence-of-harm-from-mask-use-for-specific-populations.pdf

Allen, U. D. (2020). COVID-19 among racialized communities: Unravelling the factors predictive of infection and adverse outcomes. *The Royal Society of Canada.* Ottawa. https://rsc-src.ca/en/covid-19/impact-covid-19-in-racialized-communities/covid-19-among-racialized-communities-unravelling

Archer-Kuhn, B., Allen, D., Schweizer, L., Meghji, F., & Taiwo, A. (2021). The obscure nature of signature pedagogy in social work education: A Canadian perspective. *Social Work Education, 40*(3), 383–398. https://doi.org/10.1080/02615479.2019.1677587

Archer-Kuhn, B., Ayala, J., Hewson, J., & Letkemann, L. (2020). Canadian reflections on the Covid-19 pandemic in social work education: From tsunami to innovation. *Social Work Education, 39*(8), 1010–1018. https://doi.org/10.1080/02615479.2020.1826922

Asakura, K., Todd, S., Eagle, B., & Morris, B. (2018). Strengthening the signature pedagogy of social work: Conceptualizing field coordination as a negotiated social work pedagogy. *Journal of Teaching in Social Work, 38*(2), 151–165. https://doi.org/10.1080/08841233.2018.1436635

Ayala J., Drolet J., Fulton A., Hewson J., Letkemann L., Baynton M., Elliott G., Judge-Stasiak A., Blaug C., Tétreault, G. A., & Schweizer, E. (2018). Field education in crisis: Experiences of field education coordinators in Canada. *Social Work Education 37*(3), 281–93. https://doi.org/10.1080/02615479.2017.1397109

Baird, S. L. (2016). Conceptualizing anxiety among social work students: Implications for social work education. *Social Work Education, 35*(6), 719–732. https://doi.org/10.1080/02615479.2016.11846 39.

Barlow, C., & Hall, B. (2007). "What about feelings?": A study of emotion and tension in social work field education. *Social Work Education, 26*(4), 399–413. https://doi:10.1080/02615470601081712

Billings, D. (2006). Journaling: A strategy for developing reflective practitioners. *The Journal of Continuing Education in Nursing, 37*(3), 104–105. https://doi.org/10.3928/00220124-20060301-02

Boitel, C. R., & Fromm, L. R. (2014). Defining signature pedagogy in social work education: Learning theory and the learning contract. *Journal of Social Work Education, 50*(4), 608–622. https://doi.org/10.1080/10437797.2014.947161

Calgary Transit. (2021). *Calgary Transit Access.* Retrieved from https://www.calgarytransit.com/calgary-transit-access.html?redirect=/calgary-transit-access

Canadian Association for Social Work Education. [CASWE]. (2020, March 18). *Covid-19 communication: Field education placements.* https://caswe-acfts.ca/covid-19-communication-field-education-placements/

Canadian Association for Social Work Education [CASWE]. (2021). *Vision, mission, principles and activities.* https://caswe-acfts.ca/about-us/mission/

Carlson, L. (2001). Cognitive ableism and disability studies: Feminist reflections on the history of mental retardation. *Hypatia, 16*(4), 124–146. https://doi.org/10.1111/j.1527-2001.2001.tb00756.x

Chandler, R., Guillaume, D., Parker, A. G., Mack, A., Hamilton, J., Dorsey, J., & Hernandez, N. D. (2021). The impact of COVID-19 among Black women: Evaluating perspectives and sources of information. *Ethnicity & Health, 26*(1), 80–93. https://doi.org/10.1080/13557858.2020.1841120

Council on Social Work Education [CSWE]. (2008). *Educational policy and accreditation standards.* Alexandria, VA: Author.

Council on Social Work Education [CSWE]. (2020). *CSWE COVID-19 member "pulse" survey results.* https://cswe.org/getmedia/2897bcac-7838-4104-8f9c-3d29b5fa6148/CSWE-COVID-19-Member-Pulse%e2%80%9d-Survey-Results.aspx

CTV. (2021, January 25). *Coronavirus: Grim anniversary: A timeline of one year of COVID-19.* https://www.ctvnews.ca/health/coronavirus/grim-anniversary-a-timeline-of-one-year-of-covid-19-1.5280617

Davis, A., & Mirick, R. G. (2021). COVID-19 and social work field education: A descriptive study of students' experiences. *Journal of Social Work Education, 57*(1), 120–136. https://doi.org/10.1080/10437797.2021.1929621

Day, T., Chang, I. C. C., Chung, C. K. L., Doolittle, W. E., Housel, J., & McDaniel, P. N. (2020). The immediate impact of COVID-19 on postsecondary teaching and learning. *The Professional Geographer, 73*(1), 1–13. https://doi.org/10.1080/0033012 4.2020.1823864

Dempsey, A., Lanzieri, N., Luce, V., de Leon, C., Malhotra, J., & Heckman, A. (2022). Faculty respond to COVID-19: Reflections-on-action in field education. *Clinical Social Work Journal, 50*, 11–21. https://doi.org/10.1007/s10615-021-00787-y

Didham, S., Dromgole, L., Csiernik, R., Karley, M. L., & Hurley, D. (2011). Trauma exposure and the social work practicum. *Journal of Teaching in Social Work, 31*(5), 523–537. https://doi:10.1080/08841233.2011.615261

Drolet, J., Alemi, M.I, Bogo, M., Chilanga, E., Clark, N., St. George, S., Charles, G. … & Wulff, D. (2020). Transforming field education during COVID-19. *Field Educator, 10*(2), 2–9. https://fieldeducator.simmons.edu/article/transforming-field-education-during-covid-19/

El-Lahib, Y. (2018). Social work at the intersection of disability and displacement: Rethinking our role. *Journal of Progressive Human Services, 31*(1), 1–20. https://doi.org/10.1080/10428232.2018.1531744

Farkas, K. J., & Romaniuk, J. R. (2020). Social work, ethics, and vulnerable groups in the time of the Coronavirus and COVID-19. *Society Register, 4*(2), 67–82. https://doi.org/10.14746/sr.2020.4.2.05

Garland-Thomson, R. (2002). Integrating disability, transforming feminist theory. *NWSA Journal, 14*(3), 1–32. https://doi.org/10.2979/nws.2002.14.3.1

Global News. (2021, July 14). COVID cases in Canada tracker: How many new cases of COVID-19 today? *Global News.* https://globalnews.ca/news/6649164/canada-coronavirus-cases/

Goodley, D. (2013). Dis/entangling critical disability studies. *Disability & Society, 28*(5), 631–644. https://doi.org/10.1080/09687599.2012.717884

Goodley, D., Hughes, B., & Davis, L. (2012). Introducing disability and social theory. In D. Goodley, B. Hughes, & L. Davis (Eds). *Disability and social theory: New developments and directions* (pp. 1–14). New York, NY: Palgrave Macmillan

Goodyear, R. K. (2014). Supervision as pedagogy: Attending to its essential instructional and learning processes. *Clinical Supervisor, 33*(1), 82–99. https ://doi.org/10.1080/07325 223.2014.91891 4.

Hall, M. C., & Zalta, E. N. (2019). *Clinical disability Theory.* Stanford Encyclopedia of Philosophy. https://plato.stanford.edu/entries/disability-critical/#InteAppr

Hanesworth, C. (2017). Neoliberal influences on American higher education and the consequences for social work programmes. *Critical and Radical Social Work, 5*(1), 41–57. https://doi.org/10.1332/204986017X14835298292776

Harlow, E., Berg, E., Barry, J., & Chandler, J. (2012). Neoliberalism, managerialism and the reconfiguring of social work in Sweden and the United Kingdom. *Organization, 20*(4), 534–550. https://doi.org/10.1177/1350508412448222

Hay, K., Maidment, J., Ballantyne, N., Beddoe, L., & Walker, S. (2019). Feeling lucky: The serendipitous nature of field education. *Clinical Social Work Journal, 47*, 23–31. https://link.springer.com/article/10.1007/s10615-018-0688-z

Hughes, B. (2017). Impairment on the move: The disabled incomer and other invalidating intersections. *Disability & Society, 32*(4), 467–482. https://doi: 10.1080/09687599.2017.1298991.

Knight, C. (2018). Trauma informed practice and care: Implications for field instruction. *Clinical Social Work Journal, 47*(1), 79–89. https ://doi.org/10.1007/s1061 5-018-0661-x.

Kohek, H., Seth, A., Edwards, M., & Zwicker, J. (2020). Mandatory mask bylaws: Considerations beyond exemption for persons with disabilities. *The School of Public Policy Publications, 13*(20). http://dx.doi.org/10.11575/sppp.v13i0.70911

Kourgiantakis, T., & Lee, E. (2020). Social work practice education and training during the pandemic: Disruptions and discoveries. *International Social Work, 63*(6), 761–765. https://doi.org/10.1177/0020872820959706

Lam, C. H., Wong, H., & Leung, T. T. F. (2007). An unfinished reflexive journey: Social work students' reflection on their placement experiences. *British Journal of Social Work, 37*(1), 91–105. Https://doi:10.1093/bjsw/bcl320

McGuire, L. E., & Lay, K. A. (2019). Reflective pedagogy for social work education: Integrating classroom and field for competency-based education. *Journal of Social Work Education, 56*(3), 519–532. https://doi.org/10.1080/10437797.2019.1661898

Meekosha, H., & Soldatic, K. (2014). Disability-inclusive social work practice. In L. Beddoe & J. Maidment (Eds.), *Social Work Practice for Promoting Health and Wellbeing* (pp. 162–174). Routledge.

Mian, A., & Khan, S. (2020). Medical education during pandemics: A UK perspective. *BMC Medicine, 18*(1). 1–2. https://doi.org/10.1186/s12916-020-01577-y

Minich, J. A. (2016). Enabling whom? Critical disability studies now. *Lateral, 5*(1). https://doi.org/10.25158/l5.1.9

Morgan, H. (2012). The social model of disability as a threshold concept: Troublesome knowledge and liminal spaces in social work education. *Social Work Education, 31*(2), 215–226. https://doi.org/10.1080/02615479.2012.644964

Morley, C., & Clarke, J. (2020). From crisis to opportunity? Innovations in Australian social work field education during the COVID-19 global pandemic. *Social Work Education, 39*(8), 1048–1057. https://doi.org/10.1080/02615479.2020.1836145

Moyle, J. (2016). Including disability in the social work core curriculum: A compelling argument. *Australian Social Work, 69*(4), 503–511. https://doi.org/10.1080/031240 7x.2016.1216575

Pooler, D., Doolittle, A., Faul, A., Barbee, A., & Fuller, M. (2012). An exploration of MSW field education and impairment prevention: What do we need to know? *Journal of Human Behavior in the Social Environment, 22*, 916–927. doi:10.1080/10911359.201 2.707936

Preston, S., George, P., & Silver, S. (2019). Field education in social work: The need for reimagining. *Critical Social Work, 15*(1). https://doi.org/10.22329/csw.v15i1.5908

Rogowski, S. (2011). Managers, managerialism and social work with children and families: The deformation of a profession? *Practice, 23*(3), 157–167. https://doi.org/10.1080/09503153.2011.569970

Roulstone, A. (2012). "Stuck in the middle with you": Towards enabling social work with disabled people. *Social Work Education, 31*(2), 142–154. https://doi.org/10.1080/02615479.2012.644942

Schalk, S. (2017). Critical disability studies as methodology. *Lateral, 6*(1). https://doi.org/10.25158/l6.1.13

Shakespeare, T. (2006). *Disability rights and wrongs.* New York, NY: Routledge.

Shakespeare, T., Ndagire, F., & Seketi, Q. E. (2021). Triple jeopardy: Disabled people and the COVID-19 pandemic. *The Lancet,* (London, England) *397*(10282), 1331–1333. https://www.ncbi.nlm.nih.gov/pmc/articles/PMC7963443/

Shulman, L. S. (2005). Signature pedagogies in the professions. *Daedalus, 134*(3), 52–59. https://doi.org/10.1162/0011526054622015

Sleeter, C. (2010). Building counter-theory about disability. *Disability Studies Quarterly, 30*(2). https://doi.org/10.18061/dsq.v30i2.1244

Svoboda, D., Williams, C., Jones, A., & Powell, K. (2013). Teaching social work research through practicum: What students learned. *Journal of Social Work Education, 49*(4), 661–673. https://doi.org/10.1080/10437797.2013.812889

Tortorelli, C., Choate, P., Clayton, M., el Jamal, N., Kaur, S., & Schantz, K. (2021). Simulation in social work: Creativity of students and faculty during COVID-19. *Social Sciences, 10*(1), 7. https://doi.org/10.3390/socsci10010007

Tremain, S. (2017). *Foucault and feminist philosophy of disability.* University of Michigan Press.

Ullrich, P. M., & Lutgendorf, S. K. (2002). Journaling about stressful events: Effects of cognitive processing and emotional expression. *Annals of Behavioral Medicine, 24*(3), 244–250. https://doi.org/10.1207/s15324796abm2403_10

Wayne, J., Bogo, M., & Raskin, M. (2010). Field education as the signature pedagogy of social work education. *Journal of Social Work Education, 46*(3), 327–339. https://doi.org/10.5175/jswe.2010.200900043

Woodbridge, L., & O'Beirne, B. R. O. (2017). Counseling students' perceptions of journaling as a tool for developing reflective thinking. *The Journal of Counselor Preparation and Supervision, 9*(2). https://doi.org/10.7729/92.1198

15

Supporting Spiritual Competencies in Field Education and Practice

Emma De Vynck, Jill Ciesielski, and Heather M. Boynton

Social workers entering the practice field will inevitably encounter children, adolescents, families, and/or communities dealing with adversity, and research has demonstrated spiritual strengths, crises, struggles, and distress are often intertwined with these experiences. Spirituality can arise in any practice area, and may be particularly pertinent with respect to trauma, grief, loss, life transitions, aging and end of life care, pregnancy and abortion, addictions, chronic mental health, illness, relationship issues including sexual infidelity, conflict, divorce, and 2SLGBTQ+ and other related gender and identity aspects. Spirituality is interconnected with cultural humility and competence, and ethical practice. Yet, are social work placement students sufficiently supported to consider spiritual matters arising for those they work with, as well as for themselves, as they enter practicum? While undergoing similar processes themselves, social work students may be tasked to assist clients dealing with spiritual issues, conflicts in their values and worldview, and struggles with coping. Additionally, are field educators and instructors adequately prepared to incorporate a spiritually-informed approach into their supervision of students as well as their practice with individuals, families, and communities? This chapter is written collaboratively from the perspective of three social workers and researchers at varying stages in their professional and academic paths, but we all share a passion for increasing spiritual awareness and spiritually sensitive field practice in social work. We will present relevant findings on spirituality and spiritual struggles and trauma as informed by our personal practice and research endeavours, and we will link these findings with implications for field education.

Although historically social work has roots in spirituality, explicit focus on this area was suppressed over time. If, in the past several decades, there has been a renewed interest in the necessity of integrating spirituality and religion into the social work curriculum, an important gap remains with respect to its inclusion in field education. Research has revealed that students, academics, and practitioners, as well as clients, have indicated the importance of integrating spiritual and religious aspects into academia and practice. Yet, this dimension continues to be largely unaddressed in schools of social work (Boynton, 2016; Kvarfordt et al., 2018; Moffatt et al., 2021). We contend that it is essential and past due for social work to incorporate spiritual content and pedagogy in field education.

Field educators and supervisors must be aware of the impact of spiritual aspects for both clients and for students, and should be prepared for spiritual reflection, exploration, and dialogue. We will address the importance of attending to students' spiritual needs in the field setting, as students may undergo their own spiritual challenges when they navigate the development of their professional practice identity and the shaping of their own spiritual worldview. The self-reflection and cogitative processes associated with social work education might stimulate spiritual contemplation, distress, or concerns for students, resulting in a need for supervisory support from field supervisors and instructors.

Introducing the Authors' Experience with Spirituality: Emma, Jill, and Heather

Emma

Growing up in evangelical Christianity, I was exposed to messages of service grounded in divine love and self-sacrifice. A vocation of service was compelling to me, and when I began studying social work, it felt like home. But as I dove into my first field placement, the spiritual disquietude that had begun in my teenage years only grew. Encountering individuals of all belief systems exposed me to the beauty of humanity and challenged the notions of inherent sinfulness I was raised to believe in. The focus on continued self-reflection in my courses, while edifying, contributed to my ongoing destabilization. My first field placement was at a Christian-affiliated food bank and "street church"; it felt familiar and yet entirely foreign after the tectonic shifts I had been experiencing in my worldview. I did not know where to land, how to be, or where I was going. And I certainly did not talk about it.

My own spiritual distress story may be resonant for some readers, as it is common for young people to question their worldviews. But these stories should not be chalked up to a phase, and they are not unique to emerging adults. Spiritual struggles can have profound and lasting adverse mental health impacts and affect individuals of all life stages, backgrounds, and social locations (Abu-Raiyah et al., 2015; Ano & Pargament, 2013; Wilt et al., 2021). My own story is intimately interwoven with my social work education and field practicum experiences. Through my master's thesis, these experiences help me to explore spiritual struggles in the hopes of improving support of both clients and social work students who encounter these concerns.

Jill

Being raised as an atheist in a home where spirituality was little discussed, I did not begin to explore this topic until I was an adult. Social work was one of the main factors that prompted me to consider spirituality more deeply, because it made me reflect upon my own values and motivations that brought me to the field, as well as grapple with the moral and existential issues that arose during the process. Additionally, I found that spirituality was a dimension that came up continually with many of my clients, and I felt little equipped to address it in my work with them in a competent and ethical matter. I came to believe that this was a major gap not only in my own practice, but also in the profession. Social work curriculum and field education are key components to addressing this gap.

Heather

I was raised by Catholic and Protestant parents who had turned away from their respective churches due to existential and religious questions, which were not answered by their faith. My parents conveyed that I could determine my own spiritual perspectives and practices. This led me to being exposed to many faiths, through my peers, while growing up in a multi-cultural neighbourhood in Toronto. Growing up, I heard a lot of negativities surrounding religion, although I have come to recognize the great value it holds for many individuals. Having encountered a few distressing spiritual experiences with no one to talk to about them, I blocked my spirituality for about a decade. Through my work with children and families experiencing trauma, grief, and loss I was catapulted back into the spiritual dimension of life. This triggered a renewed journey of understanding my own spirituality. I found that there was little guidance and training in the spiritual dimension, and even a lack of openness to talk about spirituality and religion with supervisors. So, I embarked on a quest to learn as much as I could in the area, which led me to explore spirituality in my master's and PhD programs. I continued this journey after two decades of learning, practice, and research in the area. This pulled me towards the many amazing experiences of my clients. I was also drawn to various organizations: I became involved with the Canadian Society for Spirituality and Social Work, I started attending and chairing conferences and symposiums, and I became the vice-president of the Society. Ultimately, I devoted my research, publishing, and teaching to matters of spirituality.

Defining Spirituality

Spirituality can be difficult to define, as it is highly personal and can vary greatly between groups or individuals (Canda et al., 2019). Within the context of social work, there is a lack of consensus around the definition of spirituality (Barker & Floersch, 2010). Hodge (2018) conveys that there is a trend within the profession to define spirituality in universal terms, with the assumption that everyone is spiritual. Additionally, while this definition is inclusive of a wide variety of spiritual or religious beliefs, the assumption that everyone can identify as being spiritual can decontextualize spirituality and may be too broad in nature. Any definition must be inclusive and respectful of a multitude of spiritual and religious beliefs, but it must also provide enough specificity for practitioners to be able to apply it in their practice (Senreich, 2013). In most definitions, core concepts of spirituality include a search for a sense of connectedness to oneself, others, the divine, beings beyond human, the natural world, the universe, and the ultimate reality. They also incorporate meaning making and a sense of purpose. Religion, rather, is concerned with spiritual matters and may be defined as institutionalized patterns of values and beliefs shared by a group and (Koenig et al., 2012). For some individuals, spirituality is associated with religion, and for others it is not.

For those individuals who find meaning in the form of religion, this should be reflected in practice. Assessments can explore spiritual and religious strengths, resources, practices, and rituals, as well as areas of challenge and struggle. For support, practitioners can consider collaborating with religious leaders, mentors, or youth groups, among others, and explore church activities for youth (Tangenberg, 2012). Social workers should also engage in an ethical reflexivity and recognize when they might need to refer to a spiritual care practitioner or clergy.

Spirituality and Culture

We contend that understandings of cultural humility and competence should be extended to include a stance on spiritual humility and competence. These should include culturally and contextually appropriate ways of practicing, as spirituality is integral to cultural beliefs and worldviews, particularly for non-Western cultures. For many individuals, spirituality is connected to their culture. Canada is a profoundly diverse country, with people of over 250 ethnic origins reported in the 2016 census (Statistics Canada, 2017a). The proportion of visible minorities is also growing, with 22.3% of the population reporting on the 2016 census to belong to one of these groups (Statistics Canada, 2017b). Canda et al. (2019) stated that the amount of diversity within countries such as the United States and Canada calls for practitioners to take a stance of cultural humility, a perspective that

> appreciates complexity and intersectionality of identities, that critically reflects on power and privilege in helping relationships while promoting collaboration and empowerment, that attends to contextual issues of social justice, and that encourages workers' continuous learning through

self-awareness and dialogue with clients and their communities. (p. 23).

We believe that this is true for social workers across the globe.

Scholars have argued for the need of practitioners to use spirituality in their work with migrants and refugees in a collaborative and client-centered manner. However, most social workers are not prepared to do this effectively (George & Ellison, 2015; Hodge, 2019; Whipple et al., 2015). Spirituality can be an important component of the worldview of marginalized peoples, such as Indigenous peoples in colonial nations, and disregarding these ways of knowing can perpetuate further harm (Lavallée & Poole, 2010). Some scholars have argued for incorporating spirituality into the profession in a way that is consistent with the principles of social justice (Belcher & Sarmiento Mellinger, 2016; Gardner, 2020).

Cultural and spiritual humility and competence involve engagement. It does not mean that a practitioner can become an expert in other cultures, but they can engage in a "never-ending process of living and learning to expand one's values, knowledge, skills, and relationships" (Canda et al., 2019, p. 400). For this reason, Canda et al. (2019) prefer the term "culturally appropriate practice" over cultural competence because the focus should be on building and maintaining relationships on an ongoing basis with a spiritually sensitive framework, rather than achieving a certain level of skill (p. 400). The clinician develops an awareness of cultural and spiritual aspects for clients, reflects on one's own spirituality, and continues to grow and develop professionally in relation to spirituality in practice. Danso (2018) noted the controversy and debate among scholars over different terms to describe this aspect of practice. Danso purported that cultural humility does not add more value to social work practice than the pre-existing concept of cultural competence, because cultural humility does not go beyond the principles of anti-oppressive practice. Regardless of which term is used to describe appropriate practice with clients from diverse cultures, spirituality certainly remains a key aspect (Canda et al., 2019).

Spirituality in Social Work

There is a well-established acknowledgment that social work as a profession has many gaps in relation to a holistic or spiritual approach (Carrington, 2013; Zapf, 2008), for it leaves those who wish to take this approach, or encounter spirituality in their practice, to "rely on their own initiative and inventiveness, with no clear theoretical, practical, or ethical guidelines" (Carrington, 2013, p. 288). Many scholars have advocated for the inclusion of spirituality in social work at a broad, macro level (Belcher & Sarmiento Mellinger, 2016; Crisp, 2020; Gardner, 2020; Zapf, 2008). Boynton (2011) conveyed that the focus on spirituality in social work at this level has centered around social justice (Coates, 2007; Lee & Barret, 2007; Nash & Stewart, 2005), ethics and ethical practice (Canda et al., 2004; Hodge, 2005a), and the need for education and training (Ai, 2002; Baskin, 2002; Coholic, 2003, 2006).

There has also been much discussion of the use of spirituality at the micro level through concepts such as "contemplative spaces" (Jacobs, 2015), mindfulness, gratitude, forgiveness, and radical acceptance, but also through spiritual assessments (Hodge, 2001, 2005b; Seinfeld, 2012). Other studies addressing issues related to practice and teaching have conveyed that spirituality is an essential component of clinical practice (Coates et al., 2007; Groen et al., 2012). Furthermore, some scholars have articulated links between trauma, grief, loss, and spirituality, itself a factor of resilience and posttraumatic growth (Boynton, 2016). They have also outlined the importance of spirituality across the lifespan and paid attention to how individuals engage in spirituality through religious practices, rituals, and creativity (Boynton, 2009, 2014, 2016; Boynton & Vis, 2011, 2017; Crisp, 2016, 2017; Vis & Boynton, 2008).

Researchers have sought the perspectives of practitioners themselves who admitted that, while being generally in favour of the inclusion of spirituality in social work practice, they do not feel equipped to do so because it is rarely included in their social work education or training (Kvarfordt & Herba, 2018; Kvarfordt & Sheridan, 2010; Oxhandler & Ellor, 2017; Oxhandler & Giardina, 2017; Oxhandler et al., 2015). A handful of studies with social work practitioners have explored practitioners' beliefs, feelings, and experiences of incorporating spirituality in clinical practice, as well as their educational and training experiences, and how their own spirituality influences, or is influenced by, their work (Bell et al., 2005; Canda & Furman, 2010; Oxhandler & Pargament, 2014; Sheridan, 2004, 2009). Social work students also think that spirituality should be included in education (Buckey, 2012; Pandya, 2018; Phillips, 2014; Senreich, 2013). A literature review of 493 articles conducted by Buckey (2012) indicated that both students and practitioners report little to no training in this area, and students were very supportive of having this material included in the curriculum.

A survey of 190 Canadian social work educators indicated that they are also largely in favour of incorporating spirituality in practice and education; only one-third of them, though, reported that this kind of material is included in their curriculum, but usually at the instructor's discretion (Kvarfordt et al., 2018). Educators raised some concerns about inserting this content into the curriculum, such as the possibility of bias by faculty or students and the lack of knowledge or experience among faculty in teaching this material (Kvarfordt et al., 2018). Social work practitioners, educators, and students have articulated the importance of spirituality within the field of practice given its significance in the lives and needs of clients, such as in meaning-making processes (Coholic, 2003, 2006; Sheridan, 2004, 2009). Several studies have found that children and adults often bring up spiritual issues in sessions, and that clients want their spiritual beliefs and practices to be recognized, honoured, and included in the counselling process (Boynton, 2016; Canda & Furman, 1998; Coholic, 2003; Sheridan, 2004). It is also apparent that practitioners are addressing and integrating spiritual interventions while lacking critical knowledge and expertise in the area (Kvarfordt & Sheridan, 2007; Oxhandler & Pargament, 2014). More importantly, Oxhandler and Pargament (2014) wondered how social workers were gaining knowledge and effectively making sound practice decisions. These limitations raise issues with self-efficacy and competence for social workers, as well as ethical concerns in practice. This body of literature clearly demonstrates an obvious need for social workers to adopt a spiritually sensitive and appropriate practice in their approach; it also underscores that the training and professional development related to spirituality is required not only for students, but for practitioners, field supervisors, and field educators.

Social Work Field Education and Spirituality

Field education is a key component of social work education, as it provides a venue for students to make links with classroom learnings and direct practice experiences. As discussed, the social work classroom rarely includes adequate exploration of spiritual and religious matters, and students may first encounter the spiritual elements of social work when they embark on their field placements and begin engaging with clients. In the field setting, students may encounter spiritual and religious matters in clients' narratives, implicitly or explicitly. Additionally, field experiences may provoke students' own spiritual cogitation, including questioning one's values, ethics, and meaning as they confront the complexities of human suffering, and encounter potential opposition to their own spiritual paradigms.

Social work literature examining field education and spirituality remains limited, and explicitly considers only a few key areas: field education with religiously affiliated agencies, challenges to students' worldviews in field education, and models for integrating spirituality into field supervision and education (see for example: Colvin & Bullock, 2017; Harris et al., 2016; Okundaye et al., 1999). A brief review of the literature revealed that many of these explorations consider Christian student experiences, Christian social service agencies, and perspectives of Christian-affiliated social work schools. This emphasis on Christian perspectives, which demonstrates the prominence of Christianity in Canadian and American religious landscapes, eclipses the true diversity of the spiritual approaches held by clients, students, and practitioners. Okundaye et al.'s (1999) model of spiritually sensitive field supervision is a departure from Christian approaches, and instead integrates Eastern spiritual traditions into field supervision. Exploring non-dominant approaches to spirituality in the field is vital for developing social work's spiritual competency and literacy beyond Christian models.

Although the social work field education and spirituality literature is limited, the possibilities for further connections and explorations are bountiful. Just as social work curriculum must respond to the call for a holistic spiritually-integrated approach, field education must consider its role in supporting the development of spiritually competent and spiritually aware social workers. This involves preparing students for spiritually sensitive work with clients, but also addressing the importance of the field education team in supporting students' spiritual needs and goals.

Spirituality is an essential element of the human experience and warrants adequate consideration across social work settings. The range of spiritual experiences for human beings can be both deeply nourishing and deeply distressing. In the following section, we explore how, for some clients and students, the spiritual realm can become a site of distress and struggle. Both Emma and Heather have considered these underexamined areas in their respective research on spiritual distress, trauma, grief, and loss in the context of spirituality and aim to provide insights from these realms for field education.

Important Research and Literature for Field Education

Spiritual Struggles, Crises, and Distress

Although there is ample literature confirming the positive impacts of religion and spirituality on coping, burnout prevention, and overall mental health and well-being, a smaller but important body of literature addresses spiritual distress and struggles (Captari et al., 2018; Exline et al., 2000). While social workers and students should consider the potential for wellness, strengths, and resources found in spirituality, a thorough discussion of spirituality must honour its potential "dark side" (Ellison & Lee, 2010, p. 501; de Souza, 2012). Acknowledging the potential harms of religion and spirituality cautions us to avoid idealizing spirituality in social work theorizing, education, and practice: we can recognize that even though "spirituality can be part of the highest of human expressions, it can also be part of the lowest" (Pargament, 2011, p. 129).

Exline and Rose (2005) outline a range of areas that are related to this dark side of spirituality and religion; some include conflicts related to one's spiritual or religious worldview, negative religious or spiritual coping, spiritual struggles and concerns, and spiritual injury. These aspects can cause great internal turmoil for individuals, for while they can impact their mental health and manifest themselves as anger, anxiety, and depression, they may also be related to trauma, grief, and loss (McConnell et al., 2006; Exline & Rose, 2005).

Spiritual struggles or distress are complex and multifaceted experiences that can have profound impacts on our well-being. Spiritual distress may include a troubled relationship with the divine, painful emotions related to one's religion and/or spirituality, chronic doubt, disillusionment with one's religious upbringing, moral and existential concerns, and interpersonal strife in religious settings (Abu-Raiyah et al., 2015; Bryant & Astin, 2008; Ellison & Lee, 2010). Although they may be difficult to put into concrete language for the sufferer, these challenges can be defined as "tension, strain, and conflict about sacred matters with the supernatural, with other people, and within oneself" (Abu-Raiya et al., 2015, p. 565). Pargament (2011), a prominent researcher in the field of spiritual struggle, proposes that if our spirituality, religion, or the organization of our worldview lacks flexibility, fails to respond to the inevitable challenges and confusions of life, and conflicts with our social environment, we may fall into distress. Such struggles are common. Anyone can experience spiritual struggles, as existential disturbances impact many of us throughout our lives regardless of explicit affiliation with a belief system or religion (Preston & Shin, 2017).

There is strong empirical evidence demonstrating linkages between spiritual struggles and distress on the one hand, and adverse mental and physical health outcomes on the other. Anger and shaken faith can result in confusion, and spiritual strife can lead to depression, anxiety, suicidality, poor recovery from illness, and even higher mortality rates (Abu-Raiyah et al., 2015; Ano & Vasconcelles, 2005; Exline & Rose, 2005; Wilt et al., 2021). In addition, research is increasingly demonstrating that spiritual distress warrants targeted attention as a distinct and complex phenomenon that "cannot merely be reduced to other psychosocial experiences" (Ano & Pargament, 2013, p. 431; Abu-Raiyah et al., 2015; Wilt et al., 2021). The spiritual aspect of struggle may be the most grievous factor in decreased well-being and, therefore, calls for a nuanced response from social workers and educators supporting clients and students with these experiences (Abu-Raiyah et al., 2015).

Spiritual struggles, distress, and concerns can be precipitated by many factors: trauma, grief, and loss events, mental health challenges, conflicts within one's spiritual community, isolation, existential meaning-making processes, lack of a sense of purpose, personal and professional identity formation aspects, the discovery of differing ideologies, questions related to religious teachings, illness or injury, etc. These varied experiences of spiritual struggles and distress may be a part of many of our stories, whether we are a client, student, or practitioner; like other emotionally fraught areas, they benefit from being named, illuminated, and nurtured. Reframing personal mental health concerns as spiritual and/or religious struggles or distress can be empowering for individuals and is more holistic than a biological or psychological perspective. Externalizing the root cause of suffering can offer a sense of relief and allow the individual to cope and make meaning of the pain, while understanding that a higher purpose of the struggle may also facilitate spiritual growth (Hefti, 2011). Exline and Rose (2005) claimed that neglecting spiritual struggles and "problems of suffering might cause us to overlook vital sources of spiritual transformation and development" (p. 335). As our spirituality and/or religion can provide the meaning system through which we find an anchor in daily events and major life hurdles, inner anguish about the spiritual realm can "deprive us of a valuable personal resource" and a coherent foundation to stand upon (Ellison & Lee, 2010, p. 505). Therefore, social workers are required to know and understand the potential for deeper spiritual aspects related to clients' and students' concerns, and the imperative need to attend to spiritual struggles for effective field practice and education.

Trauma, Grief, and Loss

Spiritual concerns, struggles, questions, and distress often arise through the experience of a traumatic event or from a significant loss. Individuals often ruminate on spiritual aspects in the process of meaning making of these difficult experiences. Pargament et al. (2014) contended that spirituality plays a critical role in major life traumas, as it helps in understanding, managing, and resolving them. Traumatic experiences can result in an existential injury affecting one's spiritual foundation and worldview, and one's sense of being in the world (Boynton & Vis, 2017; Thompson & Walsh, 2010).

Practitioners and social work students will inevitably encounter individuals dealing with trauma who may require spiritual support. However, even though "social workers are often trained in evidence-based trauma interventions and frameworks, spirituality is rarely discussed as part of these intervention frameworks" (Boynton & Vis, 2017, p. 193). The American Council on Social Work Education (2012) disseminated a competency framework for advanced social work practice which specifically outlines the need for skills and knowledge pertaining to trauma. These guidelines inform how spirituality is interrelated with trauma, and state that spirituality influences the therapeutic relationship and practitioners need to attend to spiritual development in trauma practice. Yet, in reviewing the social work literature, it becomes very apparent that there continues to be a lack of theoretical frameworks, practice guidelines, and evidence-based practices pertaining to spirituality and social work practice across the lifespan.

Incorporating spirituality is a necessary approach to trauma treatment at all developmental stages of life and may be most important for children and adolescents. Well over a decade ago calls were made to include content on spirituality for children and adolescents in social work programs, as this area was viewed to be an important practice concern (Graham et al., 2007; Cheon & Canda, 2010). Yet the gap remains. A continually growing body of research indicates that religion and spirituality is important in the lives of children and adolescents, and it is a critical component in many areas of child and adolescent development and well-being (Boynton, 2016). It also may be supportive or a factor of struggle for those who are homeless, displaced, or living in foster care; those experiencing poverty, violence, various forms of abuse, or sexual minority discrimination; and those engaging in crime or having suicidal ideation (Kvarfordt & Herba, 2018).

Research with children has found that trauma, grief, and loss can create spiritual, existential, and metaphysical challenges or struggles, which children are often managing alone (Boynton, 2016; Gabarino & Bedard, 1996; Hooyman & Kramer, 2021; Poyser, 2004). Boynton (2016) found that parents may not be aware of the extent of their children's spiritual struggles or spiritual thoughts and beliefs, and if parents themselves are struggling with these challenges, they are not able to attend to their children's needs. Furthermore, she found that practitioners reported issues with competency and mastery related to a lack of training and development in this area. These significant practice concerns expressed by social workers are relevant for supporting and fostering the development of emerging social work professionals in the field.

In an attempt to address the gap regarding children's spirituality in counselling, Boynton and Mellan (2021) proposed a framework that incorporates children's perspectives, research, and theory. Four components of their framework focused on creating space for the spiritual dimension, which can be achieved by understanding and adopting a spiritual holistic approach; four other components address how counsellors can integrate spirituality and support children through trauma, grief, and loss. These authors asserted that through suspending judgement and expecting the unexpected, social workers can "more fully embrace what emerges in the co-creative process related to the spiritual dimension" in their work with children (Boynton & Mellan, 2021, p. 2). However, there is much more research and theory to be developed in this critical area of spirituality in trauma, grief, and loss across the lifespan.

Social Work Students and Vulnerability to Spiritual Struggle

Students themselves may experience spiritual challenges throughout their social work education and field placements. Bryant and Astin (2008) discovered that spiritual struggles impact a significant population of university students compared to the general public, which may put them at higher risk for mental health challenges related to spiritual struggles. They found that students from minority religions, students who identify as women, 2SLGBTQ+, and students who encounter disorienting and challenging worldviews during their studies may be particularly vulnerable to spiritual concerns caused by marginalization. Social workers must critically examine the intersections of race, class, and gender in their work, and it can be argued that religious and spiritual identity is a key intersection that warrants further attention and appreciation (Weber, 2015). We contend that for social work students of all social locations, the unique demands of a highly self-reflective, values-based, and experiential program can certainly result in spiritual contemplation, evaluation of one's spiritual worldview, and even spiritual distress (Larkin, 2010).

Gelman (2004) reported that MSW foundation students entering their first practicum experience significant anxiety, which may include fears of inflicting harm on clients, incompetence, and inadequacy. A variety of fears can have an existential and spiritual quality, as they point to deeper concerns regarding one's personal suitability and capacity for practice, one's morality and ethics, and one's purpose and impact in the world. During their education and placements, students may confront profound questions regarding the purpose of their work and their own values and paradigms (Larkin, 2010). Working with clients who challenge one's worldview can be both disorienting and overwhelming. Additionally, as students confront the trauma experiences of clients, they may face spiritual and existential questions and emotional overwhelm. Students' own trauma histories may reemerge as they enter potentially distressing field placement settings, contributing to spiritual challenges and distress. There is some evidence that social work students have higher rates of personal trauma than students from other disciplines, an observation of certain relevance for field educators supporting students (Black et al., 1993; Sellers & Hunter, 2005). Furthermore, as new practitioners who are still developing coping strategies, social work students in field placements may be at an increased risk of emotional exhaustion and burnout, which can further precipitate or exacerbate spiritual rumination and struggle (Knight, 2010; Ying, 2008). The potentially stressful, traumatic, and spiritually impactful nature of practicum requires not only a trauma-informed approach from field educators, but also a spiritually sensitive approach. While field education can be an empowering and fruitful learning experience, the challenges and existential and spiritual quandaries that can arise cannot be minimized or ignored.

Some scholarship explores the importance of spiritual crises for growth (Magolda, 2008; Parks, 2000). Fowler's (1981) Faith Development Theory provides a helpful lens for contextualizing our spiritual development through six stages. Perhaps of most relevance among these various stages is the individuative-reflective stage. The individuative-reflective stage may occur in early adulthood, resulting in critical analysis of one's values and worldview. Spiritual distress may emerge through this experience. Magolda's (2008) work on student development describes the "shadow lands," a place where students experience ambiguity and fear as they attempt to unpack and rebuild their beliefs in a new context (p. 280). When students surface from the shadow lands, they carry clarity, confidence, and a deeper sense of personal ownership for their lives. Proponents of a growth-through-crisis approach assert that spiritual crises can have meaningful outcomes if individuals have a space or "hearth" to openly explore their struggles and integrate their new understanding of the world (Bryant & Astin, 2008, p. 6). In embracing spiritually sensitive practice, field educators and supervisors can be supporters in the shadow land and offer this hearth to students.

Case Examples

Implications for a Spiritually Sensitive Framework for Field Education
We have presented many areas of consideration for field education and practice regarding the spiritual dimension of our work. Although there are many areas of implication, the most critical is in education. It is time

Table 15.1: Case Example #1: Jon (Client)

Jon, a 17-year-old adolescent male, had been feeling depressed and anxious for a few years. He had been bullied at school and had experienced some losses of extended family members. He had been seen by a psychiatrist who recommended an antidepressant; yet Jon did not want to take medications. When the social worker met with Jon, she explored his spirituality as part of the assessment. Jon related that he was an atheist and really did not feel he was spiritual. However, through further questions Jon revealed that he was experiencing existential angst related to attempting to understand the universe and its creation, the meaning and purpose of life, and some of the traumatic experiences in his life. Through dialogue he revealed that these thoughts were overwhelming him, and that he had not discussed these with anyone. He felt he could not make sense of who he was, why he was here, and what it all meant. The social worker was able to facilitate meaning making through framing his depression and anxiety as related to spiritual distress. This allowed Jon to remove the feelings of him being flawed in some way, while it offered an avenue for working with the social worker to address his spiritual distress and anxiety. Through the opportunity to engage in discussion, Jon recognized the questions and struggles he was experiencing were part of our common humanity. The social worker validated his experience, which supported Jon in making sense of his own experiences and to come to terms with not knowing some answers. Through this, Jon was able to focus on other areas of his life that could bring meaning and purpose for him. He found that his depression and anxiety significantly lessened through engaging in spiritual meaning making processes, and by having a place of safety, authentic listening, and reflection provided by the social worker.

Table 15.2: Case Example #2: Gina (Student)

Gina is in her third month of her first BSW practicum at a child welfare organization. She was raised in a Christian home, but no longer attends church and considers
herself more spiritual than religious. As part of her practicum duties, Gina calls clients to set up appointments with their social workers. Recently, a client became very
aggravated during one of these phone calls and expressed this frustration strongly
with Gina, as she did not have ready answers to some of their questions. Gina, suddenly overwhelmed with guilt and confusion, tried to comfort the individual, but
the client only became increasingly upset and yelled at Gina until they hung up.
When she went home that evening, Gina planned to do "self-care" as discussed in
her learning agreement, as she was very upset and confused after the call. Her self-
care involved going for a walk and taking a long bath. When Gina returned to practicum the next day, she was still distraught and wracked with a sense of guilt. Her
supervisor had been in court with a client the previous day but planned a debrief
with Gina for the morning.

In their supervision and debrief meeting, Gina recounted the interaction with
the client, and how upsetting the situation was for both parties. Her supervisor
began a conversation about what the client may have been feeling. Gina and the
supervisor explored how fear and grief were present under the anger the client expressed. They discussed potential strategies for validating and responding to anger.
Following this discussion, the supervisor validated Gina's support of the client, but
suggested that in the future if a client continues to yell and get increasingly upset,
Gina could tell the client it might be better if they speak again when the client feels
calmer and end the conversation. Her supervisor also asked Gina about her guilt
response during the interaction. Gina shared that she felt frozen in the situation
and saw it as her duty to support the client selflessly. She noted that she must have
said something to upset the client, and that it was her role to continue listening
and supporting regardless of their response. The supervisor inquired where these
beliefs originated from, and Gina noted that selflessness and service were always
emphasized and praised in her Christian upbringing, although she had not originally made the connection between her background and her response to the client's
distress. Gina began to consider her religious and spiritual framework's influence
on her behaviour, including both the benefits and drawbacks of her upbringing.
This allowed for a conversation about Gina's values. The supervisor affirmed and
validated Gina's values and inquired about caring for oneself during and following
challenging practice experiences.

Through this dialogue, Gina realized that to embody the values of service she
held, she needed to care for her own spirit as well. They discussed the challenge of

Table 15.2: (*continued*)

---

balancing compassionate awareness of a client's distress with awareness of personal boundaries. Gina noted that the language of boundaries felt foreign and overly clinical. She noted that she preferred to think of it as attending to the client's spirit and needs while balancing care for her own spirit and experience. Gina and her supervisor discussed how difficult it can be to navigate this in a way that is respectful of everyone involved, and how this is an ongoing process. Her supervisor discussed what spiritual self-care could look like for Gina beyond the more surface-level self-care practices she had been practicing. They worked together to find a resonant mantra for Gina that she could repeat when she was in situations where she felt frozen and disconnected from herself. Gina chose the mantra "Protecting my spirit matters, too." Together, Gina and her supervisor created a plan to reach out to the client again in order to have a follow-up discussion about what was going on, and how Gina could support him.

Table 15.3: Case Example #3: Lyndsey (Practitioner/Supervisor)

Lyndsey, a school social worker, was assigned to work with a 12-year-old boy named Jason in a small room across the hall from his classroom. Jason had been quite aggressive and engaging in disruptive behaviours and refusing to do schoolwork. He had been exposed to domestic violence, was beaten on several occasions by his father who was struggling with substance use and mental health. He was living with his mother and a 16-year-old female sibling in a small rural town. The social worker was asked to teach the youth coping strategies and to slowly reintroduce academics in his day. The social worker had begun to develop a trusting relationship with the youth and was engaging in teaching and practicing coping strategies. She had provided the boy with a worksheet on thinking about coping at different life stages. Upon reading his responses to questions, she noted he had written that teenagers cope by "killing themselves." She was concerned about this and made her supervisor and the case manager aware of this, and she also let the boy's mother know.

The following week she was attending a psychiatric appointment for the youth and, while waiting for the family, she was notified that Jason was in hospital and had attempted suicide and was calling out for her during the night. This sparked spiritual thoughts for Lyndsey around life, death, suicide, meaning, and purpose. She recognized that she had made a significant therapeutic connection with Jason, and that he felt safe in her presence. She was supposed to attend a case conference for another

---

Table 15.3: (*continued*)

> youth right after this. She informed her supervisor of the events and was asked if she needed a couple of minutes. Lyndsey was in shock and in spiritual turmoil, and all she could respond was that she needed some water, which her supervisor got for her and then motioned for her to go into the case conference.
>
> Lyndsey struggled to focus while in the conference and returned to the school where a colleague asked her what was wrong. He told her that she needed some spiritual self-care and should go home. She took his advice, although she later learned that he received a reprimand from the supervisor for doing this. The supervisor did not speak to Lyndsey for over a week and expected Lyndsey to return to the small room to work with the boy. Her supervisor later related that she felt that maybe Lyndsey needed some space, which is why she did not call her or arrange for supervision. This was a missed opportunity to support Lyndsey and attend to the spiritual distress triggered by the work and the traumatic events.
>
> Lyndsey struggled for some time, felt exhausted, and burned out. However, through talking with a few peers and engaging in her own spiritual self-care spiritual reflection, she was able to continue working. She also was able to talk to the youth and the parent about the event, to support the family in connecting at a deeper authentic level, and to assist the parent to be aware of the child's experience and need at times for co-regulation and spiritual reflection on his experiences of trauma. She moved from working on coping and anger management skills to addressing the spiritual aspects of care and the need for processing and meaning making of the traumatic experiences. She also inquired about the spiritual strengths of the family and facilitated spiritual activities and rituals they could engage in to bring comfort and healing. This attention to spirituality enhanced her practice from both a personal and professional level.

now to orient ourselves to openly attend the spiritual domain and offer education and support within the practice realm.

Our ethical standards of practice, in particular competence, social justice, and client self-determination, apply to the relevance of spirituality for social work practice (CASW, 2005). Educators may choose to use ethical guidelines developed by scholars such as Canda and Furman (2019). A key starting point is education and training on spiritual matters for field instructors. Ensuring that future social workers who will become field instructors have spiritually sensitive practice skills, knowledge, and attitudes, in addition to a willingness to create change in policies and practices and develop spiritually informed treatment approaches, is of utmost importance. Social workers need to be cognizant of the spiritual dimension as it relates to theories such as humanistic and existential theories, transpersonal theory, and person in environment, or, as Zapf (2008) argued, person-as-environment as we are part of a larger environment of creation. Social workers should be educated on conducting spiritual assessments and the use of various models and approaches to assess for spiritual strengths, activities, practices, and resources, as well as challenges and struggles. Spirituality can readily be infused in treatment processes and frameworks, and considerations for further development in this area of practice are needed. Additionally, with appreciation for the range of cultural and religious identities clients and students may bring, spiritual pedagogy must include content on world religions, traditions, and faiths, as well as the impact of religious discrimination. Furthermore, an awareness of the roles that trauma, loss, and grief play in sparking and catapulting spiritual thoughts and reliance on spiritual beliefs and practices will inform a spiritually appropriate and competent practice (Boynton, 2016).

Field educators' roles will include preparing students for spiritually competent practice, while remaining aware of students' own spirituality, struggles, and strengths. This includes open discussion about the ethical challenges of engaging spirituality in practice and supporting spirituality in the daily life of the student. To assist students through spiritual challenges and provide a "hearth" environment, the field instructor-student relationship is critical. These matters are often deeply personal and at times ineffable. We invite supervisors and field educators to move beyond administrative and managerial approaches to supervision and be willing to enter into dialogues about spiritual, existential, and moral matters. While students are often encouraged to self-reflect during their social work training, field instructors' and educators' own self-reflection and willingness are vital for spiritual dialogue. We do not need to be experts in spiritual competency to embrace the mystery and step into dialogues on spiritual and existential matters. Incorporating spiritual awareness in practice is a lifelong learning process.

While spiritual pedagogy needs to be infused in social work program learning outcomes and standards of practice, research and development of best practices is required; in addition, there ought to be explicit attention given to spirituality in ethics, accreditation standards of schools, and organizations. Social workers should advocate for policy, practices, and procedures to include spirituality and follow holistic approaches.

Conclusion

Though spirituality has been largely neglected in the social work field and profession, spiritual issues abound for clients and students alike. Rather than avoiding these realities, social work needs to tackle such issues head on. We, as social workers, need to pull our heads out of the proverbial sand and acknowledge that this is a crucial area of practice that we must be ready to address. Spiritual struggles and distress are one area of spiritual experience that social workers may confront within themselves or with their clients. It is important for field educators to be aware that students may be particularly vulnerable to spiritual struggles, and that social work education and practicum experiences can spur on spiritual contemplation and cogitation.

We require a willingness and processes in field education to build awareness and meaningful responses to students' spiritual needs during this major transition period. Spiritual distress can emerge from trauma, grief, and loss, as well as through our development as humans when our worldviews are challenged. Both clients and students, as well as seasoned professionals, will at times face challenges to their spiritual paradigms. We recognize that there is a reciprocal nature of practice driving research and research driving practice, and thus it was our aim to impart some of the key research and practice implications related to the historically suppressed, yet emergent context of spirituality for clients, students, supervisors, and educators in field education. We hope that social workers will find supportive ways to attend to the spiritual component for clients and students and find innovative ways to integrate spirituality into their daily practice. We also hope that these aspects will drive groundbreaking research questions and support professional knowledge in this dynamic, complex, and multi-faceted area of field education.

REFERENCES

Abu-Raiya, H., Pargament, K. I., Krause, N., & Ironson, G. (2015). Robust links between religious/spiritual struggles, psychological distress, and well-being in a national sample of American adults. *American Journal of Orthopsychiatry, 85*(6), 565. https://pubmed.ncbi.nlm.nih.gov/26301940/

Ai, A. L. 2002. Integrating spirituality into professional education: a challenging but feasible task. *Journal of Teaching in Social Work, 22*(1–2), 103–130. https://doi.org/10.1300/J067v22n01_08

American Council on Social Work Education (2012). *Advanced Social Work Practice in Trauma*. [Pamphlet]. Council on Social Work Education. Retrieved from https://cswe.org/getattachment/Accreditation/Other/EPAS-Implementation/TraumabrochurefinalforWeb.pdf.aspx

Ano, G. G., & Pargament, K. I. (2013). Predictors of spiritual struggles: An exploratory study. *Mental Health, Religion & Culture, 16*(4), 419–434. https://doi.org/10.1080/13674676.2012.680434

Ano, G. G., & Vasconcelles, E. B. (2005). Religious coping and psychological adjustment to stress: A meta-analysis. *Journal of Clinical Psychology, 61*(4), 461–480. https://doi.org/10.1002/jclp.20049

Barker, S. L., & Floersch, J. E. (2010). Practitioners' understandings of spirituality: Implications for social work education. *Journal of Social Work Education, 46*(3), 357–370. https://doi.org/10.5175/JSWE.2010.200900033

Baskin, C. (2002). Holistic healing and accountability: Indigenous restorative justice. *Child Care in Practice, 8*(2), 133–136. https://doi.org/10.1080/13575270220148585

Belcher, J. R., & Sarmiento Mellinger, M. (2016). Integrating spirituality with practice and social justice: The challenge for social work. *Journal of Religion & Spirituality in Social Work: Social Thought, 35*(4), 377–394. https://doi.org/10.1080/15426432.2016.1229645

Bell, H., Busch, N. B., & Fowler, D. N. (2005). Spirituality and domestic violence work. *IDVSA Journal Articles.* https://doi.org/10.22329/csw.v6i2.5661

Black, P. N., Jeffreys, D., & Hartley, E. K. (1993). Personal history of psychosocial trauma in the early life of social work and business students. *Journal of Social Work Education, 29*(2), 171–180. https://doi.org/10.1080/10437797.1993.10778812

Boynton, H. M. (2009). Children's spirituality: An exploration of literature and a rationale for its inclusion in social work. *Child and Family Professional, 12*(1), 25–44. https://doi.org/10.1080/1364436X.2011.580727

Boynton, H. M. (2011). Children's spirituality: Epistemology and theory from various helping professions. *International Journal of Children's Spirituality, 16*(2), 109–127. https://doi.org/10.1080/1364436X.2011.580727

Boynton, H. M. (2014). The healthy group: A mind, body and spirit approach to treating anxiety and depression in youth. *Journal of Religion and Spirituality in Social Work: Social Thought, 33*, 236–253. https://doi.org/10.1080/15426432.2014.930629

Boynton, H. M. (2016). *Navigating in seclusion: The complicated terrain of children's spirituality in trauma, grief and loss* [Unpublished doctoral dissertation]. University of Calgary. http://hdl.handle.net/11023/2997

Boynton, H. M., & Mellan, C. (2021). Co-creating authentic sacred therapeutic space: A spiritually sensitive framework for counselling children. *Religions, 12*, 524. https://doi.org/10.3390/ rel12070524

Boynton, H. M., & Vis, J. (2011). Meaning making, spirituality, and creative expressive therapies: Pathways to posttraumatic growth in grief and loss for children. *Counselling and Spirituality, 30*(2), 137–159. https://psycnet.apa.org/record/2012-00594-006

Boynton, H. M., & Vis, J. (2017). Spirituality: The missing component in trauma therapy across the lifespan. In B. Crisp (Ed.), *Routledge Handbook of Religion, Spirituality and Social Work* (pp. 193–201). Routledge.

Bryant, A. N., & Astin, H. S. (2008). The correlates of spiritual struggle during the college years. *The Journal of Higher Education, 79*(1), 1–27. https://doi.org/10.1080/00221546.2008.11772084

Buckey, J. W. (2012). Empirically based spirituality education: Implications for social work research and practice. *Journal of Social Service Research, 38*(2), 260–271. https://doi.org/10.1080/01488376.2011.647979

Canadian Association of Social Workers. 2005. *CASW Code of Ethics*. [online] Available at: https://casw-acts.ca/en/Code-of-Ethics.

Canda, E. R., & Furman, L. D. (2010). *Spiritual diversity in social work practice: The heart of helping* (2nd ed.). The Free Press.

Canda, E.R., Furman, L. D., & Canda, H. J. (2019). *Spiritual diversity in social work practice: The heart of helping* (3rd ed.). Oxford University Press. USA.

Canda, E. R., Nakashima, M., & Furman, L. D. (2004). Ethical considerations about spirituality in social work: Insights from a national qualitative survey. *Families in Society: The Journal of Contemporary Social Services, 85*(1), 27–35. https://doi.org/10.1606/1044-3894.256

Captari, L. E., Hook, J. N., Hoyt, W., Davis, D. E., McElroy-Heltzel, S. E., & Worthington Jr, E. L. (2018). Integrating clients' religion and spirituality within psychotherapy: A comprehensive meta-analysis. *Journal of Clinical Psychology, 74*(11), 1938–1951. https://doi.org/10.1002/jclp.22681

Carrington, A. M. (2013). An integrated spiritual practice framework for use within social work. *Journal of Religion & Spirituality in Social Work: Social Thought, 32*(4), 287–312. https://doi.org/10.1080/15426432.2013.839206

Cheon, J. W., & Canda, E. R. (2010). The meaning and engagement of spirituality for positive youth development in social work. *Families in Society: The Journal of Contemporary Social Services, 91*(2), 121–126. https://doi.org/10.1606/1044-3894.3981

Coates, J., Graham, J. R., Swartzentruber, B., & Ouellette, B. (Eds.) (2007). *Spirituality and Social Work: Selected Canadian Readings*. Canadian Scholar's Press.

Coholic, D. (2003). Student and educator viewpoints on incorporating spirituality in social work pedagogy: An overview and discussion of research findings. *Currents: New Scholarship in the Human Services, 2*(2), 35–48.

Coholic, D. (2006). Spirituality in social work pedagogy: A Canadian perspective. *Journal of Teaching in Social Work, 26*(3–4), 197–217. https://doi.org/10.1300/J067v26n03_13

Colvin, A. D., & Bullock, A. N. (2017, November). Moral entanglements for Christian students entering field education [Conference session]. NACSW Convention 2017, Charlotte, NC, United States.

Crisp, B. R. (2016). *Spirituality and social work*. Routledge.

Crisp, B. R. (2020). Charting the development of spirituality in social work in the second decade of the 21st century: A critical commentary. *The British Journal of Social Work, 50*(3), 961–978. https://doi.org/10.1093/bjsw/bcaa015

Danso, R. (2018). Cultural competence and cultural humility: A critical reflection on key cultural diversity concepts. *Journal of Social Work, 18*(4), 410–430. https://doi.org/10.1177%2F1468017316654341

De Souza, M. (2012). Connectedness and *connectedness*: The dark side of spirituality-Implications for education. *International Journal of Children's Spirituality, 17*(4), 291–303. https://doi.org/10.1080/1364436X.2012.752346

Ellison, C. G., & Lee, J. (2010). Spiritual struggles and psychological distress: Is there a dark side of religion? *Social Indicators Research, 98*(3), 501–517. https://link.springer.com/content/pdf/10.1007/s11205-009-9553-3.pdf

Exline, J. J., & Rose, E. (2005). Religious and spiritual struggles. *Handbook of the Psychology of Religion and Spirituality*, 315–330.

Exline, J. J., Yali, A. M., & Sanderson, W. C. (2000). Guilt, discord, and alienation: The role of religious strain in depression and suicidality. *Journal of Clinical Psychology, 56*(12), 1481–1496. https://doi.org/10.1002/1097-4679(200012)56:12%3C1481::AID-1%3E3.0.CO;2-A

Fowler, J.W. (1981). *Stages of faith the psychology of human development and the quest for meaning*. Harper Collins.

Gabarino, J., & Bedard, C. (1996). Spiritual challenges to children facing violent trauma. *Childhood, 3*(4), 467–478. https://doi.org/10.1177%2F0907568296003004004

Gardner, F. (2020). Social work and spirituality: Reflecting on the last 20 years. *Journal for the Study of Spirituality, 10*(1), 72–83. https://doi.org/10.1080/20440243.2020.1726054

Gelman, C. R. (2004). Anxiety experienced by foundation year MSW students entering field placement: Implications for admissions, curriculum, and field education. *Journal of Social Work Education, 40*, 39–54. https://doi.org/10.1080/10437797.2004.10778478

George, M., & Ellison, V. (2015). Incorporating spirituality into social work practice with migrants. *British Journal of Social Work, 45*(6), 1717–1733. https://doi.org/10.1093/bjsw/bcu035

Graham, J. R., Coholic, D., & Coates, J. (2007). Spirituality as a guiding construct in the development of Canadian social work: Past and present considerations. *Spiritual and Social Work: Selected Canadian Readings*, 23–46. https://ojs.uwindsor.ca/index.php/csw/article/download/5774/4713?inline=1

Groen, J., Coholic, D., & Graham, J. R. (Eds.). (2012). *Spirituality in education and social work: Theory, practice, and pedagogies.* Wilfrid Laurier University Press.

Harris, H., Yancey, G., & Myers, D. (2016). Social work field education in and with congregations and religiously-affiliated organizations in a Christian context. *Religions, 7*(5), 52. https://doi.org/10.3390/rel7050052

Hefti, R. (2011). Integrating religion and spirituality into mental health care, psychiatry and psychotherapy. *Religions, 2*, 611–627. https://doi.org/10.3390/rel2040611

Hodge, D.R. (2001). Spiritual assessment: A review of major qualitative methods and a new framework for assessing spirituality. *Social Work, 46*(3), 203–214.

Hodge, D.R. (2005a). Spirituality in social work education: A development and discussion of goals that flow from the profession's ethical mandates. *Social Work Education, 24*(1), 37–55.

Hodge, D.R. (2005b). Developing a spiritual assessment toolbox: A discussion of the strengths and limitations of five different assessment methods. *Health and Social Work, 30*(4), 314–323.

Hodge, D. R. (2018). The evolution of spirituality and religion in international social work discourse: Strengths and limitations of the contemporary understanding. *Journal of Religion & Spirituality in Social Work: Social Thought, 37*(1), 3–23. https://doi.org/10.1080/15426432.2019.1597663

Hodge, D. R. (2019). Spiritual assessment with refugees and other migrant populations: A necessary foundation for successful clinical practice. *Journal of Religion & Spirituality in Social Work: Social Thought, 38*(2), 121–139. https://doi.org/10.1080/15426432.2017.1350125

Hooyman, N.R., Kramer, B.J., & Sanders, S. (2021). *Living through loss: Interventions across the life span.* Columbia University Press.

Jacobs, C. (2015). Contemplative spaces in social work practice. *Journal of Pain and Symptom Management, 49*(1), 150–154. https://doi.org/10.1016/j.jpainsymman.2014.10.004

Knight, C. (2010). Indirect trauma in the field practicum: Secondary traumatic stress, vicarious trauma, and compassion fatigue among social work students and their field instructors. *The Journal of Baccalaureate Social Work, 15*(1), 31–52. https://psycnet.apa.org/record/2011-19774-003

Koenig, H., Koenig, H. G., King, D., & Carson, V. B. (2012). *Handbook of religion and health.* OUP, USA.

Kvarfordt, C. L., & Herba, K. (2018). Religion and spirituality in social work practice with children and adolescents: A survey of Canadian practitioners. *Child and Adolescent Social Work Journal, 35*(2), 153–167. https://doi.org/10.1007/s10560-017-0513-5

Kvarfordt, C. L., & Sheridan, M. J. (2007). The role of religion and spirituality in working with children and adolescents: Results of a national survey. *Journal of Religion & Spirituality in Social Work: Social Thought, 26*(3), 1–23. https://doi.org/10.1300/J377v26n03_01

Kvarfordt, C., & Sheridan, M. J. (2010). Predicting the use of spiritually-based interventions with children and adolescents: Implications for social work practice. *Currents: Scholarship in the Human Services, 9*(1), 1–30. https://cdm.ucalgary.ca/index.php/currents/article/view/15885

Kvarfordt, C. L., Sheridan, M. J., & Taylor, O. (2018). Religion and spirituality in social work curriculum: A survey of Canadian educators. *The British Journal of Social Work, 48*(5), 1469–1487. https://doi.org/10.1093/bjsw/bcx069

Larkin, S. (2010). Spiritually sensitive professional development of self: A curricular module for field education. *Social Work & Christianity, 37*(4). https://www2.simmons.edu/ssw/fe/i/17-157.pdf

Lavallée, L. F., & Poole, J. M. (2010). Beyond recovery: Colonization, health and healing for Indigenous people in Canada. *International Journal of Mental Health and Addiction, 8*(2), 271–281. https://link.springer.com/article/10.1007/s11469-009-9239-8

Lee, E. K. O., & Barrett, C. (2007). Integrating spirituality, faith, and social justice in social work practice and education: A pilot study. *Journal of Religion & Spirituality in Social Work: Social Thought, 26*(2), 1–21. https://doi.org/10.1300/J377v26n02_01

Magolda, M. B. B. (2008). Three elements of self-authorship. *Journal of College Student Development, 49*(4), 269–284. https://doi.org/10.1353/csd.0.0016

McConnell, K. M., Pargament, K. I., Ellison, C. G., & Flannelly, K. J. (2006). Examining the links between spiritual struggles and symptoms of psychopathology in a national sample. *Journal of Clinical Psychology, 62*(12), 1469–1484. https://doi.org/10.1002/jclp.20325

Moffatt, K. M., Oxhandler, H. K., & Ellor, J. W. (2021). Religion and spirituality in graduate social work education: A national survey. *Journal of Social Work Education, 57*(2) 287–298. https://doi.org/10.1080/10437797.2019.1670307

Nash, M., & B. Stewart (2005). Spirituality and hope in social work for social justice. *Currents 4*(1). Retrieved June 12, 2010 from http://wcmprod2.ucalgary.ca/currents/files/currents/v4nl_nash.pdf.

Okundaye, J. N., Gray, C., & Gray, L. B. (1999). Reimaging field instruction from a spiritually sensitive perspective: An alternative approach. *Social Work, 44*(4), 371–383. https://doi.org/10.1093/sw/44.4.371

Oxhandler, H. K., & Ellor, J. W. (2017). Christian social workers' views and integration of clients' religion and spirituality in practice. *Social Work & Christianity, 44*(3), 3–24. http://www.nacsw.org/Publications/SWC/SWC44_3Sample.pdf

Oxhandler, H. K., & Giardina, T. D. (2017). Social workers' perceived barriers to and sources of support for integrating clients' religion and spirituality in practice. *Social Work, 62*(4), 323–332. https://doi.org/10.1093/sw/swx036

Oxhandler, H. K., & Pargament, K. I. (2014). Social work practitioners' integration of clients' religion and spirituality in practice: A literature review. *Social work, 59*(3), 271–279. https://doi.org/10.1093/sw/swu018

Oxhandler, H. K., Parrish, D. E., Torres, L. R., & Achenbaum, W. A. (2015). The integration of clients' religion and spirituality in social work practice: A national survey. *Social Work, 60*(3), 228–237. https://doi.org/10.1093/sw/swv018

Pandya, S. P. (2018). Students' views on expanding contours of social work practice through spirituality. *Journal of Religion & Spirituality in Social Work: Social Thought, 37*(3), 302–322. https://doi.org/10.1080/15426432.2018.1485072

Pargament, K. I. (2011). *Spiritually integrated psychotherapy: Understanding and addressing the sacred*. Guilford Press.

Pargament, K. I., Desai, K. M., & McConnell, K. M. (2014). Spirituality: A pathway to posttraumatic growth or decline? In Calhoun, L. G., & Tedeschi, R. G. (Eds.), *Handbook of posttraumatic growth* (pp. 121–137). Routledge.

Parks, S. D. (2000*). Big questions, worthy dreams: Mentoring young adults in their search for meaning, purpose, and faith*. Jossey-Bass.

Phillips, C. (2014). Spirituality and social work: Introducing a spiritual dimension into social work education and practice. *Aotearoa New Zealand Social Work, 26*(4), 65–77. https://doi.org/10.11157/anzswj-vol26iss4id27

Poyser, M. (2004). Healing trauma and spiritual growth: the relevance of religious education to emotionally and behaviourally disturbed children looked after by local authorities. *Support for Learning, 19*(3), 125–131. https://doi.org/10.1111/j.0268-2141.2004.00334.x

Preston J., & Shin F. (2017). Spiritual experiences evoke awe through the small self in both religious and non-religious individuals. *Journal of Experimental Social Psychology 70*: 212–221. https://doi.org/10.1016/j.jesp.2016.11.006

Seinfeld, J. (2012). Spirituality in social work practice. *Clinical Social Work Journal, 40*(2), 240–244. https://doi.org/10.1007/s10615-012-0386-1

Sellers, S. L., & Hunter, A. G. (2005). Private pain, public choices: Influence of problems in the family of origin on career choices among a cohort of MSW students. *Social work education, 24*(8), 869–881. https://doi.org/10.1080/02615470500342223

Senreich, E. (2013). An inclusive definition of spirituality for social work education and practice. *Journal of Social Work Education, 49*(4), 548–563. https://doi.org/10.1080/10437797.2013.812460

Sheridan, M. J. (2004). Predicting the use of spiritually-derived interventions in social work practice: A survey of practitioners. *Journal of Religion & Spirituality in Social Work: Social Thought, 23*(4), 5–25. https://doi.org/10.1300/J377v23n04_02

Sheridan, M. J. (2009). Ethical issues in the use of spiritually based interventions in social work practice: What are we doing and why. *Journal of Religion & Spirituality in Social Work: Social Thought, 28*(1–2), 99–126. https://doi.org/10.1080/15426430802643687

Statistics Canada. (2017, October 25a). *Ethnic and cultural origins of Canadians: Portrait of a rich heritage*. Statistics Canada. Retrieved June 27, 2021 from https://www12. statcan.gc.ca/census-recensement/2016/as-sa/98-200-x2016016/98-200-x2016016-eng.cfm

Statistics Canada. (2017, October 25b). *Number and proportion of visible minority population in Canada, 1981 to 2036*. Statistics Canada. Retrieved June 27, 2021 from https://www.statcan.gc.ca/eng/dai/btd/othervisuals/other010

Tangenberg, K. (2012). Congregational mentoring and discipleship: Implications for social work practice. *Journal of Religion & Spirituality in Social Work: Social Thought, 31*(3), 285–302. https://doi.org/10.1080/15426432.2012.679844

Thompson, N., & Walsh, M. (2010). The existential basis of trauma. *Journal of Social Work Practice, 24*(4), 377–389. https://doi.org/10.1080/02650531003638163

Varrella, S. (2021, March 9). *Number of immigrants in Canada 2000-2020*. Statista. Retrieved June 27, 2021 from https://www.statista.com/statistics/443063/number-of-immigrants-in-Canada/

Vis, J. A., & Marie Boynton, H. (2008). Spirituality and transcendent meaning making: Possibilities for enhancing posttraumatic growth. *Journal of Religion and Spirituality in Social Work: Social Thought, 27*(1–2), 69–86. https://doi.org/10.1080/15426430802113814

Weber, B. M. (2015). Gender, race, religion, faith? Rethinking intersectionality in German feminisms. *European Journal of Women's Studies, 22*(1), 22–36. https://doi.org/10.1177/1350506814552084

Whipple, E. E., Hall, R. E., & Sustaita, F. L. (2015). The significance of family and spirituality vis-à-vis Southeast Asian clients: Culturally sensitive social work practice with refugee populations. *Journal of Religion & Spirituality in Social Work: Social Thought, 34*(4), 356–371. https://doi.org/10.1080/15426432.2015.1067584

Wilt, J. A., Exline, J. J., & Pargament, K. I. (2021). Daily measures of religious/spiritual struggles: Relations to depression, anxiety, satisfaction with life, and meaning. *Psychology of Religion and Spirituality*. https://doi.org/10.1037/rel0000399

Ying, Y. W. (2008). The buffering effect of self-detachment against emotional exhaustion among social work students. *Journal of Religion, Spirituality, and Social Work: Social Thought, 27*(1–2), 127–146. https://doi.org/10.1080/15426430802114051

Zapf, M. K. (2008). Transforming social work's understanding of person and environment: Spirituality and the "common ground." *Journal of Religion & Spirituality in Social Work: Social Thought, 27*(1–2), 171–181. https://doi.org/10.1080/15426430802114200

How to Enhance Brain Potential in Fieldwork Education? The Multimodal Integration of Imagination and Trauma (MIIT) Framework

Ricardo Diego Suárez Rojas

Humans are capable of both involuntary and voluntary acts of imagination: for example, dreaming of a dystopia and writing about a utopia (Vyshedskiy, 2020). The neuroscientific discovery of our conscious and unconscious creativity has several implications for improving health and social conditions (Agnati et al., 2013; Fox, 2013; Vyshedskiy, 2019). For example, voluntary imaginative actions are necessary to empower clients and transform systems in the social work profession. However, chronic and toxic exposure to stressors can harm practitioners' inventive performance, in turn impacting their adaptability and spontaneity (Ashley-Binge & Cousins, 2020; Parker & Maestripieri, 2011; Sapolsky, 2004; Vyshedskiy, 2020). As a sign of concern, there is growing research regarding social work students in the United States who experience vicarious trauma, discrimination, and isolation caused by interpersonal and institutional factors (Cowie et al., 2018; Evans et al., 2018; Garcia-Williams et al., 2014; Rasheem & Brunson, 2018). How can social work students remain creative to navigate the challenges of their training and future professional practice?

The signature pedagogy in social work education is the field placement experience. Students can apply concepts and techniques learned in the classroom, alongside clients, under the guidance of an experienced field instructor (Bogo, 2020; Hummell et al., 2010; Wayne et al., 2010). However, besides field placement's potential to be a site for learning and growth, students also may face challenges beyond their capacities, inadequate supervision, and suffer from demoralization and exhaustion (Bogo, 2015; Wayne et al., 2006). Given how challenging it is to become a trauma-informed social worker, field education must be preventive, healing, and stimulating.

How is the study of imagination relevant for developing trauma-informed education and practice? To address this question, the present chapter introduces the novel *Multimodal Integration of Imagination and Trauma (MIIT) framework*. As a theory in development, it seeks to understand how perception relates to the evolution of imagination types. The purpose of this research is to contribute to the healing of psychosocial and historical trauma. The MIIT framework was developed by synthesizing the author's years of interdisciplinary and community practice with collaborators in Chiapas, Mexico City, Chicago, and Boston. Furthermore, its evolution is continuously disseminated through social media (Suárez Rojas, 2022).

The MIIT framework seeks to provide a schematic logic for interpreting and enhancing human development. Moreover, it intends to produce a methodology for integrating healing and learning in various settings and among diverse populations (see Figure 16.1). Therefore, this chapter introduces the MIIT framework's nine working principles, accompanied by respective recommendations for field education. In addition, each section is prefaced by a transdisciplinary dialogue, intending to situate this work in a larger intellectual context, synthesize findings, and derive implications (Anastas, 2014). Lastly, the recommendations for unleashing brain potential may be adapted, with congruent modifications, to other academic disciplines, workplace training settings, and age groups.

Figure 16.1: Conceptual Model of the Multimodal Integration of Imagination and Trauma (MIIT) Framework

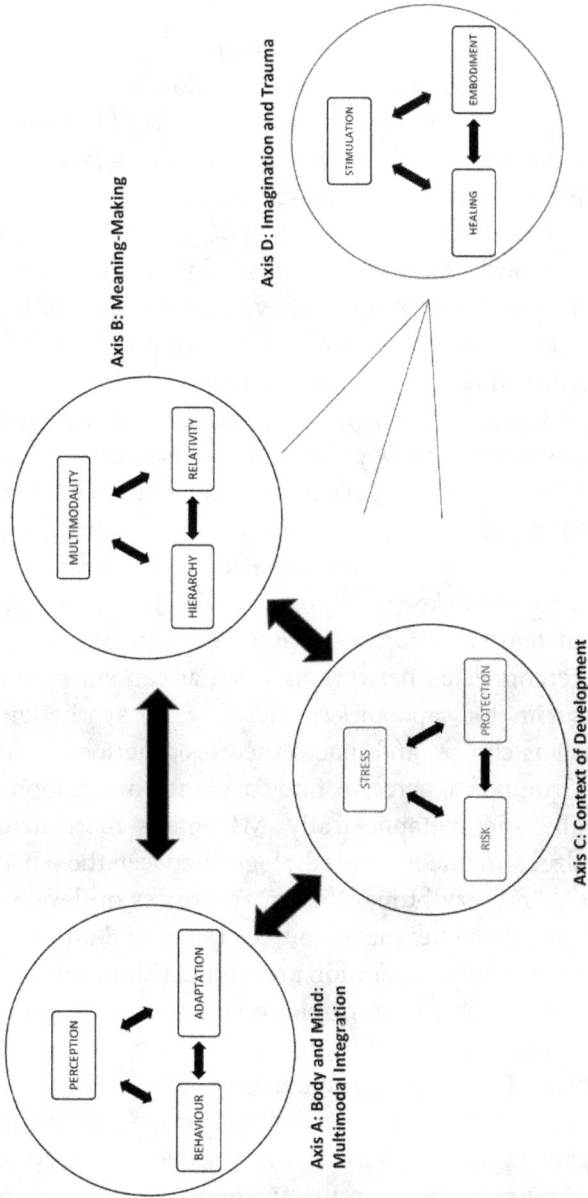

Note: The MIIT Framework seeks to offer a comprehensive view of human development. Axis A represents how multimodal integration is essential for perception and behaviour, thus allowing countless species to adapt in novel ways. Axis B touches on the social world of meaning (multimodality), recognizing the vastness of possibilities while also being mindful of power dynamics that privilege certain modalities over others. Finally, Axis C establishes that an individual may be exposed to protective and risk factors, and the stress response system can result in distinctive coping mechanisms. In turn, the synthesis from this theoretical dialogue informs an approach for intervention and implementation that considers imagination and trauma in a continuum (Axis D). Stimulation is a catalyst for healing and embodiment as long as the specific stimuli lead to growth.

Unity Principle: Commonalities Among Learners, Educators, and Clients

How is it possible that social workers can imagine a better future for society? For understanding the voluntary imagination, it is necessary to start from perception, an evolutionary older mechanism (Thomas, 1999). *Multisensory* or *multimodal integration* (MI) is the name given to how the nervous system differentiates and processes multisensory stimuli automatically and reflectively (Stein & Stanford, 2008). MI allows processing sensory inputs, consciously and unconsciously, by integrating types of data and thus reacting with a motor or behavioural response (Gingras et al., 2009). If a coherent representation of experience gets produced, performance in a determined task can improve (Stein et al., 2020).

The remarkable velocity in which neuronal ensembles arrange categories and reactions may partially be thanks to *schemas* — representations of data structures and types of events — that facilitate success in future problems based on past experiences (Gick & Holyoak, 1980; Richland et al., 2012). Moreover, schemas are conceptual and embodied: our bodies create and enact blueprints to keep our posture, allowing us to move with naturality and even mastery effortlessly (Reinersmann & Lücke, 2018). Maintaining an interconnected network of schemas can enhance several cognitive and sensorimotor capabilities. Therefore, by synthesizing relevant schemas (such as clinical and macro theories), the social work student may be better equipped to perceive, find coherence, and respond (MI).

Both biologically and metaphorically, MI entails motivated communication, a mindful and unconscious dialogue between the self and the world. MI is present in every human being, regardless of developmental capabilities, culture, or contextual resources (Stein & Stanford, 2008). Moreover, MI is essential for cooperation and competition across species, from social mammals to worms with relatively simple nervous systems (Ghosh et al., 2017; Viaud-Delmon et al., 2011). MI is also a relevant system in artificial intelligence (AI), robots, and machines (Zeng et al., 2020).

How is it possible that MI is so prevalent across life and technology? The answer is elegant in its simplicity: the intersection between sensory and motor maps. Any perception occurs in the space-time continuum, even if distorted or virtual (Stein et al., 2020). MI is involved in how a bat navigates the darkness, the mantis shrimp recognizes colours beyond the human visual spectrum, or a social worker makes a judgment call. By considering the previous insights from the neuroscientific literature, the first principle of the MIIT framework states:

1. **Unity Principle**: "Unity" refers to the commonalities concerning perceptual systems across living beings and machines, robots, and AI. Multimodal Integration (MI) names the capacity to perceive multisensory inputs and respond with an output. Perception is simultaneously a conscious and unconscious process, which actively differentiates and integrates data to form conceptual and embodied schemas. Any perceptual event happens in the space-time continuum, even those distorted or virtual.

Informed by the unity principle, the first recommendation for field education is to *avoid categorizing students, as they are all capable of integration.* Students arrive at an agency with different trajectories and capabilities, making it compelling to classify them under the maxim that "everyone learns differently." However, if a field instructor conceives a student as a "visual, interpersonal learner," does that not entail reducing that person's potential? Learning styles lack empirical evidence to firmly prove their existence (Kirschner, 2017). Moreover, their arbitrary definitions are mutually exclusive, making us believe that we are incapable of anything beyond our box, thus limiting exploration and discovery (Newton & Miah, 2017). Instead of classifying students, or clients, through inconsistent categorizations, the alternative is to recognize that differences arise from the same source: an evolutionary system that allows us to perceive, integrate, and respond.

It is essential to underscore that the MIIT framework's first principle and recommendation by no means intend to reduce the complexity inherent to diversity — an issue covered in the next section. Furthermore, the framework does not suggest the possibility of instituting a mechanistic academic structure that can be appropriate to the vast variety of field placement contexts (Andharia, 2011). Instead, the emphasis of this section is to present unity concerning perception (multimodal integration) and its extended presence across the life continuum. By recognizing commonalities, social workers will be better equipped to understand differences — and vice versa.

Divergence Principle: Differences among Learners

MI is present in all perceptual scenarios, building from a complex blueprint. And yet, there are countless gradations in how living and artificial beings perceive, integrate, and act. This recognition leads to the MIIT framework's second principle:

> 2. **Divergence Principle**: "Divergence" refers to the countless variations in perceptual systems. Anatomical and behavioural gradations influence the perception of multisensory stimuli, data integration, and performance in the space-time continuum.

Divergence leads to the second recommendation for field education: *respect differences, but do not obviate power disparities.* Being capable of MI does not mean that every student and staff member in the agency has the same preferences, resources, and motivations. Flexibility and inventiveness are always a requirement for an instructor who wishes to honour the particularity of each individual. Despite field placement being regulated by academic institutions and, allegedly, uniform administrative frameworks, fieldwork learning is highly heterogeneous and intricate — thus mirroring the students and instructors themselves (Bogo, 2020).

Furthermore, it is essential to challenge how racism and interrelated inequities created by capitalism and patriarchy impact social work education and practice (Rao et al., 2021). This reckoning requires courage and embracing discomfort. If a student or group feels that their identities are not recognized, misrepresented, or outright threatened, the teaching experience will become traumatizing. Establishing rapport with students through an intersectional logic (Atewologun, 2018) is one of the most important goals for a field instructor. Therefore, it is imperative to create a space that respects differences while not ignoring them.

Semiotic Infinity Principle: Humanity's Double-Edged Sword

The differences in MI across species may partially explain survival and domination. According to the *semiotic relativity hypothesis*, humans have a particular evolutionary advantage in creating collective meaning (Lucy, 2016). How else can we hold the potential to produce art, scientific break-throughs, and technology to save or destroy lives if not by perceiving and communicating? The evolution of language, intertwined with that of MI, partly explains such abilities: linking words to objects (Broca's area in the brain) and organizing grammatical sentences (Wernicke's area) to share complex thoughts (Lucy, 1997; Mufwene, 2013; Vyshedskiy, 2019).

Language evolution also has relied on the most advanced form of voluntary imagination: *prefrontal synthesis*, the conscious juxtaposition of mental images, which activates the lateral prefrontal cortex (Vyshedskiy et al., 2020). This imaginative faculty is the basis for synthesizing objects from memory into a novel production. Furthermore, it leads to complex operations such as self-reference: how words themselves provide the means to think about the nature of words. For example, prefrontal synthesis allows the social work intern to engage with clients and institutions, recognize patterns and exceptions, and act on critical awareness of self and society.

Furthermore, meaning-creation is also a cultural phenomenon. *Semiotic modes* are material resources agreed upon socially to communicate — e.g., speech, written word, gestures, numbers, images, colour, music, and virtual coding, to name a few. Despite ecological variations, every culture creates *signs* (a concurrence of form and meaning), motivated by their members' interests and composed with available resources (Kress, 2010). By bearing in mind these insights, the MIIT framework's third principle is:

3. **Semiotic Infinity Principle**: "Semiotic infinity" refers to how human beings are different than other species given their endless capacity for meaning-creation. Multimodal integration (MI) in humans is distinctive owing to the emergence of complex language, prefrontal synthesis, and self-awareness. This evolutionary advantage makes

Figure 16.2: How to Encourage Students to Co-create Solutions in Their Field Placements

	Remembering	Understanding	Applying	Analyzing	Evaluating	Creating
Clinical Social Worker	Identify symptoms. Recall how they relate to disorders and empowering treatments.	Interpret and summarize a client's narrative.	Implement clinical techniques into the ways you listen and ask questions.	Develop self-awareness. Distinguish risk from protective factors.	Monitor your biases and your performance.	Generate an action plan alongside your client.
Macro Social Worker	Identify organizational practices. Recall relevant policies.	Interpret and summarize the organization's functions.	Implement a cost-benefit analysis and a budget plan.	Organize observations. Distinguish risk from protective factors.	Introduce strategies to monitor organizational biases and performance.	Generate a logic model alongside your client.

Note: An example of how the revised Bloom's Taxonomy can guide field educators in encouraging the creation of solutions. This example represents a continuum, where each dimension may require factual, procedural, conceptual, or metacognitive knowledge.

humans capable of countless forms of creation, destruction, and reconfiguration through diverse modalities.

By understanding what makes human beings unique, the third recommendation for field education is : *encourage students to co-create solutions alongside their clients*. According to Bloom's revised taxonomy of education, creativity is a rigorous process that requires mastery of several cognitive skills: higher learning areas (where voluntary imagination is located) depend on previous foundations (Armstrong, 2016). From the bottom to the top, the taxonomy includes the following cognitive dimensions: Remembering > Understanding > Applying > Analyzing > Evaluating > Creating (Forehand, 2010). Furthermore, the following types of knowledge are present in each area: factual (e.g., terminology), conceptual (e.g., theories), procedural (e.g., techniques), and metacognitive (e.g., thinking about our own thinking). Importantly to note, the elements of both the cognitive and knowledge dimensions are related in a continuum, rather than simply being superior or inferior to others (Stanny, 2016).

In contrast to faculty liaisons, field instructors who supervise students in practicum do not have a syllabus. Therefore, the revised Bloom's taxonomy can assist the latter in measuring progress with concrete verbs (e.g., remembering, understanding, etc.) while maintaining a flexible structure. For the MIIT framework, "solutions" are conceptualized as a joint effort between different agents in a system (e.g., students and supervisors). This critical awareness is crucial, as clients have the same potential as social workers to create meaning that leads to further healing or trauma — yet with different power dynamics. Instead of conceiving students as vessels to be filled and tested (Freire, 1996; Kress, 2009), field instructors should facilitate engagement with multiple sources of meaning. Through a continuum logic, the goal of experiential learning should be empowering students' creative potential (see Figure 16.2).

Imperative Congruency Principle: Intersection of Theory and Practice

How can field instructors further emphasize meaning-creation among students? The discovery of the superior colliculus in cats, a structure in the midbrain capable of combining visual, auditory, and somatosensory stimuli (May, 2006; Wallace & Stein, 1997), offers answers for this question. The superior colliculus led scientists to realize how multisensory structures combine inputs to orient individuals in space and time. Across species, the predominant modality system varies (e.g., eyesight in humans and smell in mice), thus producing very distinctive behaviours.

These inquiries led to a unified principle: *MI follows an intuitive logic to improve behaviour as long as sensory inputs are perceived congruently* (Stein & Stanford, 2008). Congruency in perception means the degree to which stimuli get arranged cohesively. If a clear picture of the situation gets produced, the more likely that brain plasticity and performance will improve. Such enrichment will be proportionally higher thanks to blends of less effective stimuli in an *inverse-effectiveness logic*. In other words, when attention toward an individual sensory stimulus decreases, the capacity for integrating multiple inputs increases. For example, a social worker may better understand a problem and propose solutions by gathering different data types rather than just focusing on quantitative variables. Therefore, the inverse effectiveness mechanism is the reason why some authors say that MI can produce "something" from "nothing" (Stein et al., 2020).

However, suppose a social worker's perception develops an incongruent representation of reality by failing to understand the complexity of a client or institution; their performance will in turn degrade. The success of a stronger synaptic connection, and thus the action taking place, depends on whether the stimuli get derived from the same source and how advantageous it would be to combine information from independent sources (Stein & Stanford, 2008). For a social worker trying to grasp a specific context, multiple data sources also can introduce noise into a conclusion. Therefore, expertise and wisdom entail knowing when and how to apply theory and (or) intuition into a professional experience. As such, the MIIT framework's fourth principle emerges:

4. **Imperative Congruency Principle**: "Imperative congruency" refers to the need of a perceiver to process sensory inputs and produce a successful output. Multimodal Integration (MI) follows an intuitive logic to enhance performance and neural connections, depending on whether

data get arranged congruently. If attention to one stimulus decreases, the odds of integrating multisensory stimuli increase (inverse-effectiveness). Therefore, congruent multisensory stimulation may improve human potential.

The fourth recommendation for field education is: *amplify congruency between theory, practice, and self.* For a fruitful practicum, field instructors must establish a close relationship with faculty liaisons who serve as consultants and who understand a given school's curricula design and objectives. With the help of both types of educators, it is expected that students will learn how to practice the profession through two interwoven processes: a subjective reflection about ongoing field experiences and connections between practice events and acquired knowledge (Wayne et al., 2010).

However, what if the relationship between field instructors, faculty liaisons, and students gets precluded by personal or institutional factors? As field instructors naturally spend more time with practicum students, they are in a privileged position to encourage a more congruent understanding of the profession. Supervision times, either group or individual, should include a discussion concerning how the learning in the classroom mirrors or not the events in the placement. If there is no congruency between the two realms, the MIIT framework's fourth principle leads us to believe that the perception and performance of social workers in training will erode. Therefore, field instructors are responsible for providing continuous feedback to the faculty liaisons and, if possible, to field education coordinators and directors.

Furthermore, field instructors should also reflect on how concepts and procedures are congruent with students' identities, skillsets, and experiences. If becoming a social worker relies on data saturation (an excess of information from training, class contents, and clients' experiences), students will get overwhelmed and their retention and recall will diminish (Bjork & Bjork, 2011; Bjork et al., 2012). The better alternative is to approach learning via the inverse-effectiveness logic discussed in this section: congruently combine elements from independent sources (field, classroom, personal life) to improve perception and behaviour. These changes will allow students to navigate vast information networks with less stress, making practice meaningful and studying less cumbersome.

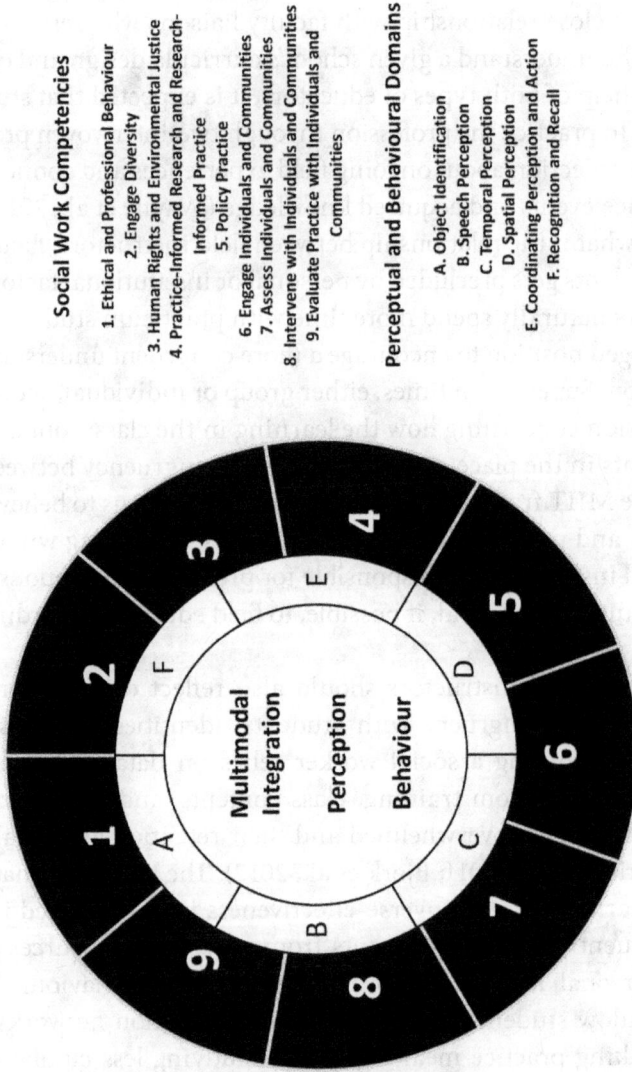

Figure 16.3: Multimodal Integration and the Development of Social Work Competencies

Social Work Competencies

1. Ethical and Professional Behaviour
2. Engage Diversity
3. Human Rights and Environmental Justice
4. Practice-Informed Research and Research-Informed Practice
5. Policy Practice
6. Engage Individuals and Communities
7. Assess Individuals and Communities
8. Intervene with Individuals and Communities
9. Evaluate Practice with Individuals and Communities

Perceptual and Behavioural Domains

A. Object Identification
B. Speech Perception
C. Temporal Perception
D. Spatial Perception
E. Coordinating Perception and Action
F. Recognition and Recall

Note: Multimodal Integration (MI) enhances performance in several perceptual and behavioural domains (represented by letters A to F, Stein et al., 2020). In turn, these abilities may inform the social work competencies, represented by numbers 1 to 9 (Council on Social Work Education, 2020). The idea of this figure is that of a roulette: one may argue that "Engage Diversity" benefits from any of the domains enhanced by MI, as long as the data are perceived congruently (e.g., speech perception). This image means to show the relevance of MI for the social work profession.

These assertions illustrate why multimodal integration (MI) is highly relevant for cultivating social work competencies (see Figure 16.3).

Disintegration Principle: Lost Communication

If integration is a synonym for communication, I define multimodal disintegration as the broken dialogue between body, brain, and the world. Such rupture brings in turn great suffering to individuals and groups. This working definition makes sense concerning relevant scientific literature. There is a growing trend in how MI's deterioration, which I take as a synonym for "disintegration," is associated with aging decay (de Dieuleveult et al., 2017) and specific disorders, including anxiety (Viaud-Delmon et al., 2011); schizophrenia (Tseng et al., 2015); autism spectrum disorder (Feldman et al., 2018); traumatic brain injury (Sarno et al., 2003); distortions in perception that result in delusions (Wallace et al., 2020); and post-traumatic stress disorder (Rabellino et al., 2018), to name a few. These studies do not assume simple causality between less effective MI and a particular condition. However, they may help us unravel how suffering and resiliency play out.

Furthermore, relevant to the MIIT framework's understanding of suffering, "trauma" has been defined as a loss of integration: a bio-psychological response created by a past injury, which overwhelms the self-defense system (Briere & Scott, 2014; Ford & Courtois, 2020). People who undergo traumatic experiences may present distortions in perception, emotional regulation, and memory recall, given the impairment in brain areas such as the thalamus, the amygdala, and the hippocampus (Van der Kolk, 2015). By losing integration between their minds and bodies, traumatized individuals grapple with a pessimistic or shameful personal narrative plagued by nightmares (acts of imagination). Problematically, the stories they tell themselves affect how they navigate daily life and think about the future (embodied and conceptual schemas).

In addition, there is a growing literature that defines the injuries provoked by colonialism and corruption on mental health as *psychosocial trauma* (Martín-Baró, 1989), *historical trauma* (Conching & Thayer, 2019; Gone et al., 2019), or *indigenous historical trauma* (Middelton-Moz et al., 2021; Panofsky et al., 2021). These authors have in common the recognition of the ripple effects of oppression on health and learning disparities. They also agree that our ancestors' experiences and living environments can predispose us to specific adaptations, as past and present events influence the *epigenome* — which regulates gene expression and its influence on phenotypes and behaviours (Singh, 2012; Thayer & Non, 2015). Consequently, the distribution of these "social injuries" largely depends on differences in the constraints and opportunities that people experience. Therefore, those who benefit or suffer from any political order embody varying degrees of resiliency and vulnerability.

As a biomedical concept, disintegration can contribute to the etiology and treatment of several mental and motor disorders. Furthermore, disintegration (in its political significance) also can help us interpret inequality, polarization, and violence. The MIIT framework's fifth principle summarizes these insights:

5. **Disintegration Principle**: "Disintegration" represents miscommunication between the body, the mind, and the world. This concept helps to understand several mental disorders, aging decay, and trauma. However, it has not only a biomedical but political dimension as well. Exploitative systems thrive by systematically diminishing creative potential, and isolating institutions and individuals. Moreover, past disintegration does not simply vanish in future generations, as historical trauma threatens the healthy development of oppressed populations around the globe.

By recognizing the dangers of disintegration, the fifth recommendation states: *hold space for tension and healing.* Social workers have an ethical obligation to observe and assess oppressive systems and seek transformations through various means (Andharia, 2011). Field instructors and faculty liaisons must grapple with how educational structures can harm students, and devise and implement strategies to mitigate such adverse effects. For immediate practices, field instructors should create space for self-care during placement hours, rather than asking students to be fully responsible for such an essential practice. For long-term strategies, one may suggest having a robust conversation regarding unpaid internships (Burke & Carton, 2013), expanding on tuition remissions, or turning the first-year placement into lab simulations and agency visits — so students lose only one year of income (Wayne et al., 2006).

Field supervision and assignments should not be stressful or dull. The consequences of being so can be damaging for health (Lee & Zelman, 2019; Sapolsky, 2001). Furthermore, field instructors must recognize the tremendous effort students make to complete their degrees while providing unpaid labour (Burke & Carton, 2013). Given the unrelenting demands of the job market, students require skills beyond menial administrative tasks — a need that can often be impeded by unstructured supervision. Therefore, field education must provide excellent training for future caregivers while building a considerate and stimulating environment. Such a mission cannot be fully accomplished without recognizing and openly discussing oppressive practices and structures.

Reimagination Principle: Boundless Potential for Healing or Trauma

If the disintegration principle makes us reflect on continuing injuries, conversely, what does continuing health entail? Imagination is the answer, yet its definition is complicated (Dor, 2017; Gerard, 1946). Importantly, MI is crucial for understanding its evolution. For example, the discovery of *mirror neurons* and their role in empathy (Gallese, 2011) and *Von Economo Neurons* and their importance to self-awareness (Butti et al., 2013) shed light on humanity's inventiveness. Significantly, these insights may help explain how *imagery* (the production of explicit and implicit mental pictures that we have experienced before) gave evolutionary rise to our creative drives.

As mentioned throughout this chapter, imagination is an umbrella term for voluntary, involuntary, and hybrid mechanisms. These types depend on the brain's functional modules, comparable to Russian dolls: a top-down series of nested structures that control various vital functions, from the autonomic ("bottom-up," brainstem to cortex signals) to the conscious ("top-down," cortex to brainstem signals).

Involuntary imagination types follow a bottom-up brain logic, depend on the posterior cortex, and develop early in a baby's life (e.g., REM dreaming and amodal completion). Voluntary types of imagination follow a top-down brain logic, activate the lateral prefrontal cortex, and develop once children engage with symbolic play (e.g., mental rotation, prefrontal analysis, and prefrontal synthesis). Lastly, hybrid types require interaction between previous mechanisms, such as lucid dreaming and categorically primed spontaneity popularly known as "eureka moments" (Vyshedskiy, 2019; 2020; Vyshedskiy et al., 2020).

Imagination types likely developed when existing imagery skills transformed through *exaptation*: an evolutionary trait that consists of manifesting a different function from its original purpose (e.g., using language for satires). Moreover, these novel possibilities appeared without affecting previously existing neural networks. Instead, the initial potential gets reused via *redeployment* (Agnati et al., 2013), as in the case, for example, of interns developing a new tactic based on their studies (exaptation) and integrating various elements from past training (redeployment), as if they were in a schema game where unlocking new abilities depends on how well past skills get rearranged.

The complex brain architecture behind creativity leads to a crucial question for social work: what are the social determinants of imagination? Neural circuitry depends on *myelin*, a fatty substance that coats axons and ensures a faster and more integrated flow of nerve impulses. Therefore, myelin is crucial for healthy brain functions and plasticity. Moreover, environmental influences continuously impact myelin integrity, as well as developmental trajectories (Forbes & Gallo, 2017). Consequently, numerous elements can either enhance (e.g., healthy diet, cognitive stimulation, loving relationships) or degrade (e.g., poor nutrition, social isolation, discrimination, boredom) myelination, which is essential for creative potential (Hackman et al., 2010; Lee & Zelman, 2019).

Thanks to these clarifications, now we can define a *thriving imagination* as a state of gray and white matter integrity, which may lead to increasingly effortless synthesis and mastery (voluntary imagination) and dreaming that does not disrupt well-being (involuntary imagination). Moreover, proper myelination could facilitate a more robust and integrated network, thus increasing the chances of developing spontaneous insights to solve problems (hybrid imagination). Therefore, imagination has specific properties to promote human potential, which can get harnessed through policy.

However, prefrontal synthesis, the most advanced type of voluntary imagination, has a strong critical period, which ends between five years old and puberty: children require recursive conversations to promote myelination of frontoposterior connections between the lateral prefrontal cortex and the posterior cortex (Vyshedskiy et al., 2020). Moreover, traumatic stress can reshape brain anatomy (Van der Kolk, 2015), thus wreaking havoc through nightmares and intrusive symptoms (involuntary imagination), eroding spontaneity (hybrid imagination), and engendering self-loathing and despair instead of positive narratives about the self and the world (voluntary imagination).

In brief, the boundless potential of imagination can be either for the benefit or detriment of an individual or group (Van der Kolk, 2015; Walsh, 2020). The sixth principle of the MIIT framework states:

6. **Reimagination Principle**: "reimagination" encapsulates the tension between healing and further trauma concerning humans' inventive capabilities. More specifically, imagination is an umbrella term for voluntary, involuntary, and hybrid abilities related to creating meaning. Imagination's types depend on the brain's functional modules on both a bottom-up and top-down structural logic, and they likely evolved through exaptation and redeployment.

The sixth recommendation for field education is: *promote the development of metaknowledge through analogical reasoning*. As stated previously, metaknowledge is a component of the revised Bloom's taxonomy (Stanny, 2016). It refers to the capacity to recognize the origins and consequences of phenomena (e.g., asking how instead of what). If students engage with second-order thinking, they can monitor their beliefs and judgments while controlling their behaviours. In other words, thinking about our thinking (metacognition) and memories (metamemory) can improve adaptability (Schwartz et al., 2011). Therefore, metaknowledge is heavily associated with self-awareness and voluntary imagination, which is essential for social work interns to mitigate their psychological stress.

For promoting metaknowledge, the MIIT framework endorses *analogical reasoning*, the process of identifying similarities between a familiar source and a less known target (Gick & Holyoak, 1980; Richland et al., 2012). Given how challenging it can be to bridge theory, practice, and self in field placements (Bogo, 2020), students may benefit from a model that explicitly endorses articulating multiple definitions, meaningful relations, and procedures to solve problems. During supervision times, field instructors can motivate students to establish analogical reasoning as a basic logic to approach every experience with clients. As an interdisciplinary field, social work requires thinking across systems of knowledge in connection with the lived experiences of community members. Moreover, research has shown that students greatly enjoy and benefit from peer learning (Hummell et al., 2010). Thus, field instructors and faculty liaisons can create plenty of opportunities for peers to interact and build complex webs of analogies together, rather than relying upon traditional teacher-centered learning.

If students struggle with analogical reasoning, Bloom's taxonomy can orient which areas need reinforcing so they can handle intricate maps of analogies without much effort. For example, understanding might be a weak link in the chain, thus requiring patience, support, and a progressive flow towards developing metaknowledge.

Multimodal Dialogue Principle: Methodology for the Healing Imagination

If imagination represents hope for historical healing, what else can we do to unleash it? This section will discuss how an educational model built on the biological basis of perception has higher chances to motivate voluntary, involuntary, and hybrid imagination while combating trauma from a bottom-up, top-down brain logic (Van der Kolk, 2015; Vyshedskiy, 2019, 2020).

Despite the infinite possibilities to transmit wisdom, some ways of creating meaning get valued higher than others. There are modes, such as literacy and numeracy, that provide higher rewards to those who can master them while punishing those who fail to conform (Benjamin, 1986; Freire, 1996; Gee, 1989). Knowledge hierarchies maintain oppression: those who cannot follow the expectations (either due to capabilities or ideology) are explicitly or implicitly branded as *maladapted*, being more likely to experience stigmatization and traumatic stress (Gravlee, 2009; Romero et al.,

2009; Parker & Maestripieri, 2011; Rangel & Keller, 2011; Sapolsky, 2004; Singh, 2012; Spencer, 2007). Suppose administrators and educators fail to understand the reductive nature of unimodal models (e.g., assessing students only on their literacy or numeracy skills): In that case, they will perpetuate an unjust education system that excludes millions (Hamilton et al., 2015; Lankshear et al., 1996).

Besides stressful learning conditions, other dominant emotional states in learning — confusion, frustration, boredom, absence of engagement, delight, and surprise (Graesser, 2011) — represent a danger for congruency. To counter such realities, students and instructors require *enhanced cognitive stimulation*: the participation in appealing and challenging activities that reinforce executive functioning, associated with a decrease in rates of brain decay and dementia. Furthermore, stimulation may even buffer the effects of low socioeconomic status (SES) on development, increase self-esteem, and reduce aggression, especially on those students who have suffered from trauma and deprivation (Hackman et al., 2011). In the case of field education, if the learning experience results in a tedious or stressful event, brain potential will be compromised (Sapolsky, 2001; Lee & Zelman, 2019).

To counter such a problem, *multimodal pedagogy* (MP) is an educational approach that encourages meaning-creation through diverse modalities while recognizing the oppressive nature of unimodal learning. MP deploys several multisensory stimuli and modes for instruction and assessment, emphasizing learners' agency (Kress, 2013).

Due to its person-centered nature and enriched stimulation, the MIIT framework hypothesizes that MP may promote *neurogenesis*, the generation of new neurons, in the hippocampus. This brain area in the limbic system contributes to perception, emotional regulation, memory formation, and discrimination between similar information units. Moreover, it is one of the only structures of the adult brain where new neurons arise, a fact also relevant for treating and preventing anxiety and depression symptoms (Lima & Gomes-Leal, 2019; Sapolsky, 2001). In conclusion, the MIIT framework assumes that congruent multisensory stimulation in a caring environment may promote daily neurogenesis, which will have an impact in several cognitive, sensorimotor, and emotional dimensions.

Congruent multisensory stimulation also may increase *brain diffusion*, consisting of tissue connections and white matter integrity (Black & Conway, 2018). Further studies are needed to investigate if MP affects the activation of the reward circuitry, communication between the left and right hemispheres, and top-down, bottom-up trauma healing via neurogenesis in the hippocampus.

Aided by multimodality, education can become preventive, stimulating, and healing. From these considerations, the MIIT framework's seventh principle emerges:

7. **Multimodal Dialogue Principle**: "multimodal dialogue" refers to how human communication integrates and produces multisensory inputs and outputs. Instruction and assessment should reflect the rich nature of the world and focus on learners' agency. Such a pedagogy may help students and teachers tap into their creative potential, resulting in a caring and challenging environment. Significantly, congruent multisensory stimulation may have preventive and healing effects across the life course by promoting neurogenesis in the hippocampus and brain diffusion.

The resulting recommendation elaborates further on pedagogy: *introduce and value multimodality in supervision and process recordings.* For the former, field instructors and faculty liaisons should not limit engagement with students through verbal and written mediums only. Each semiotic mode has different affordances and limitations (e.g., music can tap into brain circuits that writing alone cannot, and vice versa). The critical element for field instructors to remember is that multimodal resources may strengthen arguments and analogies if combined congruently (Ross et al., 2020).

Alternating during supervision between videos, songs, images, small group discussions, games, and other modalities follows the inverse-effectiveness logic. This assertion means that different sensory inputs in tandem are more likely to enhance integration, inviting students to pay attention to a more complete picture (Stein et al., 2020). Moreover, these multimodal activities have different effects in both a bottom-up (e.g., dance, music, meditation) and top-down (e.g., reflection, debate, writing) logic (Van der Kolk, 2015), thus potentially stimulating imagination types. However, such improvements are contingent on students experiencing congruency. For example, a field instructor may include music in meditation exercises. Still, if the students dislike the chosen song or think the exercise is shallow, a congruent engagement will not ensue. Nevertheless, further research is required.

Social work students are constantly asked to produce written content in their field placements, such as process recordings and competency papers. Students often consider these administrative tasks "busy work," yet field coordinators and directors may find it difficult to challenge the standards due to accreditation constraints (Wayne et al., 2006). As a countermeasure, field instructors can implement low-scale changes and allow students to go beyond the written medium to produce their process recordings: podcasts, diagrams, poems, dance, etc., that integrate social work theory and their passions. Field instructors can appreciate these multimodal productions as integrated wholes rather than isolating their components.

The goal of multimodal education is the expansion of students' semiotic resources by engaging them with specific aspects of the world, rather than just making them regurgitate the learning contents (Kress, 2013). Therefore, field instructors should invite their students to implement multimodal resources in their dialogues with clients, expanding their range of strategies into developing confidence in conversation.

Importantly, MP is not simply adding pictures and music to a slide presentation; it represents a paradigm change. To further clarify this recommendation, one may imagine being interested in testing the positive effects of *multimodal pedagogy* (independent variable) in students' *brain diffusion* (dependent variable). The MIIT framework underscores mediators that can be measured quantitatively and qualitatively (e.g., learning satisfaction and stress perception) to show treatment effects. Moreover, institutional resistance and confusion about multimodality get hypothesized as potential moderators. Thanks to the theoretical principles, if there is a change in the mediators, one could assume a transformation on the dependent variable (see Figure 16.4).

Figure 16.4: Logic Model for Interventions Employing Multimodality

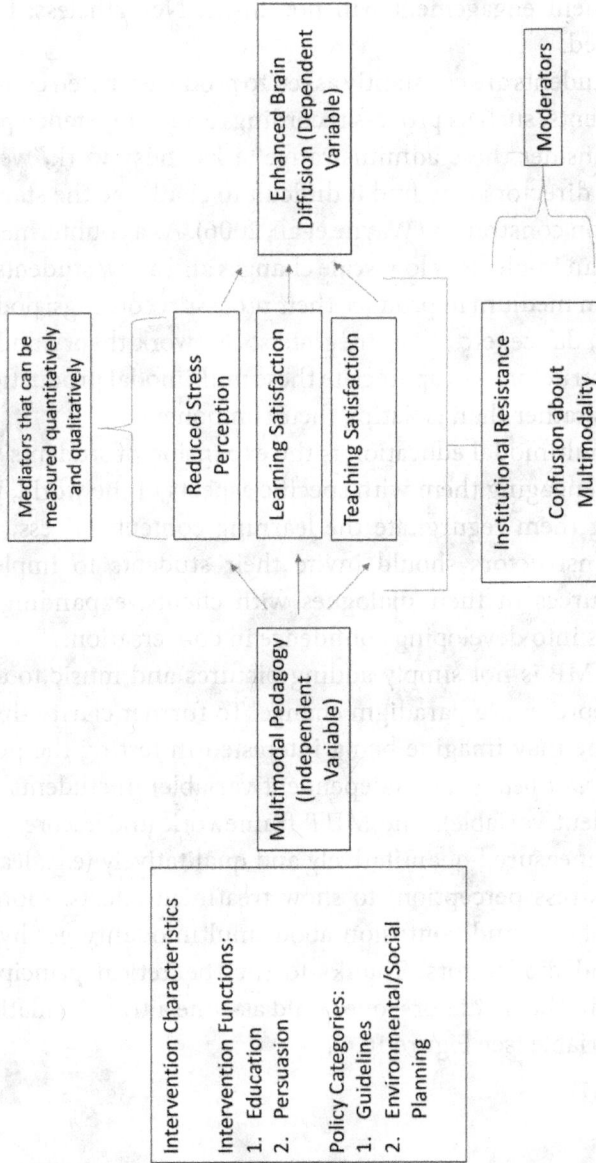

Note: This conceptual model represents an intervention where multimodal pedagogy gets tested to influence the brain diffusion of both the instructor and the students. The intervention characteristics are in accordance with the "behavior change wheel" framework (Michie et al., 2011). Researchers, supervisors, and teachers can adapt this model to either formal or informal education settings. There is an inclusion of mediators that can be easily measured if there is insufficient funding or a lack of technical knowledge/collaboration to obtain biomarker data. However, thanks to the MIIT's framework working principles, if mediators show improvement, one could argue that the dependent variable will change for the better.

Intervention Integrity Principle: Philosophy and Implementation

MP has been thoroughly studied (Kress, 2009, 2010, 2013); however, the MIIT framework integrates it with biosocial evidence and expands its implications for field education. Finally, by following the "behavior change wheel" (Michie et al., 2011), multimodality can be relevant for various intervention with an educational function (Suárez Rojas, 2019), thus showing its versatility and relevance for social workers and researchers alike (see Figure 16.5).

The MIIT framework emphasizes interventions with a participatory design for challenging intergenerational trauma and promoting imagination. Its working principles intend to expand our understanding of human development and contribute to preventive and healing training for social workers in their field placements. The following principle represents a stance towards the production of knowledge:

8. **Intervention Integrity Principle**: "intervention integrity" refers to three philosophical considerations in intervention design. (1) Ethics: self-awareness is an ongoing and perpetual component to identify oppressive practices, values, and institutional frameworks; (2) Epistemology: knowledge is multimodal by nature. Therefore, mixed methods, biomarkers, longitudinal mindsets, and techniques beyond one discipline are required to tackle complex problems; (3) Aesthetics: academics should consider how to reach wider audiences to share their insights and resources.

From this principle, the following recommendation arises: *inspire your students to consider ethics, epistemology, and aesthetics to create meaning.* For ethics, field instructors can confront students with the harsh realities in the field of social work, such as how researchers are failing to confront structural inequality by focusing primarily on micro-level interventions (Corley & Young, 2018). Therefore, field instructors should encourage their students to pursue transforming actions and forming trust. And for

Figure 16.5: Intervention Rationale

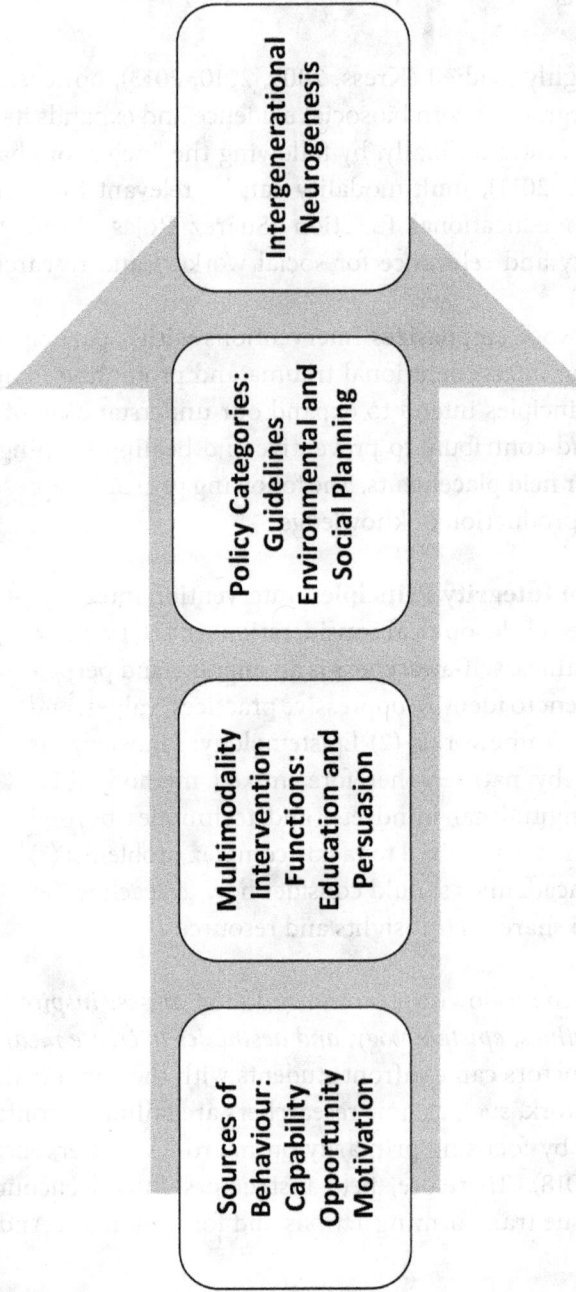

Note: By expanding on the "behavior change wheel" framework (Michie et al., 2011), this image represents the characteristics of an intervention that may have an educational and persuasive function. The sources of behaviour refer both to the individual (conscious and unconscious) and contextual elements behind any given action. The third box shows the policy categories meant to be influenced. The last box touches on the intergenerational transmission of human potential, particularly on brain plasticity. The MIIT framework affirms that any intervention with an educational component may use multimodality, given the certainty concerning how multimodal integration is a fundamental perceptual and learning system for any human being. Thus, the expectation is that researchers can implement multimodal pedagogy and expect the promotion of neurogenesis, regardless of the population and research questions.implement multimodal pedagogy and expect the promotion of neurogenesis, regardless of their population of interest and research questions.

those interns with more modest ambitions, supervision can become an avenue to practice self-awareness.

For epistemology, field instructors must underscore how knowledge is multimodal by nature. Given that each mode has virtues and limitations, academic language is just one among many ways to create meaning. In contrast, field education gets centered around clients' perceptions and narratives. Therefore, social workers in training will benefit if their instructors privilege the integration of different data types, thus conveying a more congruent representation of reality.

Finally, field instructors must underscore that social workers need to take on the aesthetic challenge of translating science to larger audiences. A social work student must learn to communicate clearly with clients and diverse communities while also thinking about the inequities concerning access to educational resources. Field instructors should remind their students of other ways of presenting knowledge beyond academic journals and books, seeking manners to fuse science and art (Boehm, 1961). For example, social work theories and findings can be transformed into virtual content to share on social media platforms, making knowledge freely accessible. For a specific example, one may review the social media contents of *Laboratorio en Movimiento*, an initiative launched in 2018 to develop the MIIT framework (Suárez Rojas, 2022).

Motivated Uncertainty Principle: Finding a Purpose Amidst Tragedy

The intricate relationship between MI and imagination brings clarity and hope to challenge trauma and disintegration. Yet, in recognizing its limitations, potential, and ongoing refinement, the MIIT framework's last principle consists of embracing uncertainty without losing its purpose:

9. **Motivated Uncertainty Principle**: "motivated uncertainty" refers to the tension between acknowledging the countless ambiguities in life while maintaining our purposes. Embracing uncertainty entails recognizing knowledge revision in degrees of confidence without intellectual arrogance or determinism. Thus, the MIIT framework remains

open to confirming or disconfirming data without losing sight of their purpose: dismantling historical trauma by developing a methodology for therapeutic imagination.

In turn, the last recommendation for educators is to *instill a sense of tragic hope*. Field instructors cannot thoroughly plan the transmission of knowledge given the indeterminate nature of field education. Students can get disheartened in the face of adversity, the death of a client, or despair at the thought of facing a monstrous system (Andharia, 2011; Baum, 2011; Millard, 1977). Instead of relying on cruel optimism or cynicism, field instructors should support their students through tragic hope. By this, I mean a stance towards history that believes in how the most mature utopias do not close their eyes to horror, but rather face it and find wisdom in it. No baby can fully understand how complex cruelty and hate can be, and there is a promise in this realization. The motivation to transform and create goes beyond a mere lifetime. Resistance is a tradition.

Conclusion

Field education is the signature pedagogy of the social work profession, as it represents the space where students integrate theory and practice. Yet, despite the merits of this approach, fieldwork also can become a challenging and even traumatic experience for students, thus underscoring the need for a preventive and healing training process. Moreover, despite the heterogeneous nature of field education, administrative constraints have harmed the profession by forcing such vast divergence into a rigid mold.

Therefore, to address these issues, I present the original *Multimodal Integration of Imagination and Trauma* (MIIT) *framework* and its nine working principles, which have several implications for expanding imagination and healing trauma (see Figure 16.6). Moreover, specific recommendations for field education got intertwined with the theoretical assumptions, with a particular emphasis on prevention, stimulation, and healing (see Figure 16.7).

The MIIT framework recognizes that perception and movement depend on multimodal integration (MI), a structure and mechanism present in countless species. Therefore, studying MI helps to understand commonalities and differences across the life continuum. Furthermore,

Figure 16.6: The Working Principles of the Multimodal Integration of Imagination and Trauma (MIIT) Framework

1. Unity: multimodal integration (MI) is an essential perceptual and behavioural system for countless species, thus helping us to understand commonalities across the life continuum.

2. Divergence: MI also allows us to understand differences in adaptation across and within the same species.

3. Semiotic Infinity: MI in humans has evolved to allow complex symbolization and language, distinguishing us from other species, given our creative and destructive capabilities.

4. Imperative Congruency: if there is data congruency, MI enhances perception and behaviour. Therefore, life gets enriched by congruency — an ethical imperative for any society.

5. Disintegration: multimodal disintegration represents miscommunication between the body, the brain, and the world. This fragmentation is biomedical and political, as historical trauma exemplifies.

6. Reimagination: imagination can either bring healing or further trauma. Imagination is an umbrella term for different mechanisms which likely developed via exaptation and redeployment.

7. Multimodal Dialogue: humans learn by integrating multisensory stimuli and communicating through diverse modalities. Education that expands this basis may have clinical effects by promoting neurogenesis.

8. Intervention Integrity: to implement interventions that promote MI and imagination, researchers must accept ongoing self-awareness, the multimodal nature of knowledge, and the translational challenge.

9. Motivated Uncertainty: the MIIT framework embraces uncertainty and remains open to confirming or disconfirming data (degrees of confidence) without losing its goal of enhancing life through multimodality.

Figure 16.7: The Nine Recommendations for Social work Educators, as They Relate to Each One of the Principles of the Multimodal Integration of Imagination and Trauma (MIIT) Framework

1. Avoid categorizing your students, as they are all capable of integration.

2. Respect differences but do not obviate power disparities.

3. Encourage students to co-create solutions alongside their clients.

4. Amplify congruency between theory, practice, and self.

5. Hold space for tension and healing.

6. Promote the development of metaknowledge through analogical reasoning.

7. Introduce and value multimodality in supervision and process

8. Inspire your students to consider ethics, epistemology, and aesthetics to create meaning beyond the classroom.

9. Instill a sense of tragic hope.

human beings are exceptional in producing complex communication through several modalities. This evolutionary advantage also helps understand the emergence of imagination types. Therefore, the MIIT framework concludes that individuals can strengthen their neural pathways through multimodal stimulation as long as congruency expands. Through numerous examples and recommendations, these ideas were shown to be relevant for field education.

The main limitation of the MIIT framework is its lack of extensive empirical testing, given that it is in its early stages of development. Future studies should test the relationships between imagination types with other health and performance outcomes. Another rich area of application of the

MIIT framework is examining how multimodal pedagogy could improve learning patterns (memory, recognition, recall, perception) across the life course while slowing cognitive and sensorimotor decay. Finally, the MIIT framework requires further investigation into replicating multimodal interventions across academic disciplines and beyond classrooms (e.g., informal learning contexts).

Overall, the MIIT framework offers insights to transform social workers' education by focusing on the congruency between the classroom and the field agency. This novel approach will be open to refinement and intellectual dialogue, while continuously recognizing the corrosiveness of historical trauma and the healing potential of imagination. As they evolve into a schematic theory, the working principles and recommendations may contribute to education across fields. By implementing multimodal integration, experiential instructors can become imagination architects.

REFERENCES

Agnati, L. F., Guidolin, D., Battistin, L., Pagnoni, G., & Fuxe, K. (2013). The neurobiology of imagination: Possible role of interaction-dominant dynamics and default mode network. *Frontiers in Psychology, 4*, 296. https://doi.org/10.3389/fpsyg.2013.00296

Anastas, J. W. (2014). The science of social work and its relationship to social work practice. *Research on Social Work Practice, 24*(5), 571–580. https://doi.org/10.1177/1049731513511335

Andharia, J. (2011). Fieldwork education in community organization: Privileging the process of political engagement. *Community Development Journal, 46*(suppl_1), i96-i116. https://doi.org/10.1093/cdj/bsq045

Armstrong, P. (2016). *Bloom's taxonomy.* Vanderbilt University Center for Teaching. https://cft.vanderbilt.edu/guides-sub-pages/blooms-taxonomy/

Ashley-Binge, S., & Cousins, C. (2020). Individual and organisational practices addressing social workers' experiences of vicarious trauma. *Practice, 32*(3), 191–207. https://www.tandfonline.com/loi/cpra20

Atewologun, D. (2018). Intersectionality theory and practice. *Oxford Research Encyclopedia of Business and Management.* https://doi.org/10.1093/acrefore/9780190224851.013.48

Baum, N. (2011). Social work students' feelings and concerns about the ending of their fieldwork supervision. *Social Work Education, 30*(1), 83–97. https://www.tandfonline.com/loi/cswe20

Benjamin, W. (1986). *Illuminations* (H. Arendt, Ed.). Schocken Books. (Original work published 1968).

Bjork, E. L., & Bjork, R. A. (2011). Making things hard on yourself, but in a good way: Creating desirable difficulties to enhance learning. *Psychology and the real world: Essays illustrating fundamental contributions to society, 2*(59–68). https://teaching. yale-nus.edu.sg/wp-content/uploads/sites/25/2016/02/Making-Things-Hard-on-Yourself-but-in-a-Good-Way-2011.pdf

Bjork, R. A., Dunlosky, J., & Kornell, N. (2013). Self-regulated learning: Beliefs, techniques, and illusions. *Annual review of psychology, 64*, 417–444. https://doi.org/10.1146/annurev-psych-113011-143823

Black, J. M., & Conway, A. (2018). The utility of neuroscience for social work research and practice with children and adolescents. *Journal of the Society for Social Work and Research, 9*(2), 261–284. https://doi.org/10.1086/698166

Boehm, W. W. (1961). Social work: Science and art. *Social Service Review, 35*(2), 144–152. https://www.jstor.org/stable/pdf/30017235.pdf

Bogo, M. (2015). Field education for clinical social work practice. Best practices and contemporary challenges. *Clinical Social Work Journal, 43*(3), 317–324. https://doi.org/10.1007/s10615-015-0526-5

Bogo, M. (2020). *Achieving competence in social work through field education*. University of Toronto Press. https://doi.org/10.3138/9781442699939

Briere, J. N., & Scott, C. (2014). *Principles of trauma therapy: A guide to symptoms, evaluation, and treatment (DSM-5 update)*. Sage Publications.

Bronfenbrenner, U. (1977). Toward an experimental ecology of human development. *American psychologist, 32*(7), 513. https://doi.org/10.1037/0003-066X.32.7.513

Burke, D. D., & Carton, R. (2013). The pedagogical, legal, and ethical implications of unpaid internships. *Journal of Legal Studies Education, 30*, 99. https://heinonline.org/HOL/P?h=hein.journals/jlse30&i=103

Butti, C., Santos, M., Uppal, N., & Hof, P. R. (2013). Von Economo neurons: clinical and evolutionary perspectives. *Cortex, 49*(1), 312–326. https://doi.org/10.1016/j.cortex.2011.10.004

Conching, A. K. S., & Thayer, Z. (2019). Biological pathways for historical trauma to affect health: A conceptual model focusing on epigenetic modifications. *Social Science & Medicine, 230*, 74-82. https://doi.org/10.1016/j.socscimed.2019.04.001

Corley, N. A., & Young, S. M. (2018). Is social work still racist? A content analysis of recent literature. *Social Work, 63*(4), 317–326. https://doi.org/10.1093/SW/swy042

Council on Social Work Education. (2020). *2019 statistics on social work education in the United States*. Retrieved from https://cswe.org/getattachment/Research-Statistics/2019-Annual-Statistics-on-Social-Work-Education-in-the-United-States-Final-(1).pdf.aspx

Cowie, M. E., Nealis, L. J., Sherry, S. B., Hewitt, P. L., & Flett, G. L. (2018). Perfectionism and academic difficulties in graduate students: Testing incremental prediction and gender moderation. *Personality and Individual Differences, 123*, 223–228. https://doi.org/10.1016/j.paid.2017.11.027

de Dieuleveult, A. L., Siemonsma, P. C., van Erp, J. B., & Brouwer, A. M. (2017). Effects of aging in multisensory integration: A systematic review. *Frontiers in aging neuroscience, 9*, 80. https://doi.org/10.3389/fnagi.2017.00080

Dor, D. (2017). From experience to imagination: Language and its evolution as a social communication technology. *Journal of Neurolinguistics, 43*, 107–119. https://doi.org/10.1016/j.jneuroling.2016.10.003

Evans, T. M., Bira, L., Gastelum, J. B., Weiss, L. T., & Vanderford, N. L. (2018). Evidence for a mental health crisis in graduate education. *Nature Biotechnology, 36*(3), 282–284. https://doi.org/10.1038/nbt.4089

Feldman, J. I., Dunham, K., Cassidy, M., Wallace, M. T., Liu, Y., & Woynaroski, T. G. (2018). Audiovisual multisensory integration in individuals with autism spectrum disorder: A systematic review and meta-analysis. *Neuroscience & Biobehavioral Reviews, 95*, 220–234. https://doi.org/10.1016/j.neubiorev.2018.09.020

Forbes, T. A., & Gallo, V. (2017). All Wrapped Up: Environmental Effects on Myelination. *Trends in Neurosciences, 40*(9), 572–587. https://doi.org/10.1016/j.tins.2017.06.009

Forehand, M. (2010). *Bloom's taxonomy. Emerging perspectives on learning, teaching, and technology, 41*(4), 47–56. University of Georgia. https://www.d41.org/cms/lib/IL01904672/Centricity/Domain/422/BloomsTaxonomy.pdf

Fox, N. J. (2013). Creativity and health: An anti-humanist reflection. *Health., 17*(5), 495–511. https://doi.org/10.1177/1363459312464074

Freire, P. (1996). *Pedagogy of the oppressed (revised)*. Continuum.

Gallese, V. (2011). Embodied simulation theory: Imagination and narrative. *Neuropsychoanalysis, 13*(2), 196–200. https://www.tandfonline.com/loi/rnpa20

Garcia-Williams, A. G., Moffitt, L., & Kaslow, N. J. (2014). Mental health and suicidal behavior among graduate students. *Academic Psychiatry, 38*(5), 554–560. https://doi.org/10.1007/s40596-014-0041-y

Gee, J. P. (1989). Literacy, discourse, and linguistics: Introduction. *Journal of Education, 171*(1), 5–17. https://www.jstor.org/stable/42743865

Gee, J. P., Hull, G., & Lankshear, C. (2018). *The new work order: Behind the language of the new capitalism*. Routledge. https://doi.org/10.4324/9780429496127

Gerard, R. W. (1946). The biological basis of imagination. *The Scientific Monthly, 62*(6), 477–499. https://www.jstor.org/stable/pdf/18832.pdf

Ghosh, D. D., Nitabach, M. N., Zhang, Y., & Harris, G. (2017). Multisensory integration in C. elegans. *Current opinion in neurobiology, 43*, 110–118. https://doi.org/10.1016/j.conb.2017.01.005

Gick, M.L., & Holyoak, K. L. (1980). Analogical problem solving. *Cognitive Psychology, 15*, 306–355. http://dx.doi.org/10.1016/0010-0285(80)90013-4

Gingras, G., Rowland, B. A., & Stein, B. E. (2009). The differing impact of multisensory and unisensory integration on behavior. *Journal of Neuroscience, 29*(15), 4897–4902. https://doi.org/10.1523/JNEUROSCI.4120-08.2009

Gone, J. P., Hartmann, W. E., Pomerville, A., Wendt, D. C., Klem, S. H., & Burrage, R. L. (2019). The impact of historical trauma on health outcomes for indigenous populations in the USA and Canada: A systematic review. *American Psychologist, 74*(1), 20. https://doi.org/10.1037/amp0000338

Graesser, A. C. (2011). Learning, thinking, and emoting with discourse technologies. *American psychologist, 66*(8), 746. https://psycnet.apa.org/doi/10.1037/a0024974

Gravlee, C. C. (2009). How race becomes biology: Embodiment of social inequality. *American journal of physical anthropology, 139*(1), 47–57. https://doi.org/10.1002/ajpa.20983

Hackman, D. A., Farah, M. J., & Meaney, M. J. (2010). Socioeconomic status and the brain: Mechanistic insights from human and animal research. *Nature reviews neuroscience, 11*(9), 651–659. http://www.dcp.uzh.ch/research/groups/neuropsychopharmacology.html

Hamilton, M., Heydon, R., Hibbert, K., & Stooke, R. (Eds.). (2015). *Negotiating spaces for literacy learning: Multimodality and governmentality.* Bloomsbury Publishing.

Herman, J. L., & van der Kolk, B. A. (2020). *Treating Complex Traumatic Stress Disorders in Adults.* Guilford Publications.

Hummell, J., Higgs, J., & Mulholland, S. (2010). Models of fieldwork education: Influences and approaches. In *Innovations in Allied Health Fieldwork Education* (pp. 95–110). Brill Sense. https://doi.org/10.1163/9789460913235_010

Kirschner, P. A. (2017). Stop propagating the learning styles myth. *Computers & Education, 106*, 166–171. https://doi.org/10.1016/j.compedu.2016.12.006

Kress, G. (2009). Assessment in the perspective of a social semiotic theory of multimodal teaching and learning. In *Educational assessment in the 21st century* (pp. 19–41). Springer, Dordrecht. https://doi.org/10.1007/978-1-4020-9964-9

Kress, G. R. (2010). *Multimodality: A social semiotic approach to contemporary communication.* Taylor & Francis. https://doi.org/10.4324/9780203970034

Kress, G. (2013). Recognizing learning: A perspective from a social semiotic theory of multimodality. In *Multilingualism and multimodality* (pp. 117–140). Brill Sense.

Lee, F. K., & Zelman, D. C. (2019). Boredom proneness as a predictor of depression, anxiety and stress: The moderating effects of dispositional mindfulness. *Personality and Individual Differences, 146*, 68-75. https://doi.org/10.1016/j.paid.2019.04.001

Lima, S. M., & Gomes-Leal, W. (2019). Neurogenesis in the hippocampus of adult humans: Controversy "fixed" at last. *Neural Regeneration Research, 14*(11), 1917. https://doi.org/10.4103/1673-5374.259616

Lucy, J. A. (1997). Linguistic relativity. *Annual Review of Anthropology, 26*(1), 291–312. https://doi.org/10.1146/annurev.anthro.26.1.291

Lucy, J. A. (2016). Recent advances in the study of linguistic relativity in historical context: A critical assessment. *Language Learning, 66*(3), 487–515. https://doi.org/10.1111/lang.12195

Martín-Baró, I. (1989). Political violence and war as causes of psychosocial trauma in El Salvador. *International Journal of Mental Health*, *18*(1), 3–20. https://doi.org/10.108 0/00207411.1989.11449115

May, P. J. (2006). The mammalian superior colliculus: Laminar structure and connections. *Progress in Brain Research*, *151*, 321–378. https://doi.org/10.1016/S0079-6123(05)51011-2

Michie, S., Van Stralen, M. M., & West, R. (2011). The behaviour change wheel: A new method for characterising and designing behaviour change interventions. *Implementation Science*, *6*(1), 1–12. http://www.implementationscience.com/content/6/1/42

Middelton-Moz, J., Mishna, F., Martell, R., Williams, C., & Zuberi, S. (2021). Indigenous trauma and resilience: pathways to 'bridging the river' in social work education. *Social Work Education*, 1–18. https://doi.org/10.1080/02615479.2021.1998427

Millard, D. A. (1977). Literature and the therapeutic imagination. *The British Journal of Social Work*, *7*(2), 173–184. https://doi.org/10.1093/oxfordjournals.bjsw.a056816

Mufwene, S. S. (2013). *The origins and the evolution of language* (pp. 15–18). Oxford University Press.

Newton, P. M., & Miah, M. (2017). Evidence-based higher education–is the learning styles 'myth' important? *Frontiers in psychology*, *8*, 444. https://doi.org/10.3389/fpsyg.2017.00444

Panofsky, S., Buchanan, M. J., John, R., & Goodwill, A. (2021). Indigenous trauma intervention research in Canada: A narrative literature review. *The International Indigenous Policy Journal*, *12*(2), 1–24. https://doi.org/10.18584/iipj.2021.12.2.10936

Parker, K. J., & Maestripieri, D. (2011). Identifying key features of early stressful experiences that produce stress vulnerability and resilience in primates. *Neuroscience & Biobehavioral Reviews*, *35*(7), 1466–1483. https://doi.org/10.1016/j.neubiorev.2010.09.003

Perrotta, G. (2019). Psychological trauma: Definition, clinical contexts, neural correlations and therapeutic approaches. *Current Research in Psychiatry Brain Disorders CRPBD-100006*. https://grfpublishers.com/article/view/MTc4/Psychological-Trauma-Definition-Clinical-Contexts-Neural-Correlations-and-Therapeutic-Approaches-Recent-Discoveries

Rabellino, D., Densmore, M., Théberge, J., McKinnon, M. C., & Lanius, R. A. (2018). The cerebellum after trauma: Resting-state functional connectivity of the cerebellum in posttraumatic stress disorder and its dissociative subtype. *Human Brain Mapping*, *39*(8), 3354–3374. https://doi.org/10.1002/hbm.24081

Rangel, U., & Keller, J. (2011). Essentialism goes social: Belief in social determinism as a component of psychological essentialism. *Journal of personality and social psychology*, *100*(6), 1056. https://doi.org/10.1037/a0022401

Rao, S., Woo, B., Maglalang, D. D., Bartholomew, M., Cano, M., Harris, A., & Tucker, T. B. (2021). Race and ethnicity in the social work grand challenges. *Social Work*, *66*(1), 9–17. https://doi.org/10.1093/sw/swaa053

Rasheem, S., & Brunson, J. (2018). She persisted: The pursuit, persistence, & power of African American women in social work graduate programs at Historically Black Institutions (HBI). *Social Work Education, 37*(3), 378–395. https://doi.org/10.1080/0 2615479.2017.1401603

Reinersmann, A., & Luecke, T. (2018). Body schema, multisensory integration and developmental disorders. *Fortschritte der Neurologie-Psychiatrie, 86*(4), 233–241. https://doi.org/10.1055/s-0043-119797

Richland, L. E., Stigler, J. W., & Holyoak, K. J. (2012). Teaching the conceptual structure of mathematics. *Educational Psychologist, 47*(3), 189–203. https://doi.org/10.1080/004 61520.2012.667065

Romero, L. M., Dickens, M. J., & Cyr, N. E. (2009). The reactive scope model — a new model integrating homeostasis, allostasis, and stress. *Hormones and behavior, 55*(3), 375–389. https://doi.org/10.1016/j.yhbeh.2008.12.009

Ross, J., Curwood, J. S., & Bell, A. (2020). A multimodal assessment framework for higher education. *E-Learning and Digital Media, 17*(4), 290–306. https://doi. org/10.1177/2042753020927201

Sapolsky, R. M. (2001). Depression, antidepressants, and the shrinking hippocampus. *Proceedings of the National Academy of Sciences, 98*(22), 12320–12322. https://doi.org/10.1073/pnas.231475998

Sapolsky, R. M. (2004). *Why zebras don't get ulcers: The acclaimed guide to stress, stress-related diseases, and coping.* Holt Paperbacks.

Sarno, S., Erasmus, L. P., Lipp, B., & Schlaegel, W. (2003). Multisensory integration after traumatic brain injury: A reaction time study between pairings of vision, touch and audition. *Brain Injury, 17*(5), 413–426. https://doi.org/10.1080/0269905031000 070161

Schwartz, B. L., Son, L. K., Kornell, N., & Finn, B. (2011). Four principles of memory improvement: A guide to improving learning efficiency. *IJCPS-International Journal of Creativity and Problem Solving, 21*(1), 7. https://web.williams.edu/ Psychology/Faculty/Kornell/Publications/Schwartz.Son.Kornell.Finn.2011.pdf

Singh, I. (2012). Human development, nature and nurture: Working beyond the divide. *BioSocieties, 7*(3), 308–321. https://doi.org/10.1057/biosoc.2012.20

Spencer, M. B. (2006). Phenomenology and ecological systems theory: Development of diverse groups. In R. M. Lerner & W. Damon (Eds.), *Handbook of child psychology: Theoretical models of human development* (pp. 829–893). John Wiley & Sons Inc.

Stanny, C. J. (2016). Reevaluating Bloom's taxonomy: What measurable verbs can and cannot say about student learning. *Education Sciences, 6*(4), 37. https://doi. org/10.3390/educsci6040037

Stein, B. E., & Stanford, T. R. (2008). Multisensory integration: Current issues from the perspective of the single neuron. *Nature Reviews Neuroscience, 9*(4), 255–266. https://doi.org/10.1038/nrn2331

Stein, B. E., Stanford, T. R., & Rowland, B. A. (2020). Multisensory integration and the society for neuroscience: Then and now. *Journal of Neuroscience, 40*(1), 3–11. https://doi.org/10.1523/JNEUROSCI.0737-19.2019

Suárez Rojas, R. D. (2019). "They call us puercos and indios." A mixed-methods intervention to reduce the stress perception of police officers. *Laboratorio en Movimiento*, Vol. 2, 1–15. https://www.researchgate.net/publication/341255211_They_call_us_puercos_and_indios_A_mixed-methods_intervention_to_reduce_the_stress_perception_of_police_officers

Suárez Rojas, R. D. (2022, May 5). *Laboratorio en Movimiento*. https://www.diegosuarez rojas.com/laboratorio-en-movimiento.

Thayer, Z. M., & Non, A. L. (2015). Anthropology meets epigenetics: Current and future directions. *American Anthropologist, 117*(4), 722–735. https://doi.org/10.1111/aman.12351 https://doi.org/10.1111/aman.12351

Thomas, N. J. (1999). Are theories of imagery theories of imagination? An active perception approach to conscious mental content. *Cognitive science, 23*(2), 207–245. https://doi.org/10.1207/s15516709cog2302_3

Tseng, H. H., Bossong, M. G., Modinos, G., Chen, K. M., McGuire, P., & Allen, P. (2015). A systematic review of multisensory cognitive–affective integration in schizophrenia. *Neuroscience & Biobehavioral Reviews, 55*, 444–452. https://doi.org/10.1016/j.neubiorev.2015.04.019

Van der Kolk, B. A. (2015). *The body keeps the score: Brain, mind, and body in the healing of trauma*. Penguin Books. http://dx.doi.org/10.7812/TPP/14-211

Viaud-Delmon, I., Venault, P., & Chapouthier, G. (2011). Behavioral models for anxiety and multisensory integration in animals and humans. *Progress in Neuro-Psychopharmacology and Biological Psychiatry, 35*(6), 1391–1399. https://doi.org/10.1016/j.pnpbp.2010.09.016

Vyshedskiy, A. (2019). *Neuroscience of imagination and implications for human evolution*. Boston University.

Vyshedskiy, A. (2020). Voluntary and involuntary imagination: Neurological mechanisms, developmental path, clinical implications, and evolutionary trajectory. *Evolutionary Studies in Imaginative Culture, 4*(2), 1–18. https://doi.org/10.26613/esic/4.2.186

Vyshedskiy, A., Khokhlovich, E., Dunn, R., Faisman, A., Elgart, J., Lokshina, L., ... & Ilyinskii, P. O. (2020, December). Novel prefrontal synthesis intervention improves language in children with autism. *Healthcare, 8*(4), 566. https://doi.org/10.3390/healthcare8040566

Wallace, M. T., & Stein, B. E. (1997). Development of multisensory neurons and multisensory integration in cat superior colliculus. *Journal of Neuroscience, 17*(7), 2429–2444. https://doi.org/10.1523/JNEUROSCI.17-07-02429.1997

Wallace, M. T., Woynaroski, T. G., & Stevenson, R. A. (2020). Multisensory integration as a window into orderly and disrupted cognition and communication. *Annual review of Psychology, 71*, 193–219. https://doi.org/10.1146/annurev-psych-010419051112

Walsh, M. C. (2020). *Imagination and adolescent trauma: The role of imagination in neurophysiological, psychological, and spiritual healing*. Lexington Books.

Wayne, J., Bogo, M., & Raskin, M. (2006). Field notes: The need for radical change in field education. *Journal of Social Work Education, 42*(1), 161–169. https://doi.org/10.5175/JSWE.2006.200400447

Wayne, J., Bogo, M., & Raskin, M. (2010). Field education as the signature pedagogy of social work education. *Journal of Social Work Education, 46*(3), 327–339. https://doi.org/10.5175/JSWE.2010.200900043

Zeira, A., & Schiff, M. (2010). Testing group supervision in fieldwork training for social work students. *Research on Social Work Practice, 20*(4), 427–434. https://doi.org/10.1177/1049731509332882

Zeng, T., Tang, F., Ji, D., & Si, B. (2020). NeuroBayesSLAM: Neurobiologically inspired Bayesian integration of multisensory information for robot navigation. *Neural Networks, 126*, 21–35. https://doi.org/10.1016/j.neunet.2020.02.023

Conclusion

Sheri M. McConnell, Julie Drolet, and Grant Charles

In this book, each chapter and each author addressed privilege, oppression, and inequity at systemic, institutional, and agency levels. From their own perspective and context, the contributors did so with a focus on social work practice and field education. By acknowledging and exploring disparities resulting from social identities and intersectionality, the authors brought forth recommendations to instigate change in social work and field education, in educational institutions, and in broader social systems.

The following discussion highlights the research presented in each chapter and their ensuing recommendations. These discussions are divided into five themes, which represent the focus or location of change: (1) access to education; (2) colouring outside the lines: innovative models for field education; (3) integrating Indigenous and anti-racist knowledges, methodologies, and perspectives; (4) encouraging students to step/think outside of their comfort zone; and (5) integrating research into social work field education.

Access to Education

Several chapters addressed disparities within educational institutions, particularly those experienced in social work educational programs and within field education. Shiferaw, Asrate, and Eyasu (chapter 7) explored the impact of gender, poverty, health and disability, and geography on access to and support for education. Their research focused on the lived experiences of three women completing PhDs in Ethiopia, each of whom encountered many hurdles in completing their education. They proposed that:

> To reduce gender-based discrimination, higher education institutions need to create an empowering climate on the issues of gender and disability. They have to train their staff members and students on gender equity, and craft new policies to enhance women's involvement. (p. 153)

Sharing some of the same concerns, Aguilera, Medley, Gage, and Hutchison described economic injustice in social work educational programs and field agencies (chapter 1). They asserted that "higher education systems today replicate and reflect inequality and oppression, even though the social work departments within them teach students to fight against these social issues" (p. 23). Further, they described how, "while having academic discussions about how to serve economically oppressed people in the field, some social work students themselves are simultaneously experiencing economic oppression, which is then exacerbated by practicum requirements" (p. 24). In response to this economic oppression, the authors identified "a need to adopt more innovative and sustainable models in social work field education, as the historical model that continues today has proven to only benefit those with economic means" (p. 31). Suggesting a way forward, they asserted that "economic justice starts with us confronting our own critical issues within social work field education. As demonstrated, supporting students' material needs is imperative to their educational and professional success" (p. 31). Making concrete change in the lives of students necessitates exploring options within field agencies, universities, and government to provide financial support to social work students participating in field practicums.

The COVID-19 pandemic has made more visible the challenges and changing contexts in field education, including barriers to accessibility and inclusion. In order to respond to these challenges and barriers, it is essential to (re)imagine creative approaches and pilot new models for developing and providing field education. These new ways of thinking and doing often require revising field education processes, policies, and practices. We were reminded by Janse van Rensburg et al. (chapter 12), who described a PhD advocacy field practicum involving consultations with autistic adults, that "accessibility is not a hurdle — it is a commitment" (p. 242).

In furthering that commitment to accessibility, de Bie, Chaplin, and Vengris (chapter 3) recommended concrete, practical strategies for engaging with and supporting students and field instructors from racialized, Indigenous, 2SLGBTQ+, and disability communities. Integral to their chapter is a critical analysis of the benefits and possible pitfalls of students and field instructors discussing their intersecting identities. Noting that change processes are more complex than they anticipated, the authors provided thoughtful suggestions for how to create safety and openness within field agencies, including new practices around field orientations, student interviews and matching, field instructor recruitment and training, and pre-placement interview guides.

Gooding (chapter 8) also addressed how racialized students and field instructors discuss their intersecting identities and use of self, by integrating Critical Race Theory (CRT) and Social Identity Theory (SIT). In order to do so, the author invited

> field instructors and students to explore non-dominant ways of social work practice during supervision. ... When race is included in conversations about use of self, it gives social workers, BIPOC and otherwise, the freedom to bring race into the room explicitly because it informs social life. (p. 168)

Furthermore, Gooding

> encourage[s] field instructors to consider issues of structural and interpersonal power across difference, as well as within shared identities. ... Discussing use of self both within and across difference will allow field supervisors to support and challenge students in their development as social workers and facilitate a critical praxis. (p. 168)

Colouring Outside the Lines: Innovative Models for Field Education

Field practicums traditionally have consisted of a social worker providing field instruction to one or more students in an agency offering in-person case management or clinical services to individuals, families, or groups. However, challenges in field education, as described in the introduction and addressed in each of the chapters, demand that field coordinators explore other practicum delivery models.

As Kusari observed in chapter 14, while the pandemic "posed unique challenges for field education, as many students had to cancel their practicum placement and/or find ways to complete their hours through remote work" (p. 273), it also provided a unique context in which many longstanding field education practices were critically analyzed, and new practices emerged within a very short time frame. The author addressed the challenges and opportunities for innovation that she experienced while working within the disability sector and supervising two BSW practicum students. Kusari explained that "despite the challenges that COVID-19 presented, it also offered a space to experiment with field education opportunities which were conceptualized as unconventional" (p. 290), including remote, virtual field practicums. Her experience with Information and Communication Technologies (ICT), both in supervising practicums and in delivering services to program participants, led the author to support the implementation of a mix of in-person and virtual program/service delivery in the future. The PhD advocacy practicum, described by Janse van Rensburg et al. (chapter 12), also introduced a new model of engaging in virtual field education. This model, inspired by *Pedagogy of the Oppressed* (Freire, 2018), involves a four-phase process (problem posing to the student, student problem-solving, problem posing to the community, and community problem-solving).

Stepping outside of traditional ways of offering field education, Wong (chapter 2) invited us to consider the benefits and limitations of matching social work students with non-social work field supervisors. To illustrate her points, Wong shared her experiences of completing an MSW practicum in two agencies where there were no social workers onsite. She concluded that developing and supporting field practicums supervised by non-social workers creates opportunities to expand the number of available field agencies, opens doors to engage with non-traditional practicum sites, offers students greater access to engage with and learn from marginalized peoples and communities, and enhances interdisciplinary learning and practice.

As described in the previous section, in response to the economic barriers faced by students in unpaid practicums, Aguilera, Medley, Gage, and Hutchison (chapter 1) advocated for new models of field education that financially support economically disadvantage students. They assert that "providing an economic safety net for students will also increase diversity in the social work field, as students from underrepresented groups who previously could not afford an unpaid practicum will be able to pursue the profession" (p. 30).

In Ethiopia, like many countries across the globe, students tend to be placed in large institutions in urban centres. Shiferaw, Asrate, and Eyasu (chapter 7) advocated that "Ethiopian universities need to revisit their 'business as usual' practicum trend, by focusing on communal settings in rural areas to address the gender gaps so evident in education and in other social institutions" (p. 153). They reminded us that

> local social workers, educators, and social development practitioners are required to address local realities of personal, social, and community challenges. We can use student practicum reports to gain much wider understanding about local problems and solutions. (p. 153)

On a similar note, Ali (chapter 11) described a model of field education in community development in Pakistan and highlighted the impact of social work students on local and broader social change. The discussion "provide[d] insights into the field education model that trains practicum students in need assessment, community mobilization, participatory action research, capacity building, monitoring, evaluation, and long-term sustainability of the project" (p. 210). Building strong community development practicums requires "collaboration between social work schools and social development agencies. In the future, even more collaboration is needed to address the multi dimension challenges related to social and environmental justice" (p. 221).

Suárez Rojas (chapter 16) invited readers to ponder how, despite the merits of field education, "fieldwork also can become a challenging and even traumatic experience for students, thus underscoring the need for a preventive and healing training process" (p. 348). In response to these concerns, he introduced the novel Multimodal Integration of Imagination and Trauma (MIIT) framework to aid in developing trauma-informed field education and social work practice.

Integrating Indigenous and Anti-racist Knowledges, Methodologies, and Perspectives

Several authors envisioned achieving change through integrating Indigenous and anti-racist knowledges, methodologies, and perspectives into social work and field education curriculum. Chilanga (chapter 4) advocated for the Indigenization of social work education in Africa, in part by transitioning from a Western casework model to a developmental social work theory and practice education curriculum. In his chapter, Chilanga asserted that "the transforming from Eurocentric to Afrocentric social work pedagogies has the potential to influence Africa's social work theory, policy, and practice" (p. 70). Further, he hypothesized that such change would lead social workers to address social problems more effectively, including poverty, homelessness, unemployment, lack of access to education, food insecurity, and disease. Notably, this chapter offered that "the theory and field education curriculum of developmental social work is designed to empower social workers to advocate for economic development and confront structural systems that perpetuate social problems" (p. 73).

Also advocating for social work educators to Indigenize the curriculum and social workers to engage in social change, Ayele and Kebede (chapter 10) provided a critical overview of social work education and field education in Ethiopia. In doing so, they "consider[ed] the gaps between theory and practice in Ethiopia and explore[d] how these could be addressed in order to bring about social change in systems to promote social justice in international social work" (p. 193). Given that "field education may also play a vital role in identifying and intervening in unjust and oppressive practices at the individual, group, and community level" (p. 196), the authors also recommended the integration of social justice into social work field education and social work practice in Ethiopia.

Drawing on research that explores the provision of services to undocumented victims of interpersonal violence (IPV), Balbuena (chapter 13) described how "culturally responsive practices and policies need to be implemented to remove structural and institutional barriers" (p. 252) and recommended that "social work service providers must become aware of their service delivery and cultural responsiveness to diverse groups of undocumented immigrants who are economically, socially, and politically marginalized" (p. 267).

In a similar vein, Mack (chapter 6) discussed using culturally responsive approaches to address racial disproportionality and disparity in child welfare practices and reflected on her research-based field practicum with a child welfare agency. Her recommendations for field education included "... providing opportunities for increasing cultural awareness, engaging in skill-based interventions, seeking more profound cultural knowledge, participating in cultural encounters, cultivating cultural desire, and implementing action-oriented practices" (p. 128). Hence, "it is recommended that field education supervisors and students collaborate on ways to integrate opportunities for discussing, applying, and promoting culturally responsive practices within the field practicum setting" (p. 127). In chapter 15, De Vynck, Ciesielski, and Boynton

> contend[ed] that understandings of cultural humility and competence should be extended to include a stance on spiritual humility and competence. These should include culturally and contextually appropriate ways of practicing, as spirituality is integral to cultural beliefs and worldviews, particularly for non-Western cultures. For many individuals, spirituality is connected to their culture. (p. 299)

Greenslade (chapter 5) addressed the lack of preparedness for anti-racist social work practice among social work students, the dearth of anti-racist theory and practical skills in the curriculum, and the essential role of critical conversations in anti-racist education. Contextualizing the urgency of her recommendations, she drew links between the COVID-19 pandemic and the increased presence, visibility, and violence of racism. In doing so, she reminded us that anti-racist education does not happen in a vacuum. Instead, it is a consistent reflection of everyday encounters, rife with the subtlety of racism and Whiteness that have become so much a part of our existence that we no longer question them. (p. 106)

Greenslade recommended Critical Race Theory as a framework for engaging in conversations about race, racism, coloniality, anti-racism, and anti-coloniality. Importantly, she noted that

It is through the conversations and reflections in which we engage, with ourselves and with others, that we begin to question and comprehend years of coloniality, white supremacy, and racist systems and structures that have gone unquestioned for so long that we hardly notice them anymore. (p. 114)

On a similar note, Gooding (chapter 8) integrated Critical Race Theory (CRT) and Social Identity Theory (SIT) to discuss race as a component of "use of self." She postulated that "if use of self is truly about relationship, then there must be an understanding that relationships do not live outside of societal constructions of race, and that social worker bodies become a part of use of self" (p. 158).

Encouraging Students and Field Instructors to Step/Think Outside of Their Comfort Zone

Authors also addressed the necessity for social work field education to provide opportunities for students and field instructors to participate in uncomfortable conversations, address unspoken topics, and engage with under-served populations.

Recognizing the assumption that social workers and social work students are from dominant identity groups and that service users are not, Gooding (chapter 8) urged "field instructors and students to engage in meaningful conversations about the social construction of race, its dimensions, and the ways a racialized identity informs one's ability to use self to build relationships with clients and to advance client goals" (p. 169).

Similarly, Greenslade (chapter 5) acknowledged the dearth of anti-racist theory and practical skills in the curriculum and counselled that

> owing to the continued pervasiveness of racism, intentional and explicit anti-racist social work education is long overdue, and it is imperative that these conversations start happening in field education. Failure to do so is to severely disadvantage social work students as they graduate to practice in environments and institutions plagued by racism. (p. 114)

Kaushik (chapter 9) asserted that social work education has a responsibility to educate students about immigration, and therefore encouraged field education to enhance that learning through placements with immigrant serving agencies. Recognizing that "the challenges and issues that immigrants face are often beyond cultural or ethnicity-based discrimination or racism" (p. 187), it is essential that social work educators not limit discussions to diversity but rather focus on immigration policies and practices. She demonstrated that

> Owing to the rapid influx of immigrants, the changing demographic realities in Canada demand that the social work academic programs offer appropriate knowledge and experience on the range of issues experienced by the immigrants, and not just limit the focus on diversity and cultural competence. (p. 187)

This call for increased education around immigration is echoed by Balbuena (chapter 13) in her recommendations regarding the provision of services to undocumented victims of interpersonal violence (IPV) in the US. In her chapter, she explains that "There is a need for social work field education programs to acknowledge the importance of immigration status as a component of diversity" (p. 269).

De Vynck, Ciesielski, and Boynton (chapter 15) explored the integration of spirituality and religion into the social work curriculum, particularly field education. Addressing the absence of spirituality in most social work curriculum, the authors noted that "Although historically social work has roots in spirituality, explicit focus on this area was suppressed over time" (p. 296). They advocated for social work educators to include spirituality in their teaching and pointed out that "social workers entering the practice field will inevitably encounter children, adolescents, families, and/or communities dealing with adversity, and research has demonstrated spiritual strengths, crises, struggles, and distress are often intertwined with these experiences" (p. 295). Shiferaw, Asrate, and Eyasu (chapter 7) equally underscore the importance of spirituality in social work practice and research, noting that "a spiritual base provides them purpose, direction, focus, and a sense of fulfilling their destiny" (p. 150).

Integrating Research into Social Work Field Education

The majority of the contributors noted that there is not enough research on field education available and highlighted the importance of researching various aspects of field education. Many of the authors suggested areas for further exploration and some addressed the importance of integrating research into social work field education. De Vynck, Ciesielski, and Boynton (chapter 15) "recognize[d] that there is a reciprocal nature of practice driving research and research driving practice" (p. 315). de Bie, Chaplin, and Vengris (chapter 3) noted that

> one significant implication of our work for field education, then, is recognition and promotion of the value of field education coordinators working in partnership with students and field instructors in ongoing change-oriented research and evaluation projects to enhance equity and accessibility in placement teaching and learning. (p. 64)

Zenebe and Kebede (chapter 10) "highlight[ed] the important role of field education in addressing visible gaps while also engaging in social work research, evaluation of programs or projects, and planning social work interventions at various levels" (p. 193).

In this collection, field education research and scholarship are valued and respected, and provide a stimulating field for investigation. It is important and necessary to promote social work field education as a site for research. Prior to the COVID-19 pandemic, Asakura et al. (2018) found that field education was under intense pressure to respond to a rapidly changing environment. Today, the pressures and challenges are compounded by the impacts of the global pandemic and many interrelated social, economic, and environmental factors. New practices and perspectives are needed to drive innovation and transform social work field education. The authors call for additional resources, collaboration, social justice, accessibility, equity, new placement models and field instruction approaches, and for pedagogy informed by anti-racist and Indigenous knowledges. Social work educators must accept responsibility to maintain a strong commitment to social justice education in field programs (Levine & Murray-Lichtman, 2018). While many social work educators agree that social justice is critical in social work education, there remain significant challenges to making social justice a priority in the field placement (Levine & Murray-Lichtman, 2018). Moreover, the need for advancing environmental justice was demonstrated by contributors who addressed environmental concerns, such as clean drinking water and environmental degradation.

The Global Agenda for Social Work and Social Development, a joint commitment to action of the three global organizations of social work professionals (IFSW), educators in social work (IASSW), and activists (ICSW) adopted the 2020–2030 framework "co-building inclusive social transformation." This theme is echoed by the authors of this collection who share a concern about and share strategies to address the state of field education.

REFERENCES

Asakura, K., Todd, S., Eagle, B., & Morris, B. (2018). Strengthening the signature pedagogy of social work: Conceptualizing field education as a negotiated social work pedagogy. *Journal of Teaching in Social Work, 38*(2), 151–165. https://doi/org/10.108 0/08851233.2018.1436635

Freire, P. (2018). *Pedagogy of the oppressed*. Bloomsbury Publishing USA.

Levine, A. S., & Murray-Lichtman, A. (2018). Integrating social justice in field education. *Field Educator, 8*(1), 1–7. https://www2.simmons.edu/ssw/fe/i/18-186.pdf

List of Contributors

WASIF ALI, PHD, is a sessional instructor in the Faculty of Social Work and the Department of Sociology at the University of Calgary. He is a researcher for a SSHRC-funded project that examines diversity, inclusion, and social justice issues facing minority communities in Canada. In 2020–2021, he was a postdoctoral associate in the Transforming the Field Education Landscape (TFEL) project. His research interests include environmental justice, gender justice, green social work, and sustainable development. He established a Center for Sustainable Development in Pakistan and leads a Sustainability and Policy Network since 2017. He has previously worked for the United Nations in various capacities.

HELEN ASRATE, MA, BA, is a social psychology lecturer at Wollo University and a PhD student in social work at the University of Gondar in Ethiopia. She has a Bachelor of Arts in Psychology from the University of Gondar and a Master of Arts in Social Psychology from Addis Ababa University in Ethiopia. She previously worked in Women affairs and served as a Child Safeguarding officer.

KELEMUA ZENEBE AYELE is a PhD candidate in Social Work at the University of Gondar in Ethiopia. She completed her Master of Arts in Gender Studies from Addis Ababa University. She has served as lecturer at Haramaya University for 4 consecutive years. She is involved in developing business, as well as evaluating research and practical projects through the intersections of gender and disability for an inclusive research incubation consultancy. Her research interests include gender and disability, gender-based violence, gender and migration, and social justice for marginalized groups.

NICOLE BALBUENA is a MSW candidate and Title IV-E scholar at the University of California, Berkeley (UCB). In 2019, she earned her bachelor's degrees in Sociology, Chicanx/Latinx Studies, and Political Science at the University of California, Irvine (UCI). She is an active leader and a driven researcher with research interests in immigration, social services, and intimate partner violence. She is currently the chair of the PCW Resource Zone and Media Committees for the California Social Work Education Center (CalSWEC) Title IV-E Summit; president of the NASW CA 23 Strong Council; and communication manager of the Latinx Social Work Caucus at UCB. In 2019, Nicole's honours thesis paper entitled, "The Service Provider's Dilemma: Confronting the Challenges of Service Delivery for Undocumented Victims of Intimate Partner Violence" earned multiple writing awards, including the campus-wide 2019 Upper-Division Writing Awards in Social Sciences and Social Ecology.

MORGAN BANISTER is a 37-year-old autistic adult and is part of the Ottawa Adult Autism Initiative group, as well as two autistic adult social support groups in Ottawa. She is also an active volunteer for music festivals, Ottawa Humane Society, and has also been involved with Autism Ontario's Ottawa Chapter. Morgan has a wide range of interests in artwork, glass paper weights, pottery, tea pots, mugs, yarn, books, jigsaw puzzles, and blankets.

SHELIA BELL, MHSc, is a Speech-Language Pathologist (University of Toronto, 1983) who has been working with individuals on the autism spectrum (preschool to adult) for more than 30 years. In her private practice, she has had the opportunity to work long term with many ASD individuals. Observing how diverse autism profiles develop over time has given her a unique perspective on the autism spectrum and has led her to develop many innovative therapeutic and educational intervention strategies. She is one of the founding members of the Ottawa Adult Autism Initiative, a project that is seeking to improve the supports/services and quality of life for adults on the autism spectrum.

ALISE DE BIE, PhD, is a Postdoctoral Research Fellow in the Paul R. MacPherson Institute for Leadership, Innovation, and Excellence in Teaching at McMaster University. Working across disciplines, Alise's teaching and research have primarily contributed to Mad(ness) Studies, Critical Disability Studies, social work, and ethics. They have been a social work field instructor to five students in mad/disability-related community organizing and research placements.

EMMA DE VYNCK is a MSW thesis student and research assistant at the University of Calgary, pursuing research on the lived experiences of spiritual distress for women of evangelical Christian backgrounds. She hopes to add to the conversation on spirituality in social work and allied professions. Her work experience is in mental health, and she plans to continue applying spiritually informed learning to her professional endeavours.

MARION BOGO was a professor in the Factor-Inwentash Faculty of Social Work at the University of Toronto. She was recognized for her many contributions to the field of social work and field education.

HEATHER M. BOYNTON, PhD, is an assistant professor in the Faculty of Social Work at the University of Calgary. She is also the vice-president of the Canadian Society for Spirituality and Social Work. Her research and teaching interests include spirituality and trauma, grief and loss, post-traumatic growth, children and family mental health, holistic body-mind-spirit approaches to health and wellness, and interprofessional education. She has over 30 years of experience as a child and youth worker, social worker and child and family therapist, and manager in mental health. She also is an adjunct professor in Kinesiology at Lakehead University and a faculty member at the Northern Ontario School of Medicine.

JANICE CHAPLIN, MSW, is an associate professor (teaching) and field education coordinator in the School of Social Work at McMaster University. She teaches micro social work practice and draws on her experience as a social worker in the health sector to ground her teaching. Her current work is centred on the experiences of equity-seeking students in field placements and field instructor perspectives on supervising students and supports they need in their field placement.

GRANT CHARLES, PhD, is an associate professor in the School of Social Work and an affiliated faculty with the Division of Adolescent Health and Medicine in the Department of Pediatrics with the Faculty of Medicine at the University of British Columbia, Vancouver. He holds an adjunct appointment with the School of Child and Youth Care at the University of Victoria.

EMMANUEL CHILANGA, PHD, RSW, MSc, B.ED, is a registered social worker and a project coordinator for the Transforming the Field Education Landscape project in the Faculty of Social Work at the University of Calgary's Central and Northern Alberta Region in Edmonton. His research and teaching interests focus on social work education, child and family health, food and nutrition, and participatory action research both in Canada and in Africa. Emmanuel holds a PhD in Social Work and a master's degree in social work, a Master of Science degree in Geography and a bachelor's degree in Education.

JILL CIESIELSKI is a Master of Social Work thesis candidate at the University of Calgary. Based on her experiences working with children, youth, and families as a front-line social worker, she is interested in incorporating spirituality into the profession and in developing a holistic approach to direct practice. The use of spirituality in social work practice is the topic of her thesis research.

JULIE L. DROLET, PHD, RSW, is a professor in the Faculty of Social Work at the University of Calgary and the director of the Transforming the Field Education Landscape (TFEL) project funded by a SSHRC partnership grant. She leads an international social work research program to advance knowledge in the fields of social work and social development. She is an internationally recognized expert in international social work, and her research focuses on field education, disaster social work, social development and sustainable development, social protection, and immigrant settlement and integration. She is the author of nine scholarly books and edited collections. She has been recognized through numerous awards by the University of Calgary, the Killam Foundation, the Royal Society of Canada's College of New Scholars, and the Canadian Foundation for Innovation. She is a registered social worker with the Alberta College of Social Workers (ACSW).

Afework Eyasu, MA, BA, is a lecturer in social psychology and education at Wollo University. Afework graduated with his Bachelor of Arts and Master of Arts degree from Addis Ababa University in psychology and social psychology respectively. Currently, Afework is a PhD candidate at the University of Gondar's Department of Social Work. His research focuses on family issues such as contributing factors and consequences of divorce, youth unemployment in Ethiopia, and education.

Cyerra Gage, BSW, pronouns they/them/theirs, graduated from St. Edward's University in Austin, Texas, in 2020 with a bachelor's degree in Social Work. They presented research on gender identity and expression at the Southwestern Psychological Association (SWPA) conference in 2017 and gave an oral presentation at the 2020 Symposium on Undergraduate Research and Creative Expression on alternatives to policing in schools and the relationships between school and prison. C. has been involved in community organizing work around the Austin area and is passionate about building systems of community care that undermine current systems of oppression.

Anita R. Gooding, PhD, LCSW, MSW, BA, is a licensed clinical social worker who received a Bachelor of Arts in Women, Gender & Sexuality Studies from Trinity College, a Master of Social Work from the University of Pennsylvania, and a PhD in Social Work and Social Research from Portland State University. Her experience spans micro and macro levels of practice and includes community outreach and organizing, development and marketing, treatment education for persons living with HIV/AIDS, outpatient therapy for LGBTQIA-identified persons and service as a BSW field director. Her research centres on the subjugated knowledges of historically marginalized groups; race and social work practice, including use of self; and equity and inclusion within social work education.

Zipporah Greenslade is a Master of Social Work student at the University of Calgary. Her research interests include anti-racist and anti-colonial education as sites of transformative justice, critical pedagogies, practice with immigrants and refugees, and spirituality. Her professional practice involves Equity, Diversity, Inclusion & Decolonization (EDID) research and implementation, teaching, settlement services, and policy.

She is active in student advocacy and has been a student member of the Faculty of Social Work's Anti-Black Racism Task Force (University of Calgary). She also served as a Student Advisory Committee member and Field Research Scholar with the Transforming the Field Education Landscape (TFEL) project.

ANNELISE HUTCHISON is a student at St. Edward's University's School of Behavioral and Social Sciences in Austin, Texas, studying psychology and sociology. She will be graduating from the university in May 2022 and pursuing a Master of Social Work at the University of Texas at Austin while working full time for St. Edward's University Student Financial Services. Her research interests include working with adolescent boys in juvenile corrections, at risk adolescents in foster care, and supporting youth with incarcerated parents. She also hopes to get her PhD in social work and continue educating others on racial and social disparities in education and childcare systems.

CHRISTINE JENKINS has been an advocate for many years and most recently around issues related to late female diagnosis, gender bias, and autistic aging. Currently a community research associate at Carleton University, she is a co-author of the anthology *Spectrum Women: Walking to the Beat of Autism* (2018) and has presented in Canada and internationally. Jenkins has been a peer reviewer for the journal *Autism in Adulthood* and edits other books and articles. As she states, "Our aim is to help include autistic voices at every stage in true co-production of research." Jenkins recently started a business, the Christine Jenkins AUsome Consulting, at www.cjAUsome.ca.

VIBHA KAUSHIK, PhD, RSW, is a registered social worker in Alberta and a postdoctoral associate in the Faculty of Social Work at the University of Calgary currently working on two partnership projects: (1) Transforming the Field Education Landscape and (2) Aging in the Right Place. In addition, she teaches undergraduate and graduate courses in the Faculty of Social Work at the University of Calgary. Her current research interests include social work with newcomers, newcomer settlement and integration, homelessness and housing insecurity among older immigrants, and mixed-methods research. She has several peer-reviewed publications as first author and has presented her work at multiple national and international peer-reviewed conferences to academic and community-based audiences.

EDWARD KING is an adult who is autistic. He was diagnosed at the age of 3 and had trouble speaking. At that time, doctors said that Edward had a 50% chance of never speaking, but he overcame that challenge. After graduating from Algonquin College, he has had two jobs: working for the City of Ottawa as a custodian and weight room attendee, and at a fitness gym as a custodian. At times, he assists adults who have special needs and physical disabilities at summer camps and social nights through the City of Ottawa. Since 2011, Edward has gone to schools — from grade two to high school — and attended adult audiences at workshops to talk about overcoming challenges, bullying, and autism. Today, Edward volunteers with OAAI and is willing to help out individuals to have better futures. He enjoys biking, running, walking, listening to music, and hanging out with friends.

KALTRINA KUSARI is a PhD Candidate in the Faculty of Social Work at the University of Calgary. Her current research focuses on the experiences of return migrant women to Kosova, where she is from. She has also been involved with research projects which focus on refugee resettlement in Canada and has co-developed a training program for service providers who serve immigrants with disabilities. Her research informs her practice, her role as a field supervisor for practicum students, and her teaching at both University of Calgary and Athabasca University.

ALEXANDRA K. MACK, MSW, is a recent graduate of Howard University's School of Social Work, in Washington DC. As an MSW student, Alexandra Mack was selected as an American Evaluation Association GEDI Scholar, Howard University's School of Social Work's 2020–2021 Founders Fellow, Health Resources and Services Administration Behavioral Health Workforce Education and Training (BHWET) Scholar, and a 2020–2021 Transforming the Field Education Landscape (TFEL) Scholar. Alexandra's research interests include culturally responsive child welfare practice, the utilization of spoken word as a medium to optimize the portrayal of phenomena and enhance audience connectivity, and performance accountability and quality improvement of social and mental health services.

SHERI M. MCCONNELL, PhD, MSW, BSW, an assistant professor and former field education coordinator at the Memorial University School of Social Work, in Newfoundland and Labrador, is a queer white settler who currently resides on the traditional lands of the Beothuk. As part of her commitment to decolonization, reconciliation, and Indigenization, she chairs the team offering a BSW program in Cambridge Bay, Nunavut, through a partnership between Nunavut Arctic College and Memorial University. Dr. McConnell is a commissioner on the CASWE-ACFTS Commission on Accreditation and led the development and implementation of the CASWE-ACFTS Online Field Instructor's Course. She is a co-investigator with Transforming the Field Education Landscape (TFEL).

MARGARET JANSE VAN RENSBURG, MSW, RSW, BA, is a Social Work PhD student at Carleton University who has recently completed her MSW. She is a non-autistic ally and steering committee member of the Ottawa Adult Autism Initiative. She holds a Bachelor of Arts in archaeology and medieval studies and a graduate certificate in autism and behaviour sciences. Margaret's research interests surround promoting autistic self-determination, disability, women's safety, and eating disorders under an anti-oppressive lens. Margaret enjoys lifting weights, swimming, and playing with her gecko in her free time.

RICARDO DIEGO SUÁREZ ROJAS, MSW, MA, holds a Master of Arts in Bioethics from The University of Chicago, specializing in the evolution of capitalism and the social determinants of health. Currently, he is an MSW/PhD student at Boston College School of Social Work, and a research assistant at the Center for Work, Health, and Wellbeing at Harvard T.H. Chan School of Public Health. His research interests include stress and trauma across the life course, the neurobiology of perception and imagination and its implication for education and clinical practice, and intervention design and implementation science for fostering creativity and health in the workplace. In addition, he is the director of Laboratorio en Movimiento, an initiative that seeks to challenge historical trauma in the South of Mexico through the fusion of science and art.

Endalkachew Taye Shiferaw, MA, is an Assistant Professor in social psychology at Gambella University. Endalkachew graduated with his Master of Arts degree in Social Psychology from Addis Ababa University. He has lectured at Gambella ATVET College, Mettu University, and Gambella University. His research interests focus on the well-being of internally displaced persons and refugees.

Courtney Weaver, MA, is a self-advocate who is very much engaged in the field of autism and accessibility. After obtaining a Masters in Critical Disability Studies at York University in 2017, she has consistently done a variety of work roles in the aforementioned field. Her current ones include program support officer for the Accessibility, Accommodation & Adaptive Computer Technology (AAACT) Program, office assistant to MP Mike Lake, Housing Through an Autism Lens (HAL) Solutions Lab self-advocate advisor and project coordinator for the Canadian Autism Spectrum Disorder Alliance's (CASDA's) Work from Home project.

Karen Lok Yi Wong, MA, MSW, RSW, was trained in social policy for a Master of Arts at University of York, in the UK, and in social work for Master of Social Work at the University of British Columbia, Vancouver. She has conducted research, including analyzing policies, on older adults and healthcare with a focus on palliative care, long-term care, and family caregiving. She has also published and presented widely to academic and professional audiences. She has been an invited reviewer for academic and professional journal articles, conference presentation abstracts, and project proposals. She is currently the research scholar of Simon Fraser University Science and Technology for Aging Research (STAR) Institute. Karen is a registered social worker in British Columbia and has been practicing in diverse settings related to older adults such as community senior services centre and long-term care. She is currently practicing social work at Mount St Joseph Hospital of Providence Healthcare, Vancouver. She serves as the clinical advisor at 411 Seniors Centre Society, Vancouver. She also serves in the BC Association of Social Workers Multicultural and Anti-racist Committee, Seniors Community of Practice, and Richmond, Delta, and Burnaby Branch. She is a long-term volunteer for Alzheimer's Society BC.

Index

298, 318; connecting, 9, 102, 123, 125, 313; connectivity, 355, 377; connects, 11, 231

consent, 137, 229, 255

conservation, 218, 225

consortium, 131

consulting, 227–228, 239, 241–243, 376; consultancy, 371; consultants, 333; consultation, ix, 13–14, 63, 217, 227–228, 230, 232–245, 361, 384; consulted, 38, 63, 230, 232, 237, 241

continent, 8, 70–74, 82, 87, 91

continuum, 118, 325–328, 330–331, 348–349, 353

contribute, 2, 11, 14, 29, 35, 39, 47, 118, 152, 163, 167, 179, 202, 233, 237, 239, 241–243, 266, 274, 324, 336, 341, 345, 351; contributed, 7, 17, 43, 122, 144–145, 149–150, 152, 195, 209, 219–220, 240, 297, 373; contributing, xiii, 4, 9–10, 12, 29, 118, 200, 309, 375; contribution, xiv, 4, 8, 11, 13, 16, 30, 56, 65, 126, 146, 184, 200, 243, 352; contributor, ix, xiii, 1, 4, 16–17, 120, 146, 359, 368–369, 371, 384

controversy, 300, 354

convention, 318

coordinator, 6, 38–39, 42–43, 48, 64–65, 84, 123, 198, 200–202, 205–206, 213, 282, 291, 333, 343, 362, 368, 373–374, 377, 379; coordinate, 198, 280; coordinated, 182; coordinating, xiii, 193, 202, 212; coordination, 13, 65, 201, 212, 290

coping, 150, 228, 235, 281, 284, 295, 304, 306, 309, 312–313, 316, 325, 356

COVID, ix, 2–6, 8, 14–15, 17, 21, 29, 31, 35, 37, 58, 72, 91–93, 96, 101, 115, 204, 273–279, 281–285, 287, 289–294, 360, 362, 365, 368, 384; pandemic, 2–6, 8, 14–15, 21, 29, 31, 35, 37–38, 58, 72, 91–92, 204, 273–274, 277–281, 284–288, 290, 293–294, 360, 362, 365, 368–369

corporation, 132, 194, 206

corruption, 71, 90, 96, 335

cosmology, 79, 96

councils, 181

counselling, 41, 85, 122, 170, 185, 198, 294, 302, 308, 317; counselled, 367; counsellors, 94, 125, 294, 308

counternarrative, 161–163

counties, 28, 122, 131, 268, 270

countries, 1, 13, 27, 69, 71, 81, 86–87, 89–90, 92, 133, 151, 177–178, 194, 209, 211, 213, 216, 283, 299, 363

courthouse, 261–262, 269

courts, 197, 261–263

creativity, 30, 294, 301, 323, 331, 338, 353, 356, 378; arts, iv, 134, 153, 371, 374–375, 378–379,

384; artwork, 372; crafts, 153, 360; created, 2–3, 6–7, 13, 15, 23–24, 40, 210, 228, 231, 235, 244, 278, 280, 289, 312, 328, 335; creates, 29, 164, 169, 252, 262, 329, 363; creating, 2–4, 7–8, 29–30, 37, 89, 124, 126, 230, 232, 235, 240, 243, 277, 285, 289, 308, 317, 329, 331, 339–340, 352; creation, 54, 161, 236, 240, 310, 314, 329–331, 341

crisis, 2, 13, 17, 21, 47, 65, 67, 94, 206, 210, 213, 225, 276–277, 280, 291, 293, 295, 304, 309, 353, 368

critique, 70, 104–105, 125, 147, 160, 170, 228, 275, 277

culture, viii, 9–10, 79, 86, 95, 117, 118–131, 136, 148, 166, 168, 176, 181, 183, 185, 187, 212, 225, 246, 252, 254, 269, 299–300, 316, 322, 326, 329, 357, 365, 377, 384; intercultural, 45; multicultural, 132, 169–170, 189, 379; multiculturalism, 103; transcultural, 129

customs, 160, 261

cutbacks, 282

cuts, 47, 276

D

dance, 342–343

daughters, 150

deans, 190, 274

debt, 24, 48

decentralization, 222

declaration, 153, 203

decolonizing, 94, 116, 207; decolonial, 113; decoloniality, 96; decolonization, 94–95, 205, 375, 378

democracy, 190, 229; democratic, 134, 152–154

demographics, xii, 97, 178, 183, 187, 251, 255–257, 266, 268, 367

depoliticize, 276

deportation, 14, 252–253, 257, 260–262, 264, 266–267

deposit, 229, 233

depression, 133, 304–305, 310, 316, 318, 322, 341, 354, 356

desegregation, 61

developmental, vii, xi, 8–9, 12, 69–71, 73–93, 95–97, 245–246, 248, 307, 326, 338, 356–357, 364, 385

digital, iv, 41, 356, 385

dilemma, ix, 26, 114, 130, 169, 189, 251, 253, 255, 257, 259, 261, 263–265, 267, 269, 280–281, 372, 385

director, 25–26, 39, 54, 65, 148, 190, 274, 333, 343, 374–375, 378

sociology, 115, 145, 191, 200, 212, 219, 225, 247, 371–372, 376; sociological analysis, 221; sociologists, 215–216, 219

sociocultural, 163

socioeconomic, 69, 72–73, 83, 86, 122, 151, 183, 210, 219, 251, 254, 341, 354; socioeconomic status, 95, 341

somatosensory, 332

specialize, 135; specialist, 197, 233; specialization, 48–49, 65, 82–83, 212; specialized, 83, 90, 183; specializing, 39, 378; specialty, 29

species, 325–326, 329, 332, 348–349

spectrum, 13, 199, 231–232, 245–248, 327, 335, 353, 372, 376, 379

speech, 145, 233, 235, 238, 253, 329, 334, 372

spiritual, ix, 15–16, 137, 139, 145, 149–151, 154, 251, 295–322, 337, 357, 365, 368, 373, 386; faith, 297–298, 305, 309, 314, 318, 320–322; spirituality, 10, 15, 136, 150, 152, 155, 295–308, 310, 313–322, 365, 367–368, 373–375

stakeholder, 78, 81, 85, 90, 113, 183, 197–198, 202, 205, 277–279

standardized, 121

standards, 23, 25, 28, 32–33, 89, 93, 96, 112, 114, 130, 182, 184, 197, 200, 203, 206, 209, 291, 313–315, 343

standpoint, 120, 170

states, 10, 16, 23, 27, 33, 79, 101–102, 117, 120, 122, 129–130, 135, 157, 159–160, 166, 191, 195, 203, 252, 262, 299, 318, 323, 327, 336, 339, 341, 352, 376

statistics, 115, 154–155, 247, 299, 322, 352

status, 5, 14, 25, 56, 60, 70, 105, 120, 122, 132, 150, 160–161, 165, 182, 195–196, 210, 221, 251–254, 258–264, 266–270, 341, 354, 367

stigma, 60, 263, 283–284; stigmatized, 275, 283; stigmatization, 115, 212, 340

stipend, 6, 22, 28–30

stories, 107, 113, 161, 210, 217–220, 235, 288, 297, 306, 335

storying, 246

storytelling, 41, 162

strategies, xiii, 14, 58, 64, 80–81, 95, 122, 152, 193, 217, 221, 224, 235, 240, 242, 309, 311–312, 336, 343, 361, 369, 372

stress, xiii, 24–25, 29, 32, 138–139, 149–151, 290, 316, 319, 325, 333, 335, 339–340, 343, 354–357, 378; burnout, 304, 309; stressful, 277, 281, 294, 309, 337, 341, 355; stressor, 29, 277, 323; stress-related, 356

structural, 9, 14, 31, 70–73, 81, 105–106, 168, 204–205, 252, 254–255, 266, 339, 345, 361, 364–365; structures, 11, 55, 71, 104, 113–114,

118, 136, 160–161, 163, 167, 203, 211, 230, 240, 326, 332, 336–337, 341, 366

struggle, 15, 26, 62, 104, 157, 161, 166, 184, 282, 288, 295–297, 299, 304–310, 313, 314–318, 320, 322, 340, 368; struggling, 27, 282, 307, 312

subjects, iv, 87, 289, 386

substances, 259

Sudanese, 191

suicide, 312; suicidal, 307, 353; suicidality, 305, 318

supervise, 44, 50, 59, 87, 198, 281, 331; supervised, 3, 37, 40, 44, 84–85, 158, 233, 279, 362; supervisees, 50; supervising, 15, 43, 57, 84, 202, 274, 279, 283, 362, 373; supervision, 5, 7–8, 32–33, 36, 39–40, 43, 45, 50, 54, 56–59, 61–62, 84, 87–88, 91–92, 133, 158, 162, 166, 168, 170–171, 185, 188, 208, 216, 277, 281, 284, 292, 294–295, 303, 311, 313–314, 324, 333, 337, 340, 342, 347, 350–351, 358, 361; supervisor, vii, xii, 6–8, 12, 26, 35–45, 47, 64–66, 84, 88–89, 91, 126–127, 129, 147, 167–170, 187–188, 206, 216–217, 221, 233–234, 238, 274, 277, 280, 285–286, 289, 292, 296, 298, 302, 310–315, 331, 344, 361–362, 365, 377, 386; supervisory, 11, 158, 162–163, 166, 169, 213, 296

supremacy, 104, 114, 168, 366

survivor, 266, 268

sustainability, 17, 210, 216, 220–221, 223, 233, 363, 371

Sweden, 292

Syrian, 188–189

systems, viii, 14, 23, 28, 55, 69, 71, 73, 89, 94, 105–106, 114, 120, 122, 124–125, 128, 183–184, 193, 195, 197, 199, 201, 203, 205, 207, 253, 267–268, 273, 297, 323, 326–328, 336, 340, 356, 359–360, 364, 366, 375–376, 386; systematic, 74–75, 86, 94, 119–120, 213, 269, 353–354, 357; systematically, 5, 38, 336; systemic, 49, 103–105, 107–108, 112, 205, 264, 284–285, 359; systemically, 21, 104

T

Tanzania, 75, 89

taxonomy, 330–331, 339–340, 351, 353, 356

technocratic, 121

technology, 6, 15, 37–42, 90, 93, 219, 223, 236, 245, 274, 279, 282, 285, 287, 326, 329, 353–354, 362, 379; technological, 58, 71, 222, 236–237, 239

telehealth, 287

temporality, 116

territories, 50

terrorism, 177

www.ingramcontent.com/pod-product-compliance
Lightning Source LLC
Chambersburg PA
CBHW050624280326
41932CB00015B/2511